Albert de Belleroche

(1864 - 1944)

Works from the Artist's Studio

Acknowledgements

We are hugely indebted to George C. Kenney for his lifelong interest in Belleroche and collaboration with Liss Llewellyn in the publication of his ground-breaking catalogue raisonné *Albert de Belleroche, Master of Belle Epoque Lithography*.

We are indebted to the scholarship of Bernard Derroitte and Richard Reed Armstrong, Theodore B. Donson and especially to Steven Kern, author of *The Rival of Painting: The Lithographs of Albert Belleroche*, San Diego Museum of Art, 2001.

We are grateful to John Singer Sargent scholars, Richard Ormond, for his unwavering support and Eliane Kilmurray for her essay situating Belleroche in the wider context of his better known contemporaries. And to Trevor Fairbrother and Devon Cox.

We are grateful to members of the Belleroche family, including Nina and Evelyne Sutton, and to the family of Gordon Anderson, especially to Gordon Snell.

This publication and the catalogue raisonné, *Albert de Belleroche, Master of Belle Epoque Lithography*, that accompanies it, have both been designed by David Maes. Neither project would have come to fruition without his flair and Herculean will.

We are hugely grateful to George Richards and Eva Liss at Liss Llewellyn, and to Sarah Newman, Miranda Prescott and Helen Ivaldi at Russell-Cotes Art Gallery and Museum.

We are grateful to Rick and Rosemary Obey. We are again especially indebted to Christopher Campbell-Howes for his help with editing. And to Tom Wheare.

This publication is dedicated to Gordon Anderson, (1929-2017)

First published in 2023 by LISS LLEWELLYN

ISBN : 978-1-9993145-8-3

Text © Elaine Kilmurray & Paul Liss

Photography: Glynn Clarkson, Pierre Emmanuel Coste & Petra van der Wal

Design and Typesetting by David Maes
Printed by Zenith Media, April 2024

Albert de Belleroche

(1864 - 1944)

Works from the Artist's Studio

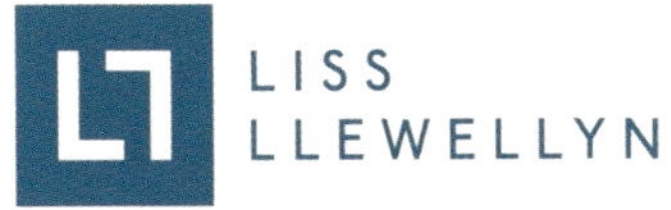

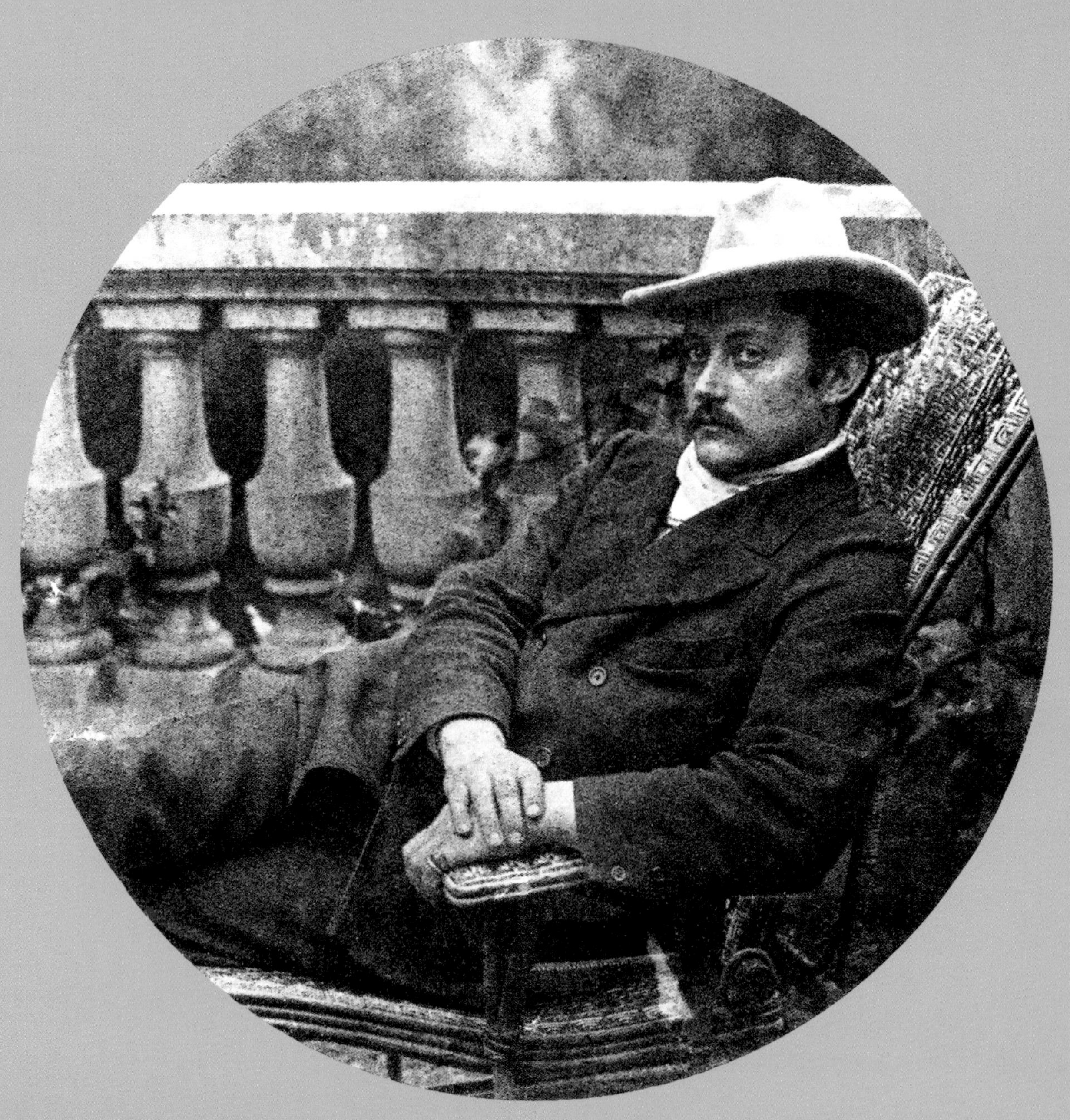

FIG. 1 – Photographic portrait of the artist as a young man.

Table of Contents

Preface / *Paul Liss*   7

Introduction / *Paul Liss*   9

Albert de Belleroche and John Singer Sargent – A Life-long Friendship / *Elaine Kilmurray*   15

Paintings   35

Drawings   81

Lithographs   113

Chronology   164

Albert Belleroche's Studio Log Book   168

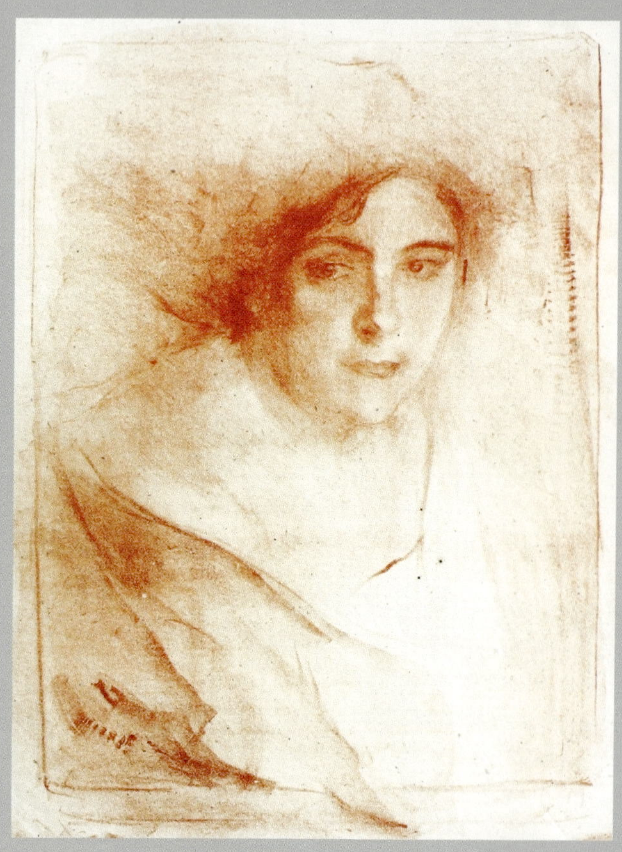

CAT. 259 – *Portrait of Julie de Belleroche,* (K121, AB 538), c.1915
lithograph, 13 ¼ x 10 ½ in. (33.5 x 27 cm). Edition: 1.

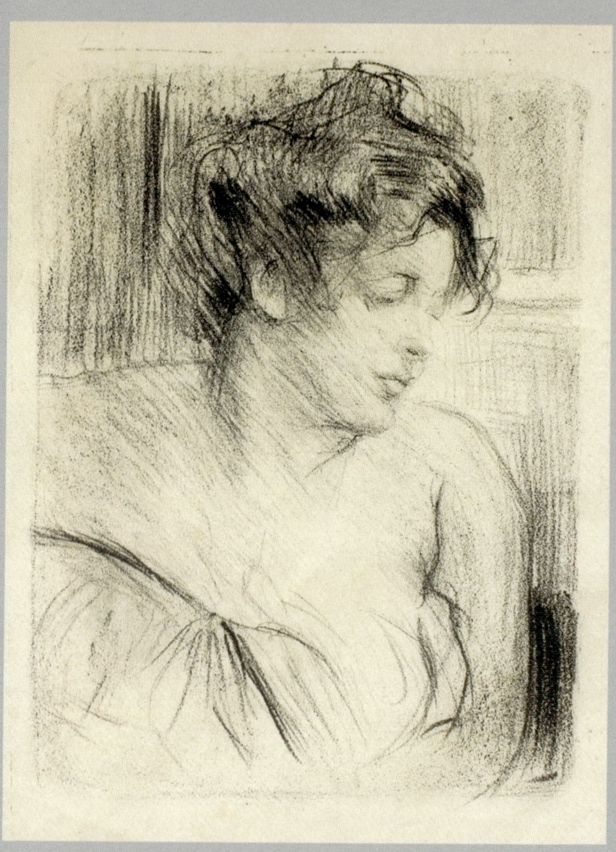

CAT. 215 – *Portrait of Lili Grenier,* (K021, AB 562), c.1903,
lithograph, 15 x 10 ½ in. (37 x 26.2 cm). Edition: 3.

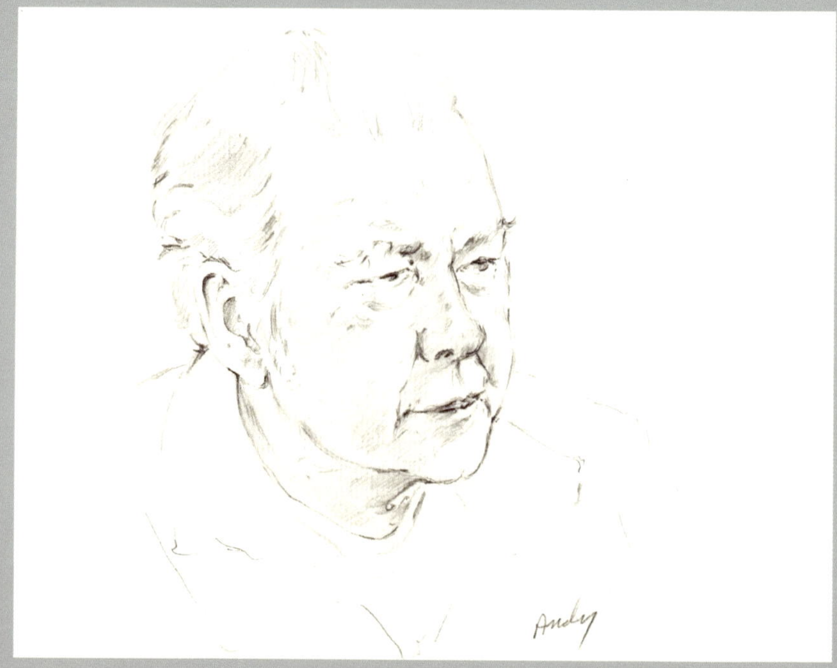

FIG. 2 – David Maes, *Portrait of Gordon Anderson (Andy),* 2006,
pencil on paper, 8 x 10 in. (20 x 25 cm).

This collection of Belleroche's work, which comprises more than three hundred paintings, drawings and lithographs, is the largest of its kind, whether in public or private hands. As a group, these works offer a striking record of the breadth and quality of Belleroche's art and an insight into his working technique, which at times was remarkably innovative. The collection includes an unrivalled number of monotypes and single edition prints. It is also unique in reuniting the preparatory graphic work with the paintings. Although Belleroche is primarily known as a print maker, for the first two decades of his professional life (1880-1900) he was a painter. After 1900 he worked as a lithographer, first and foremost, but painting and graphic art co-existed and understanding the relationship between the two is important for appreciating his extraordinary talent.

This is the first time that the unique collection of 'Works from the Artist's Studio' has been published or exhibited in public. The collection, which was put together by Julie de Belleroche (CAT. 259), the artist's wife, was subsequently inherited by their son, William ('Willy') de Belleroche (FIG. 3). Gordon Anderson (FIG. 2), who from the mid-1950s was Willy's personal secretary and romantic companion, inherited the collection when Willy died in 1969. Other works come from the collection of Lili Grenier (see FIG. 17 & CAT. 33), the celebrated model of Henri de Toulouse Lautrec.

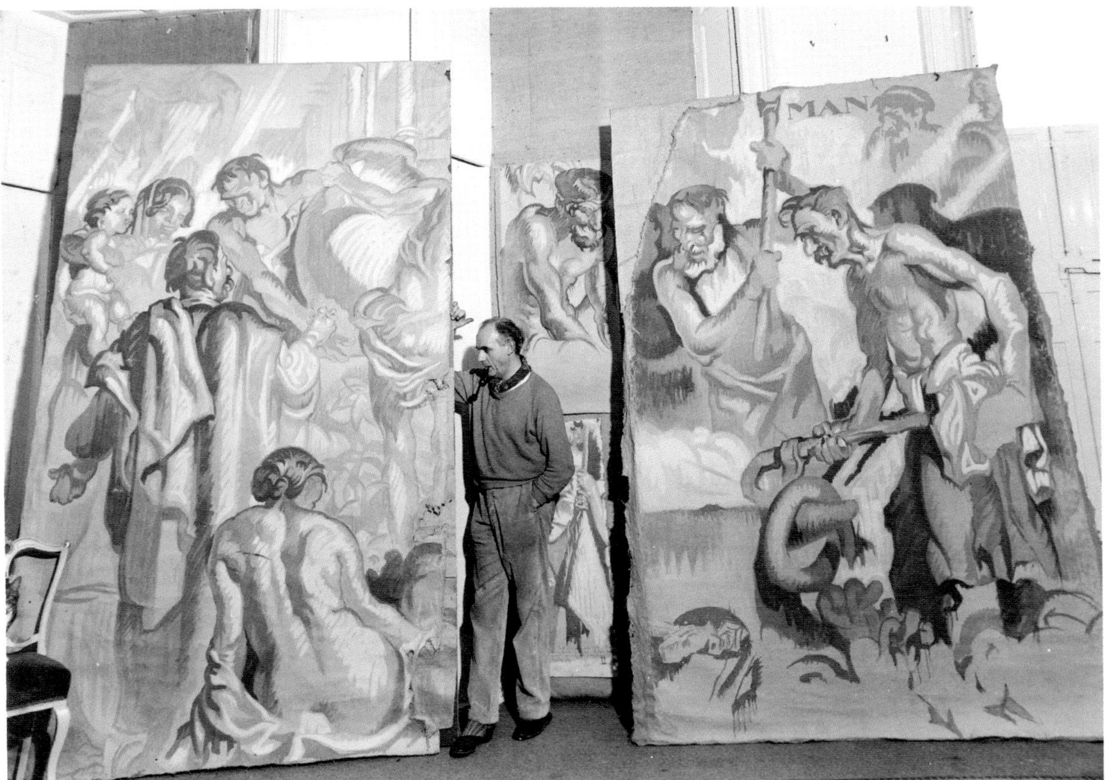

FIG. 3 – William de Belleroche in 1961 with Frank Brangwyn's studies for his Rockefeller Centre murals in New York.

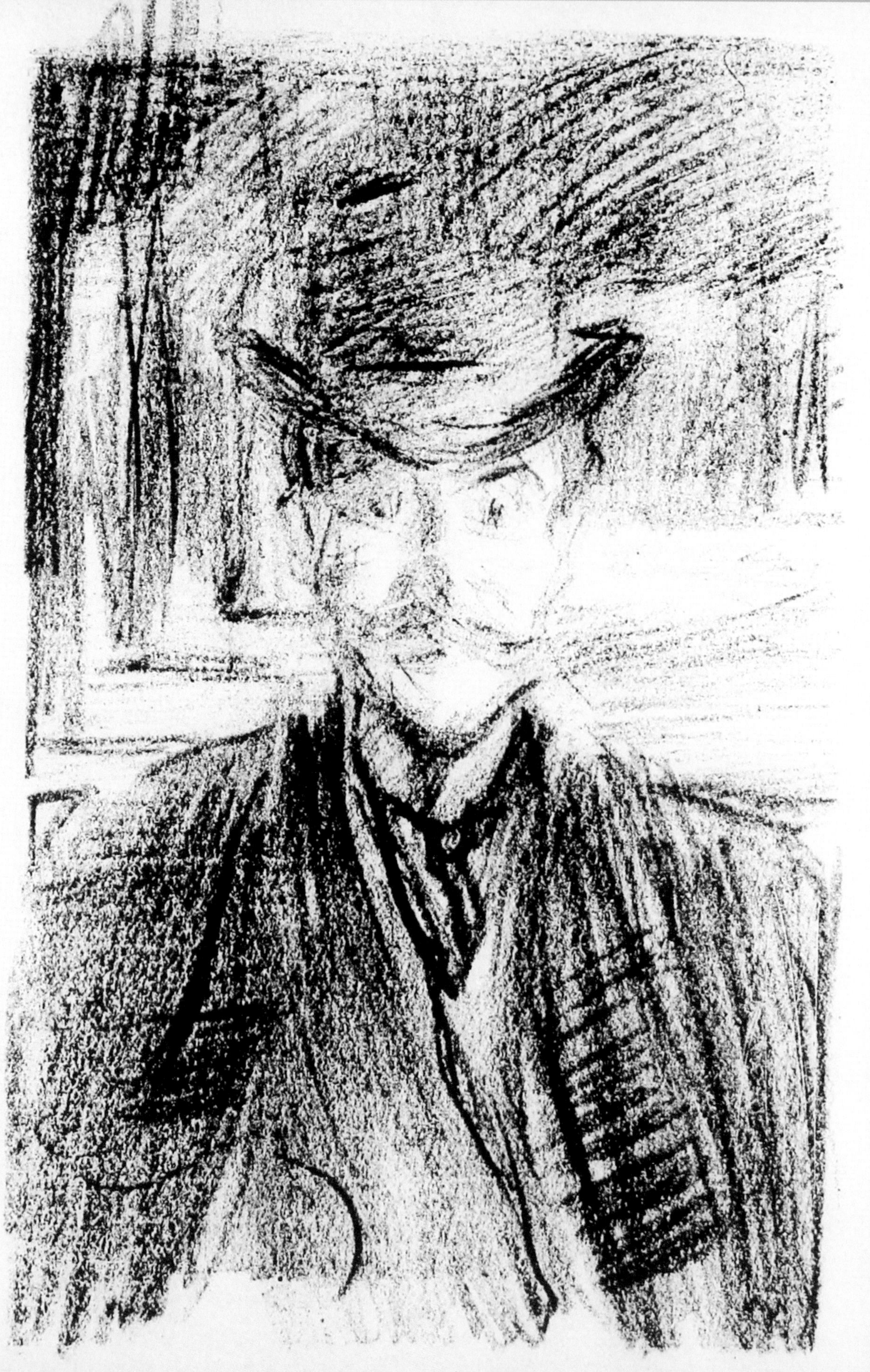

Albert de Belleroche – Artist of the Belle Epoque

Paul Liss

Artists of the Belle Epoque have received increasing attention since the dawn of the twenty-first century: Richard Ormond and Elaine Kilmurray's remarkable John Singer Sargent: The Early Portraits was published in 1998; the Palais des Beaux-Arts in Lille mounted a Carolus-Duran (Belleroche's teacher) exhibition in 2003. Jacques-Emile Blanche has been the subject of a catalogue raisonné by Jane Roberts and exhibition at the Fondation Pierre Bergé-Yves Saint Laurent (2012); Zorn (2017), Khnopff (2019), Boldini (2022), and Bernhardt (2023) have all featured in monographic exhibitions at the Petit Palais in Paris. Helleu was the subject of an exhibition at the Musée d'Orsay in 2022/3. Sargent will be fêted around the world next year, 2025 being the centenary of his death. Many similar initiatives might be mentioned here. Belleroche has yet to have his turn.

Born in Swansea in 1864, Belleroche (CAT. 151) was educated in Paris, enrolling at the studio of Carolus-Duran in 1882, where he met and became a lifelong friend of John Singer Sargent. Although Belleroche did not remain a student of Duran's for long, he adopted the master's technique of painting with a fully loaded brush, without any preparatory underdrawing. Inspired by the Dutch Old Masters, whose works Belleroche studied in museums, the fledgling artist discovered the power of light and dark chiaroscuro that would later drive his innovations in lithography.

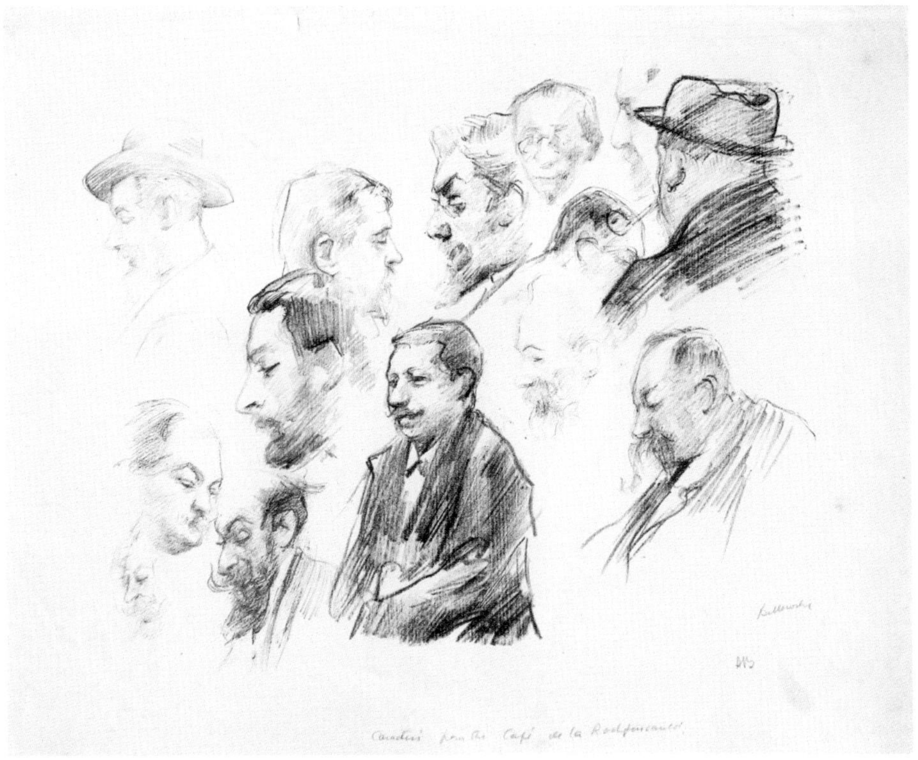

CAT. 156 – *Page de croquis d'hommes au café*, (K859, AB 564, Z06), 1905 (?),
18 x 14 in. (45.7 x 35.6 cm). Edition: 1.

CAT. 151 – *Self Portrait*, (K175, AB 568), c.1902, 6 x 4 in. (15.2 x 10.2 cm), Edition: 1.

Impatient to embark on his own career Belleroche, still in his early 20s, set up a studio in Montmartre, opposite the Moulin Rouge; he took lodgings in the nearby Place de Clichy (FIG. 18) close to the art shop M.Hennequin, the favourite paint supplier of Manet and the Impressionists. He soon became an habitué of the next door Café Guerbois, and Cafe Rouchefard, where many of the renowned artists of Montmartre gathered, (CAT. 156). Among his entourage were also celebrated literary figures of the day, including Oscar Wilde, Emile Zola (whose funeral cortège he painted in 1902) and George Moore. According to his son, Willy de Belleroche, Albert was even the inspiration for Oscar Wilde's acclaimed *The Picture of Dorian Gray* (1890).

Celebrated models of the period posed for Belleroche, among them Victorine Meurent, notorious as the model of Eduard Manet's Olympia (1863). He portrayed many of the performers of Montmartre, including Maissa, from the Moulin Rouge, famous for her 'Danse du Ventre' and Cha-hu-kao, immortalized in paintings by Toulouse Lautrec. Other celebrities from the demi-monde who posed for Belleroche included Mata Hari (of whom he produced at least four lithographs and several pencil studies) (FIG. 4), and the famous Japanese wrestler Taro Myaki.

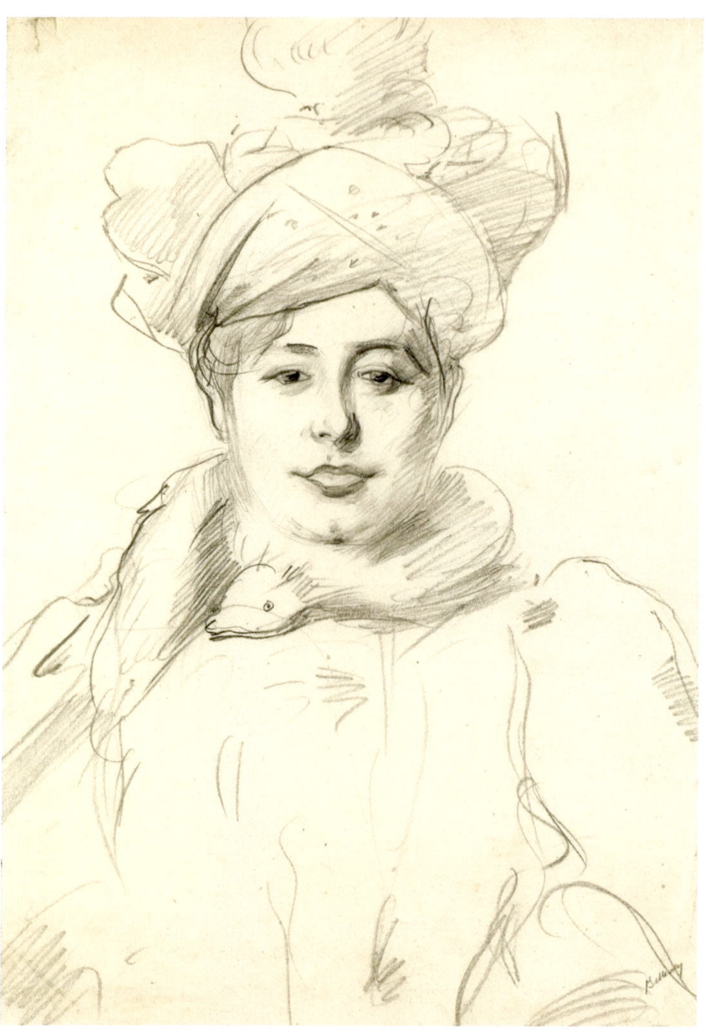

FIG. 4 – *Mata Hari*, c.1905,
pencil on paper,
14 ½ x 10 ¼ in. (36.7 x 26 cm).

Belleroche was inspired by different aesthetic currents, ranging from second generation Impressionism to Symbolism. Symbolism, the predominant movement of the Belle Epoque, placed a special emphasis on the world of dreams and mysticism, as well as on various aspects of counterculture and marginality, from which the figure of the femme fatale emerged as a leitmotif.

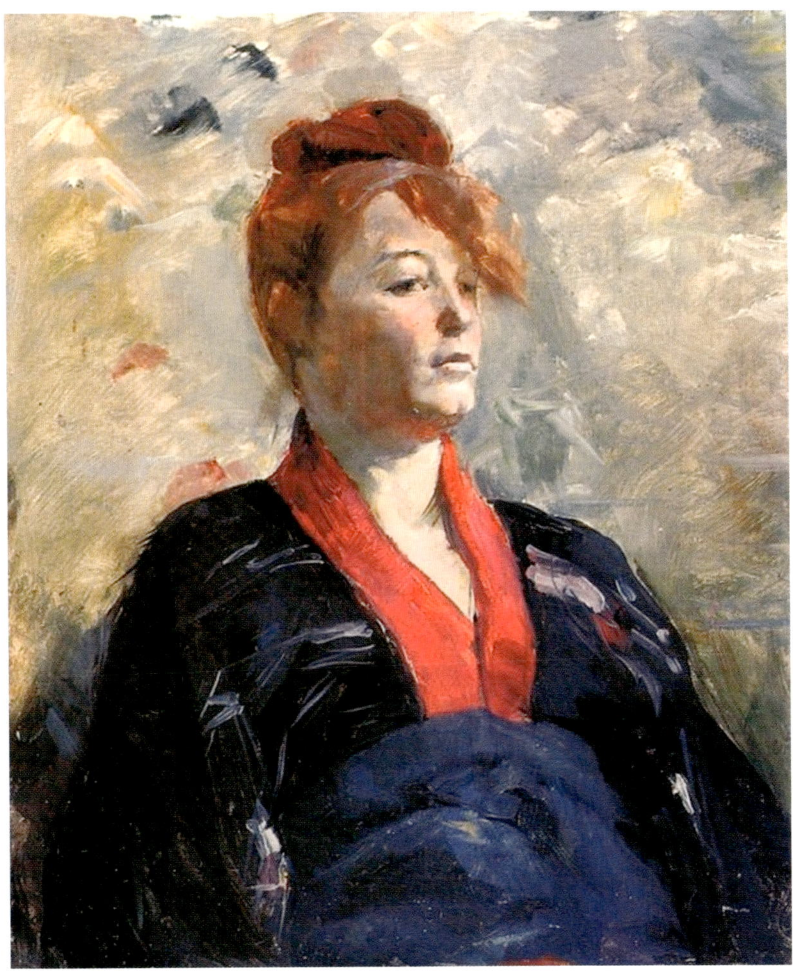

FIG. 5 – Henri de Toulouse-Lautrec (1864-1901),
Lili Grenier,1888, oil on canvas. Private Collection.

These preoccupations are especially discernible in Belleroche's graphic art, dominated by series of portraits of women in different states of reverie or melancholy, bearing titles such as *Indolence*, *Réflections* and *Résistance*.

Belleroche's longest serving model was Lili Grenier, the subject of many oils, drawings, and, between 1900 and 1908, 67 lithographs. Grenier also posed for Renoir, Cormon (FIG. 17), Degas, Fantin-Latour and Lautrec (FIG. 5). Grenier and Belleroche were lovers for seventeen years, from 1890 until 1907. According to Willy, "Lili was both intelligent and a woman of taste and acquired an important collection of paintings by artists for whom she posed. [….] The walls of her home were covered with unframed pictures by Lautrec, Degas, Fantin-Latour, Renoir and many others."

Artists were frequently the subject of Belleroche's art. Lithographic portraits that have been identified include Léandre (138), Anglada (cat 144) and Brangwyn; pencil portraits include Cassat and Sargent.

That Belleroche was immersed in the artistic milieu of the Belle Epoque undoubtedly adds attraction to his story: at times his life reads like a novel, and indeed he is one of the central characters in Deborah Davis' *Strapless* (Penguin 2004), which was later adapted by Christopher Wheeldon as a ballet for the Royal Opera House (2016). But fame by association would be a poor reason to argue that a reassessment is long overdue.

Was Albert Belleroche simply a minor figure, a *petit maître*, of the Belle Epoque, who justifiably has sunk to relative obscurity, or is his talent worthy of a more detailed examination? If so, what were his qualities as an artist that would argue in favour of such a reappraisal?

A good starting point might be to ask why Belleroche is relatively little-known today? Several reasons can be suggested. He was financially independent, and so had no need to exhibit. On leaving Paris in 1910 he was increasingly out of the public eye, and he never sought the limelight. In 1924, at the age of 60, Belleroche appears to have largely retired from producing lithographs. Only 12 lithographs are known to have been produced after 1924, most of them of the artist's daughter Alice. He finished his life in relative obscurity in Nottingham.

Nevertheless, during his lifetime Belleroche's achievements did not go unnoticed. He exhibited at the Salon from 1887, with the Société des Artistes Français from 1891, in England at the Royal Academy and, from 1894, the more progressive New English Art Club. In 1903, alongside Henri Matisse, André Derain and Georges Roualt, he became a founding member of Société du Salon d'Automne, and had a room dedicated to his work in 1904. This honour was only ever accorded to 5 other artists: Cézanne, Puvis de Chavannes, Redon, Renoir and Toulouse-Lautrec. On the occasion of this solo exhibition, the French state acquired his oil *Printemps* – painted in his studio opposite the Moulin Rouge – which entered the Luxembourg Museum and afterwards hung in the British Section of the Musée du Jeu de Paume (now in Musée d'Art et d'Histoire, Orange).

Amongst Belleroche's admirers were Degas, Renoir and Sargent. In an article written in 1935 ('Albert Belleroche', *Apollo*, Vol. XXI, no. 203, April 1935), Brangwyn recalled that Degas admired the way Belleroche painted reflections of light. Degas is known to have owned at least three of Belleroche's lithographs (Colta Ives, Susan Stein et al, 'The Private Collection of Edgar Degas, A Summary Catalogue', New York, Metropolitan Museum, 1997, no 14, p. 4.) and Degas freely offered his advice: in his Log Book Belleroche noted that for *La Femme Arabe* (K547, AB 168.1), Degas insisted that the print 'show pubic hair' and Belleroche obliged. Roger Marx, the champion of Renoir, credited Belleroche as playing 'a leading role in the renaissance of lithography' and as 'a pioneer of innovative techniques'.

Belleroche's lifelong friendship with Sargent is especially fascinating. Sargent and Belleroche met in 1882 at the studio of Carolus-Duran where they both trained. They shared studios in Paris and London and made painting trips together, including in 1883 a seminal trip to Harlem to Harlem in the company of Helleu (CAT. 19, opposite page and page 56). In 1905 Belleroche declined joining Sargent on another painting trip to the Middle East fearing that Sargent might overly 'influence me in my art and affect my personal expression'.

Correspondence shows that Sargent acted as Belleroche's mentor, offering him advice about his paintings and exhibiting his work. Belleroche was the subject of numerous portraits in both pencil and oil by Sargent. Eight years his senior, Sargent affectionately referred to Belleroche as 'baby Milbank', Milbank being the name of Belleroche's stepfather. The closeness of the friendship between Sargent and Belleroche has given birth to intense speculation as to whether their relationship was purely professional. In *John Singer Sargent: The Sensualist* (Yale University Press, 2000), Trevor Fairbrother has suggested otherwise. Elaine Killmurray's essay, *Albert de Belleroche and John Singer Sargent – A Life-long Friendship*, commissioned for this catalogue, discusses in depth the nature of their amity.

Belleroche scholarship is dependent on two principal sources: the first is the artist's studio Log Book documenting his production as a print maker; the second is a series of 1955 interviews with Julie de Belleroche undertaken by Willy and Gordon Anderson. On the basis of notes taken, Willy had hoped to write a book about his father. Although this project never came to fruition it has been the main source of the artist's biography and of many amusing anecdotes. Trying to separate the myth from the facts has been a constant challenge.

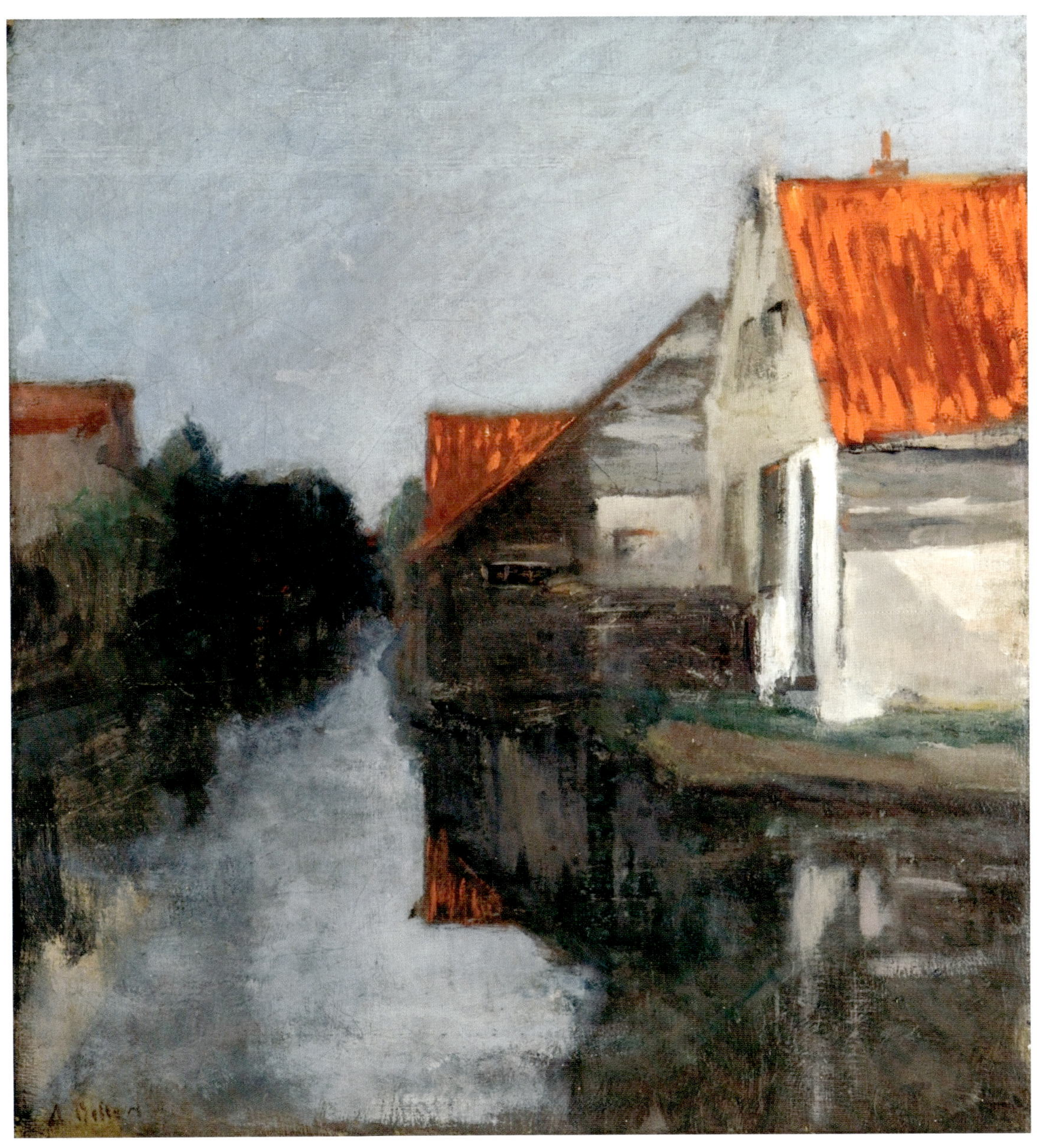

CAT. 19 – *Haarlem*, c.1883, oil on canvas, signed, 15 x 14 in. (38 x 35.5 cm).

The 2001 San Diego exhibition, with its excellent catalogue by Steven Kern, marked the first modern milestone in Belleroche scholarship. George Kenney's 30 year research project into the lithographic art of Belleroche, resulting in the catalogue raisonné of Belleroche's lithographs, *Albert de Belleroche, Master of Belle Epoque Lithography*, (Liss Llewellyn, 2024) as the companion to this publication, marks a second defining moment, mapping for the first time the full extent of Belleroche's career as a lithographer. In a period of less than 25 years he produced nearly 1000 images of remarkable innovation. Steven Kern has even argued that 'it is reasonable to place Belleroche amidst the most influential of the Impressionist printmakers, for his habitual reworking of an image directly echoes the monotypes of Mary Cassatt, Camille Pissarro and Edgar Degas, whilst pushing this aesthetic to an even more radical extreme'. Belleroche's art only occupies a very small place in what was arguably the richest period of French art, but even if he is considered a *petit maître*, this publication hopes to argue that posterity owes him more than this modest honour.

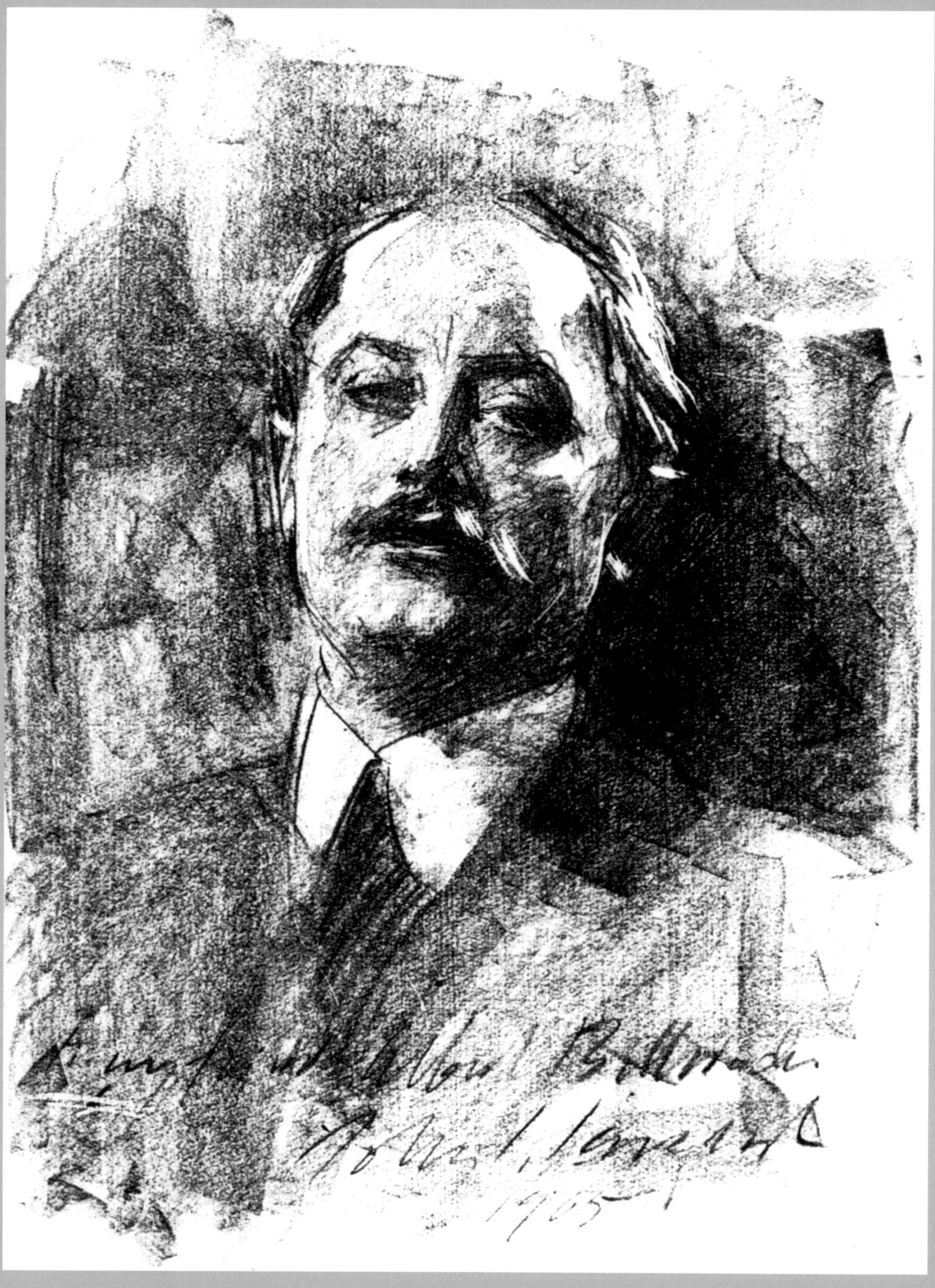

Albert de Belleroche and John Singer Sargent – A Life-long Friendship

Elaine Kilmurray

Albert Gustavus de Belleroche (1864-1944) was born in Swansea, south Wales, to parents of continental European descent and he spent most of his life in Paris and London. Albert's father, Edward Charles, Marquis de Belleroche, came from a noble French Huguenot family, and his mother, Alice Sidonie Van den Berg, daughter of Desire Baruch, was Belgian. Albert maintained a close relationship with his parents' native countries throughout his life. The Marquis de Belleroche died in 1867, when Albert was a young child. A few years later, Alice married Harry Vane Milbank, son of the Liberal Member of Parliament Sir Frederick Milbank and a well-known adventurer, huntsman and gambler. In 1871, the couple moved to Paris where Alice entertained in style in their house on the Avenue Montaigne. (FIG. 7) The young Albert took his stepfather's name for some years.[2]

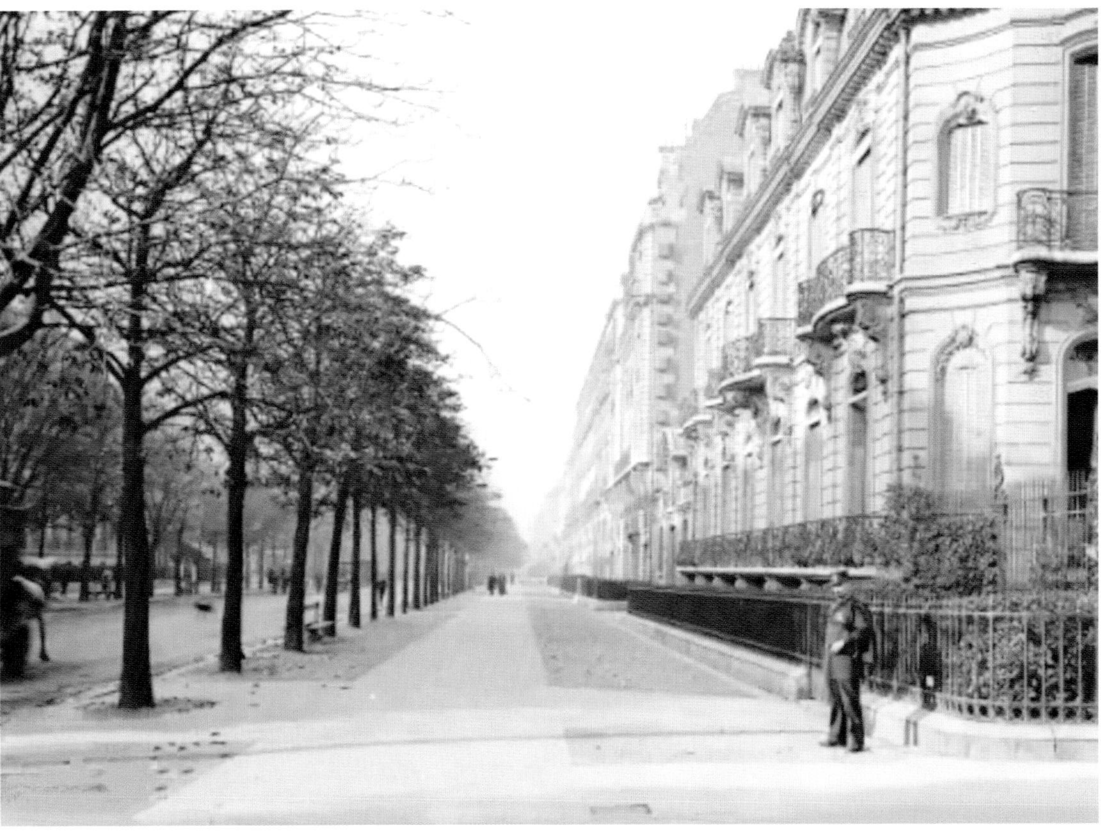

FIG. 7 – Avenue Montaigne, Paris, c.1900.

FIG. 6 – John Singer Sargent, *Portrait of Albert de Belleroche*, 1905, transfer lithograph, 20 ½ x 15 ½ in. (52 x 39.4 cm), Inscribed: "To my friend Albert Belleroche, John S. Sargent, 1905".

Albert Belleroche grew up in a Paris magnificently and efficiently rebuilt under Baron Haussmann, a city with long, wide boulevards, elegant squares and parks, a modern railway network, department stores, a café culture, theatres and a lively, illustrated press. It was confident and vibrant, the capital of culture, luxury and pleasure, and the centre of the art world. Paris offered young artists the best art education and an experience of art ranging from the academic to the avant-garde, and it provided them with a popular and broad exhibition forum, from the prestigious annual Salon held on the Champs-Elysées to private galleries showing experimental work, including that of the artists who would come to be known as the Impressionists.

In 1882, Harry Milbank commissioned Carolus-Duran (1837-1917), one of the most fashionable and successful portraitists in Paris, to paint a portrait of his wife.[3] At around this time Carolus-Duran, at a dinner in honour of the Prince of Wales (later King Edward VII), was shown some sketches by Belleroche and was so impressed that he suggested that the young man should come to study at his atelier, then one of the most progressive in Paris.[4] It was, for Belleroche, a singular foray into formal art education. In his short time as a student in Duran's atelier, he absorbed the master's progressive technique, dispensing with preliminary under-drawing and underpainting – the basis of traditional academic training – in favour of a more immediate *au premier coup* method. This involved working with a loaded brush applying flowing pigment directly onto the canvas. Carolus had been deeply influenced by the painting style of the seventeenth century Spanish painter Velázquez and he encouraged his students to build up the form and modelling of the face by describing the principal planes in their fundamental tonal values, laying in the half-tones first, followed by the darker accents and then the highest lights. Carolus also advocated the facture of the Dutch painter Frans Hals, laying touches one on top of the other without blending, creating a more textured surface and fleeting effects. To contemporary artists keen to forge a new style, the suggestivebrushwork and painterly realism of these Old Masters were among the qualities which were signifiers of modern art. Carolus's emphasis on tonal painting influenced Belleroche's understanding of the relative values of light and dark and would inform his experiments with lithography, the expressiveness of his treatment of blacks and greys.

The rising star from Carolus's atelier was a young American artist John Singer Sargent (1856-1925), who so impressed his fellow students that some among them 'watched his growth and wondered whether Carolus were teaching him or he were stimulating Carolus'.[5] Sargent's style was reminiscent of his master's, but 'the reminder became so faint as to be negligible, for Sargent sublimated the texture of Carolus's handling into something more felt and distinguished'.[6] In 1879, Sargent won an Honourable Mention at the Salon for a stylish three-quarter length portrait of his master (FIG. 8) (Sterling and Francine Clark Art Institute, Williamstown, Massachusetts) and, in 1881, he was awarded a second-class medal for a portrait of the wife of a Chilean diplomat, Madame Ramón Subercaseaux (private collection). These were extraordinary accolades for a young American to receive from the French art establishment

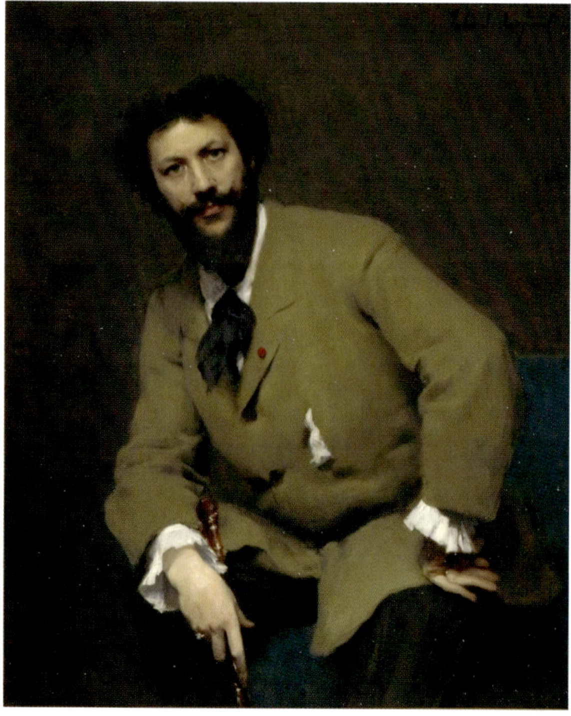

FIG. 8 – John Singer Sargent, *Carolus-Duran*, 1879, oil on canvas, 46 x 37 ¾ in. (116.8 x 95.9cm). Sterling and Francine Clark Art Institute, Williamstown.

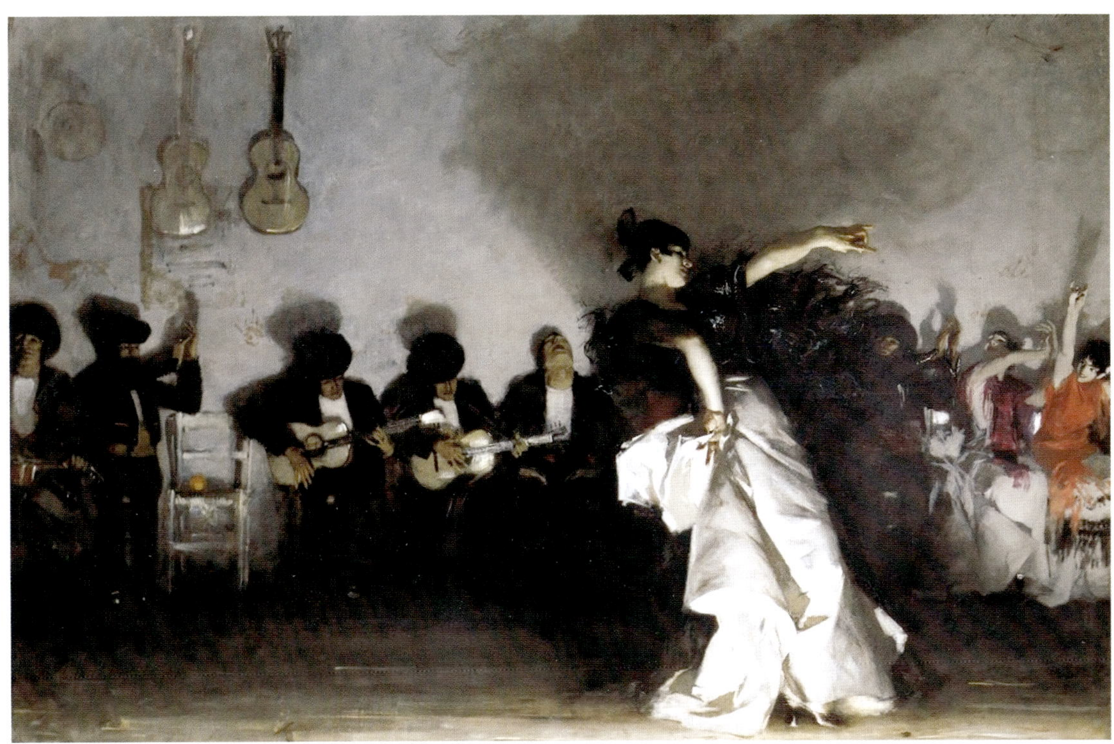

FIG. 9 – John Singer Sargent, *El Jaleo*, 1882,
oil on canvas, 91 ¼ x 137 in. (232 x 348 cm). Isabella Stewart Gardner Museum, Boston.

and they indicated that Sargent was on the brink of international success and fame. His submissions to the Salon of 1882 were a monumental but daringly sketchy study of a Spanish dancer in performance, *El Jaleo; – danse de Gitanes* (FIG. 9) (Isabella Stewart Gardner Museum, Boston) and a more traditionally charming Velázquez-inspired portrait, *Lady with the Rose* (The Metropolitan Museum of Art, New York). The raw energy, flagrant theatricality and apparently reckless paint handling of *El Jaleo* were uncompromising; they provoked intense discussion among the critics and the exhibition-going public, making Sargent one of the bright, controversial young artists of the moment. It was at around this time that he and Belleroche met. According to Belleroche's account, it was 'some time in the year 1882, at an annual dinner offered to Carolus Duran by his pupils' when he himself was a new boy in Duran's atelier.[7] He then met the American artist informally in the Restaurant l'Avenue, where Sargent was sketching in an album, which became known as 'L'album Sargent'. With regard to Belleroche, these early Paris years are poorly documented, but it was a heady artistic environment: he came to know Henri de Toulouse Lautrec and the pastellist and etcher Paul-César Helleu (1859-1927), and he crossed paths with Pierre-Auguste Renoir and the writers George Moore, Emile Zola and Oscar Wilde.

In 1883, Sargent, Belleroche and Helleu made a short visit to Haarlem in The Netherlands to see the work of Frans Hals. The pencil sketch of Sargent asleep on a train (reproduced as the frontispiece to Belleroche's article on Sargent's lithographs and dated 1883) was probably done on the journey to or from Haarlem. Although Belleroche was only eight years younger than Sargent, the older artist referred to the younger as 'Baby Milbank'. Sargent painted a series of portraits of Belleroche (two of them inscribed 'to Baby Milbank') in oil.[8] He depicted him as a sitter in conventional day dress (FIG. 10) and as an artist with a sketchbook in front of him respectively. In two other oils he represented him as a model. In a half-length study, he wears a costume similar to that worn by the musicians in *El Jaleo*. Since Sargent and Belleroche did not meet until 1882, this portrait was painted when Sargent had finished or was finishing work on *El Jaleo* and possibly around the time of its exhibition at the Salon in 1882, where it attracted lively critical attention. It shows Sargent depicting Belleroche *in persona*, playing with studio props to create an informal, collaborative portrayal of a friend.[9] In what was conceived as the most ambitious portrayal, Belleroche is wearing a tunic with the square-cut neckline associated with Renaissance costume (FIG. 11). In his description of the picture, Belleroche does not identify himself as the model: 'Amongst the other pictures which Sargent painted in this new studio I will mention a three-quarter life-size portrait of a young man in a Florentine costume. This picture which was originally intended to represent an Italian gentleman holding a large double-handed sword, was finally cut down to the bust and the theatrical accoutrements removed'.[10] It remained in Sargent's possession throughout his life and hung in his dining room in Tite Street, Chelsea.[11] A drawing showing Belleroche standing (almost) full-length with a sword probably represents the original idea for the picture (Yale University Art Gallery, New Haven).[12]

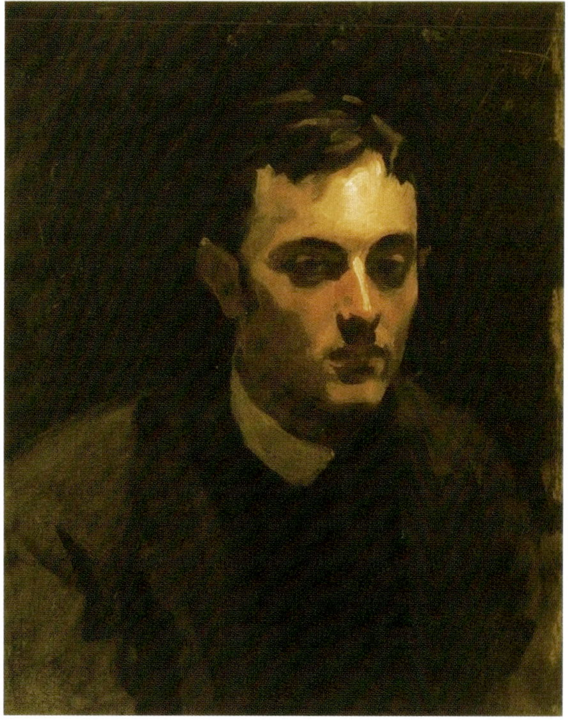
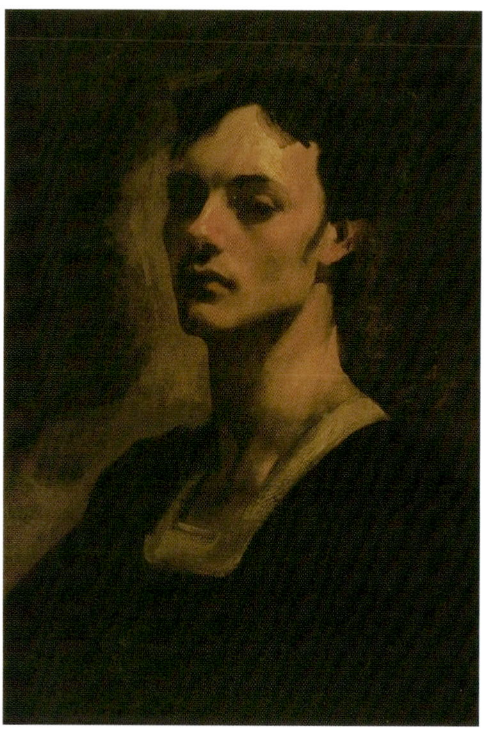

FIGS. 10 & 11 – John Singer Sargent,
Portrait of Albert de Belleroche, c.1882, oil on canvas, 24 x 18 in. (61 x 45.7 cm).
Portrait of Albert de Belleroche, 1883, oil on canvas, 25 x 16 ½ in. (63.5 x 41.9 cm).

According to Belleroche, sittings for this portrait took place at Sargent's studio at 41 Boulevard Berthier near the Batignolles (Sargent had moved there from his studio near the Luxembourg Gardens at some point in the middle of 1883). Belleroche's son, Count William de Belleroche, has recorded that his father told him that the portrait required twenty sittings and was painted during intervals between sittings for Sargent's most celebrated work, the portrait of Madame Pierre Gautreau (*Madame X,* 1883-84, The Metropolitan Museum of Art, New York) (FIG. 12).This portrayal of an American-born beauty wearing a severely elegant black dress with one jewelled shoulder strap slipped was a *succès de scandale* at the Salon in 1884. Her tightly-fitting, skin-revealing dress and the flagrant artifice of her make-up – a whitening cosmetic powder – challenge conventional ides of womanhood. The portrait was seen to be a flamboyantly transgressive work, aesthetically and societally, and it became one of the defining works of Sargent's career.[13]

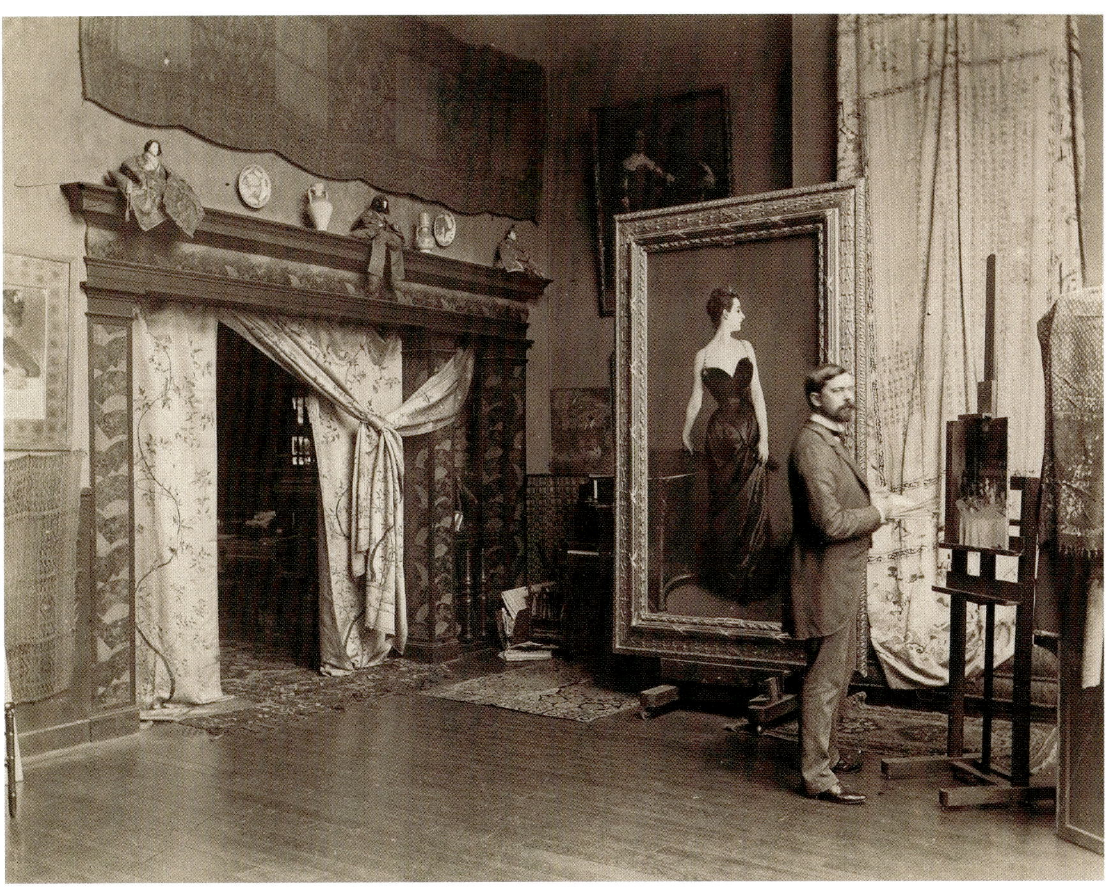

FIG. 12 – John Singer Sargent in his studio, 41 Boulevard Berthier, Paris, with the portrait of Madame X,1884. Photograph attributed to A. Giraudon.

Sargent painted Madame Gautreau at her country estate, 'Les Chênes' at Paramé, near Saint-Malo in Brittany and in his Paris studio. He wrote to Belleroche from Paramé on 'Les Chênes' headed notepaper. The letter, on which Sargent has drawn a sketch of Madame Gautreau's head peering above the back of a piano, is undated, but the envelope is dated '7 Sept 83'. It is quoted in full to indicate the teasing tone of the relationship between Sargent and Belleroche:

> Dear Baby
>
> In spite of the ridiculousness of corresponding with a child, here I am answering your letter. But please don't write me any more! Oh no.
> I am still at Paramé, basking on the sunshine of my beautiful model's countenance. I suppose I shall be here at least two weeks more and then I must be off to Italy. So no Scotland for me. Please tell your mother that I regret it very much.
> Helleu is at 41 Boulevard Berthier. I hear from him now and then. Sometimes cheerful letters and sometimes a 'grand emmerdement seems to tomber sur Leu Leu' I shall see him in a day or two for I am going to spend 24 hours in Paris and then coming back here.
> Mme Gautreau is at the piano and driving all my ideas away.
> Hoping not to hear from you any more, dear duck,
>
> Yours,
>
> John S. Sargent[14]

This letter is one of a number of tantalising connections between Belleroche and the portrait of Madame Pierre Gautreau. Sargent's oil portraits of Belleroche and several drawings portray a beautiful young man with delicate but clearly defined features and soulful, hooded eyes. Belleroche's sensuous, androgynous beauty and the fact that Sargent was painting him at the same time as he was working on the 'unpaintable beauty' that was Amélie Gautreau has led to some discussion about artistic conflation and gender ambiguity.[15] The features in one drawing in particular, of a head, tilted and in profile, bears such a close relationship to images of both Gautreau and Belleroche that it has been claimed as a depiction of both sitters, or a blurring of the two.[16] Dorothy Moss reads this facial merging as a reflection of the 'heightened emotion that reveals [Sargent's] intense friendship and identification with Belleroche'. She stops short of suggesting a homosexual relationship, adopting the term "'homosocial' bond", and she makes the point that male bonding that was neither overtly romantic nor sexual, particularly when one of the men was in a mentoring role, was not uncommon in the culture of the period.[17] There has been considerable discussion about Sargent's sexuality in recent literature, led by the research and insights of the Sargent scholar Trevor Fairbrother, and a reading of the artist's intense studies of Belleroche as expressions of an erotic response or of sublimated desire is persuasive.[18] The idea of a homosexual relationship between Sargent and Belleroche was given a fictional reality in Deborah Davis's successful biographical novel about Amélie Gautreau, *Strapless* (2003), and physical form in Christopher Wheeldon's ballet, based on Davis's book, which premiered at the Royal Opera House, London in 2016. The ballet features the dancers representing Sargent and Belleroche engaged in a brief *pas de deux* shot through with suppressed yearning. The writer Colm Tóibín has noted Belleroche's 'sultry sexual presence' in his discussion of Sargent's sexuality, suggesting that 'the masked sensuality in some of the work or the sense of the face and the pose as filled with an aura of performance' stems from the artist's desire for secrecy or concealment.[19]

Sargent's portrait of Madame Gautreau may also inform the unfinished full-length portrait of Belleroche's mother (FIG. 13), which Sargent was probably working on at around the same time. Alice Milbank, wearing a black evening gown with a décolleté neckline, stands against a neutral background, her left hand on her hip, her right hanging by her side, in an approximate mirror-image of *Madame X*. The similarities between the two works in terms of pose and dress are indicative of Sargent's pictorial preoccupations at the time. [Compare with Belleroche's potrait of his mother. (FIG. 14)]

It is possible to trace something of the history of Sargent's association with Belleroche through surviving letters. In an enigmatic, undated letter, headed 'Boulevard Berthier', Sargent wrote: 'A lot of things have turned up to prevent me having a sitting tomorrow. So please put it off till some other day. I have got a wig!'[20] The letter must date from between 1883, when Sargent moved to Boulevard Berthier, and 1886, when he left Paris for London. There is nothing to suggest to which portrait Sargent is referring and no clues as to the significance of the wig! Sargent moved to England around 1886 and there is very little in the later 1880s to give substance to the relationship. Sargent did write to Belleroche from Russell House, Broadway on 6 October 1886, at the time he [Sargent] was working on his beautiful study of two young girls lighting oriental lanterns in a twilit garden, *Carnation, Lily, Lily, Rose* (1885-86, Tate, London) (FIG. 15), but it is simply a letter about their failure to cross paths when Belleroche was visiting London and Sargent in the Cotswolds. The most important reference point at this approximate date is not a document but a painting, and an intriguing one. A charming oil study by Belleroche of two young girls in sailor dresses leaning over a table with a sheet of paper on which one of them is sketching depicts Sargent's dining room (FIG. 16). An oil study by Sargent depicts the same room from an approximately similar angle; the table, chairs and dresser are the same in both works as are some of the paintings hanging on the walls. Another interior by Sargent, *The Blue Bowl*, probably represents the same room from a different angle.[21] All the works are undated (Sargent's two oils probably date from around the mid 1880s to the mid 1890s on

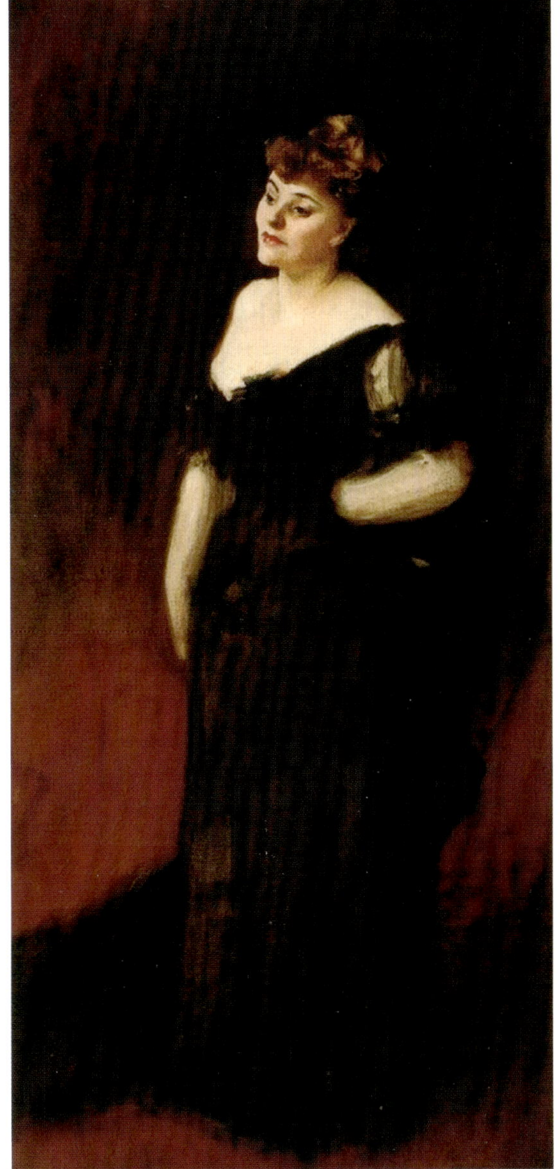

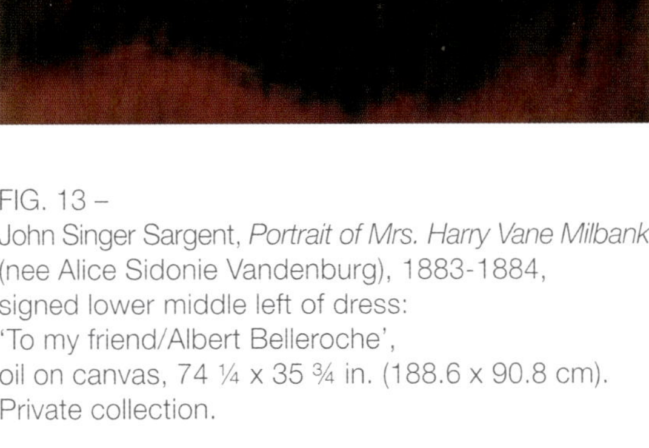

FIG. 13 –
John Singer Sargent, *Portrait of Mrs. Harry Vane Milbank*
(nee Alice Sidonie Vandenburg), 1883-1884,
signed lower middle left of dress:
'To my friend/Albert Belleroche',
oil on canvas, 74 ¼ x 35 ¾ in. (188.6 x 90.8 cm).
Private collection.

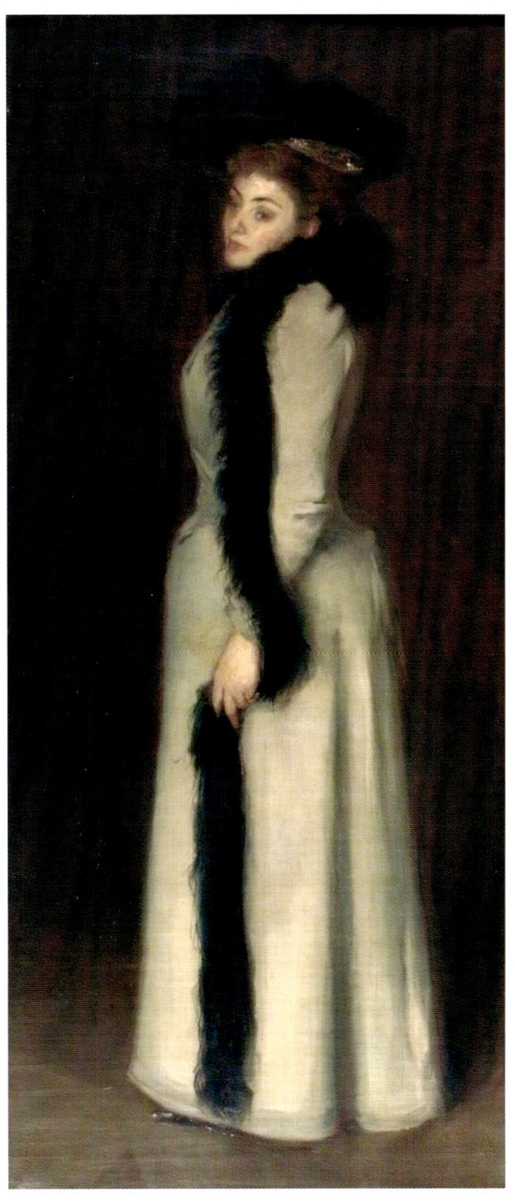

FIG. 14 –
Mrs H. V. Milbank (The Artist's Mother), early 1900s,
oil on canvas, 76 x 33 in. (193 x 84 cm),
Amgueddfa Cymru – National Museum Wales,
National Museum Cardiff (gift from the artist, 1942).

stylistic grounds) and it is uncertain whether the dining room is that in Boulevard Berthier in Paris or Tite Street in London. Belleroche's painting gives a physical reality to the continuing, if intermittent, artistic relationship between the two men.

The artists were on familiar enough terms to share each other's studios when it was convenient. In the summer of 1891, Sargent travelled back from a lengthy trip to Egypt, Greece and Turkey, where he had been doing research for a mural project he had recently undertaken for the Special

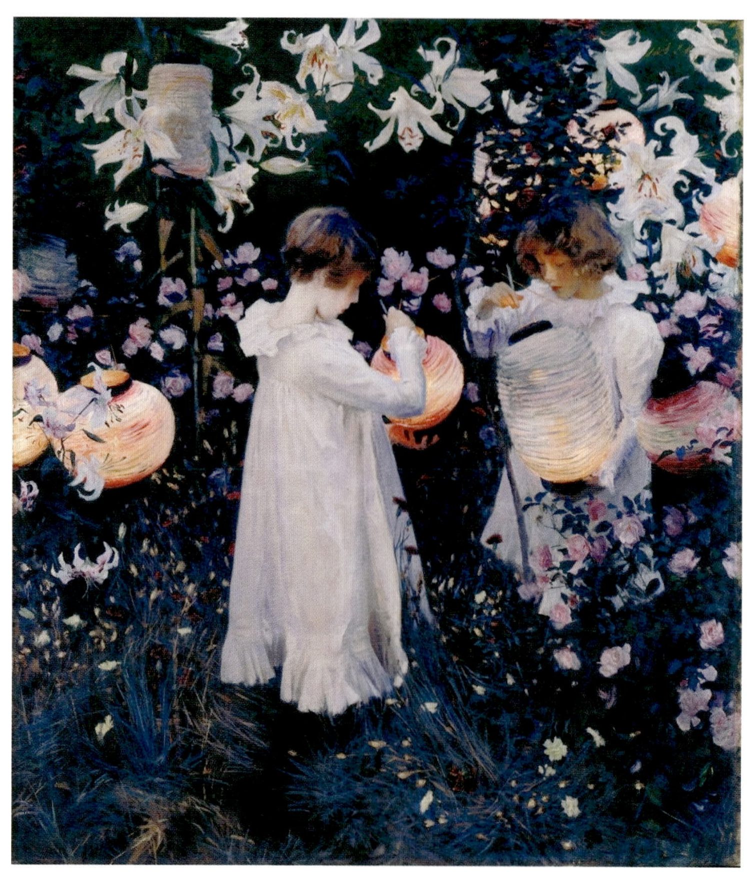

FIG. 15 – John Singer Sargent, *Carnation, Lily, Lily, Rose*, 1885, oil on canvas, 68 ½ x 60 ½ in. (174 x 153.7 cm). Collection: Tate, London.

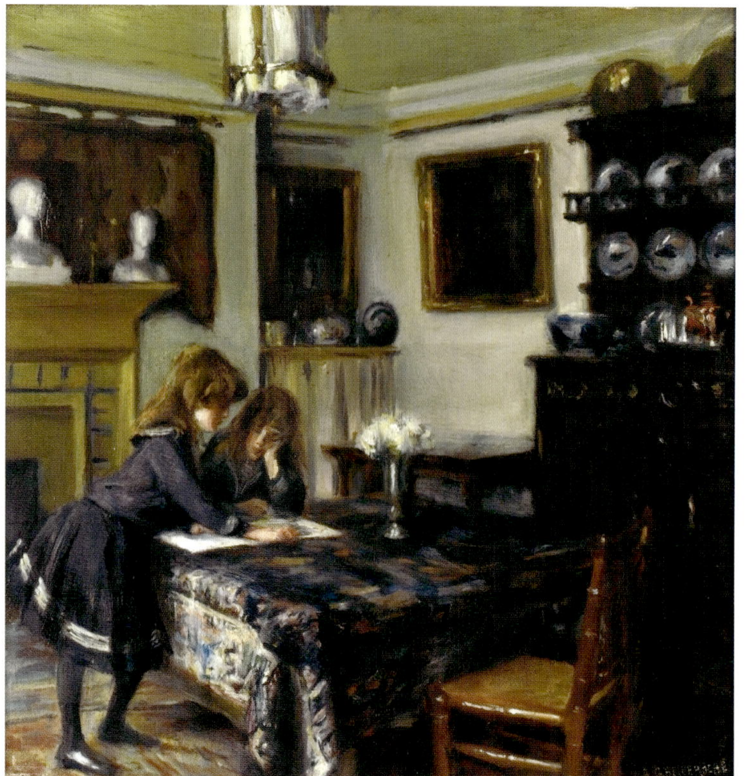

FIG. 16 – *The Dining Room of John Singer Sargent,* c. 1884, signed, oil on canvas, 17 ¼ x 16 ¾ in. (43.5 x 42.5 cm). Provenance: Julie de Belleroche; William de Belleroche, Ruth Wittman.

Collections Hall of the Boston Public Library. He made an extended stopover in Paris, staying there for some weeks and attending the wedding of his younger sister Violet. While in Paris he borrowed Belleroche's studio to paint a portrait of Thomas Brackett Reed, Speaker of the House of Representatives in Washington (Collection of the US House of Representatives).[22] Belleroche used Sargent's studio in London from time to time: at least two letters from Sargent to Belleroche were addressed to him at 33 Tite Street.[23]

Early in 1891, Sargent's friend, the American painter and illustrator Edwin Austin Abbey (1852-1911), who had also been commissioned to create a mural cycle for the Boston Public Library (*The Quest and Achievement of the Holy Grail*) had taken a lease for twenty-one years on a house, Morgan Hall in Fairford, Gloucestershire. Abbey built a studio in the grounds big enough for him and Sargent to work on a large scale – Sargent described it as a space 'where a two-metre canvas looks like a postage stamp'.[24] Living and working deep in the Gloucestershire countryside, Sargent became enthusiastic about country pursuits. He was a passionate but far from gifted rider. In one instance, he got into trouble when he was on horseback and – unintentionally – crossed a local farmer's field of winter wheat. An unpleasant episode ensued, the farmer took legal action and all was resolved when Sargent, represented by the celebrated lawyer Sir George Lewis, paid the farmer damages of £50.[25] During his hunting phase, Sargent called on Belleroche, whose step-father was an accomplished horseman and hunter, to visit him in the country and help him improve his equestrian skills.

Sargent's tone to Belleroche can be brusque to the point of hectoring. His seniority (by eight years) and perhaps his professional success seems to have shaped their relationship and determined the tone of Sargent's letters. On 15 February 1892, he wrote to Belleroche:

> Where the devil are you — and why don't you answer my note and telegram? I have written to Mackellan and to Tite Street? Will you come down next week? There is a [hunting] meet Tuesday here . . . [26]
> And
> You can always have my studio, and if you come over – let me know, so I can have you down here. I expected to have some good rides with you, and that you would teach me to jump hedges and hunt.[27]

Several letters refer to administrative matters. On 20 February 1892, Sargent was writing to Belleroche in Paris (at 7 rue de Tourlaque): 'I am glad your picture is appreciated at the Volney'.[28] There are a few sustained passages of artistic comment and advice:

> You ask me if I think the little gaio [?] will be accepted at the R.A. Of course I should vote for it, but there are eight others, [illegible] whom I cannot promise for. They would consider it a study and reject it on those grounds. And if it did get in it would certainly be slayed [skied?] because it is not a picture with a subject. I think it would be much better seen at the New English Art Club. This is my advice. But if you prefer sending it to the Academy, send me the title etc right away. I will fill up a notice and send it on. The sending in day is Monday, March 28th. I have not got a notice, but I will get one. It would save time for you to dictate it to me, and I will attend to the sending in of the picture.[29]

> Your big picture isn't half as far advanced as I expected to find it — it is a kind of thing that will depend entirely on the execution. If those biceps and rumpsteaks are very well painted, it will be interesting.
> I think the general tone – especially in the flesh, is a little 'lie de vin' [wine-coloured] and I don't like the way the tail of the dress hangs down in a point. It makes a very meagre and insignificant drapery for such a strapping girl. I should try a much bigger, thicker drapery

that would take big folds, and simplify the red if you must, even if you are very fond of it, for the sake of more character and form. And above all, execute the head, and throat, and arms, and make a fine 'morceau' and try to impart your own [illegible] to the spectator, by sheer strength of painting. Those parts are well indicated, but very sketchy and 'lie de vin'. I daresay, if I had seen the model sitting there, I would have given a much better criticism. Take it for what it is worth.[30]

Although Belleroche was largely based in Paris, he maintained a foothold in London, joining the New English Art Club in 1894:

What do you want to see me most particularly about? I am going to Paris for a long time. So you had better write, and spell correctly.
Your things at the New English Art Club are well placed on the line. You ought to come over to see them before the show closes, which will not be for a month I suppose. It might teach you something. They look a little juvenile. Do you send your 'Red Girl' any-where?[31]

In 1905, Sargent was planning to visit Palestine to do some painting research for his work on the Boston Public Library murals. There is a small group of letters in which he invites Belleroche to accompany him and goes into some detail about travel arrangements, routes, passports etc.:

Do you care to go to Palestine and Syria in the autumn with me? . . .
The travelling, and hotel expenses from Brindisi, through Palestine and Syria and back to Brindisi, would be mine. I mean you would take the trip as my guest, if you will do me the pleasure of coming along. I shall take lots of painting things . . . Part of the journey will be done in tents and on horseback if it is not too hot. I hope you will [come]. If you won't, I will try to get somebody else – but I should prefer a painter and an old friend. Please let me know soon – for I don't want to go alone, and will invite someone else, who might not agree as well as we should as to where to stop and work.[32]
On this early part of the trip, which may be partly done in tents, it would have been particularly agreeable to have had a companion. As you cannot come for the whole journey, I will try to get an Italian artist who is here and who knows our journey to Palestine. If he cannot come, I will still be very grateful if you will join me out there as soon after the 20th of September as possible. I will write you again in a day or two and tell you the result of this new demarche. It seems to me so important that one should have a companion on such a journey . . . So please do not abandon on the idea of coming until you hear from me again . . .
As for money, you can paint a small picture for me if you have scruples about my financing the trip.[33]

In the event, Sargent travelled to Palestine with an Italian artist, Alberto Falchetti (1878-1956). Issues of logistics and timing may have prevented Belleroche from making the journey to Palestine, but he was also wary of being in Sargent's shadow. Years later, Belleroche gave the reason for his declining: 'I realized that a journey like that with Sargent might influence me in my art and affect my personal expression'.[34]

Sargent and Belleroche almost certainly came to lithography independently of each other. Sargent executed the first of his six lithographs around 1895, while Belleroche began working in the medium in 1899 after being disappointed by the quality of a reproduction of one of his works. Sargent adopts a different tone to Belleroche when he is discussing lithographs:

I like that drawing very much – particularly the darked proof on yellow paper, I don't know how many proofs one can take from a lithograph, but I would like to have six others – dark

ones, if possible. Pity the mouth is bad – the light on both lips is too bright.
If you were here, I should do lots of these – Why?[35]

Sargent has also written on the back of the envelope: 'Just darken lights on lips'.
Sargent's notes can be so brief as to be cryptic:

Many thanks for the lithographs. They are quite enough. I have hardly had time to look at them. They are just like the others – aren't they? Pity one eye is too high up.[36]

Sargent's forays into lithography were short-lived and relatively provisional, whereas Belleroche's technical experiments and commitment to the medium were such that he was deemed to have played 'a leading role in the renaissance of lithography'.[37] Sargent's six lithographs are catalogued and illustrated in an article that Belleroche wrote for *The Print Collector's Quarterly* after the older artist's death. They comprise two studies of a draped young man, presumably a model; two portrait studies of Belleroche (FIG. 6); one of William Rothenstein at work and a portrait of a young woman. Sargent's lithographs were all done on transfer paper rather than directly onto stone. Belleroche may have seen himself as part of a great French tradition. According to William de Belleroche, his father owned a press from the Imprimerie Lemercier in Paris, the press which 'printed the works of Delacroix, Daumier, and many of the French Impressionists'.[38] Belleroche printed the two portraits Sargent made of him on his own press.[39]

Lithography was invented in 1796 by Alois Senefelder of Solnhofen in Germany. It involves drawing on fine-grained porous limestone or on a zinc plate with greasy material, then wetting the stone or plate and applying greasy ink, which adheres only to the drawn lines. Dampened paper is applied to the stone and is rubbed over with a special press to make the final print. In the hands of Honoré Daumier, Théodore Géricault and Eugène Delacroix, lithography had a great artistic flowering in France, but it suffered some decline in the latter decades of the nineteenth century, when it was too closely associated with the reproduction of images. To a new generation, however, lithographic crayon and ink (or *tusche*) offered expressive possibilities that spoke to contemporary interest in the artist's individual stroke, the signature *touche*. Belleroche was acquainted with Henri de Toulouse-Lautrec (1864-1901); they were fellow aristocrats and Lili Grenier, one of Lautrec's favourite models, became model, muse and mistress to Belleroche.[40] (FIG. 5) During a brief but intense career, Lautrec's innovative style and commitment to the medium ensured that popular advertising lithography was taken seriously rather than being dismissed as commercial ephemera. Although Toulouse Lautrec worked assiduously and inventively on his lithographic drawing and directed the process of production, he left the actual printing in the hands of a skilled technician. In order to get the most out of the materials, exploit their expressive qualities and ensure the 'artistic integrity of the work', Belleroche became involved in and responsible for the entire process and production to such an extent that his technical experiments and innovations extended the scope of the medium. In 1933, Louis Lebeer, curator of the Bibliothèque Royale in Brussels, organised an exhibition of Belleroche's work. In an essay published in the catalogue, with input from the artist, Lebeer details some of Belleroche's experimental trials and what he concluded from them:

He declared that the stone is a material with which the artist must have direct contact in order to take advantage of its full potential. Each stone has its own characteristics: its grain, whether heavy or light; its receptivity to the grease of the crayons or wash that the artist must take into consideration. At the press, the stone responds to both ink and pressure – sometimes slowly, sometimes in a wink – that the artist himself must regulate to obtain the desired results.[41]

Belleroche's free drawing with the crayon makes for a range of markings, from broad, sweeping lines to apparently intentional scribbles, trails and spatters, exploiting the inherent physical qualities of the stone and producing nuanced textures. His manipulation of light and shade creates powerful tonal contrasts and effects, and his figures are more physically present than, for example, the aerial figures of Paul Helleu. Belleroche's sureness of touch and his drawing directly onto the stone might derive from his encounter with Carolus's teaching methods and the emphasis he placed on values and half-tones in painting.

Belleroche produced over 960 lithographs which are varied in subject, but he was principally a portrayer of women, from society ladies of the Belle Epoque to nudes.[42] Claude Roger-Marx called his work 'powerful and tender, celebrating the women of our time', while noting that the sensuousness of his nudes might have interested Degas and Rodin.[43] Commentators pointed to Belleroche's responsiveness to the potential of the limited palette, his skill in manipulating it and his painterly use of the crayon. These are some representative comments: 'his strong whites and luxurious blacks'; 'more colourist than draughtsman, but . . . a colourist in white and black'; 'his richly nuanced palette is at the service of a highly sensitive intelligence'.[44] 'It is possible, using nothing but whites and blacks, to show oneself to be the equal of the most wide-ranging colourist; the spectrum of ash greys to downy greys, the deep blacks, velvety, matt or shining, is so subtle and so diverse'.[45] Critics noted the significance of French influences on Belleroche's work, some of them obvious – Sargent, Helleu, Albert Besnard, Eugène Carrière – and some more surprising, for example the comparison of his still-lifes to those of Jean-Baptiste-Siméon Chardin (1699-1779).[46] The obituarist writing for *The Times* noted that Belleroche's lithographic work was probably most remarkable for its 'sympathetic and expressive handling of the medium'.[47]

Belleroche's geographical relationships – France, England, Belgium – continued, with shifts in emphases, throughout his life. In 1887, he sent his first contribution (a self-portrait) to the Salon in Paris (Société des Artistes Français) and he continued to exhibit works there. In 1903, he was a Membre-Fondateur of the Salon d'automne, established as an alternative to the official and conservative Salon, exhibiting there from 1903 to 1906. A room was dedicated to his work in the 1904 Salon d'automne exhibition, from which his *Printemps,* a female nude, was purchased by the French state.[48] Belleroche also exhibited at the Galerie Henry Graves (1906 and 1908) and the Galerie Devambez (1908,1909). He joined the progressive New English Art Club in London in 1894 and exhibited there until 1899, and in smaller London venues (Goupil & Cie and Dowdeswell among them). There was the major exhibition in Brussels in 1933 and a show at Colnaghi in London in 1941 (11 oils and 30 drawings). Belleroche had made a decisive break with Paris in 1910, when he ended his ten-year relationship with Lili Grenier (FIG. 17) and married Julie Emilie, daughter of his friend, the sculptor Jules Edouard Visseaux and seventeen years Belleroche's junior. The couple travelled to Brussels (Belleroche contributed to the Universal Exposition in Brussels in 1910) and the following year moved to London. In 1918, they settled in Rustington on the Sussex coast, where they lived quietly and raised their family. Belleroche continued to work, concentrating on lithography, but he largely removed himself from the public sphere of art.

FIG. 17 – Fernand Cormon (1845-1924), *Portrait of Lili Grenier*, c.1885.

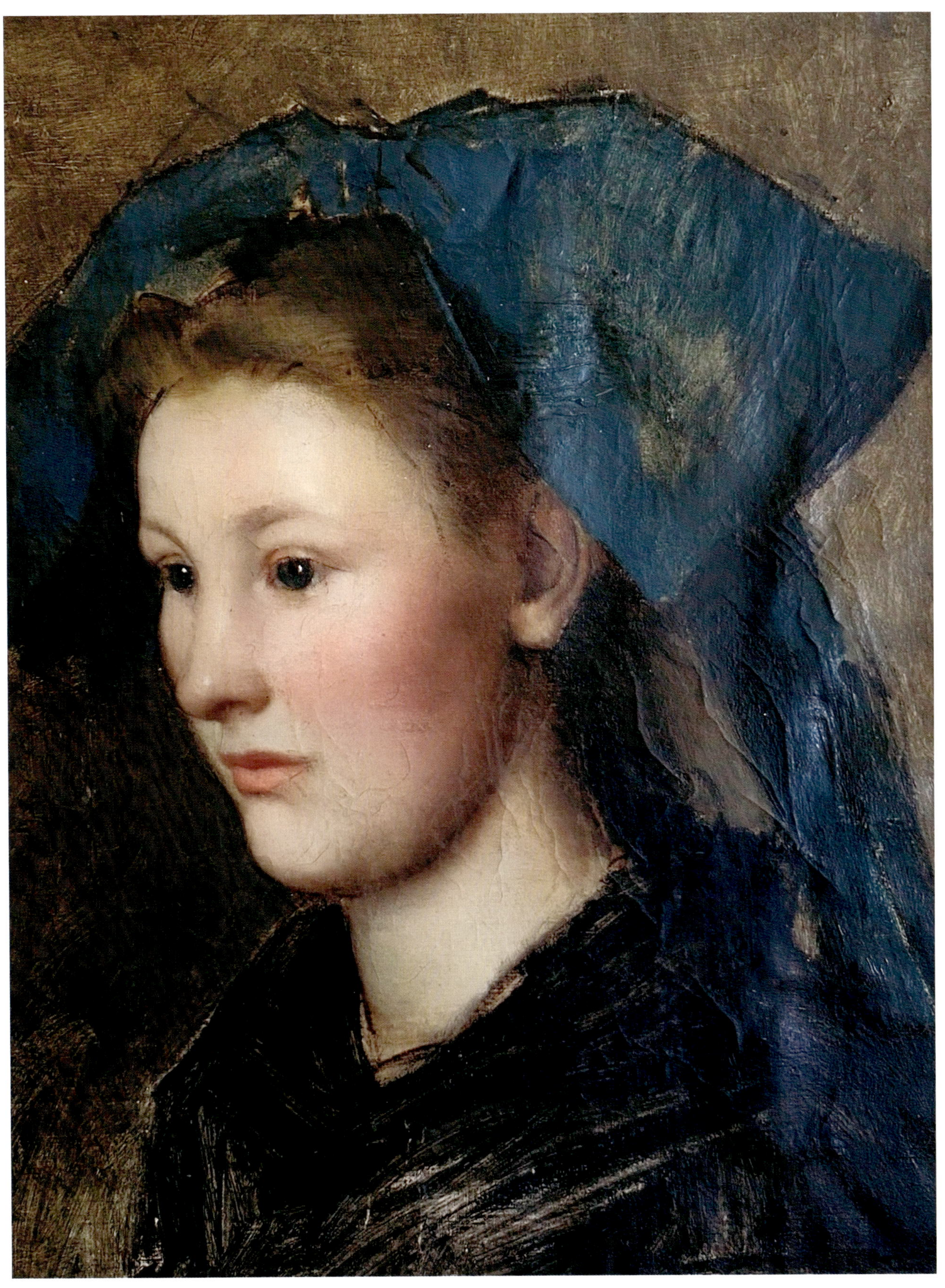

ENDNOTES

1   'disciple and close follower of Sargent'. Louis Vauxcelles, 'La Vie artistique', *Gil Blas,* 27 January 1908 [p.2].

2   Belleroche used the surname 'Milbank' until he was around thirty years old. He preferred 'Belleroche' to 'de Belleroche'. His son, William, chose to use 'de Belleroche'.

3   A three-quarter length portrait of Alice seated with a fan by Carolus-Duran, dated 1877, was sold at Bonham's, London, 2 March 2016, lot 73.

4   There is very little documentation recording Belleroche's early career. The story about his meeting Sargent is anecdotal. William de Belleroche, Albert's son, gave the account to the painter Frank Brangwyn. See William de Belleroche, *Brangwyn's Pilgrimage: The Life Story of an Artist*, London, 1948, p. 234.

5   Edwin H. Blashfield. 'John Singer Sargent—Recollections', *North American Review*, vol. 221 (June 1925), pp. 641-42. The American artist and muralist Edwin Howland Blashfield (1848-1936) was studying in Paris with Léon Bonnat when Sargent entered Carolus's studio in 1874.

6   Blashfield 1925, p. 642.

7   Albert Belleroche, 'The Lithographs of Sargent', *Print Collector's Quarterly*, vol. XIII [1926], p. 32

8   See Richard Ormond and Elaine Kilmurray, *John Singer Sargent: The Early Portraits*, New Haven and London, 1998, pp. 97-100 (nos 96-99). For a later lithographic portrait of Belleroche by Sargent. (See FIG. 6.)

9   This portrait is in the collection of the Colorado Springs Fine Arts Center at Colorado College, Colorado Springs, USA.

10   Belleroche 1926, p. 34.

11   The portrait was in Sargent's studio sale held at Christie's, London on 24th and 27th July 1925, lot 139, as 'Study of a Young Man'. It is now in a private collection.

12   For an illustration of this drawing, see Dorothy Moss, 'John Singer Sargent, "Madame X" and "Baby Millbank"', *Burlington Magazine,* vol. 143, no. 1178, May 2001, p. 275, fig. 22.

13   Letter from William de Belleroche to David McKibbin, 16 June 1968, John Singer Sargent Archive, Museum of Fine Arts, Boston.

14   This address on the envelope reads; 'Albert Milbank Esq/Dunain House/ Inverness N.B./ Ecosse/ Grand Bretagne. Sargent's letters to Belleroche are in a private collection. The author has not seen them in recent years and, with the exception of the letter written from Paramé, does not have copies. The transcriptions are made from notes taken some time ago. The French phrase translates as: 'a great affliction seems to fall on Leu Leu'. 'Leu Leu' was Sargent's nickname for Paul Helleu.

15   The phrase 'unpaintable beauty' in a letter from Sargent to his friend, the writer Vernon Lee, quoted in The Hon. Evan Charteris, K.C., *John Sargent*, London, 1927, p. 59. Moss 2001, pp. 268-75.

16   For illustrations of drawings of Belleroche by Sargent, see Ormond and Kilmurray 1998, p. 100, no. 99 and figs 45, 46, and Moss 2001, p. 271, figs. 9, 10,11. For the profile drawing which has been identified as both Belleroche and Madame Gautreau (Yale University Art Gallery, New Haven, Connecticut, 1931.26), see Ormond and Kilmurray 1998, p. 98, fig. 44, and Moss 2001, p. 269, figs 3 and 5.

17   Moss, 2001, pp. 273, 274.

18   Trevor Fairbrother has done extensive work on Sargent and the male-directed gaze, including a discussion of an album of his studies of male figures in the Fogg Art Museum, Harvard University ArtMuseums, Cambridge, Massachusetts, see *John Singer Sargent: The Sensualist*, Seattle Art Museum and Yale University Art Gallery, New Haven and London, 2000, pp. 104-111 and pp. 180-211.

19   Colm Tóibín, 'Henry James: Shadow and Substance', *Henry James and American Painting*, The Pennsylvania State University Press and The Morgan Library and Museum, 2017, pp. 44, 45.

20   This letter is addressed to Albert Milbank Esq/483 Fulham Road/London S.W., private collection.

21   For a detailed discussion of Sargent's *My Dining Room* and *The Blue Bowl*, see Richard Ormond and Elaine Kilmurray, *John Singer Sargent: Figures and Landscapes, 1883-1899*, New Haven and London, 2010, pp. 92-95, nos 853, 854.

22   Belleroche 1926, p. 44.

23   The numeration of Sargent's Tite Street studio can be confusing. He settled at 13 Tite Street, Chelsea in 1886. It was later renumbered 33. In 1900, he expanded to 31 Tite Street, knocking the connecting walls through and combining the buildings. He used 31 as his residence and 33 as his studio.

24   'où une toile de deux mètres a l'air d'un timbre-poste'. Undated letter from Sargent to Paul-César Helleu, formerly collection Madame Paulette Howard-Johnston.

25   For an account of Sargent's and his brush with the law, see Stanley Olson, John *Singer Sargent: His Portrait*, London, 1986, pp. 176-77.

26   Letter from Sargent to Belleroche, 15 February 1892, sent from Morgan Hall, Fairford, Gloucestershire to Belleroche at 33 Tite Street, London, private collection. Another letter, written two days later, was also sent to Belleroche at Sargent's studio. The identity of Mackellan is unknown, but it is likely that he was a porter or valet.

27   Letter from Sargent to Belleroche, January 1894, sent from Morgan Hall and addressed to Belleroche at New Club, 4 Grafton Road, London, W., private collection.

28   This is probably the Cercle artistique et littéraire, rue de Volney, one of a number of 'cercles' (smaller exhibition venues in Paris) at this period.

29   Undated letter from Sargent to Belleroche. Headed 'Friday', sent from 33 Tite Street, private collection.

30   Letter from Sargent to Belleroche, 17 May 1894, sent from 33 Tite Street, private collection.

31   Undated letter from Sargent to Belleroche. Headed 'Monday', private collection.

32   Letter from Sargent to Belleroche, 31 July 1905, sent to 30 Rue de Bruxelles, Paris. Letter re-addressed to: Poste St Hubert, Villers Cotteret, France, private collection.

33   Letter from Sargent to Belleroche, 22 August 1905, sent to Poste St Huber, Foret de Villiers Cotteret, Aisne, France, from Grand Hotel, Mont Cervin, Peraldo Proprietaire, Giomein, private collection.

34   Belleroche 1926, p. 38.

35   Letter from Sargent to Belleroche, 10 February 1905, sent to 30 Rue de Bruxelles, Paris, private collection.

36   Letter from Sargent to Belleroche, 8 March 1905, private collection.

37   'une place de premier plan dans la renaissance de la lithographie'. Claude Roger-Marx, 'Peintres-Lithographes contemporains: Albert Belleroche', *Gazette des beaux-arts*, I, vol. 39, 1908, p. 74.

38   William de Belleroche, *Brangwyn Talks*, London, 1944, p. 7.

39   In 2001, an exhibition of Belleroche's lithographs was assembled at the San Diego Museum of Art in California (the museum holds the largest collection of Belleroche's lithographs in the United States). See Steven Kern, *The Rival of Painting: The Lithographs of Albert Belleroche*, San Diego Museum of Art, San Diego, California, 2001. Kern's essay in the catalogue is a distinguished and valuable contribution to the literature on Belleroche and lithography.

40   A portrait of Toulouse-Lautrec in profile by Belleroche was sold at Bonham's, London, 11 December 2008, lot 17.

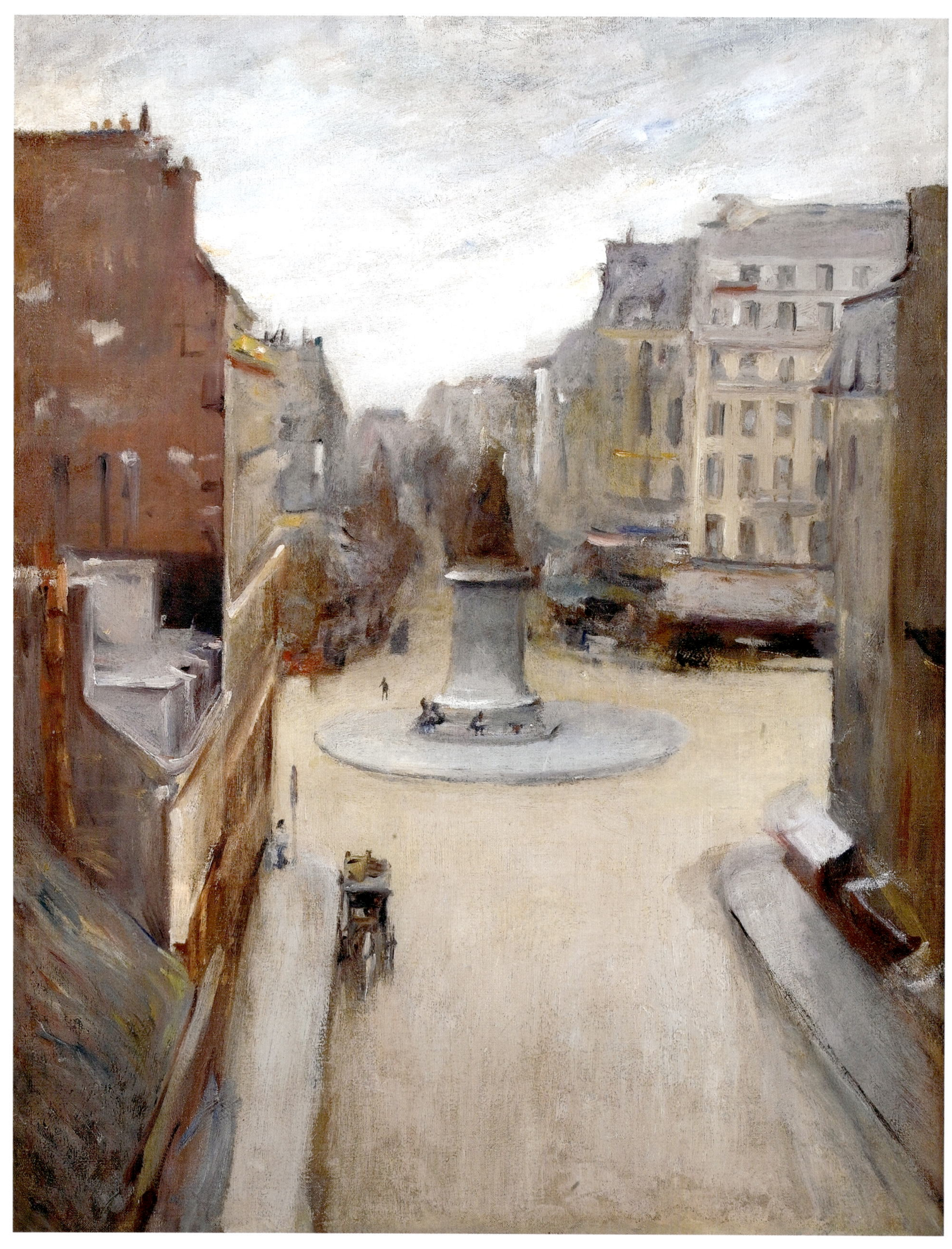
FIG. 18 – *Place de Clichy*, c.1890, oil on canvas, 28 x 24 in. (71 x 61 cm).

41 Louis Lebeer, Exposition de l'oeuvre lithographique d'Albert Belleroche, Brussels, Bibliothèque Royale de Belgique, 1933, pp. 10-12. A lengthy passage is quoted in Kern 2001, pp. 12-13.

42 The number of lithographs is an estimate made by George Kenny, who is, at present, working on a catalogue raisonné of Belleroche's work.

43 'Oeuvre puissant et tendre qui célèbre la femme de notre temps'; 'une suite de nus don't la volupté forte sut intéresser naguère Degas et Rodin . . . '. Claude-Roger Marx, 'Peintres-Lithographes contemporains: Albert Belleroche', *Gazette des Beaux-Arts*, vol. 39, 1908, pp. 76, 77.

44 'ses blancs vigoureux et ses noirs opulents; '. . . est plus coloriste que dessinateur, mais . . . coloriste en blanc et noir'; 'Sa palette riche en nuances est au service d'une intelligence riche en flexions'. Pierre Hepp, 'Exposition Albert Belleroche (Galerie Henry Graves)', *La Chronique des arts et de la curiosité*, no. 5, 1 February 1908, p. 39.

45 'On peut, rien qu'avec les blancs at les noirs, de montrer l'égal des plus varieé coloristes; la gamme des gris cendres des gris duveteux, des noirs profonds, veloutés, mats ou brillants, est si souple et si diverse'. Louis Vauxcelles, 'La Vie artistique', *Gil Blas*, 27 January 1908 [p.2].

46 The comparison with Chardin comes from a review of Belleroche's exhibition (11 oils and 30 drawings) at Colnaghi's on New Bond Street. See 'Art Exhibition: Mr A de Bellroche's Works', *The Times*, 22 October 1941, p. 6.

47 'Mr A. de Belleroche: Lithographer and Painter', *The Times*, 15 July 1944, p. 7.

48 *Printemps* (a female nude) hangs, at present, in the Musée d'Art et d'Histoire in Orange.

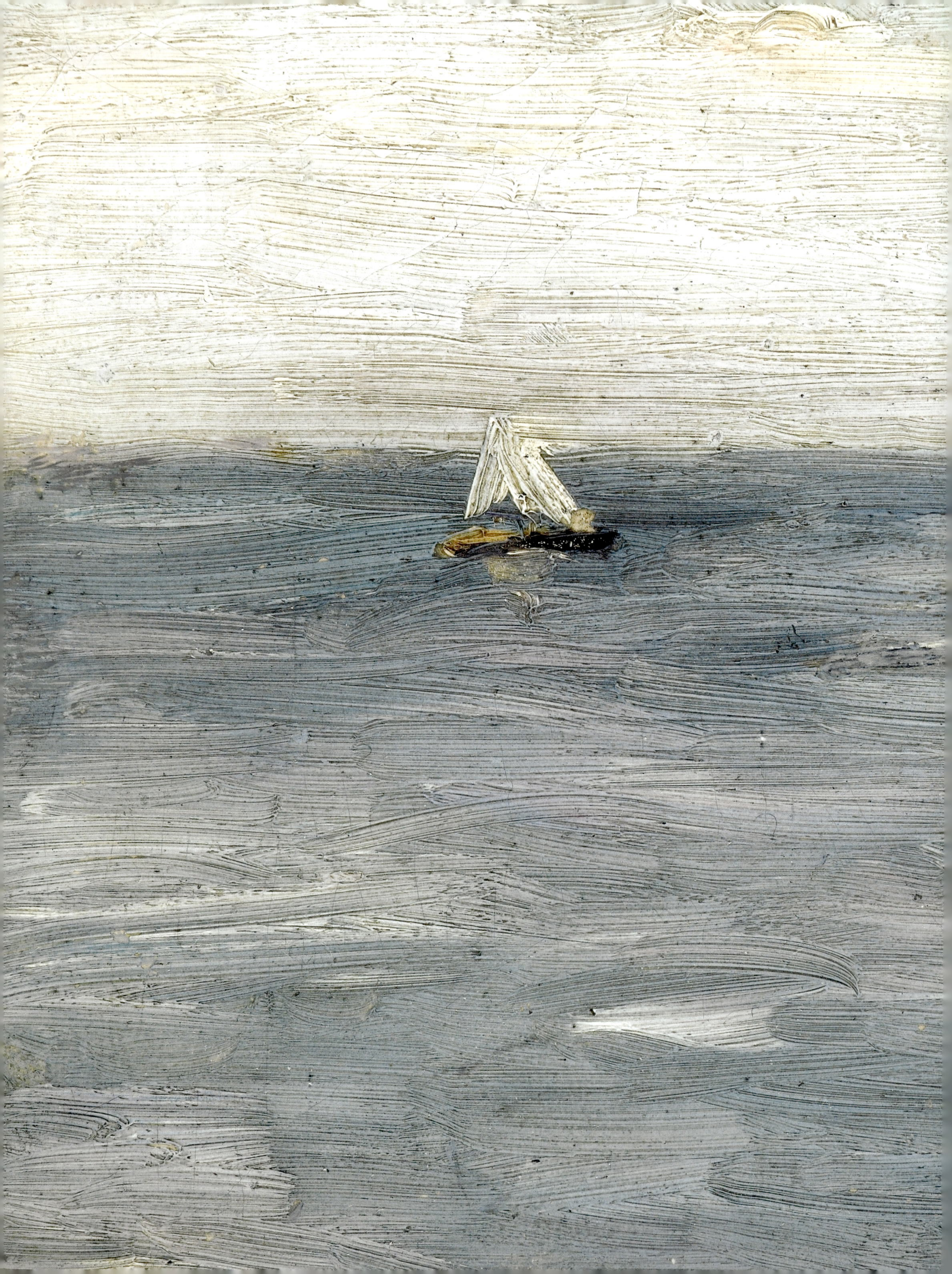

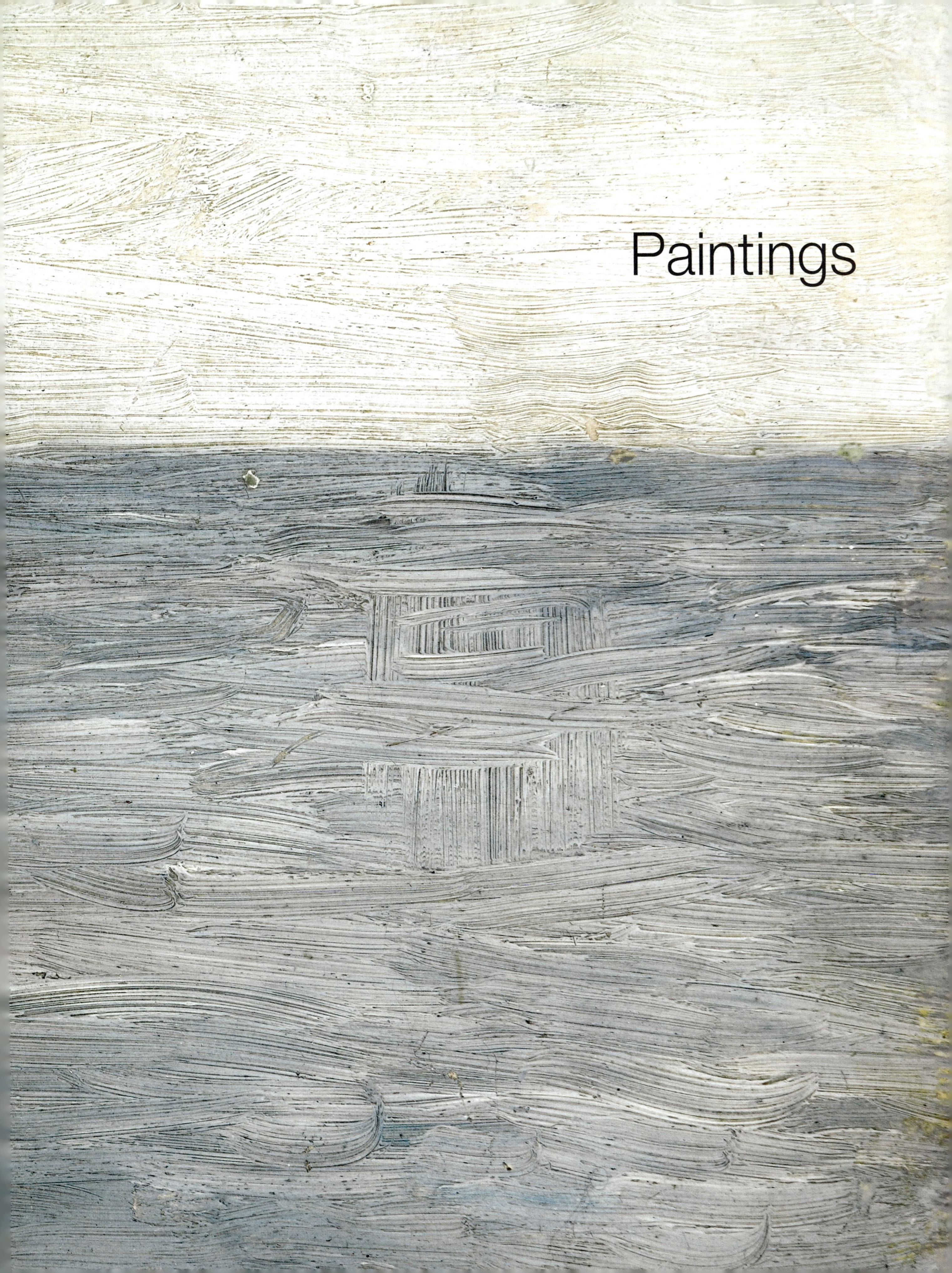
Paintings

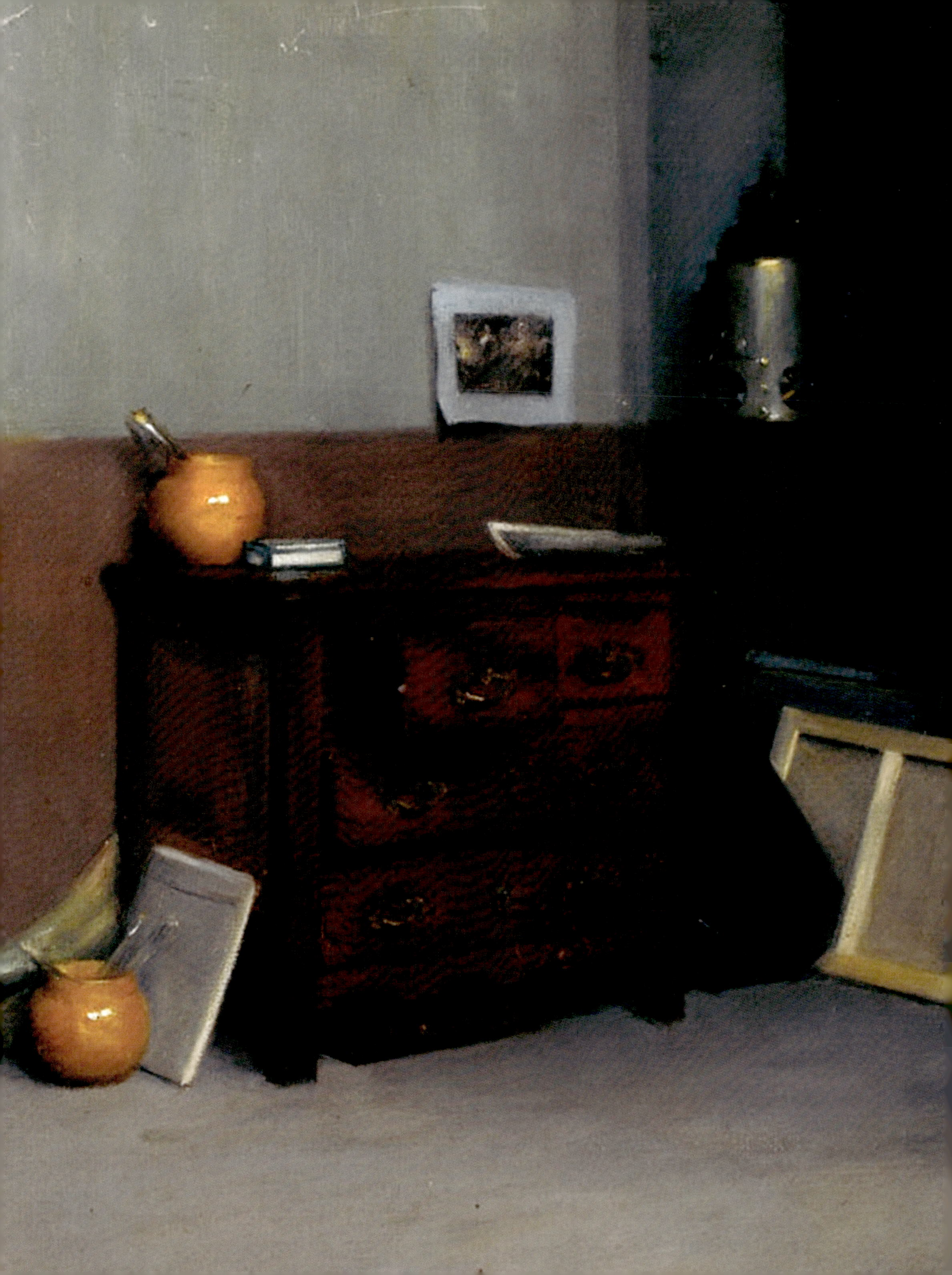

'In his painting he belongs in spirit to the Impressionists: not in the narrower technical meaning of the title but in the sense that Sargent described himself as such in the eighties of the last century.'

A M Hind, Keeper of Prints and Drawings at The British Museum (1933-1945),
Foreword to *Exhibition of Paintings and Drawings by Albert de Belleroche*, October/November 1941.

In 1882, aged 18, Albert de Belleroche enrolled at the studio of Carolus-Duran, one of the most progressive artists in Paris. It was here that Belleroche met John Singer Sargent (1856-1925), 8 years his senior. Albert de Belleroche's career as a painter has been consistently overlooked. Most narratives seem to suggest that upon discovering lithography in 1899 – and receiving widespread acclaim for his printmaking – he subsequently de-emphasized painting. His reputation as a lithographer, though justly deserved, frequently ensconces the true figure of Belleroche and his contribution to the arts across several media. Furthermore, the idea that Belleroche's career could be so neatly bifurcated is inaccurate, and one only needs to look at his prints to debunk this myth, and realise that his painting played an active, complementary role in redefining lithography at the turn of the twentieth century. His prints were often inspired by his painting, and through the process of sketching in oil, Belleroche was able to explore the qualities of light and colour which he sought to use in his lithography.

This experimentation reveals an artist who could create fully-fledged canvases for public exhibition, but who might just as easily invert established conventions and hierarchies by using painting as a precursor to printmaking. This was a revolutionary approach, and as Julian Millest remarked in 1935: 'Although he (Belleroche) is probably the greatest living exponent of this beautiful art, (lithography), he has not scrificed his painting for it but has always treated the two together.' (Apollo 1935 XII, 24 April.)

Part of Belleroche's approach to painting can be attributed to his apprenticeship with Carolus-Duran. While the academy of the *Ecole des Beaux-Arts* emphasised drawing as the foundation of good art, Carolus-Duran favoured direct painting, without under drawing, using technique inspired by Velazquez, building up form through tonal values. Colour was applied without blending, with pigments laid on top of one another to create fleeting effects, similar to the paintings of Frans Hals, and in tune with the wet on wet techniques being championed by the impressionists.

Such an education – partly trained, in part autodidactic – readied Belleroche to make an impact upon the exhibition scene. He repeatedly exhibited at the *Paris Salon* from 1887, the *Société des Artistes Français* from 1891 and the *Salon d'Automne* from 1903. Between 1894 and 1899, he also sent paintings to be exhibited at the great bastion of Impressionist painting in Britain, the *New English Art Club* in Piccadilly.

CAT. 32 – *Les deux petits pots (Les pots jaunes)* (DETAIL), c. 1889, signed, oil on canvas, 18 ¼ x 15 ¼ in. (46.5 x 38.5 cm).

Life Studies & Portraits

'That, in my opinion, is one of the finest examples of flesh painting that I have ever seen; it is not paint but real flesh'.

Sir Frank Brangwyn, *The Times*, 22 October 1941

The life studies in this collection rank amongst the earliest known paintings by Belleroche, and date to his training under Carolus-Duran. The palette used, with subtly modulated flesh tones set against rich and contrasting background colours, especially dark reds, are typical of Carolus-Duran's signature portraits, yet bear the hallmarks of an artist striving for individuality. Duran's technique of directly painting with a fully loaded brush on canvas, without any preparatory under-drawing, was inspired by Velazquez and the Dutch Old Masters.

As his painting technique developed Belleroche began to produce flamboyantly elegant works, echoing not just those of Sargent but also of Lavery, Walton and Peploe. As his palette lightened he learnt to build up soft grey and pink tones, with dark shadows painted in rich black, through which combination he was able to capture the passing effects of flickering light on flesh with remarkable skill.

In 1887, five years after studying in Duran's studio, Belleroche made his debut with a self portrait at the Paris Salon's annual exhibition at the Académie des Beaux-Arts. The Salon continued to accept his paintings, and in 1894 Belleroche joined the New English Art Club so that he could exhibit his paintings in London. His portraiture is all the more striking, for being of independent means he could afford to be selective in terms of the sitters that he portrayed. Nevertheless Belleroche actively sold over 1000 lithographs and some paintings with Paris, London and New York galleries. (See George C. Kenney: *Albert de Belleroche, Master of Belle Epoque Lithography,* Liss Llewellyn, 2024, p.65.)

Belleroche's portrait output suggests a cronyistic approach with depictions of close friends and influencers within his social circle, as in his portraits of Sargent, or the large oil sketches of Emile Zola's funeral procession (Musée d'Art et d'Histoire, Orange). On other occasions, these works were more idiosyncratic, recording figures of the time such as the Japanese wrestler, Taro Miyake, who popularised Judo across Europe. More frequently however, he was able to capture the doyennes of le Tout-Paris, and immortalise their beauty in unrivalled terms. A.M. Hind would later write that 'the lack of necessity for the sale of his works and a reluctance to seek for portrait commissions, in spite of his special faculty in portrait painting, may have lost him immediate repute, but his industry and single-minded devotion to his art, combined with a rare sensibility, will assure his later fame.' Hind's words may not ring true just yet, but the revaluation of Belleroche is long overdue.

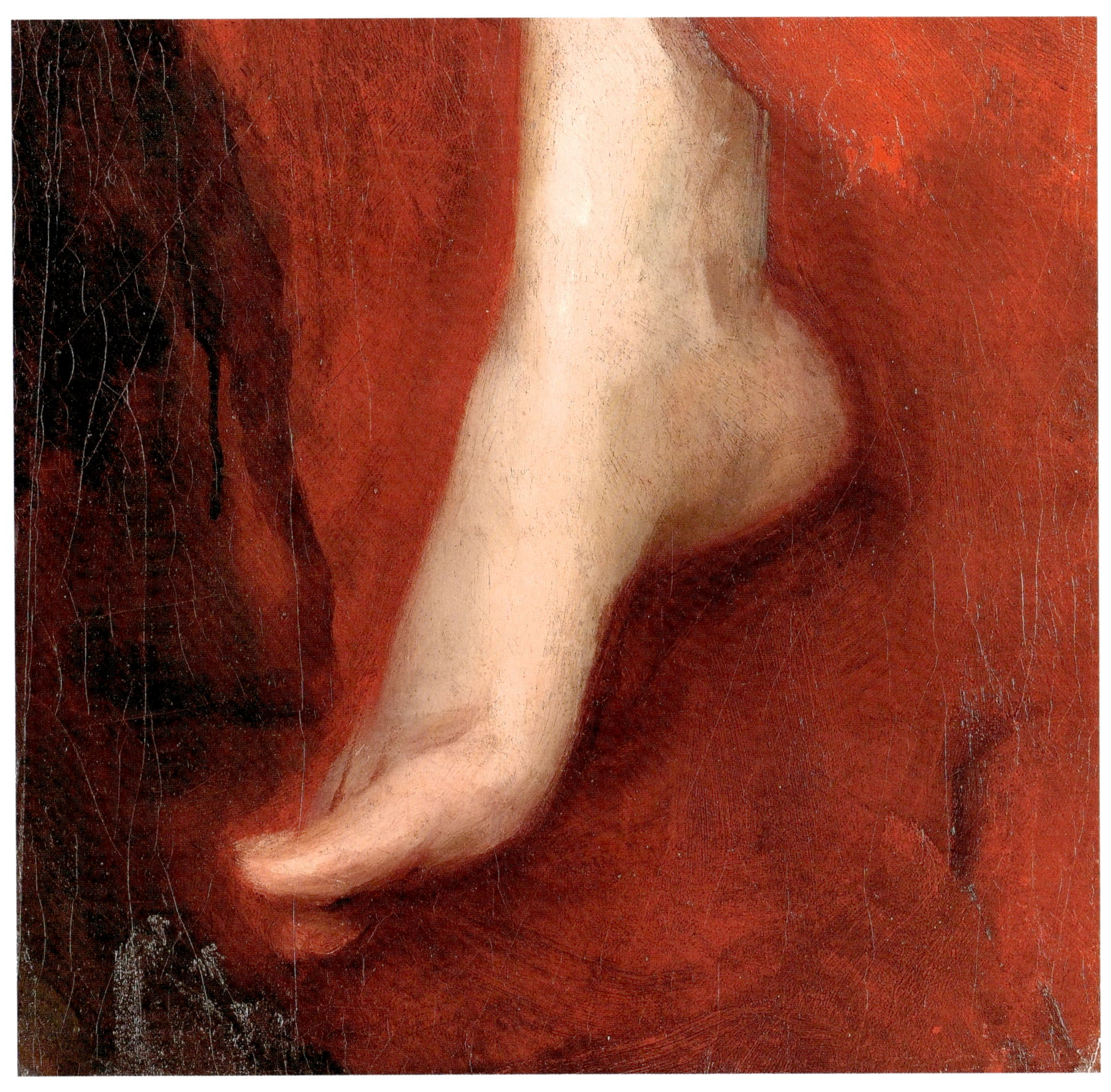

CAT. 1 – *Study of a Foot*, early 1880s, oil on canvas, 11 ½ x 12 ¼ in. (29.3 x 31 cm).

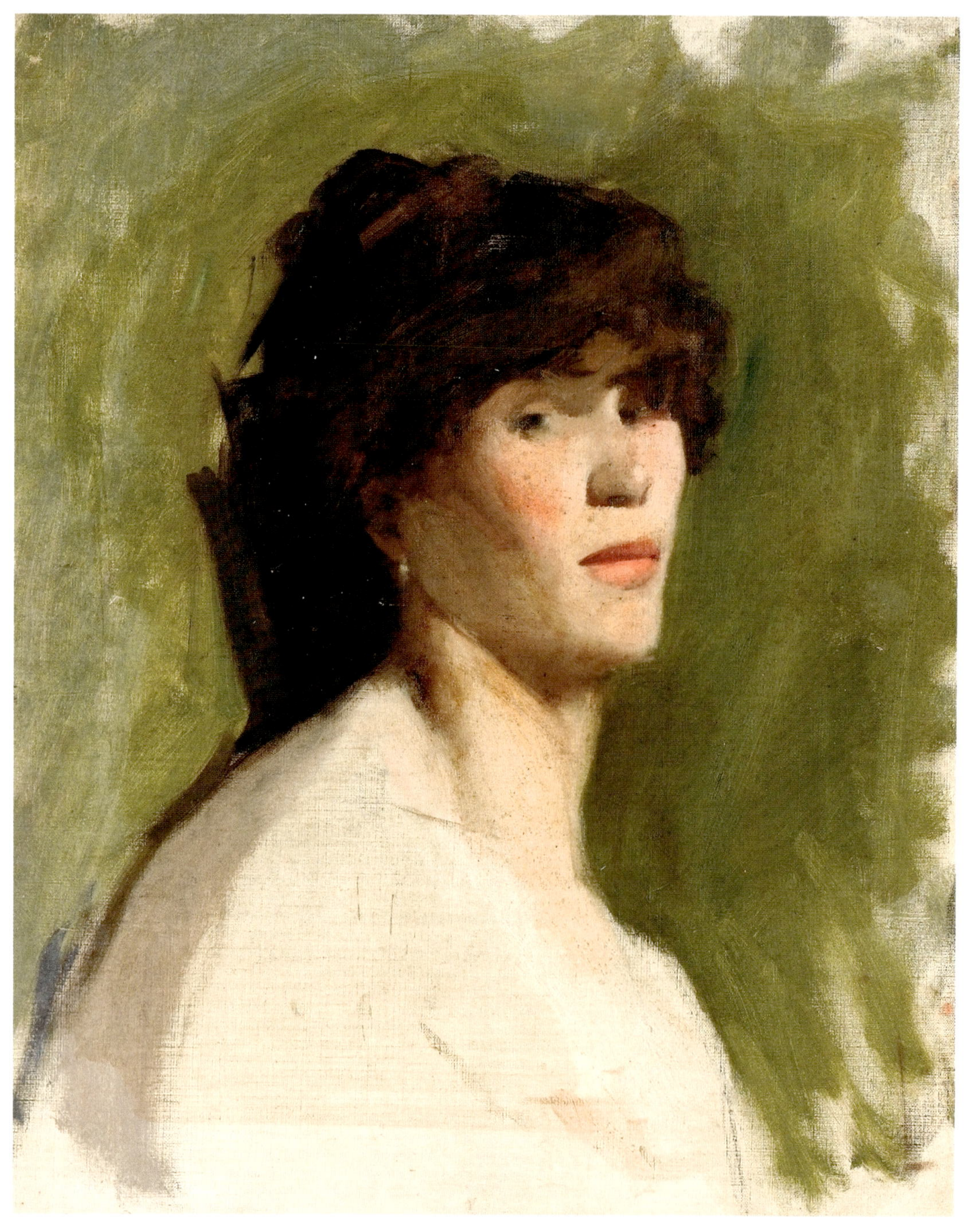

CAT. 2 – *Portrait of a Woman,* early 1880s, signed on the reverse,
oil on canvas (stamped Paul Foinet), 20 ¼ x 16 ¼ in. (51 x 41 cm).

CAT. 3 – *Female Nude*, early 1880s, inscribed on reverse, oil on canvas, 22 x 17 ½ in. (56 x 44.5 cm).

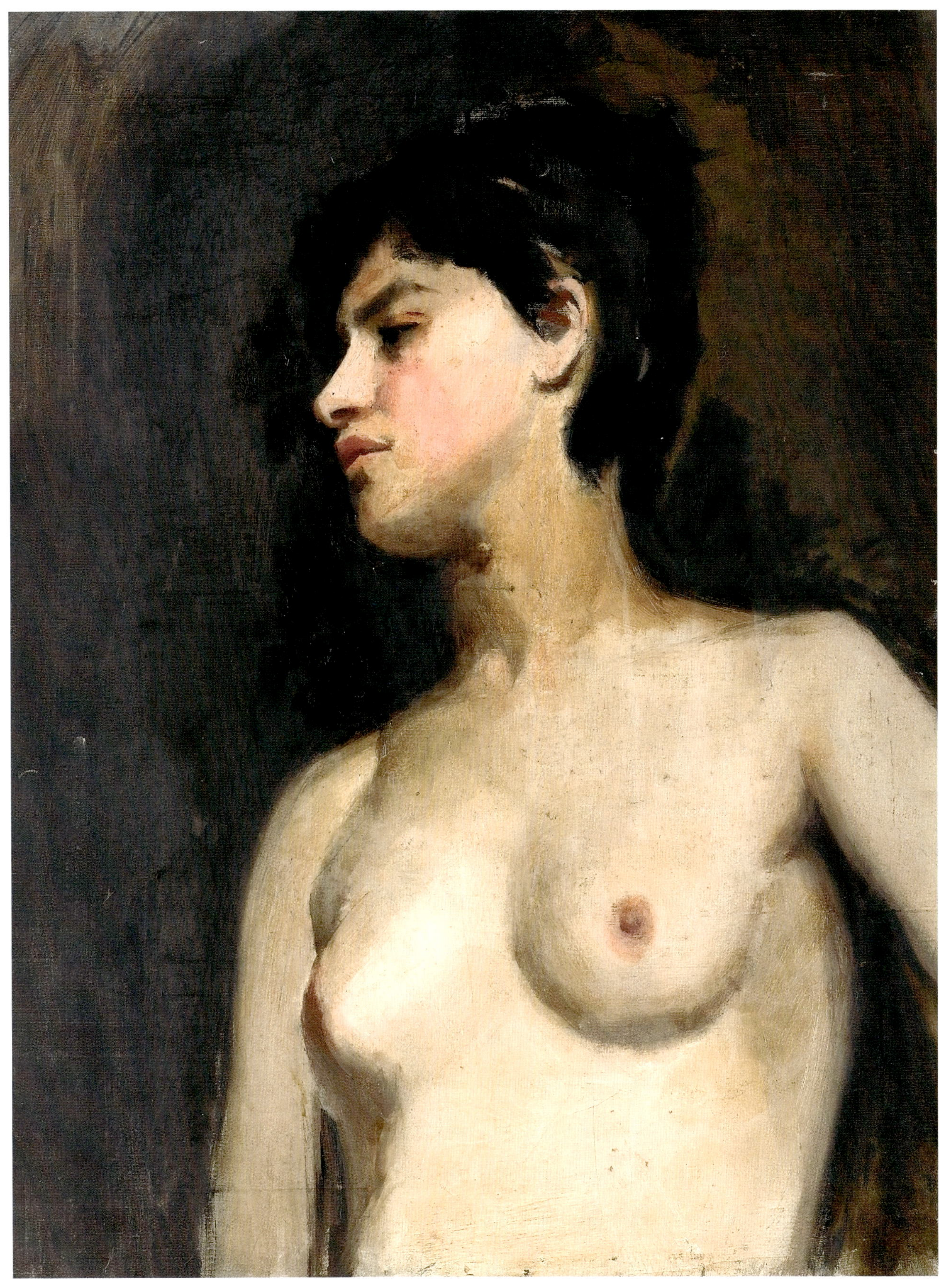

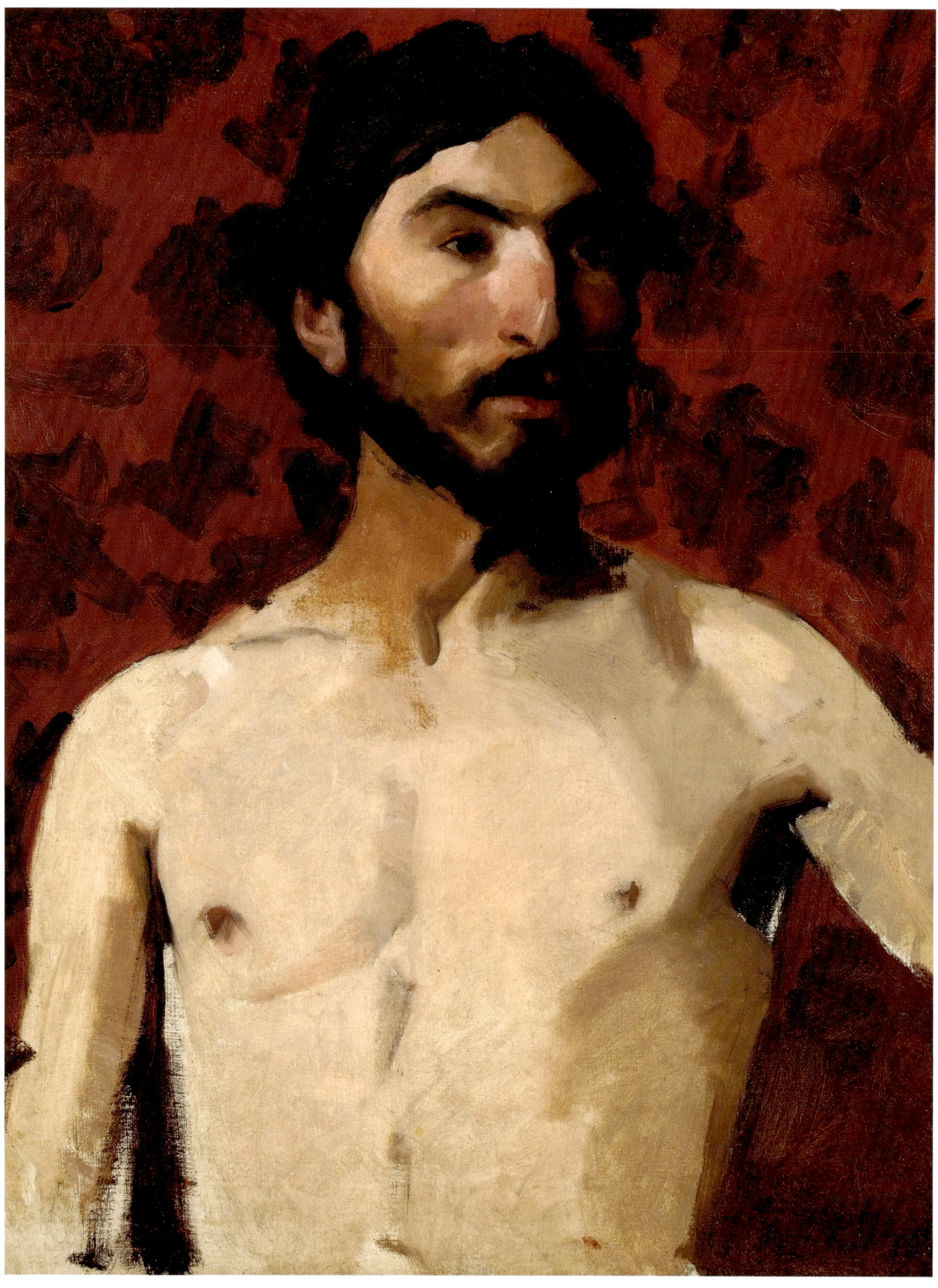

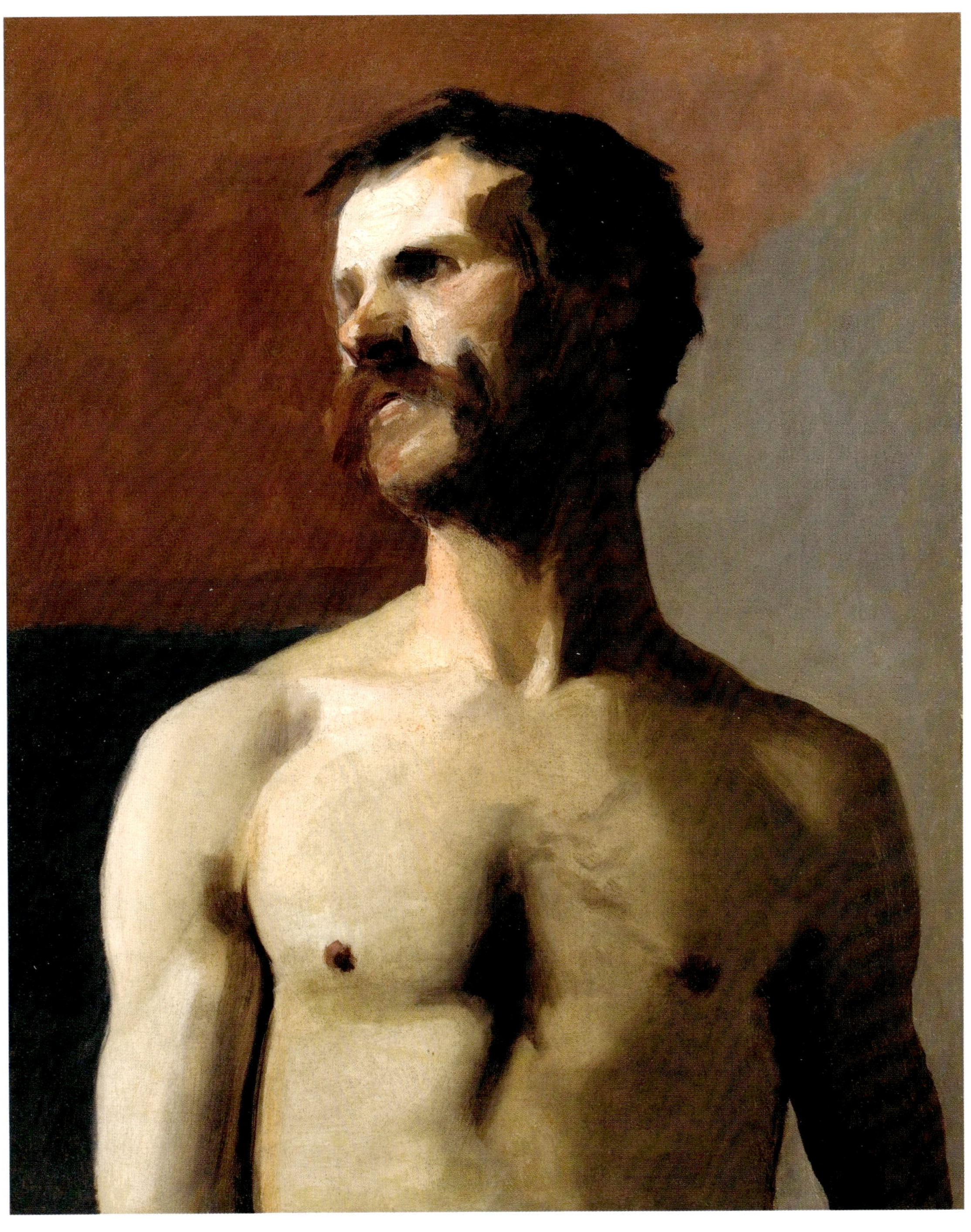

CAT. 5 – *Male Nude*, early 1880s, signed on reverse,
oil on canvas (canvas stamped Paul Foinet), 24 x 20 in. (61 x 50.8 cm).

CAT. 4 – *Life study – Bearded Man*, early 1880s, signed on reverse, oil on canvas, 24 x 18 ½ in. (61 x 47 cm).

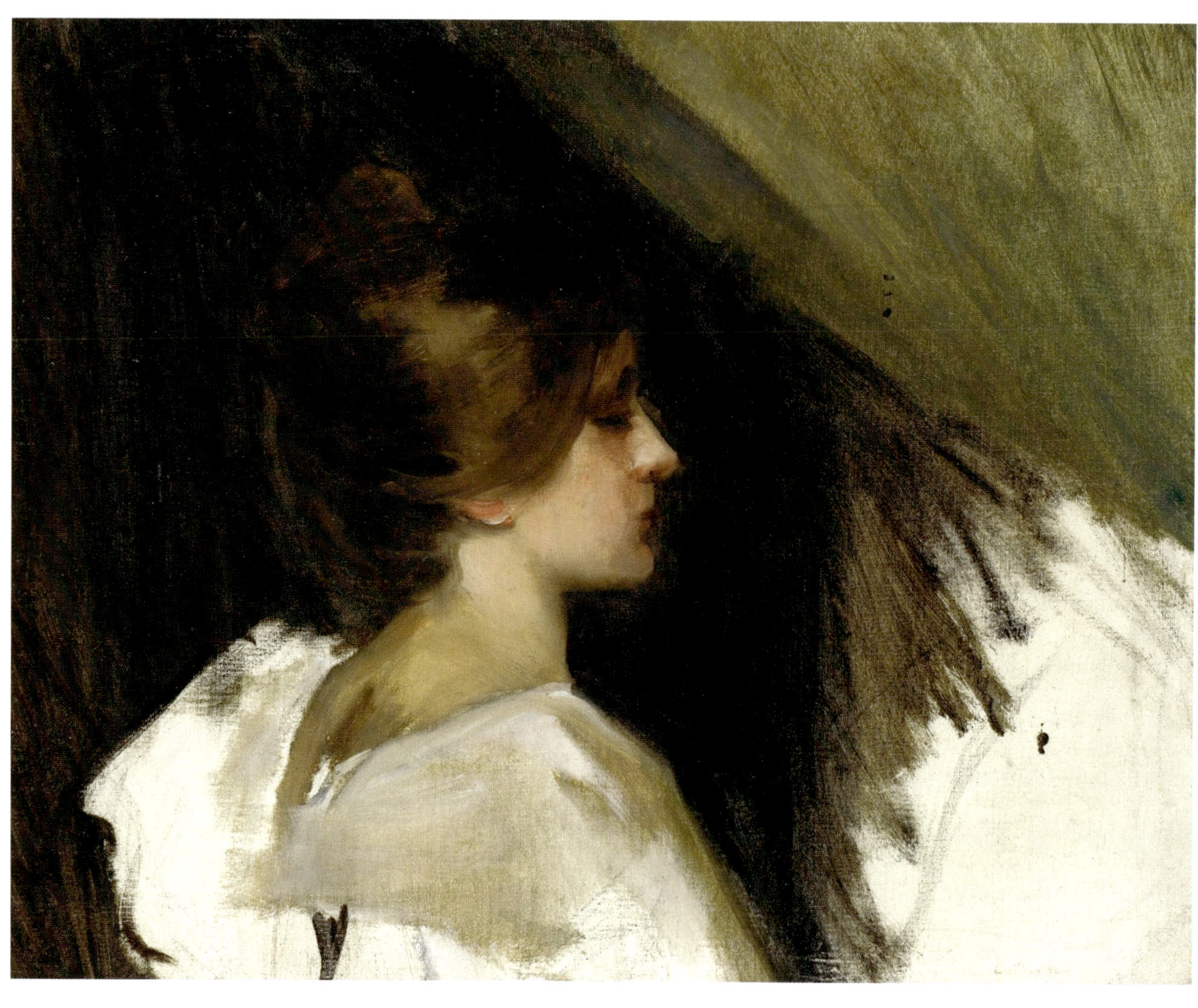

CAT. 6 – *Profile portrait of Julie Visseaux*, c.1908, signed in pencil, oil on canvas, 21 x 26 1/4 in. (53.2 x 66.5 cm).

CAT. 7 – *Life Study in Silhouette,* 1890s, oil on canvas, 30 x 20 (76 x 51 cm).

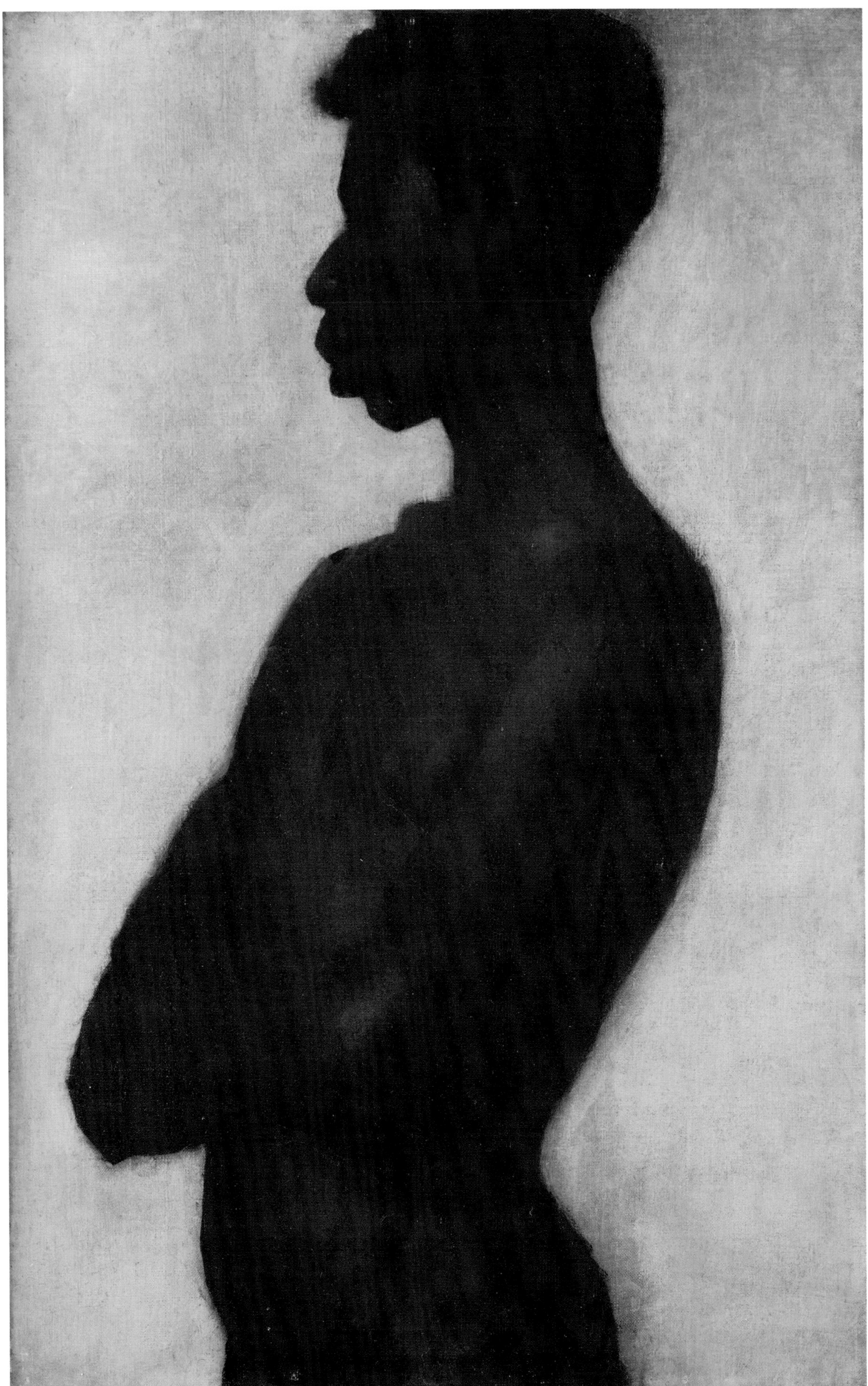

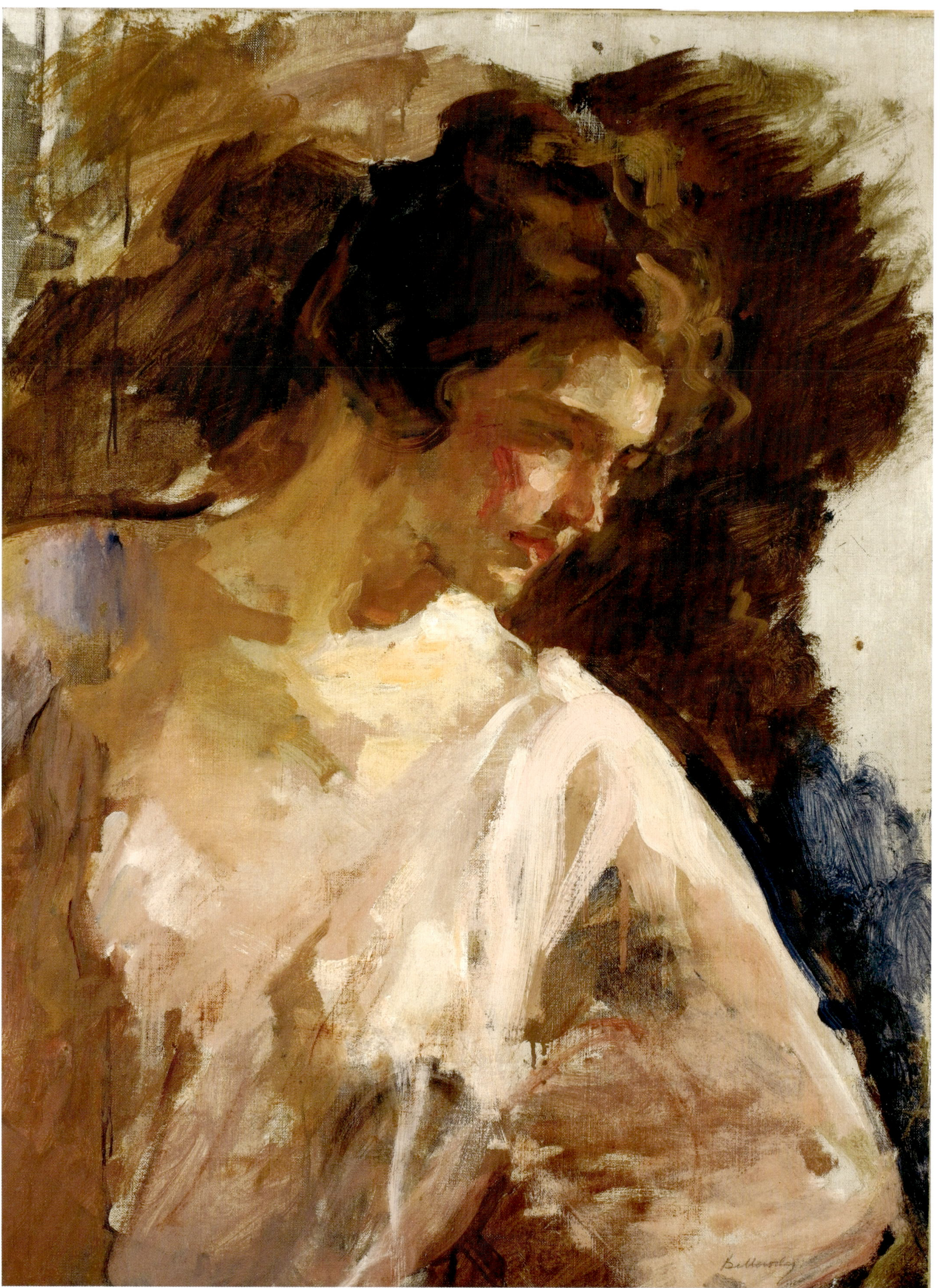

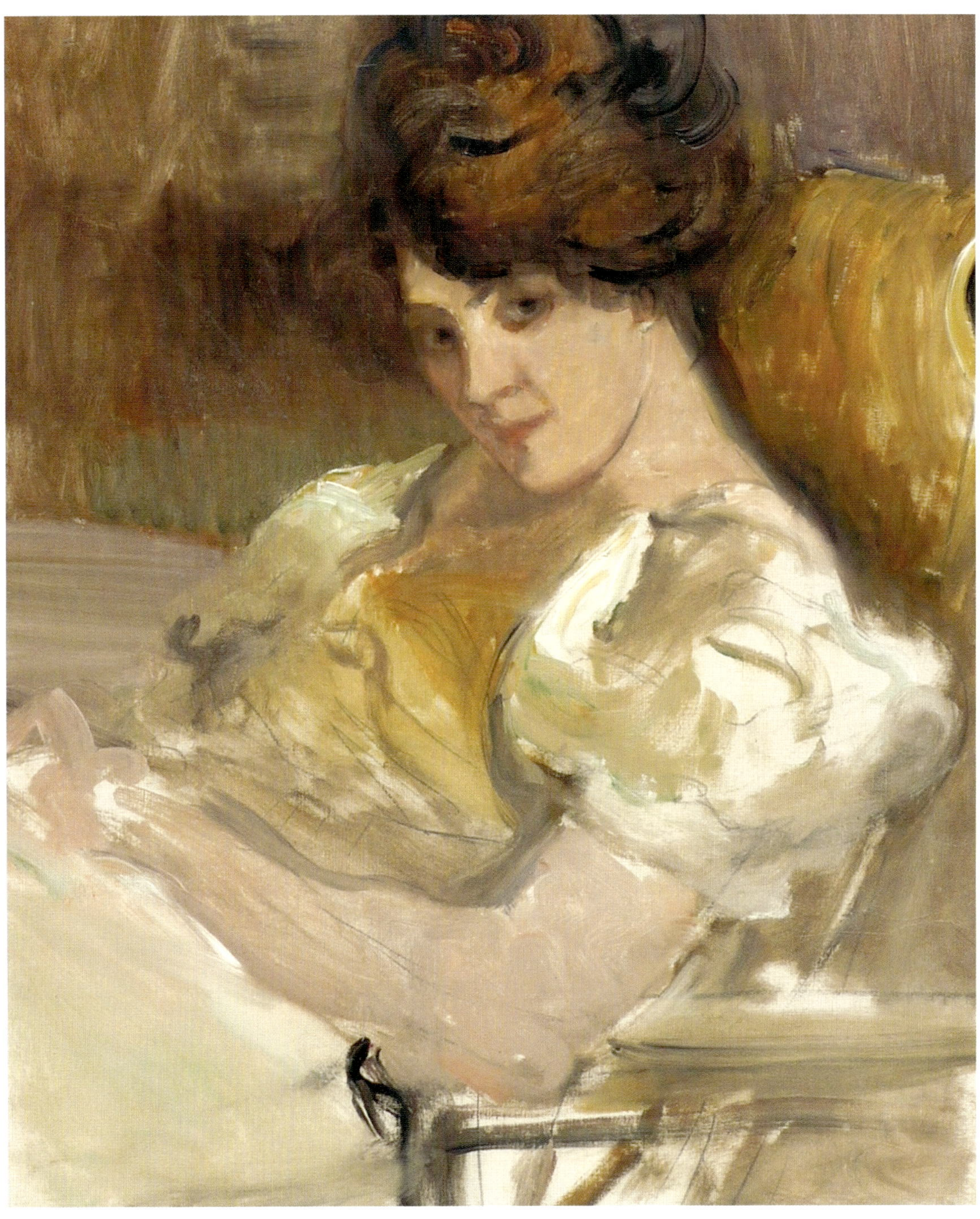

CAT. 9 – *Portrait of Julie Visseaux, seated*, c.1908, inscribed with inventory number to reverse, oil on canvas, 30 x 25 in. (76 x 63.5 cm).

CAT. 8 – *Portrait of Julie Visseaux*, c. 1908, signed, oil on canvas, 26 ½ x 20 ½ in. (67.3 x 52 cm).

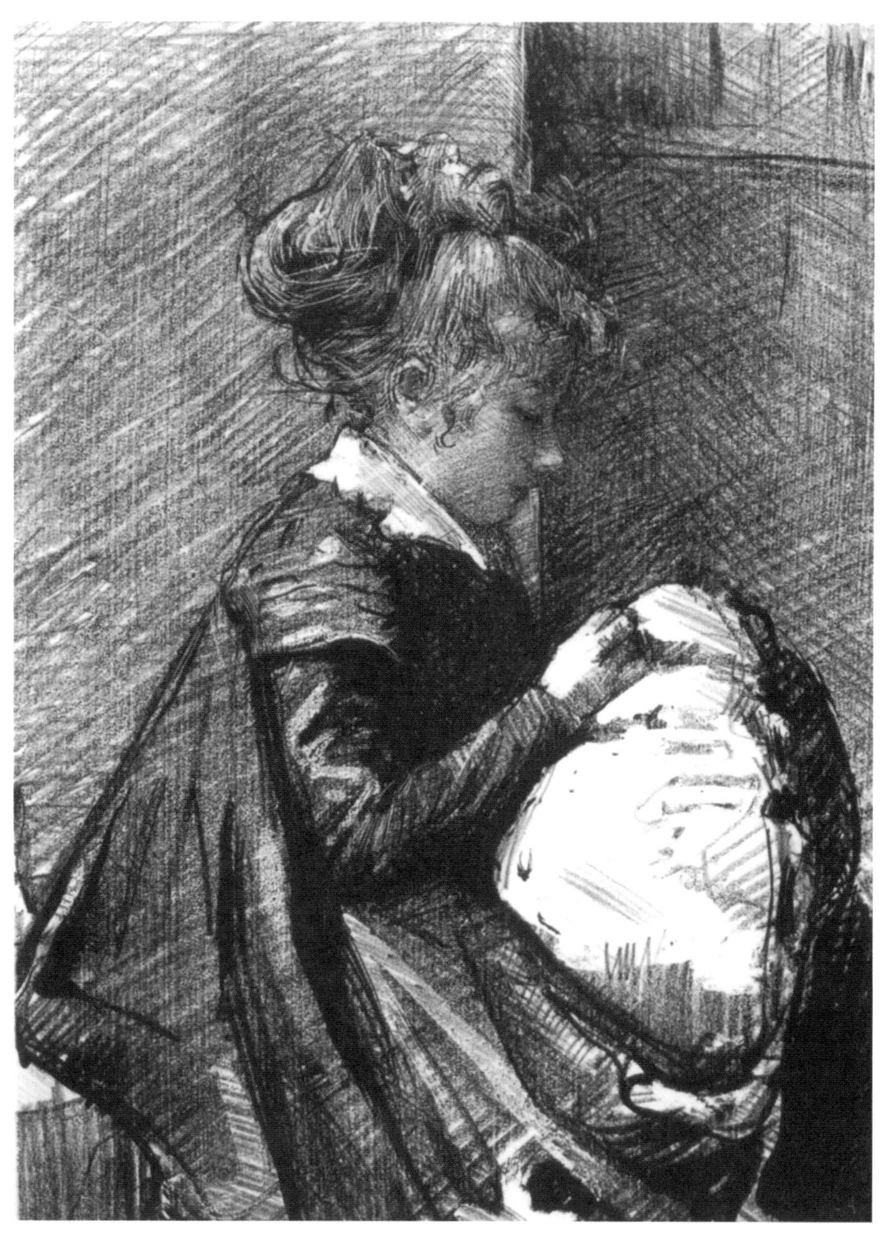

CAT. 10 – *La Couseuse*, (K400, AB 37.2), 1901,
lithograph, 14 1/2 x 11 3/4 in. (36.8 x 29.8 cm). Edition: 15.

CAT. 11 – *La Couseuse*, 1901, oil on board, 21 ¾ x 16 ½ in. (55.5 x 41.5 cm).

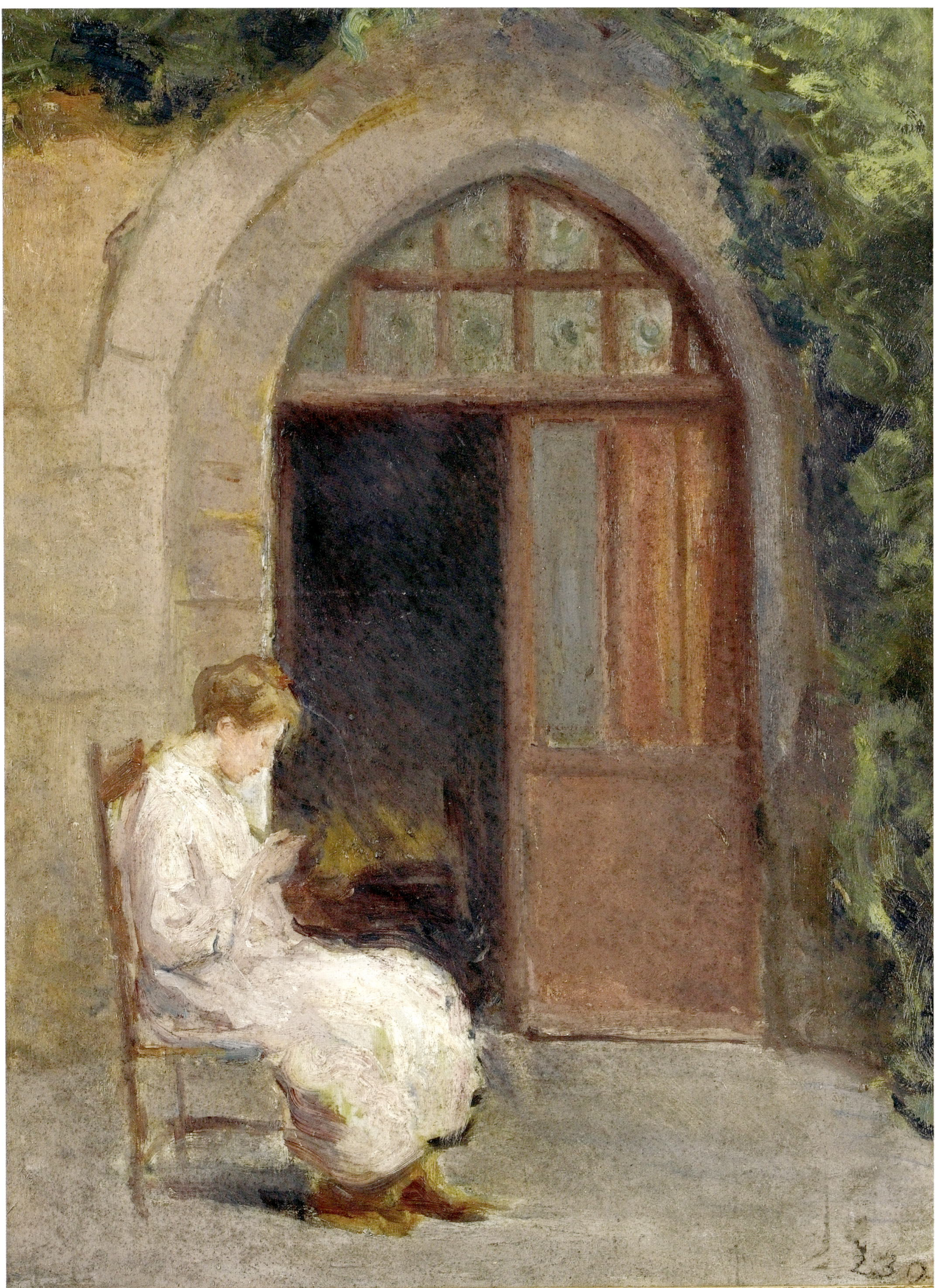

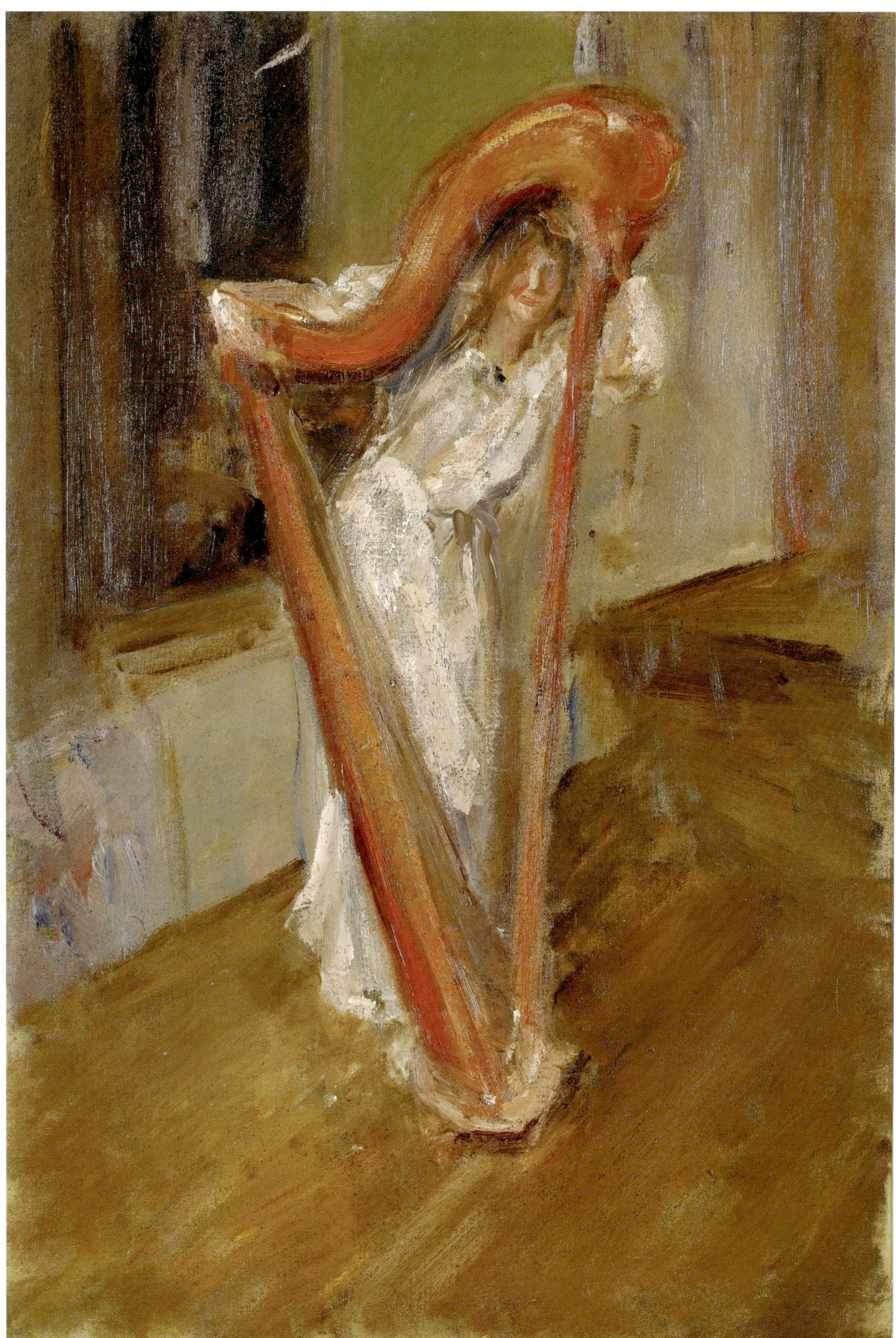

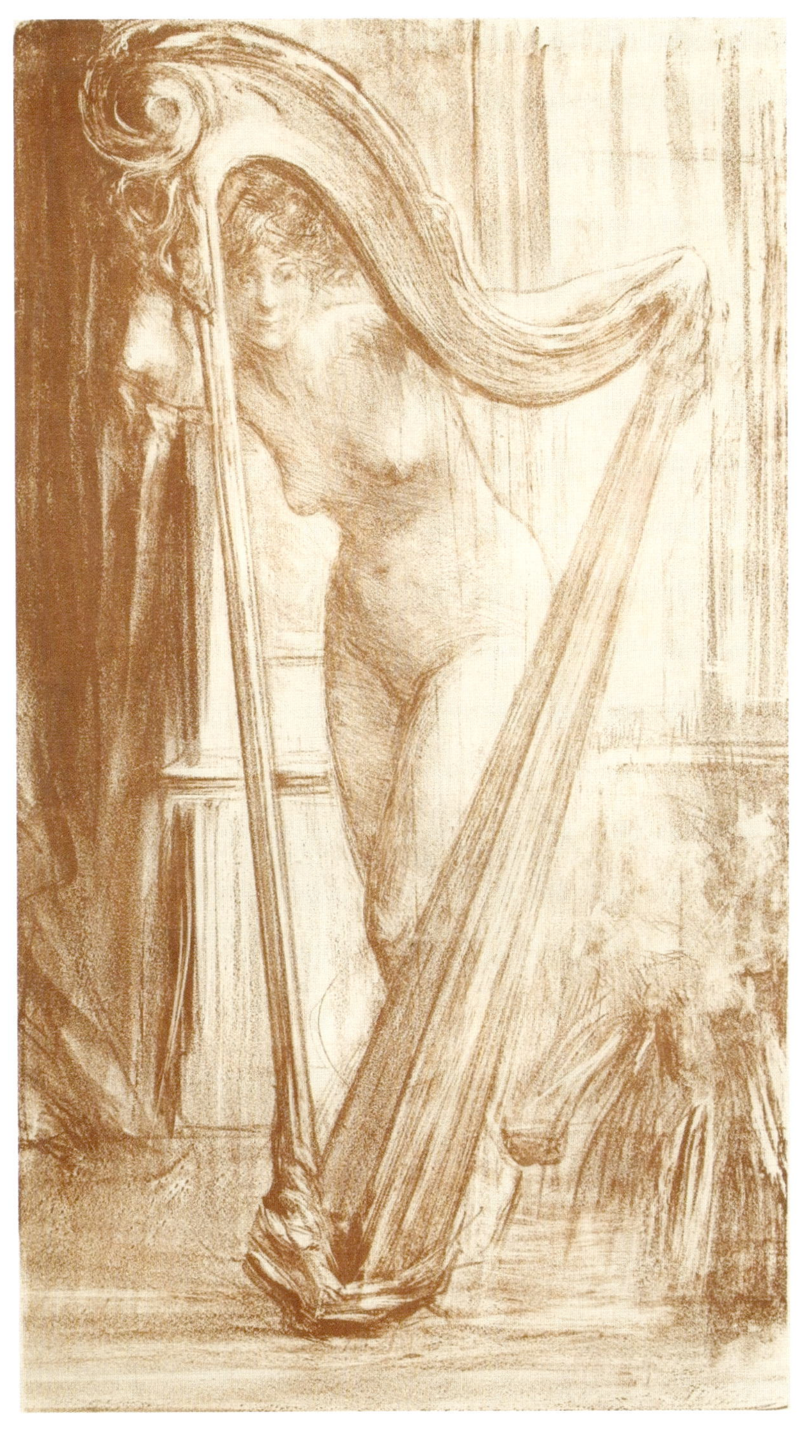

CAT. 13 – *Petite Lili* (?) *à la Harpe*, (K011, AB 51), 1903, signed lithograph, 28 ½ x 22 ½ in. (72.4 x 57 cm). Edition: 30.

CAT. 12 – *Petite Lili à la Harpe*, c.1903, signed with initials, oil on canvas, 24 x 15 ¾ in. (61 x 40 cm).

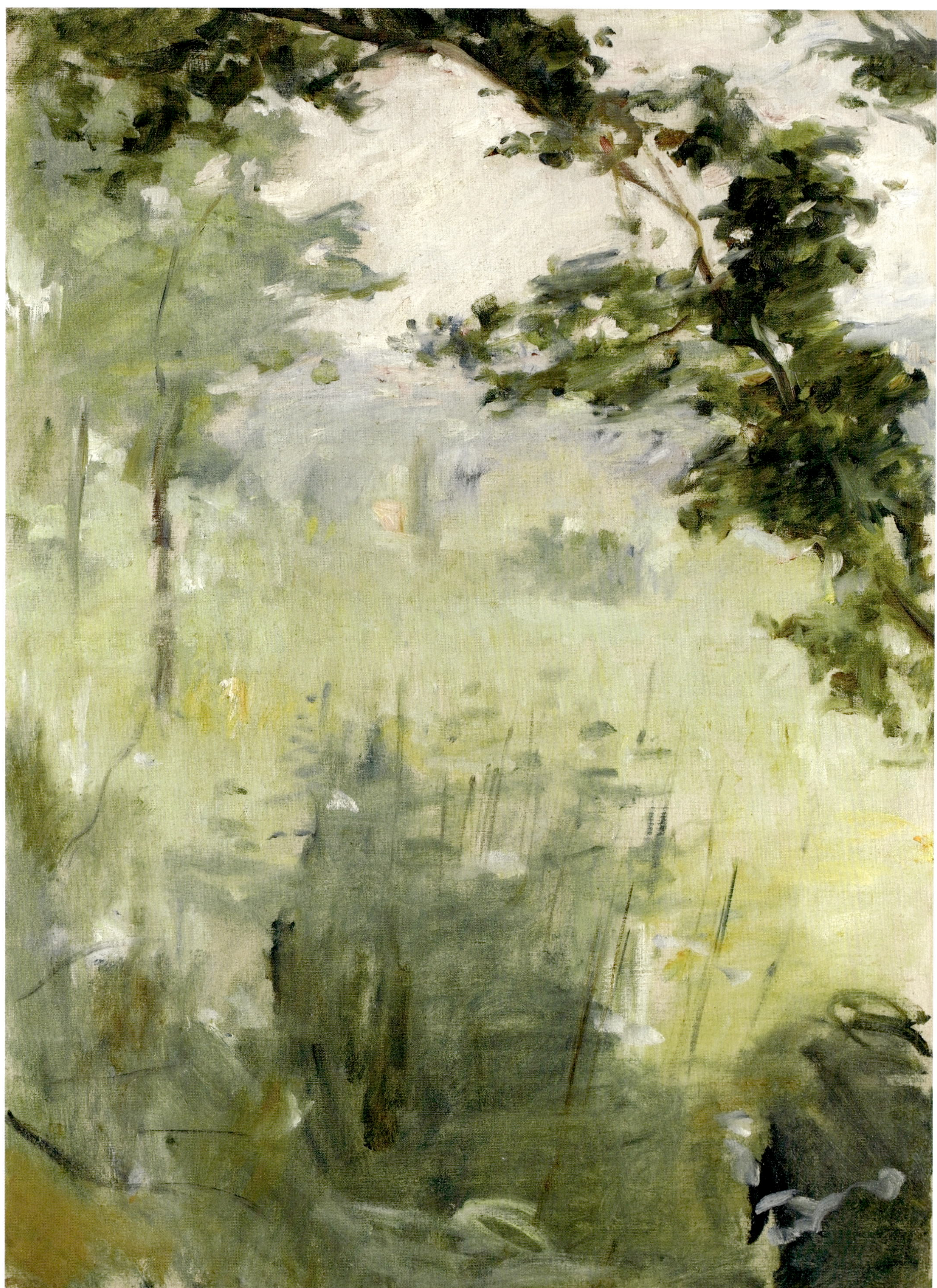

In their choice of subject matter and technique, Belleroche's landscapes, seascapes and cityscapes reveal the strong influence of the Impressionists. He enjoyed painting en plein air, and employed a wet-on-wet painting technique favoured by contemporaries such as Sargent, Monet, and Renoir. The daring compositional devices, as well as the striking economy and sparseness of his views, may betray a debt to advances in contemporary photography, in addition to a knowledge of Ukiyo-e printmaking, which was enjoying widespread popularity and distribution throughout Paris, due to the endeavours of Tadamasa Hayashi.

Among Belleroche's favourite sketching grounds were Châteaudun, 130 km from Paris, where he rented La Vieille Chapelle as a studio spacious enough to house his huge Imprimerie Le Mercier printing press, and Villiers-sur-Morin, where his frequent model and mistress Lili Grenier had a farmhouse. Other scenes include ports, such as Dover and Boulogne, and railway stations, among them Charing Cross, and other staging posts that were essential to his frequent crossing of the Channel.

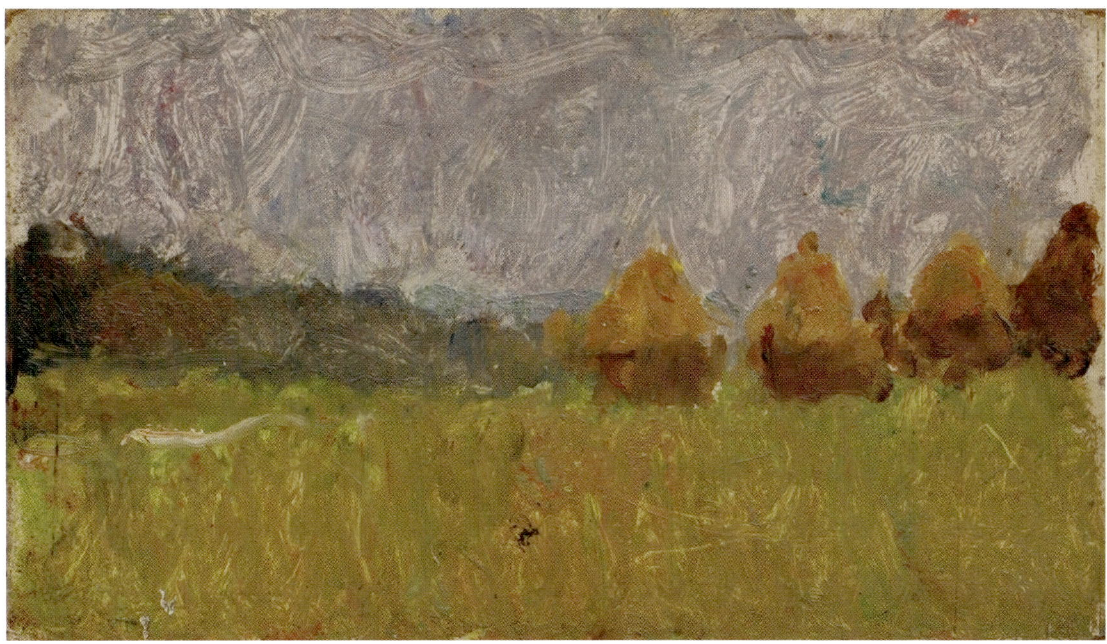

CAT. 15 – *Landscape with Haystacks*, oil on board with scratching out, 8 x 14 in. (20.3 x 35.5 cm).

Overleaf:

CAT. 16 – *Landscape with Green Meadow and Gated Wall*, c. 1900, inscribed on reverse, oil on panel, 6 ¼ x 9 ¼ in. (16 x 23.5 cm).

CAT. 14 – *Landscape Study,* oil on canvas, 24 ½ x 12 ½ in. (62 x 32 cm).

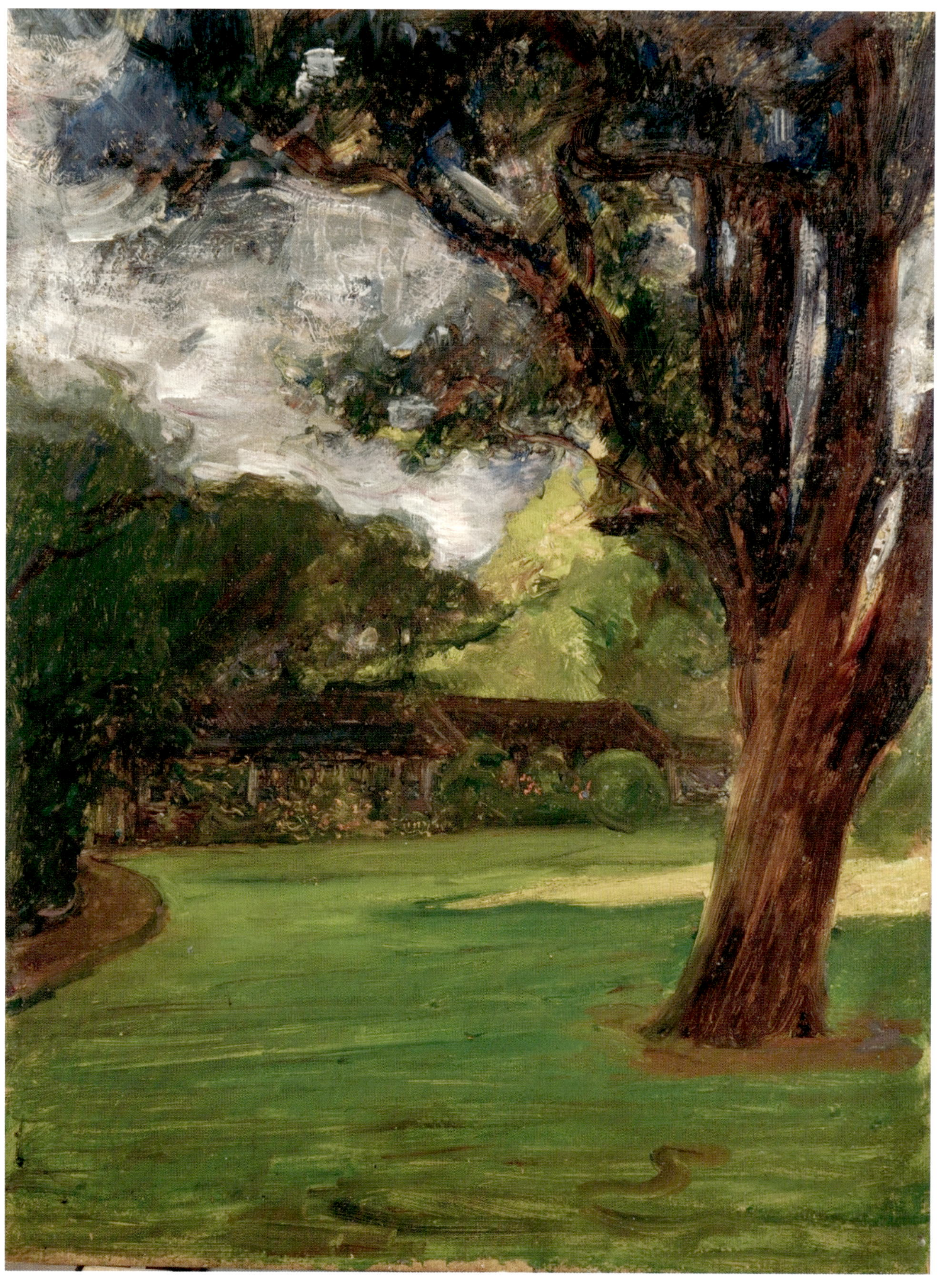

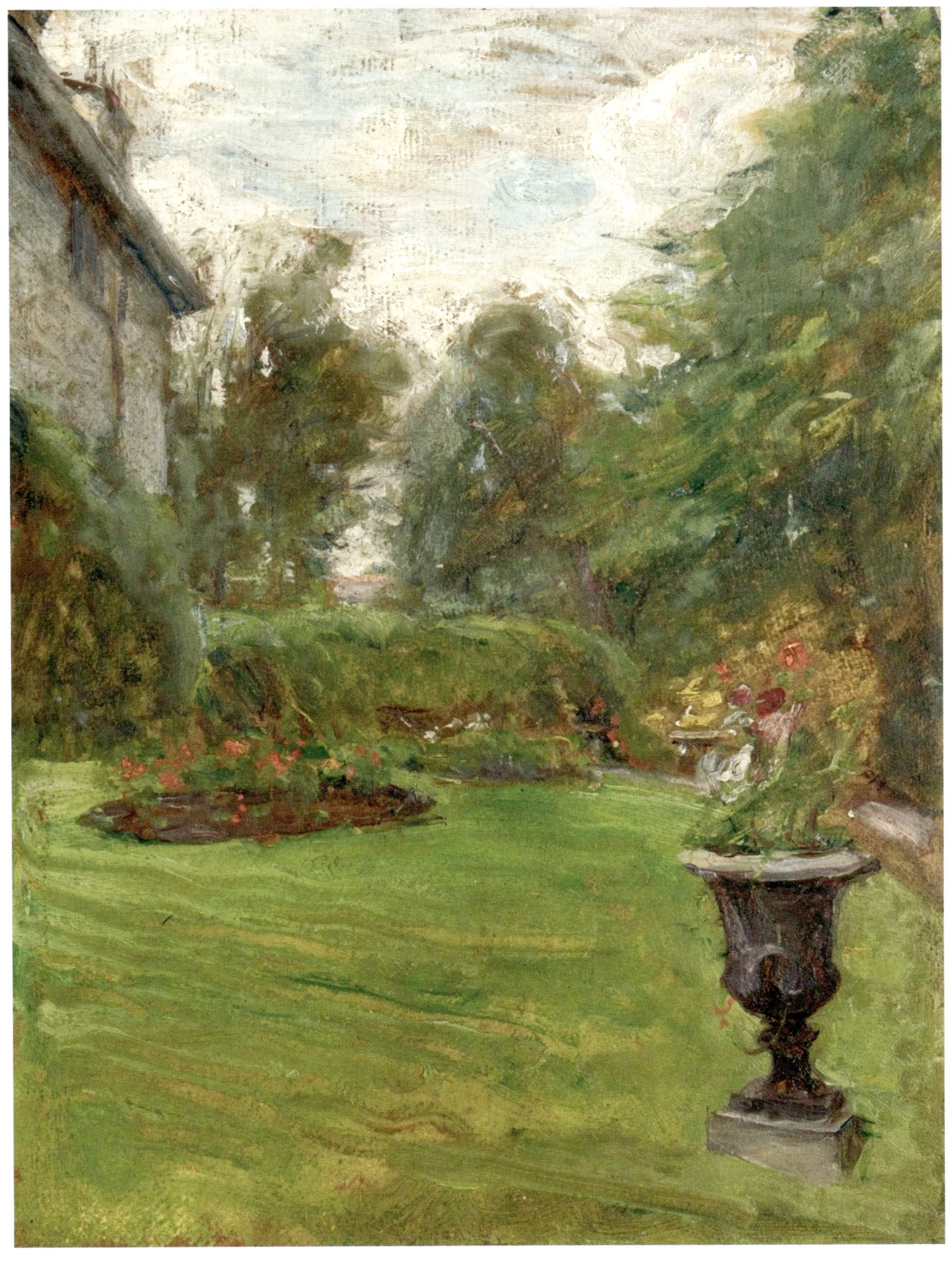

CAT. 18 – *The Artist's Garden with stone flowerpot, Hampstead*, oil on panel, 17 ¾ x 13 ¾ in. (45 x 35 cm).

CAT. 17 – *The Artist's Garden with Yew tree*, oil on panel, 17 ¾ x 13 ¾ in. (45 x 35 cm).

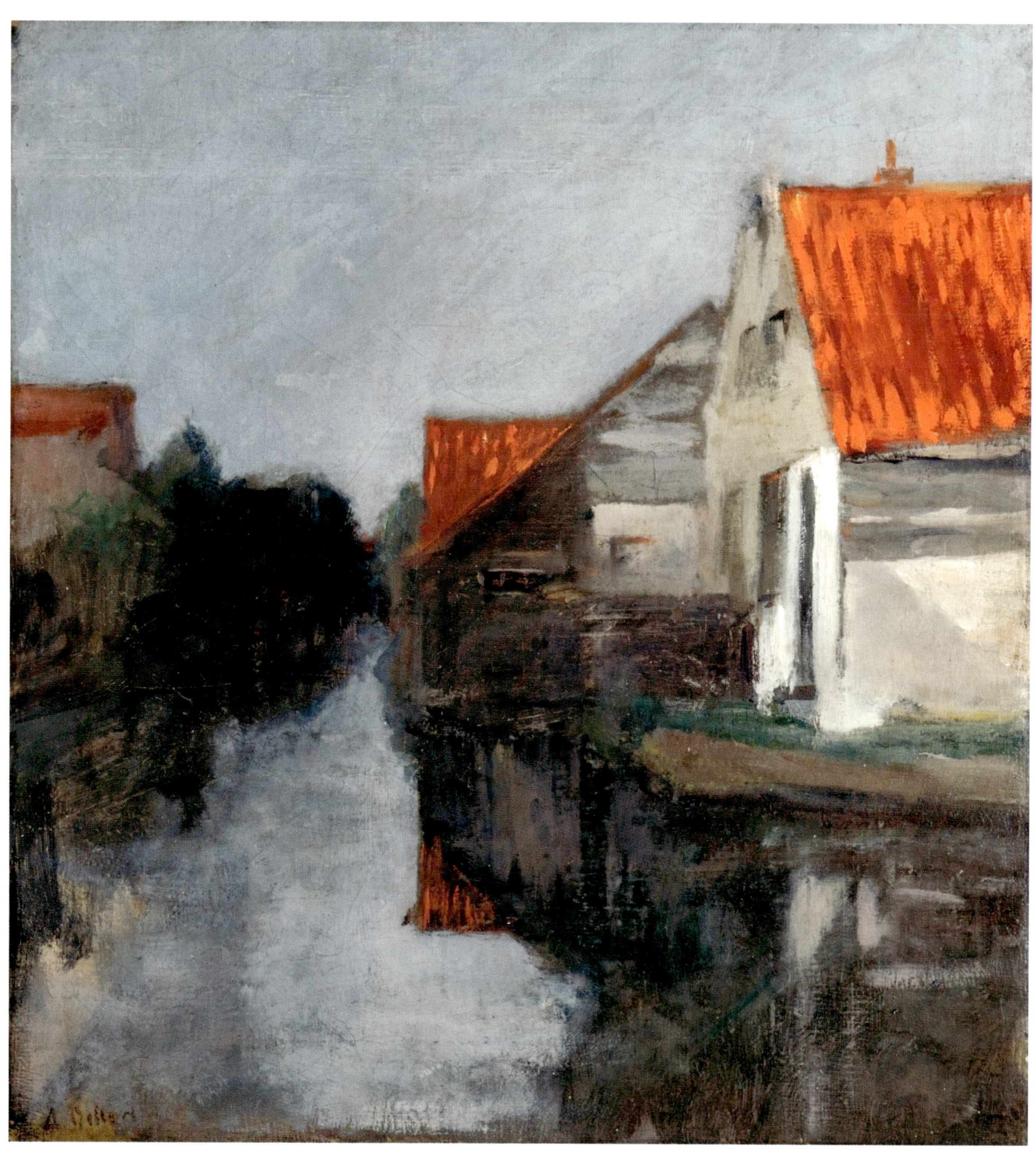

CAT. 19 – *Haarlem*, c.1883, oil on canvas, signed, 15 x 14 in. (38 x 35.5 cm).

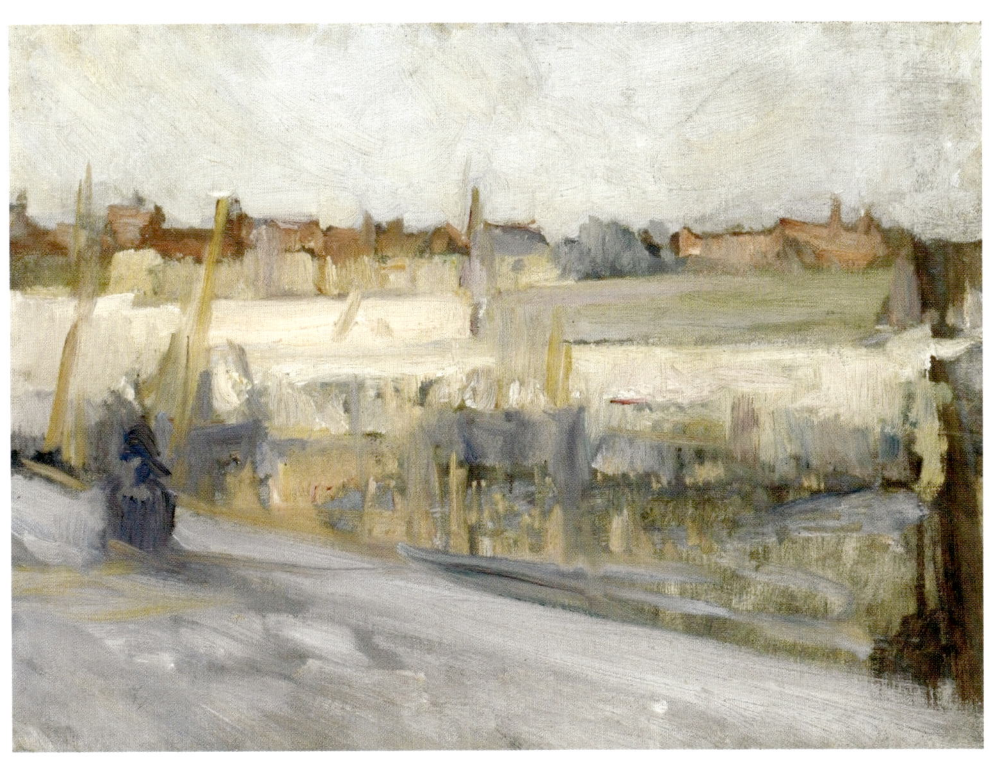

CAT. 20 – *View Across a Harbour,* (possibly Boulogne sur Mer), oil on canvas, 13 x 18 in. (33 x 45.8 cm).

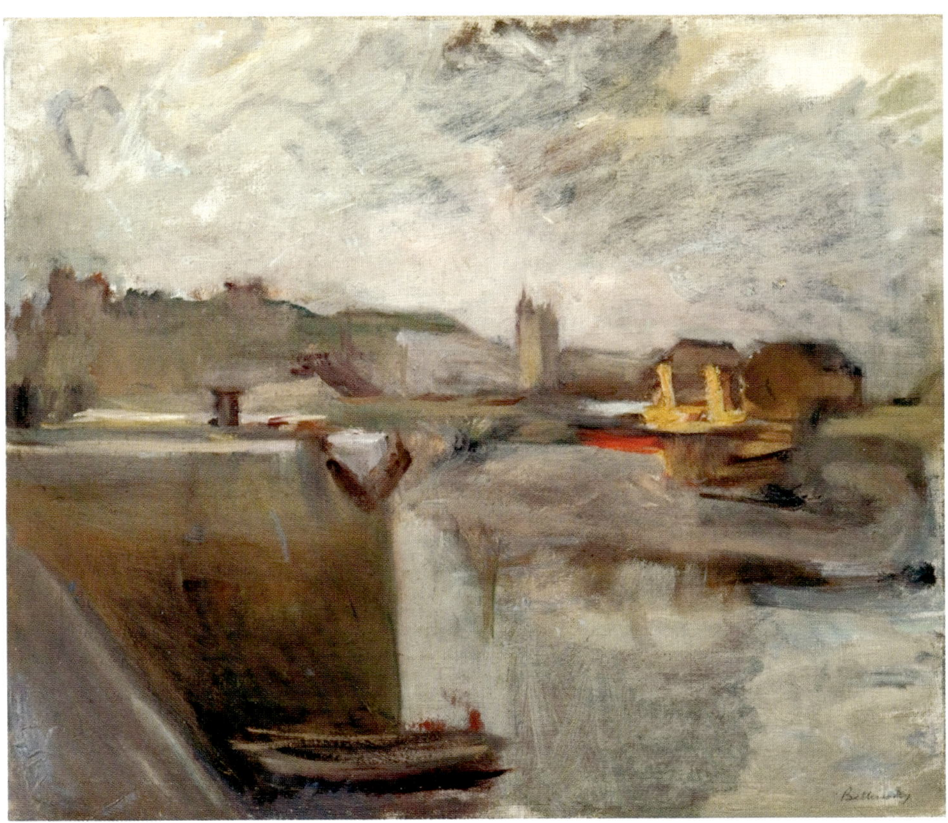

CAT. 21 – *On the Quayside, Boulogne sur Mer*, oil on canvas, signed, 15 x 18 in. (38 x 45.5 cm).

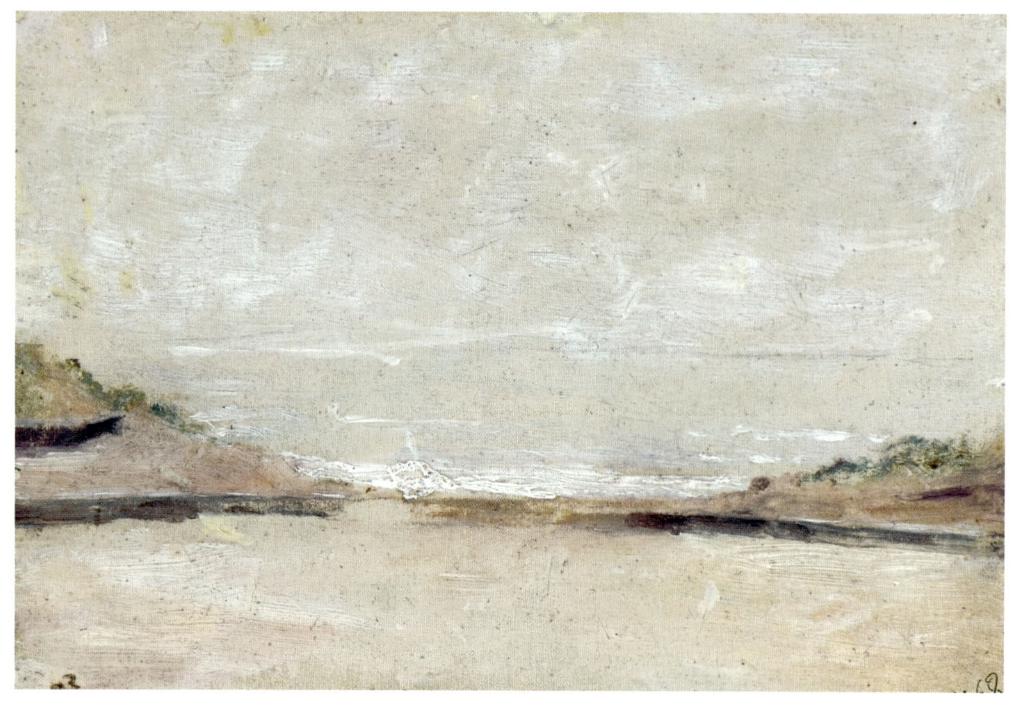

CAT. 22 – *Seascape with Waves*, 1885, signed with initials and inscribed 19.6.85,
oil on panel, 5 ¼ x 7 ¾ in. (13.5 x 19.5 cm).

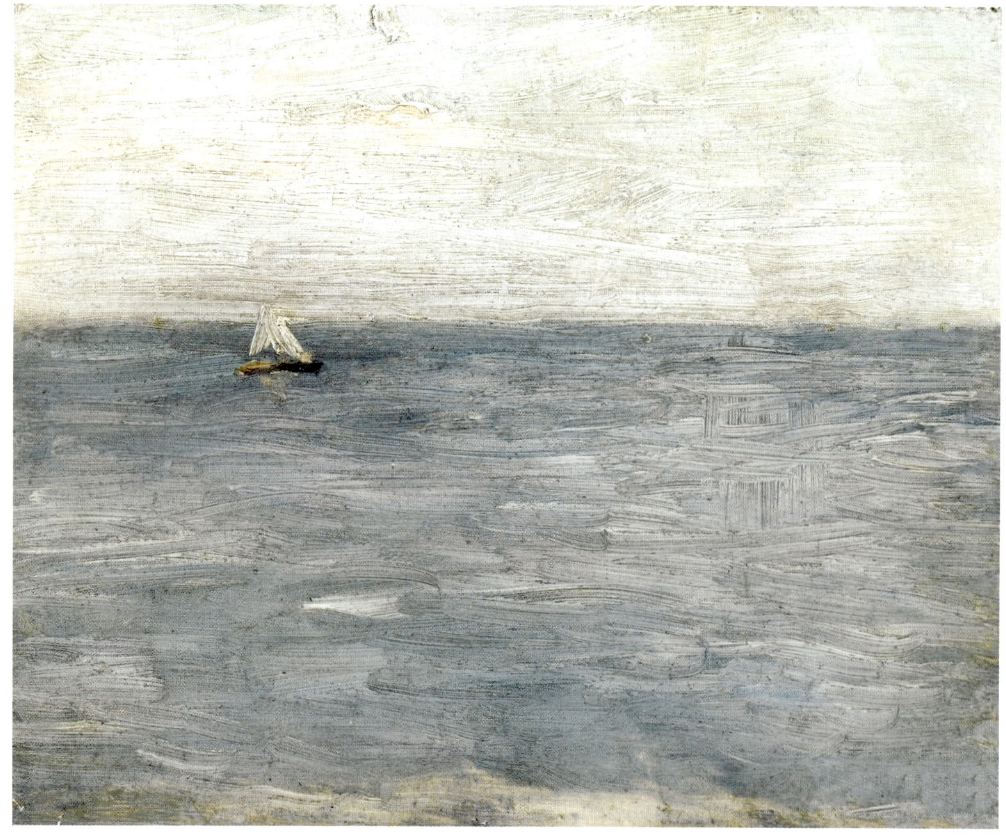

CAT. 23 – *Seascape with Sailing Boat*, oil on prepared millboard, 8 x 10 in. (20.3 x 25.5 cm).

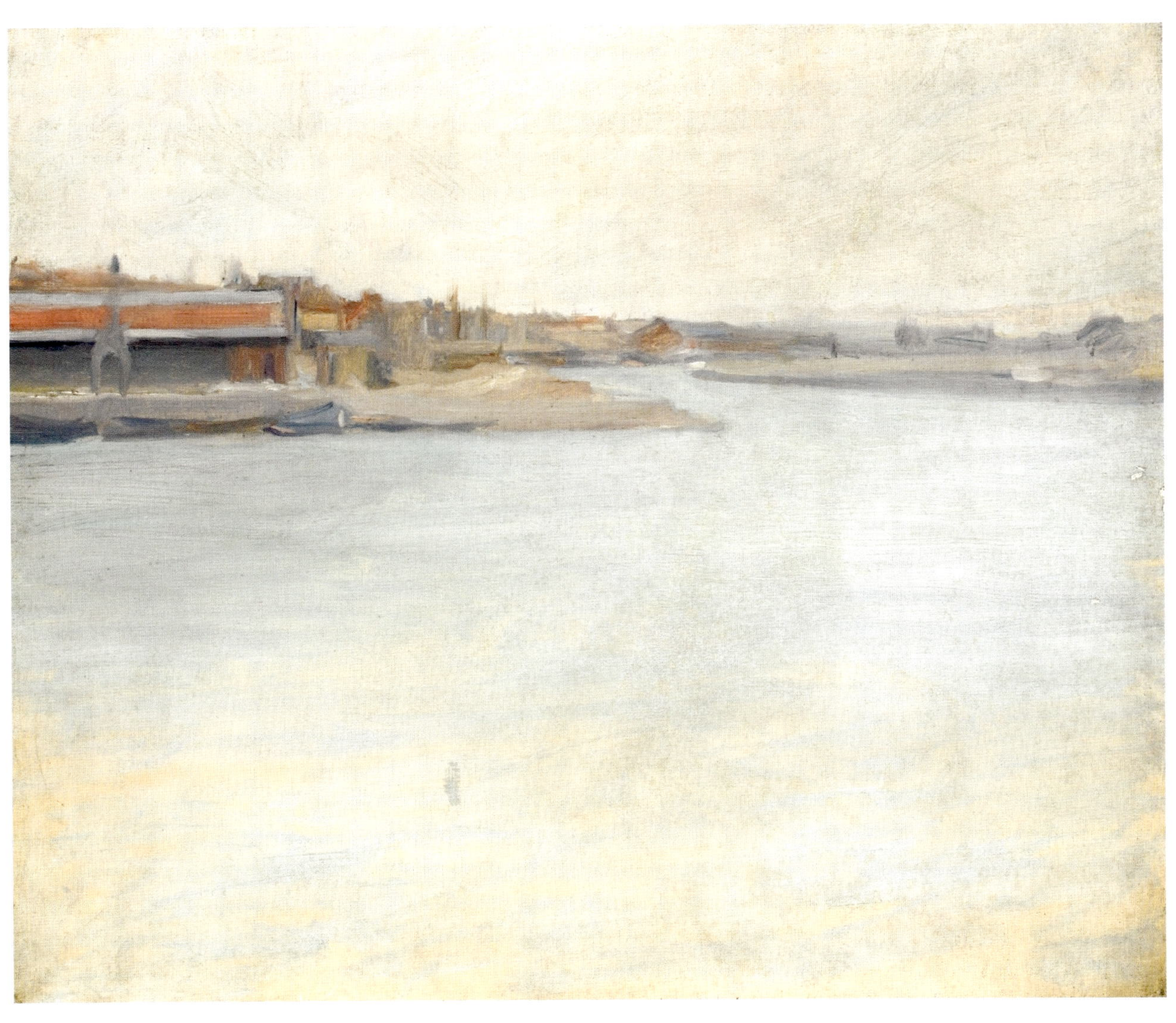

CAT. 24 – *Boulogne sur Mer – A View of the Port*, oil on canvas, 21 x 25 ¼ in (53.2 x 64 cm).

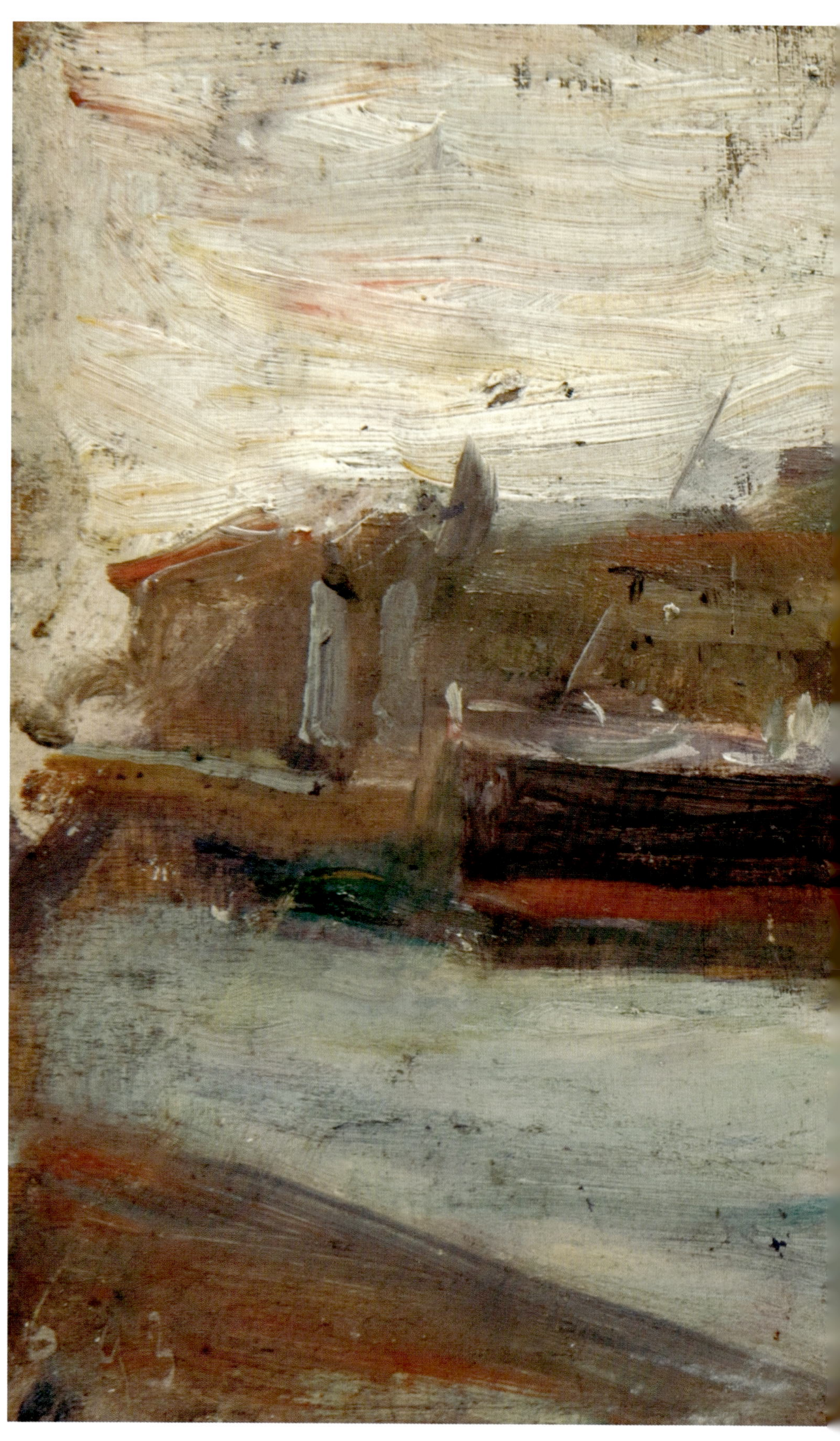

CAT. 25 – *Steam Engine Tug Boats on the Quayside*, 1893,
signed with initials,
oil on panel,
6 x 9 ½ in. (15.5 x 24 cm).

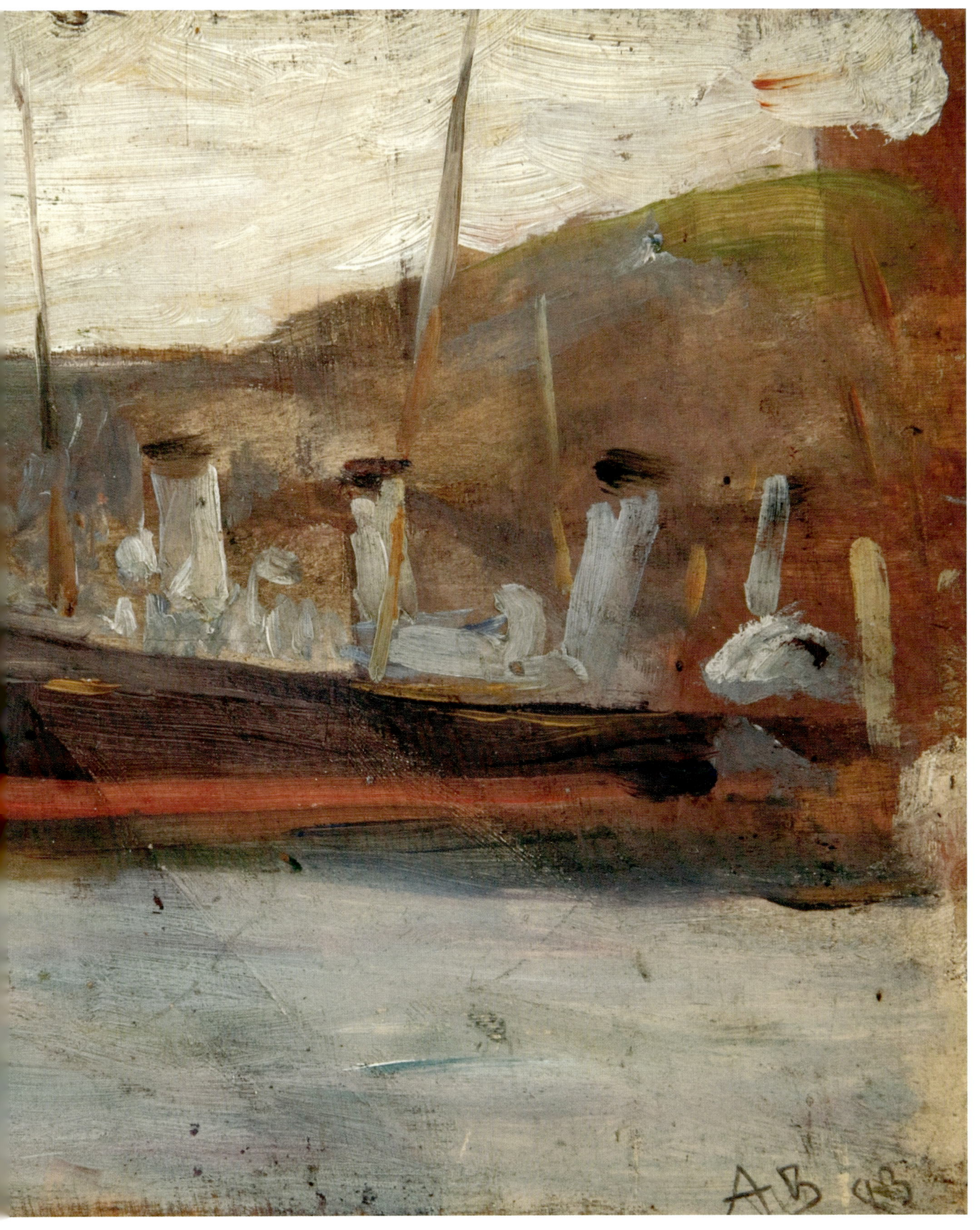

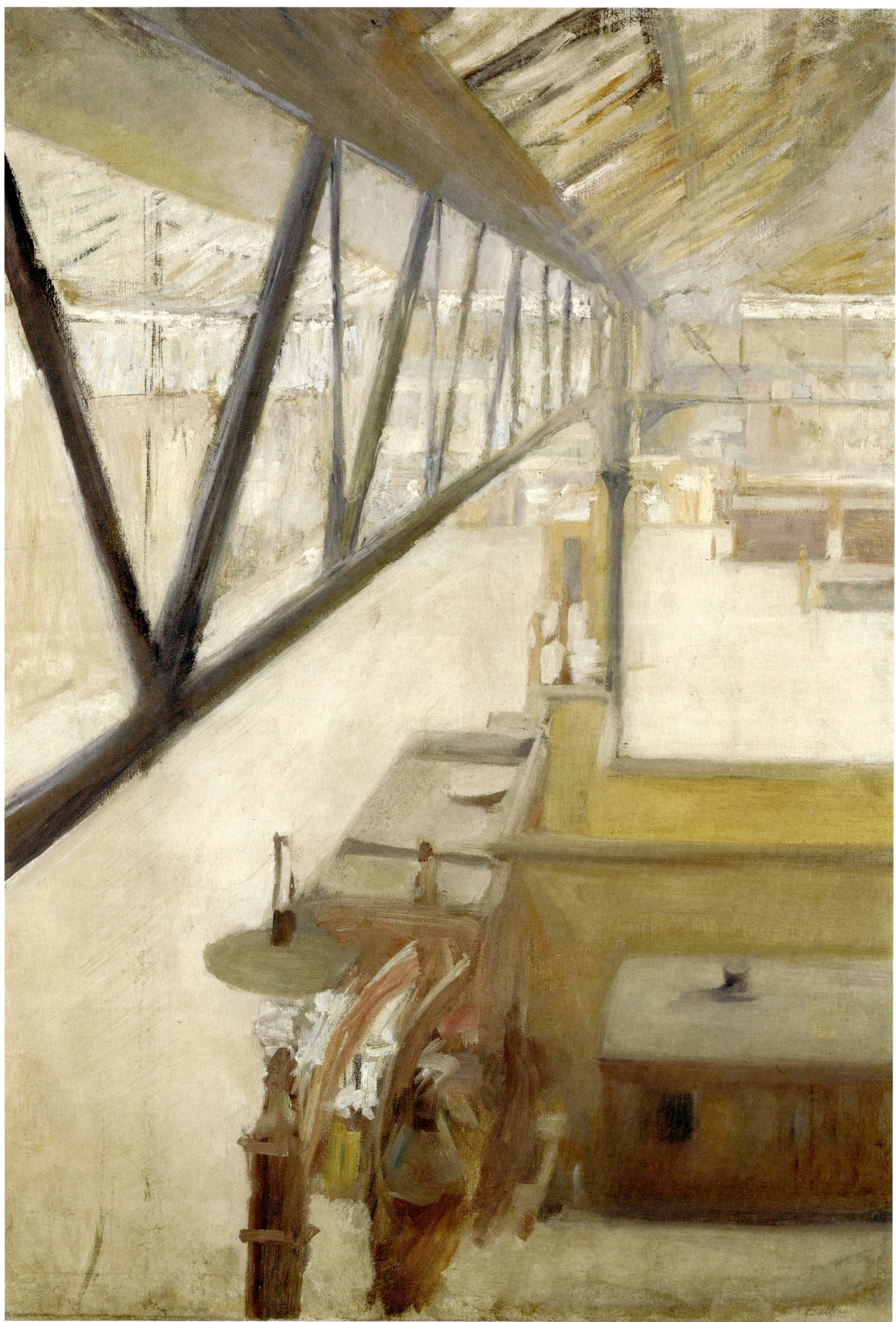

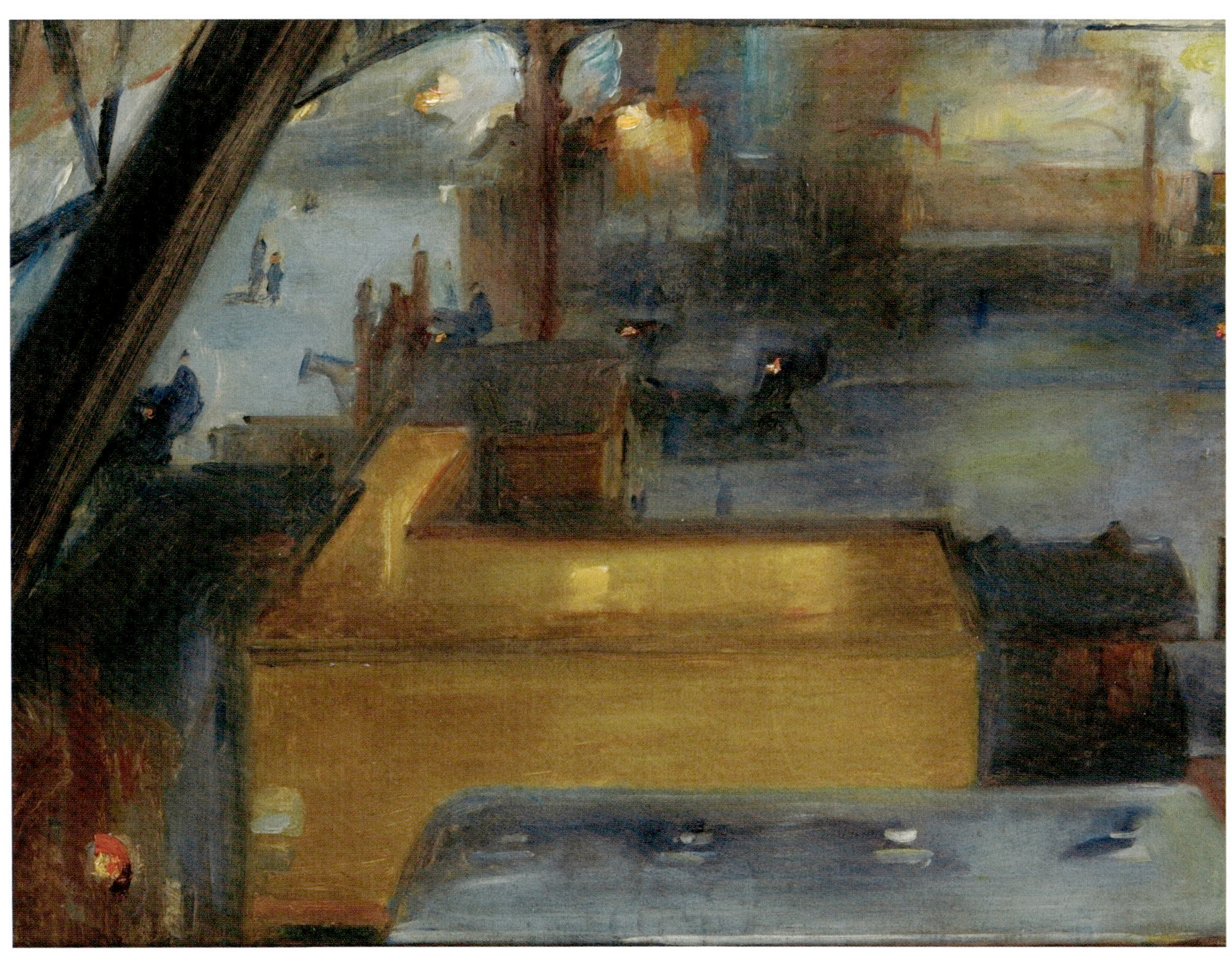

CAT. 27 – *Nocturn at Charing Cross Station*, c.1890, oil on canvas. 21 x 28 ¼ in. (53.5 x 72 cm).

CAT. 26 – *Early Morning, Charing Cross Station*, c.1890, signed in pencil,
oil on canvas, 30 x 21 ½ in. (76.3 x 54.5 cm).

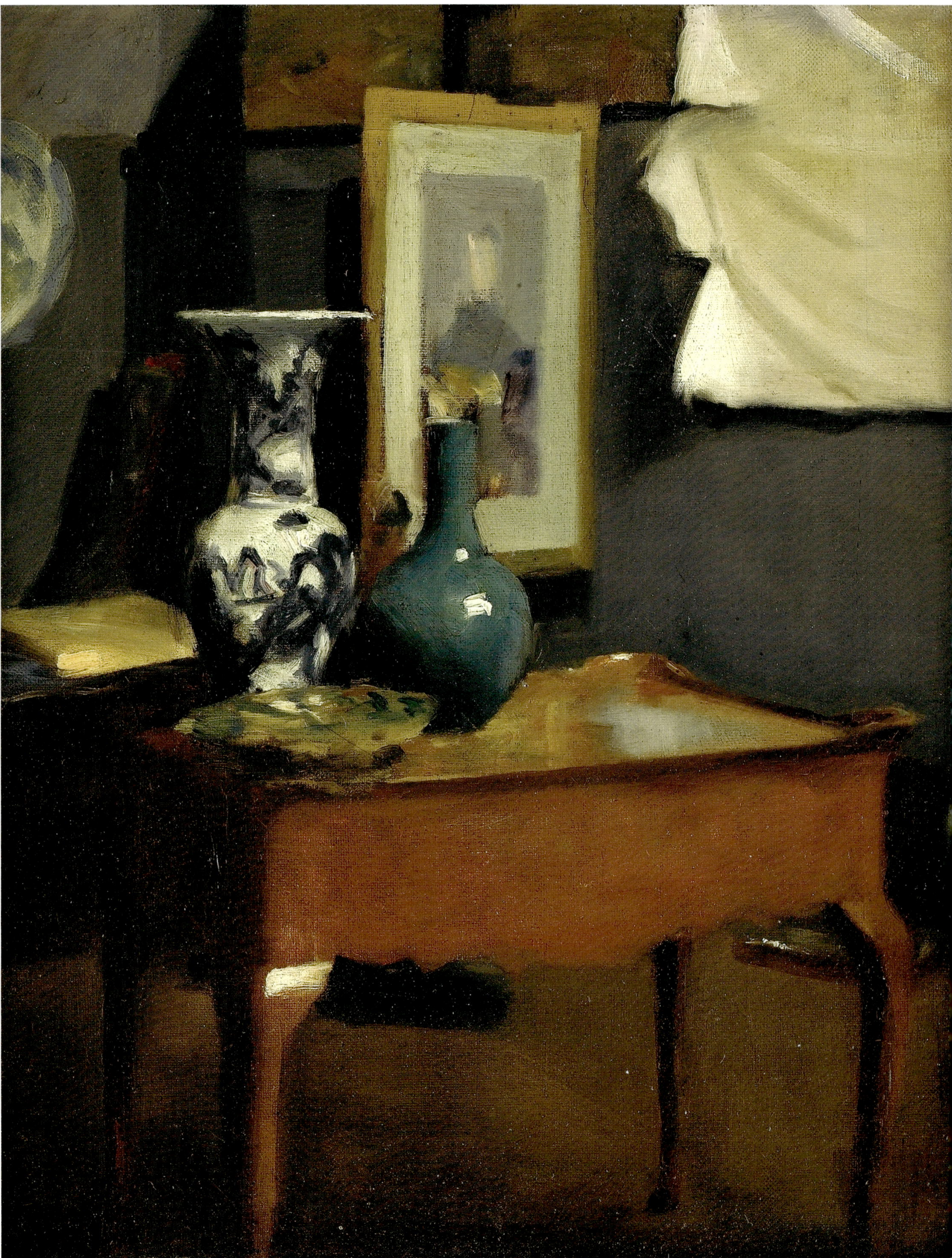

'His still life pictures – with the glimmer of light on silver and other objects, the shadows full of rich and reflected tones – has brought a new note into this kind of painting. One might say that he has carried the tradition of Chardin a step further, giving immediacy to his efects of light and colour, crystallizing the emotion of a particular moment. In this work one feels that, with his lively and nervous handling of paint, he makes the objects before him live in the moving light that plays on them, and it is not surprising that Degas thought so highly of these works.'

Frank Brangwyn,

Foreword to *Albert de Belleroche* by Julian A Millest, *Apollo* 1935 XII, 24 April.

'The most interesting work shown this season is the study of an interior by M. Belleroche. Its interest consists int he fact that it is a piece of painting that is absolutely modern – impressionistic if you prefer – in its technique. The painter has completely mastered and comprehended the qualities and possibilities of his material under modern conditions.'

'The New English Art Club', *The St James Gazette*, April 6 1895.

Belleroche's profound admiration of Dutch paintings from the Golden Age was crystalised by the visit he made to Harlem in 1883 in the company of fellow students John Singer Sargent and Paul César Helleu. He was also admirative of the works of Fantin-Latour and Toulouse-Lautrec, Belleroche's exact contemporary. Belleroche always retained in his studio, La Vieille Chapelle at Chateaudun, Lautrec's iconic 1895 lithographic poster of La Revue Blanche (see CAT. 29). In Lautrec's 'Portrait of Lili Grenier', 1888 (FIG 5), the Japanese kimono that she is wearing was in fact a studio prop of Belleroche.

CAT. 28– *Le Secretaire Louis XVI,* oil on canvas, 18 ¾ x 15 ¼ in. (46.5 x 38.5 cm).
Exhibited: Arthur Tooth and Sons Ltd, London.

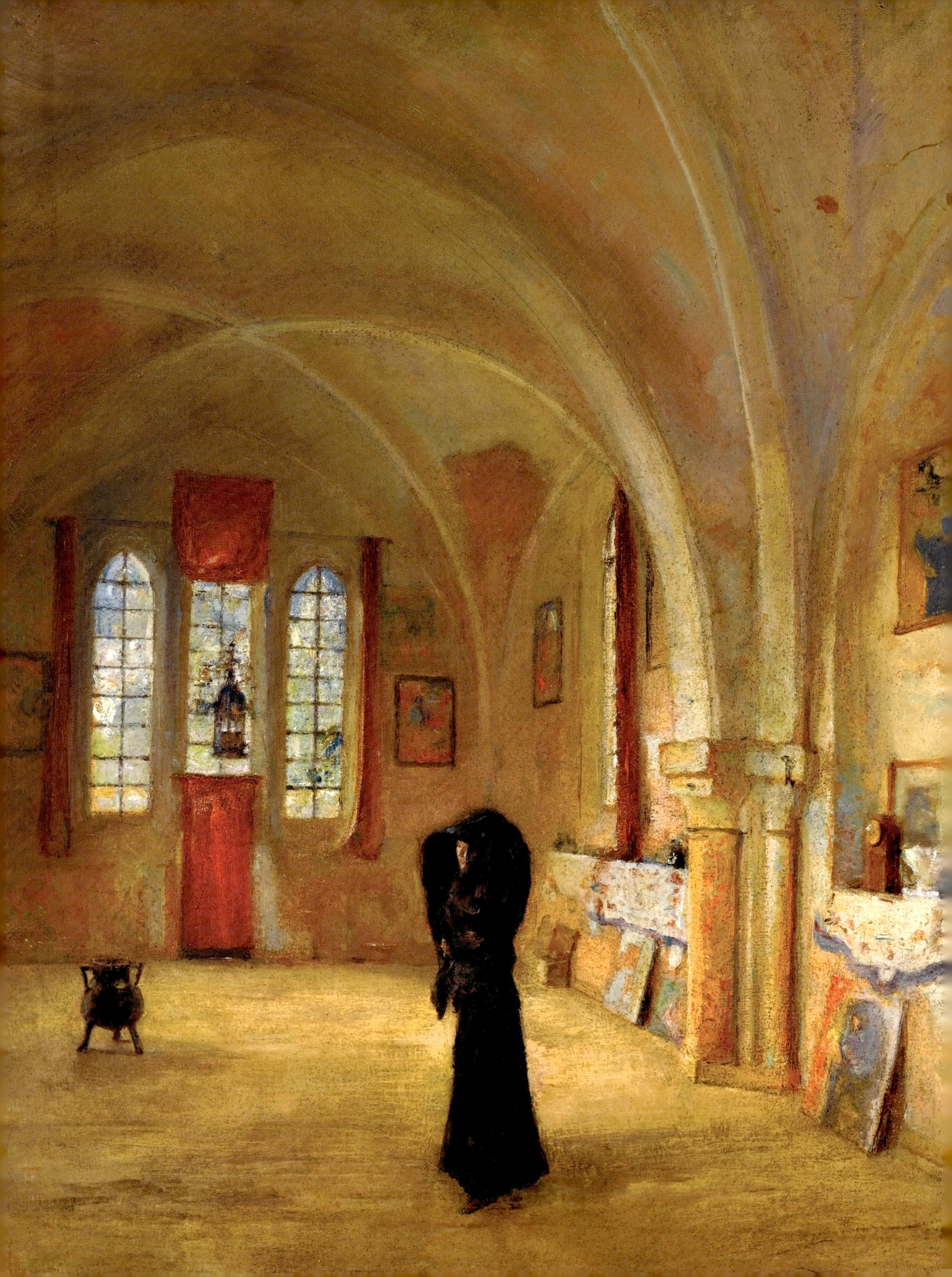

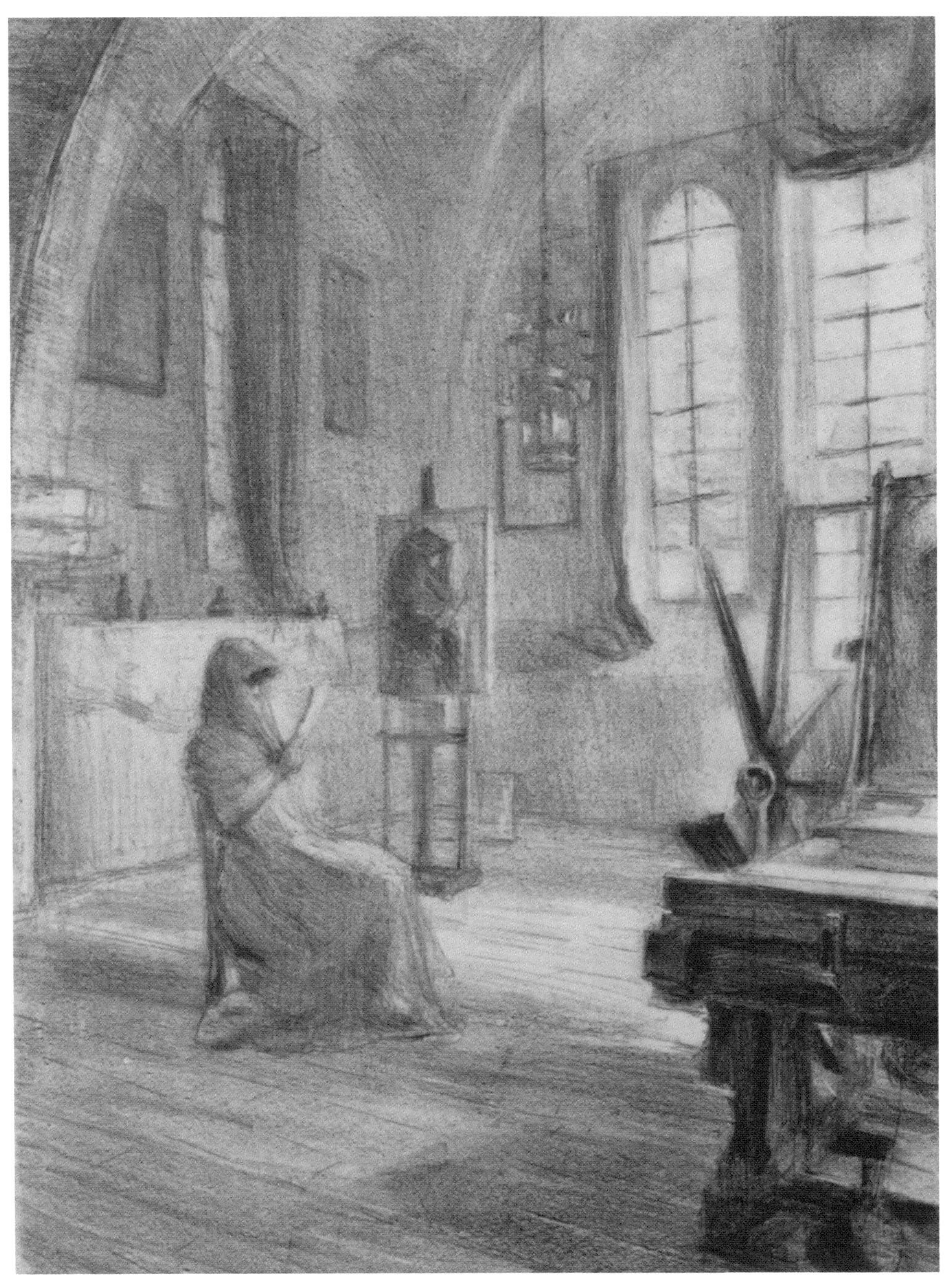

CAT. 30 – *Intérior à la Bossière*, 1909, (K876, AB 313),
lithograph. Edition: 10.

CAT. 29 – *The Artist's Studio, La Vielle Chapelle, La Boissiere, Chateaudun*, c. 1909, oil on canvas, 30 x 24 in. (76.2 x 61 cm).

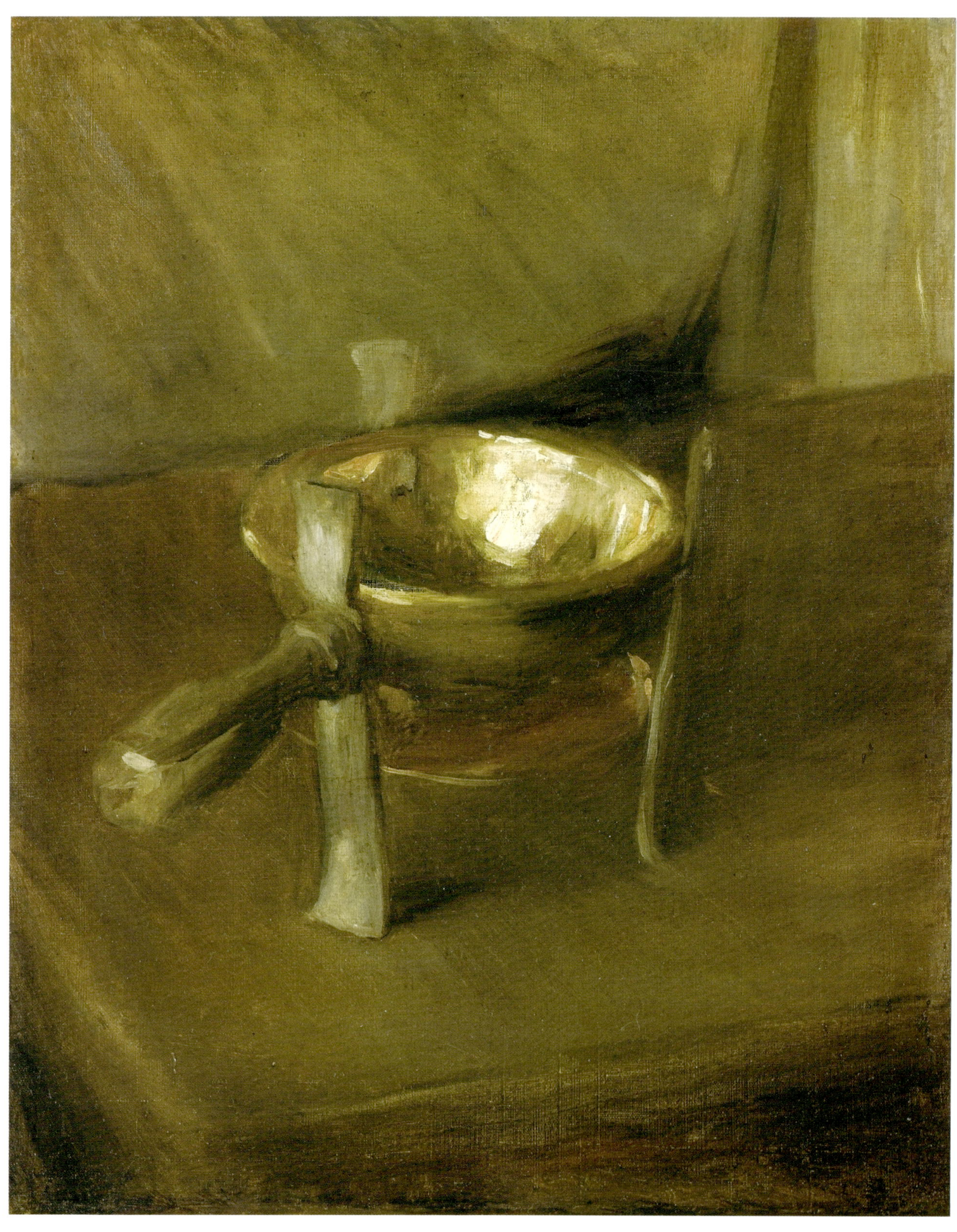

CAT. 31 – *Still Life with Crucible*, c. 1890, signed on reverse,
oil on canvas (P. Aprin, Paris), 19 x 15 ½ in. (48.2 x 39.5 cm).

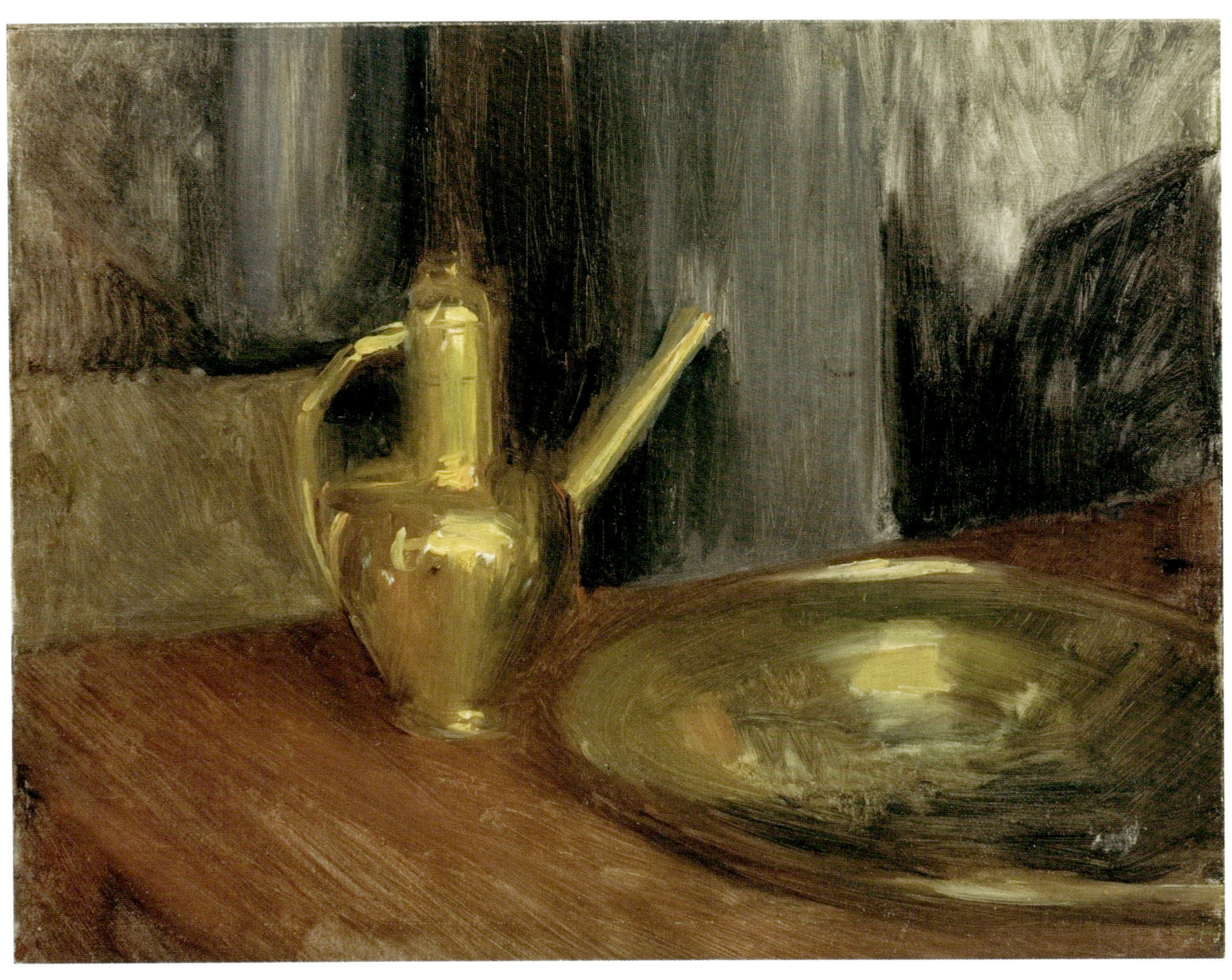

CAT. 32 – *Still Life with Coffee Pot and Bowl,* c.1890, oil on canvas, 19 x 25 ½ in. (48 x 65 cm).

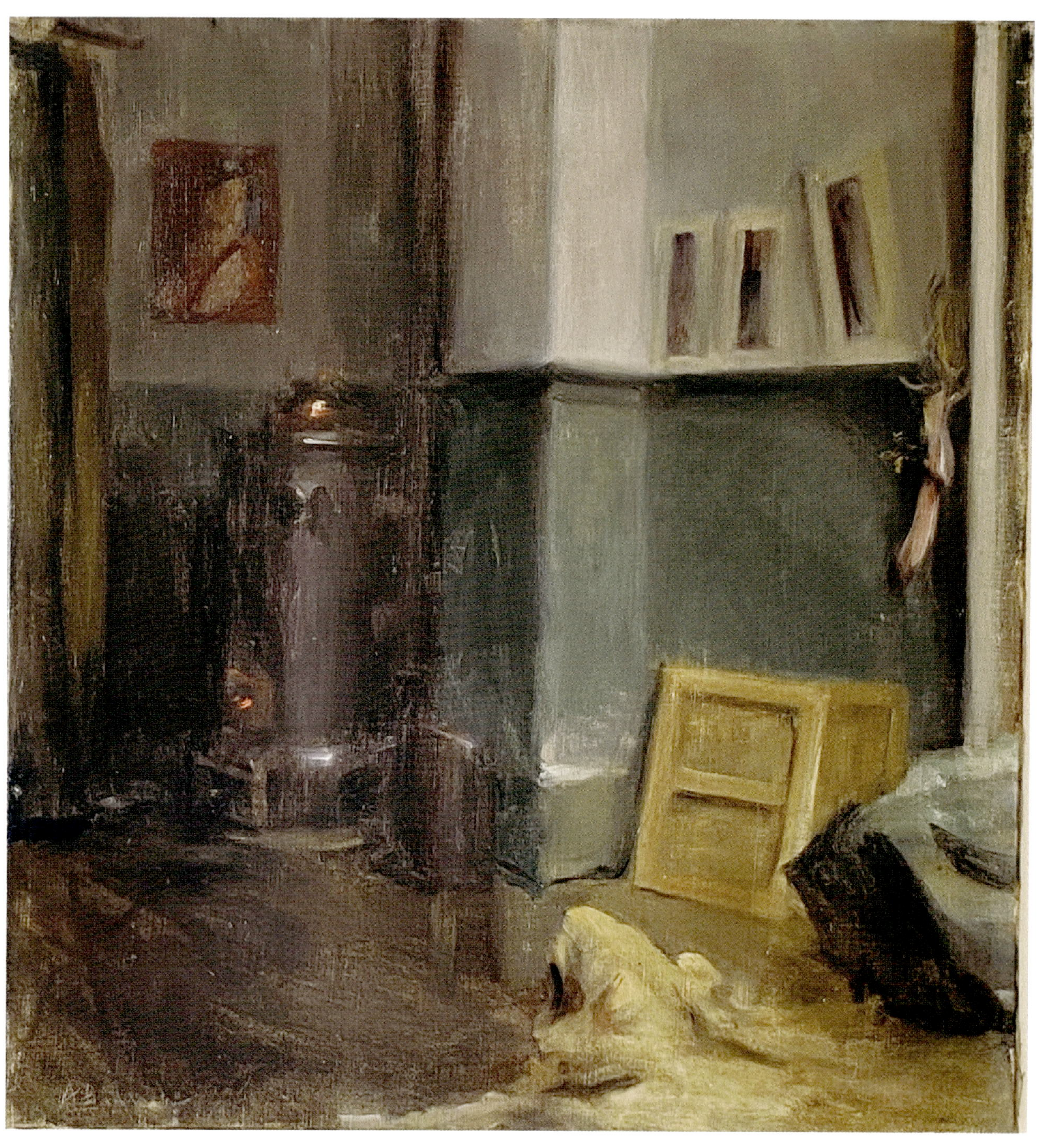

CAT. 33 – *Studio Interior with Canvases*, c.1889, oil on canvas, 17 ¼ x 16 in. (44 x 41 cm). Provenance Lili Grenier.

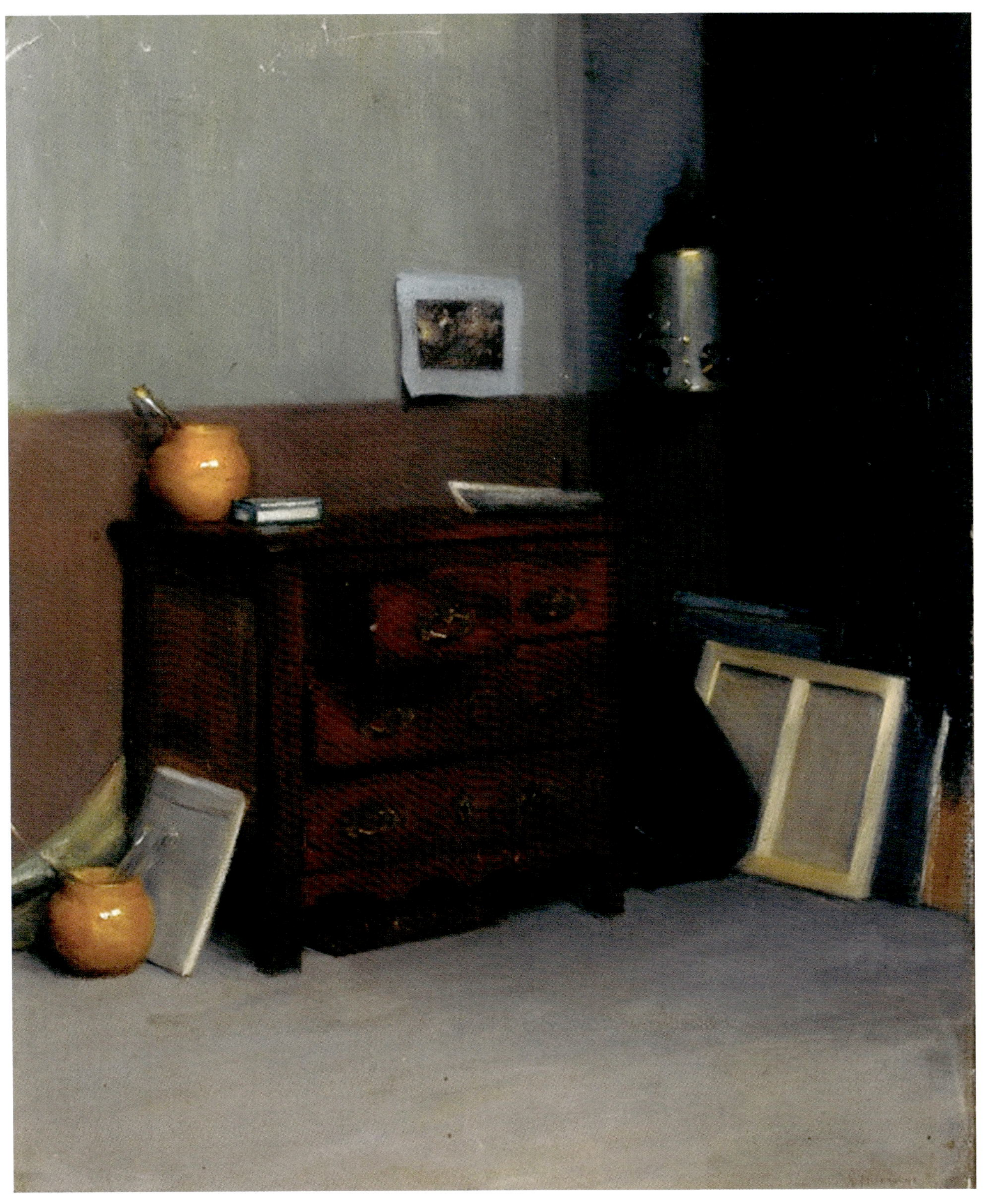

CAT. 34 – *Les deux petits pots (Les pots jaunes)*, c.1889, signed, oil on canvas, 18 ¼ x 15 ¼ in. (46.5 x 38.5 cm).
Exhibited: Arthur Tooth and Sons Ltd, London.

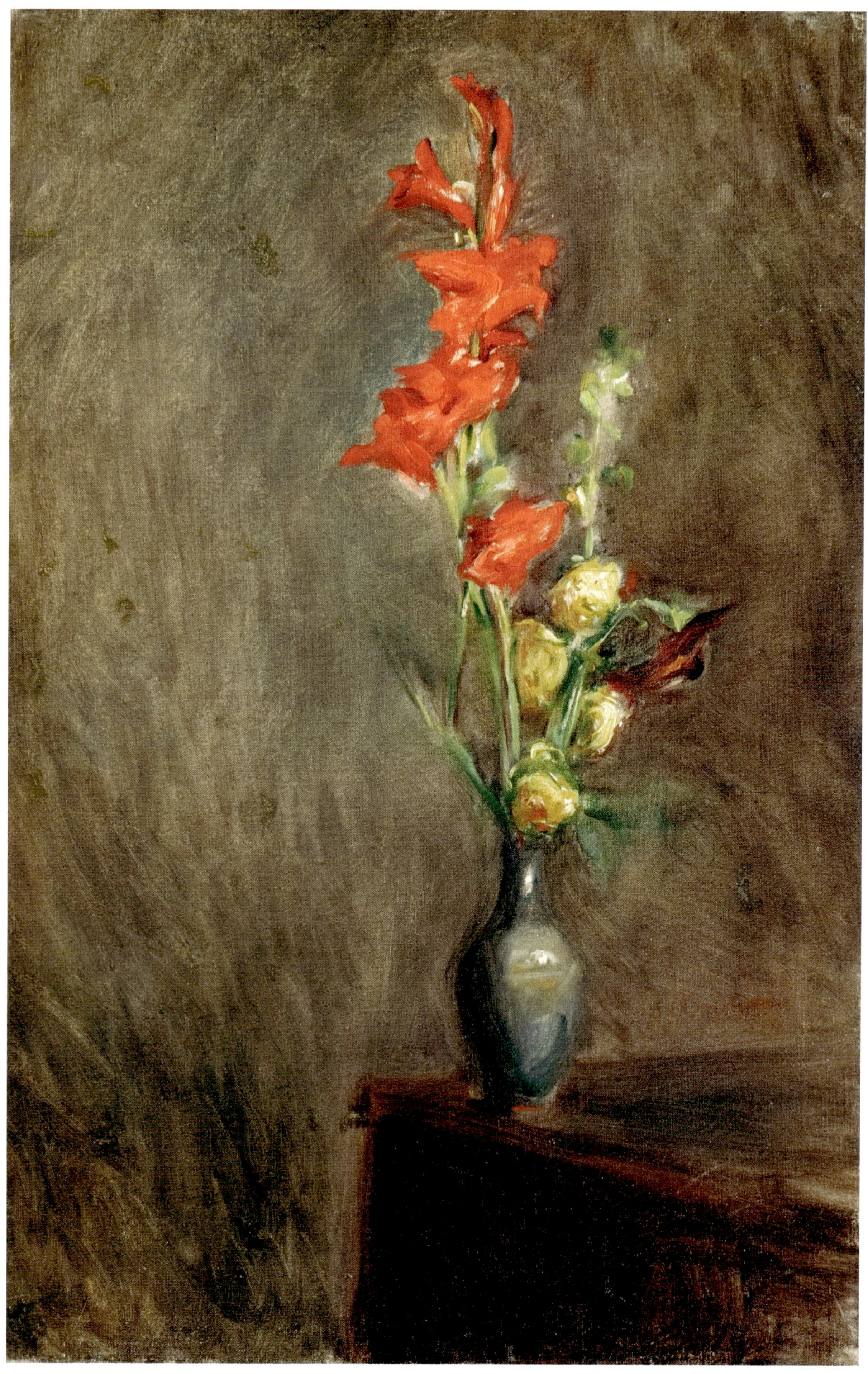

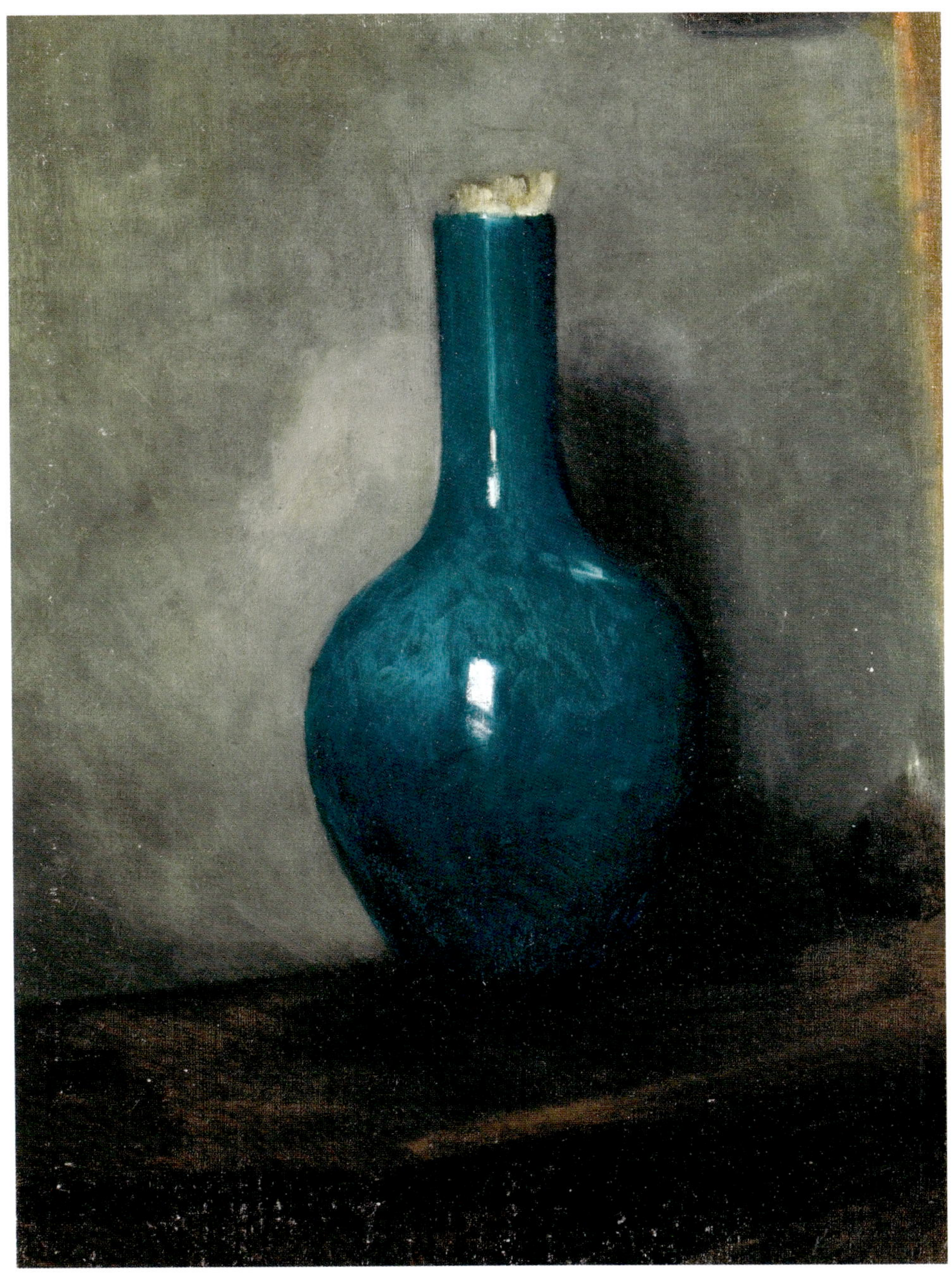

CAT. 36 – *Blue Vase on Grey Background*, c. 1885,
signed in pencil, oil on canvas, 21 ¼ x 16 ½ in. (54 x 41.5 cm).

OVERLEAF:

CAT. 35 – *Gladioli, Roses and Stocks in a Vase*, c.1885,
oil on canvas, 28 ¾ x 19 in. (73 x 48 cm).

CAT. 37 – *Discarded Slippers*, c. 1890,
oil on canvas, 11 ¾ x 16 in. (30 x 40.4 cm).

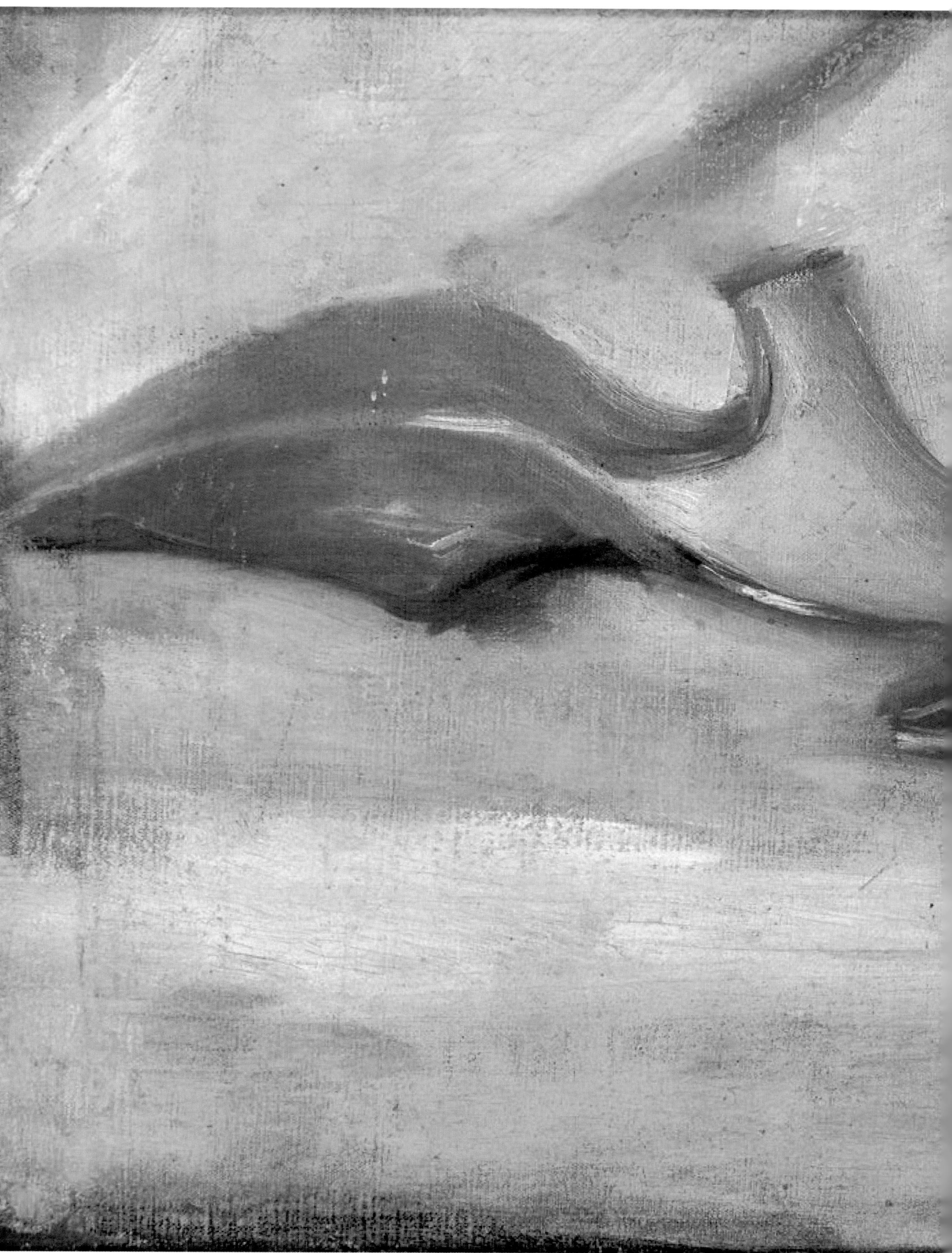

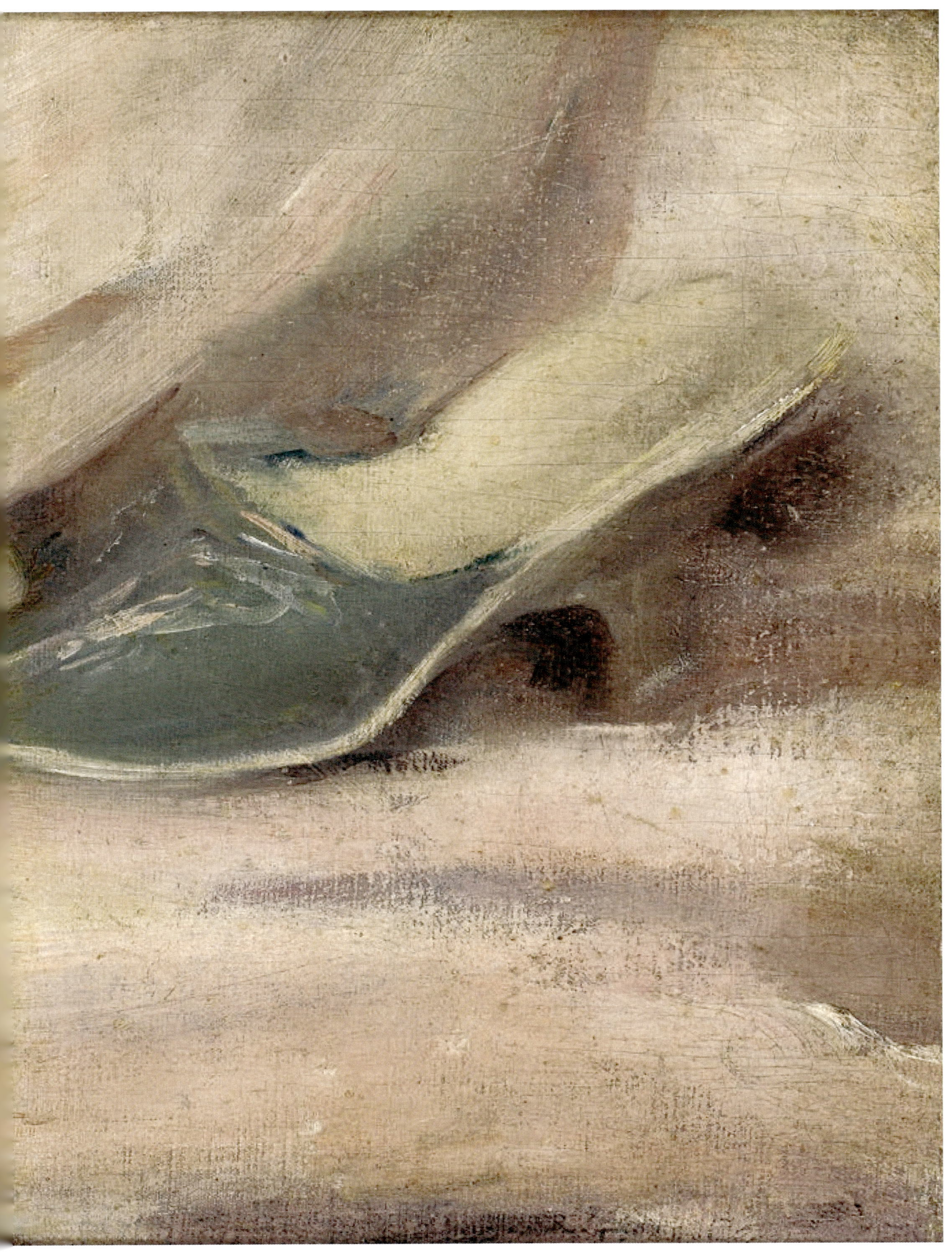

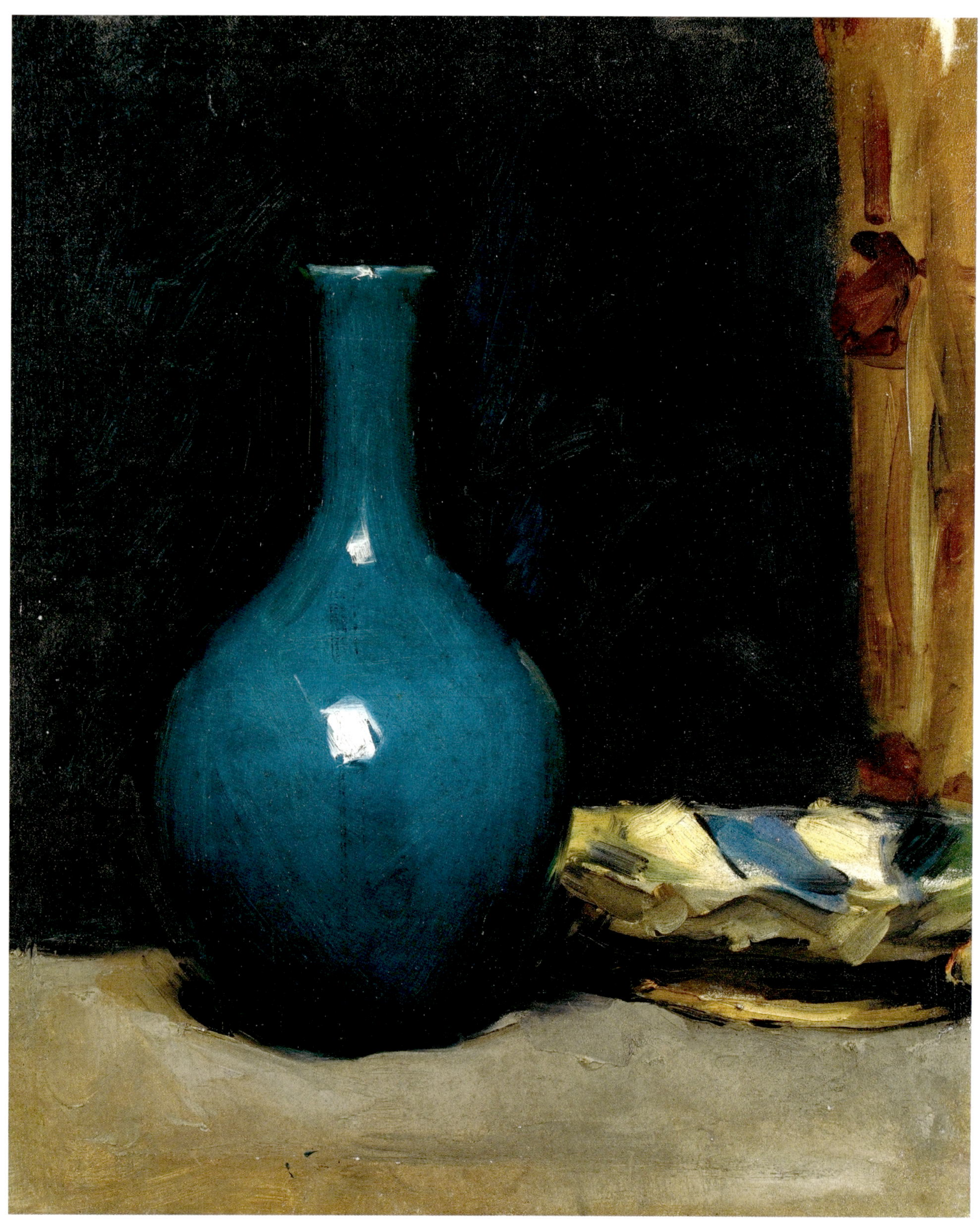

CAT. 38 – *Still Life with Blue Vase and Folded Cloth*, late 1880s, signed with initials,
Oil on canvas, 21 ½ x 18 in. (54.5 x 45.8 cm).

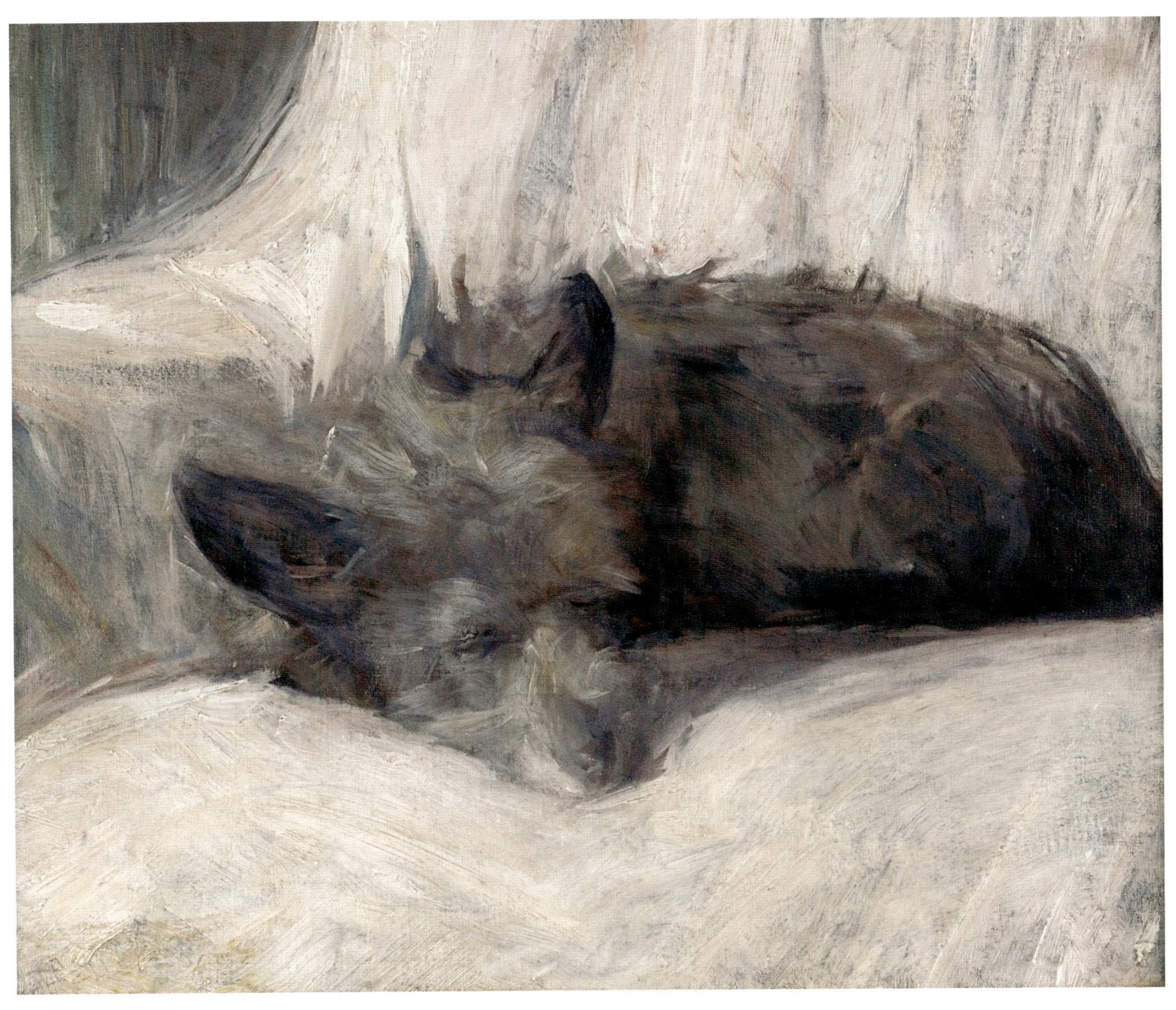

CAT. 39 – *Lance at Dunain House*, early 1880s, oil on canvas, 14 ¾ x 17 ½ in. (37.4 x 44.5 cm).

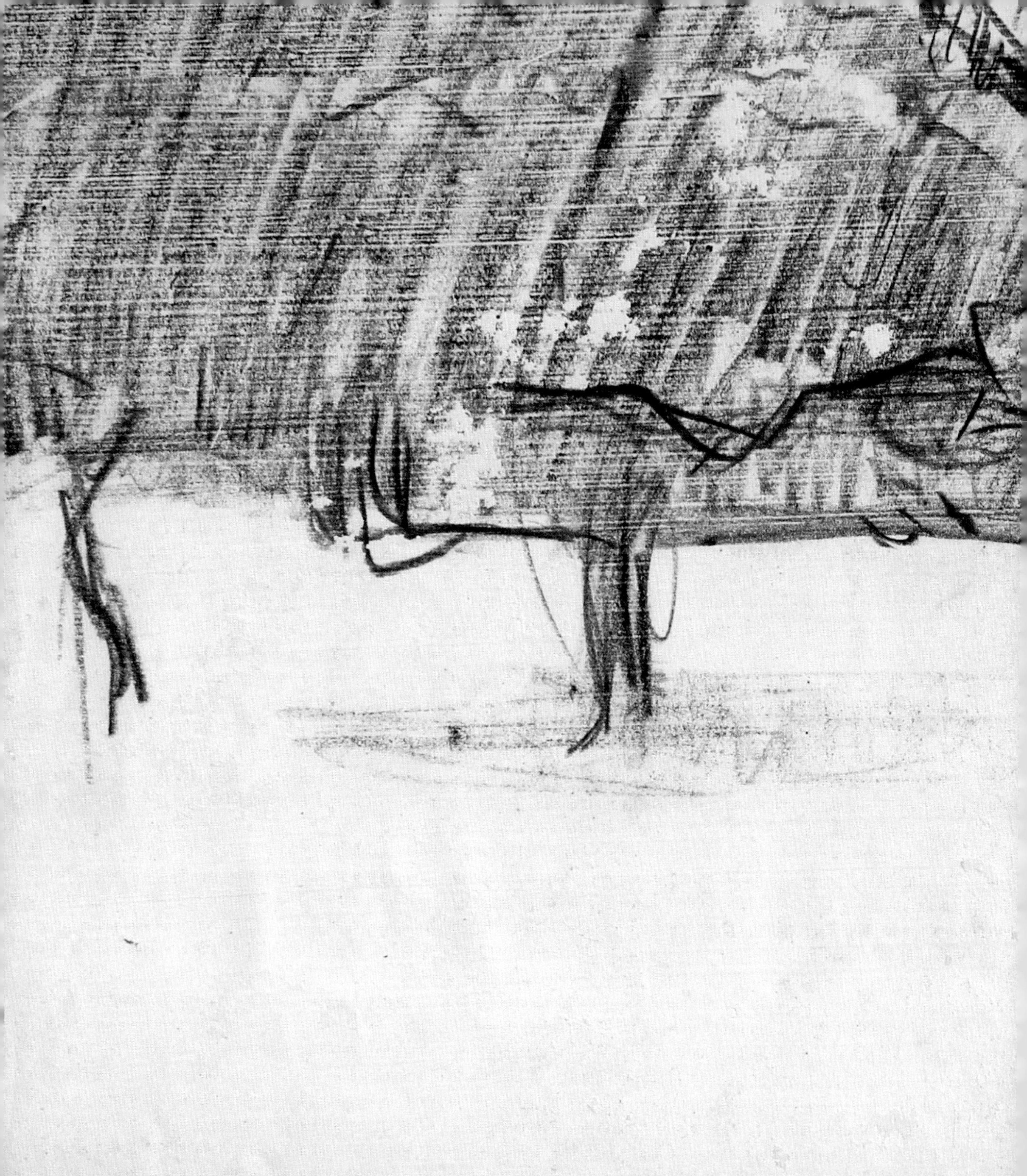

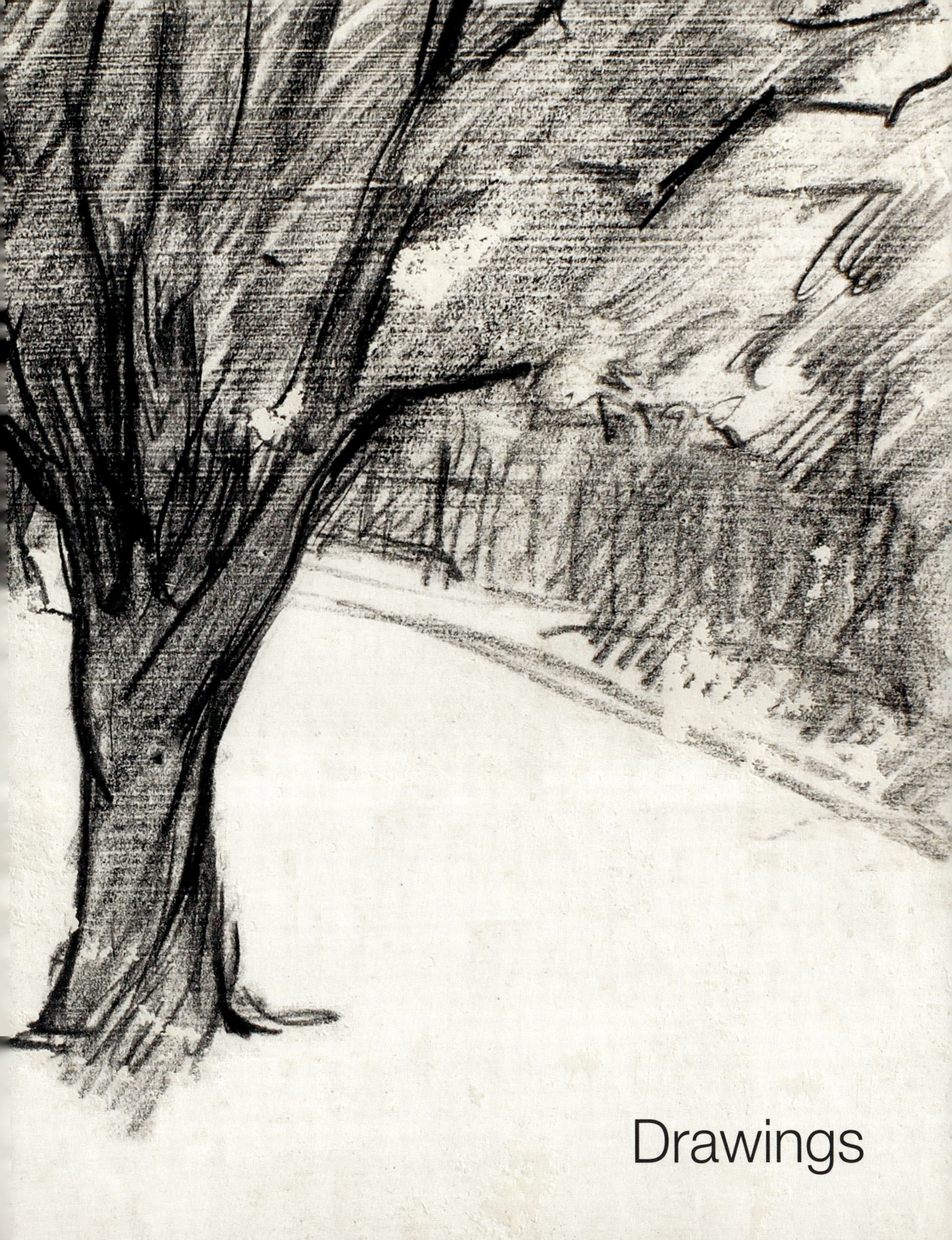

Drawings

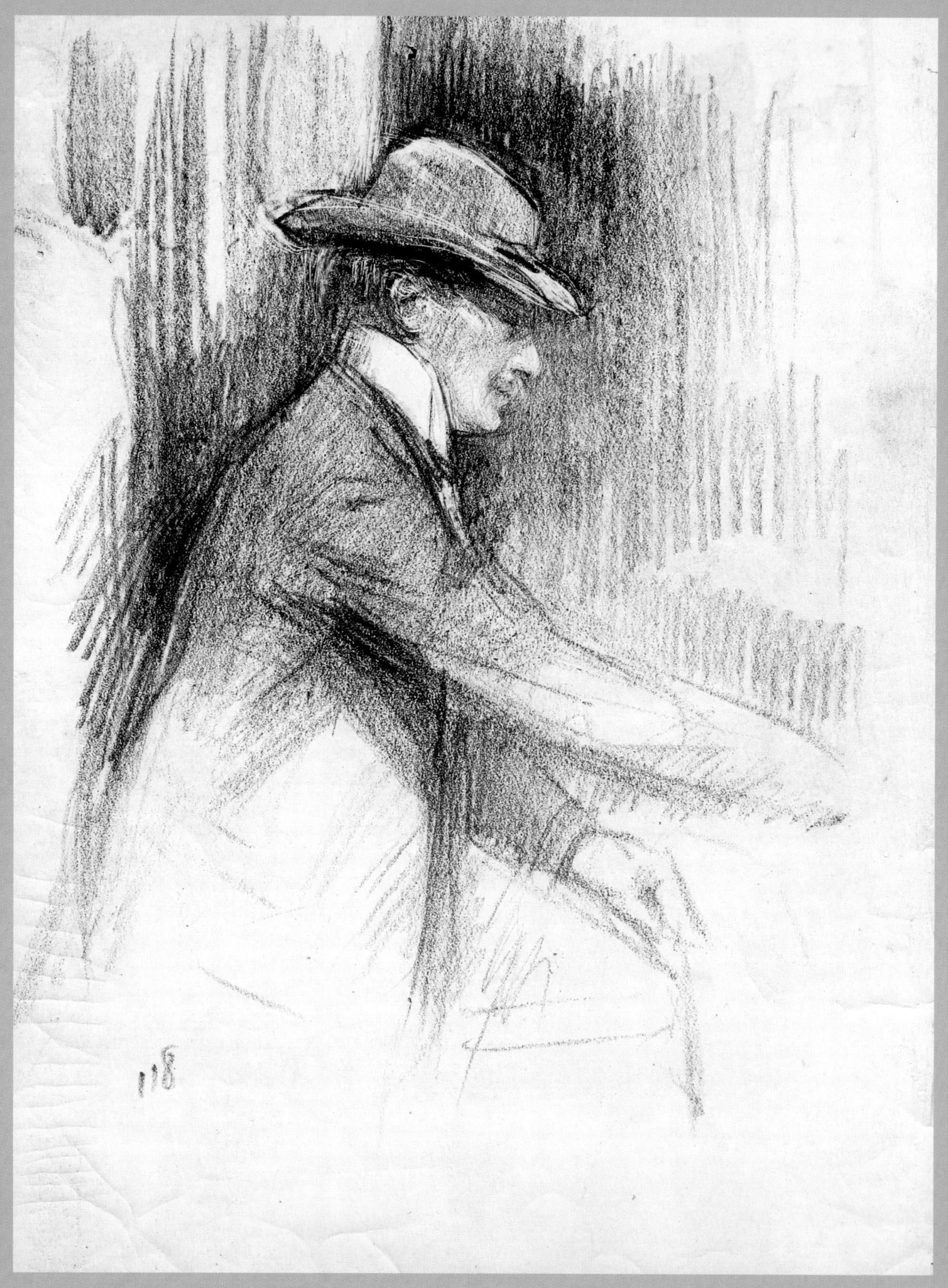

Inspite of the fact that drawing was an essential process for Belleroche, relatively few drawings survive. As an artist he painted directly onto canvas, without any underdrawing, and as a print maker he drew directly onto the stone matrix. Lithographic stones were wiped clean after printing, so that the stone could be reused or the limited edition reprinted.

Like all students of the period Belleroche did make life-drawings, and learnt to sketch on the spot, en plein air. Throughout his life he also made accomplished portrait drawings, in parallel to his exquisite lithographs. Only occasionally did he exhibit drawings. A Colnaghi exhibition of 1941 included 32 drawings, but as A.M.Hind observed in the catalogue foreword, "Belleroche's drawings are rare, for he prefers to sketch on canvas and draw on stone." Occasionally Belleroche drew on transfer paper, working in lithographic crayons, pencil and tusch (a black pigment used in the production of lithographs). Many printmakers of the period, for instance Daumier and Lautrec, used this medium because it had two advantages over lithographic stone: it was portable, (it could be used to record subjects outside the studio) , and the drawn image was not reversed through printing. Once passed through the press, however, the original drawing from the transfer paper would be lost. A number of drawings on transfer paper by Belleroche survive – as such it would appear that he did not always intend that these drawings were to be printed from, which would have resulted in their destruction. A drawing on transfer paper can be difficult to distinguish from a single edition lithograph. George Kenney has pointed out that Belleroche's earliest experiments with lithography, in 1899, involved transfer paper, but that Belleroche was unhappy with the results. In 1933, Louis Leeber, (curator of the Royal Museums of Fine Arts Belgium) asserted that Belleroche felt strongly that he needed to always draw directly on his stone to maintain the utmost quality and control.

Belleroche's drawings range from rapid sketches, made on the spot, to more formal portraits. The studio interiors are particularly noteworthy, not only for their technical excellence but also as important historical records of spaces that Belleroche shared with Sargent.

Belleroche's studies of flowers – especially single stem roses – also bring to mind the exquisite drawings of Fantin-Latour, himself an early pioneer of lithography as an art form in its own right.

CAT. 40 – *Half Length Profile Portrait of a Gentleman*, black crayon on paper, 17 ¼ x 11 ¼ in. (44 x 28.5 cm).

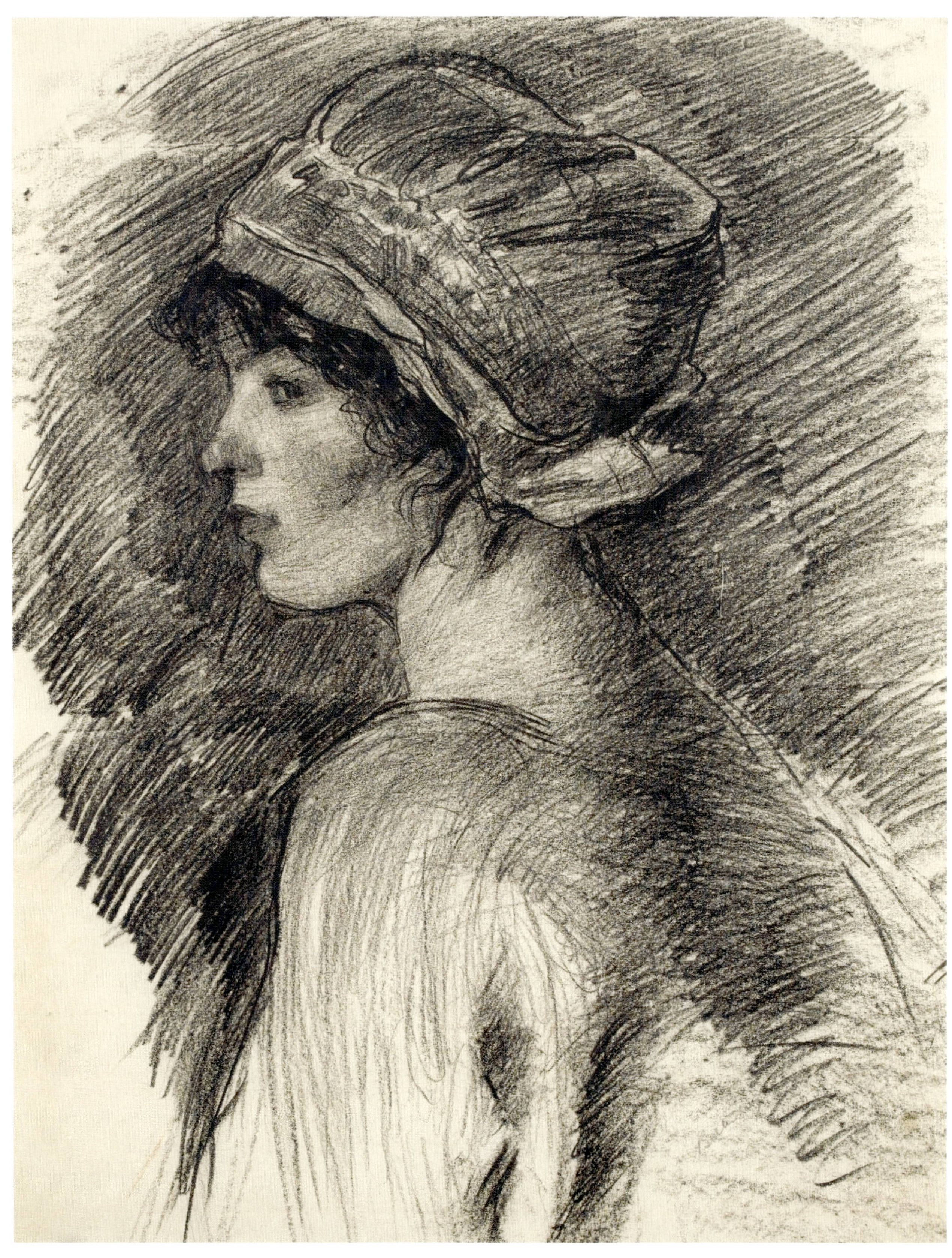

CAT. 41 – *Dorothy*, black crayon on paper, 21 ¾ x 16 ¾ in. (55 x 42.5 cm).

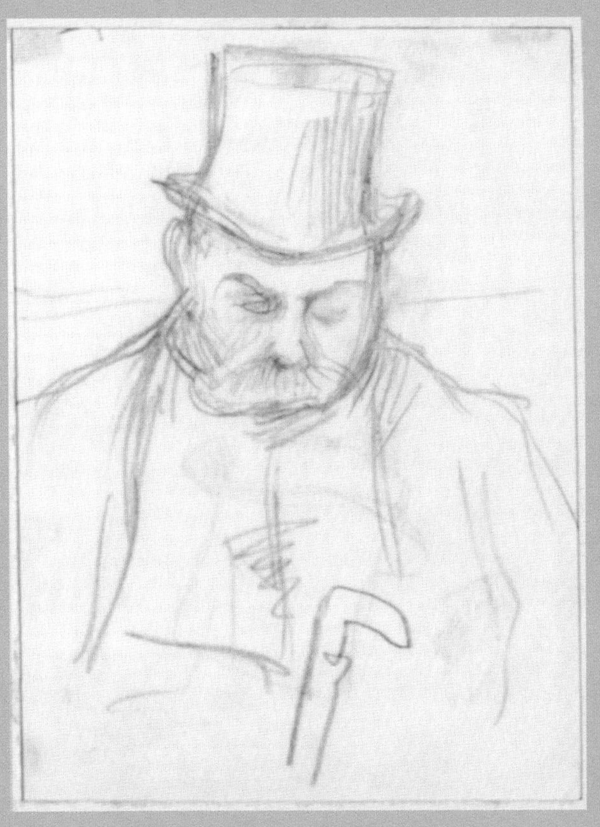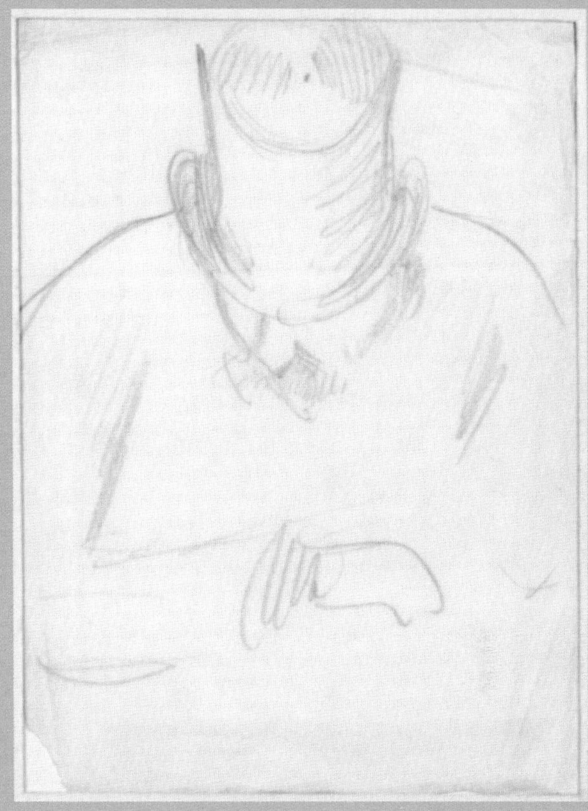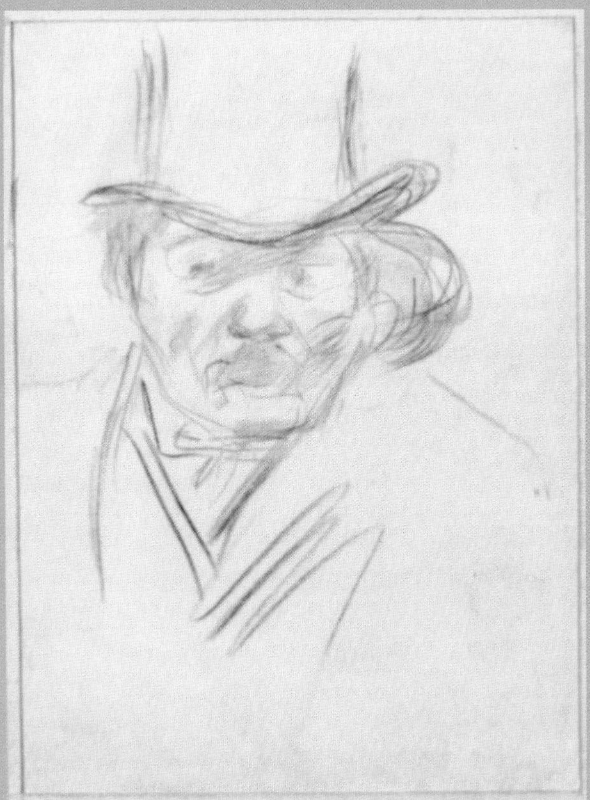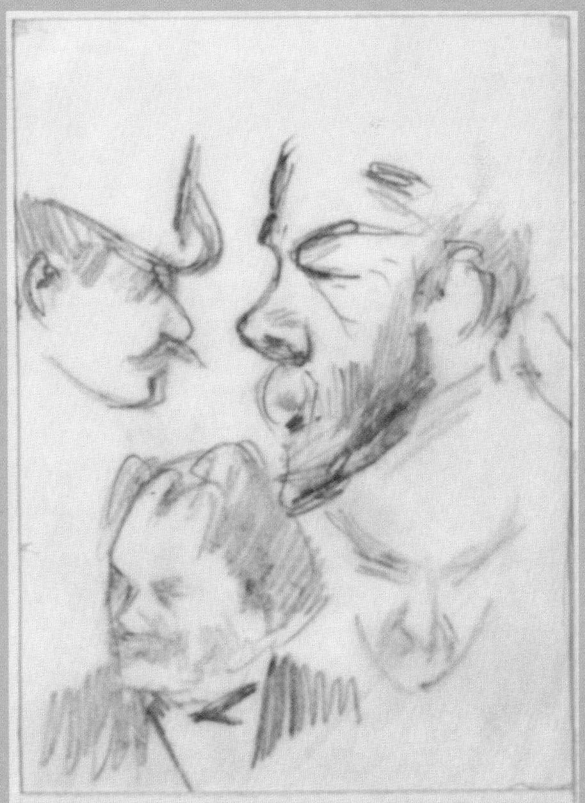

CAT. 42 - 45 – *Four Portrait Studies*, (four drawings mounted together), pencil on paper, each 6 ¼ x 4 ½ in. (16 x 11.5 cm).

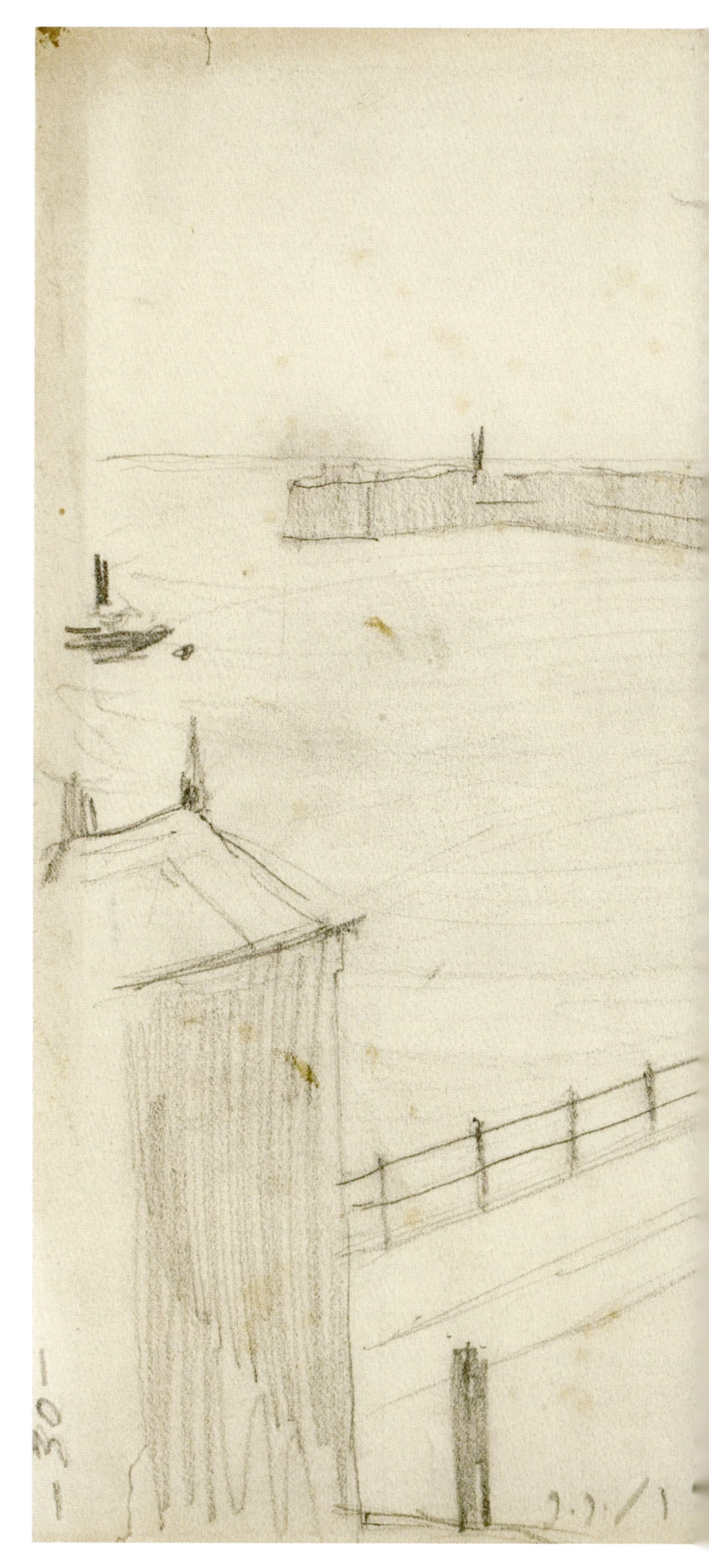

CAT. 46 – *Pier at Dover*, signed,
inscribed: "Dover July 19th",
pencil on paper, 9 ¾ x 13 ½ in. (25.2 x 34.5 cm).

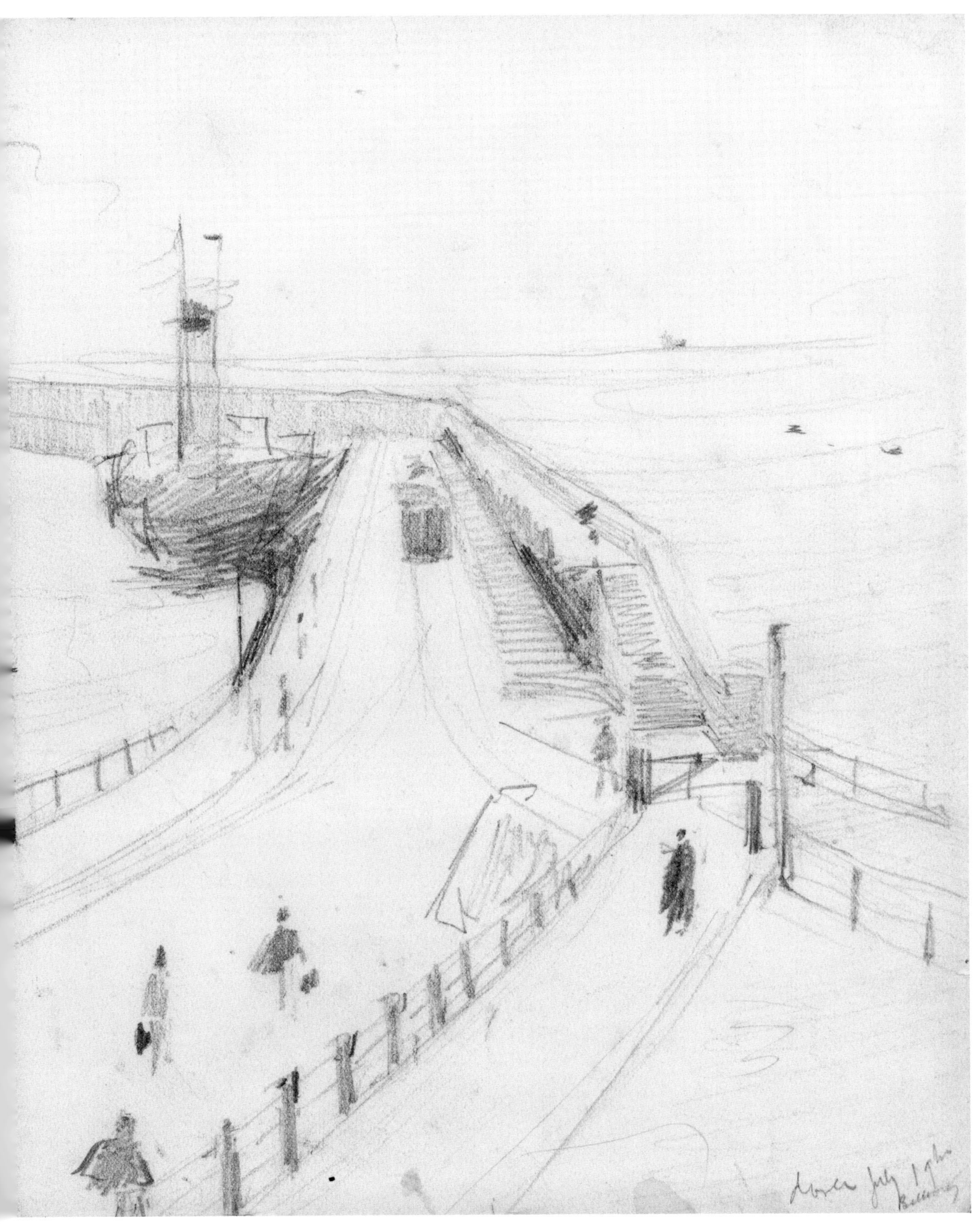

Dover July 1 96

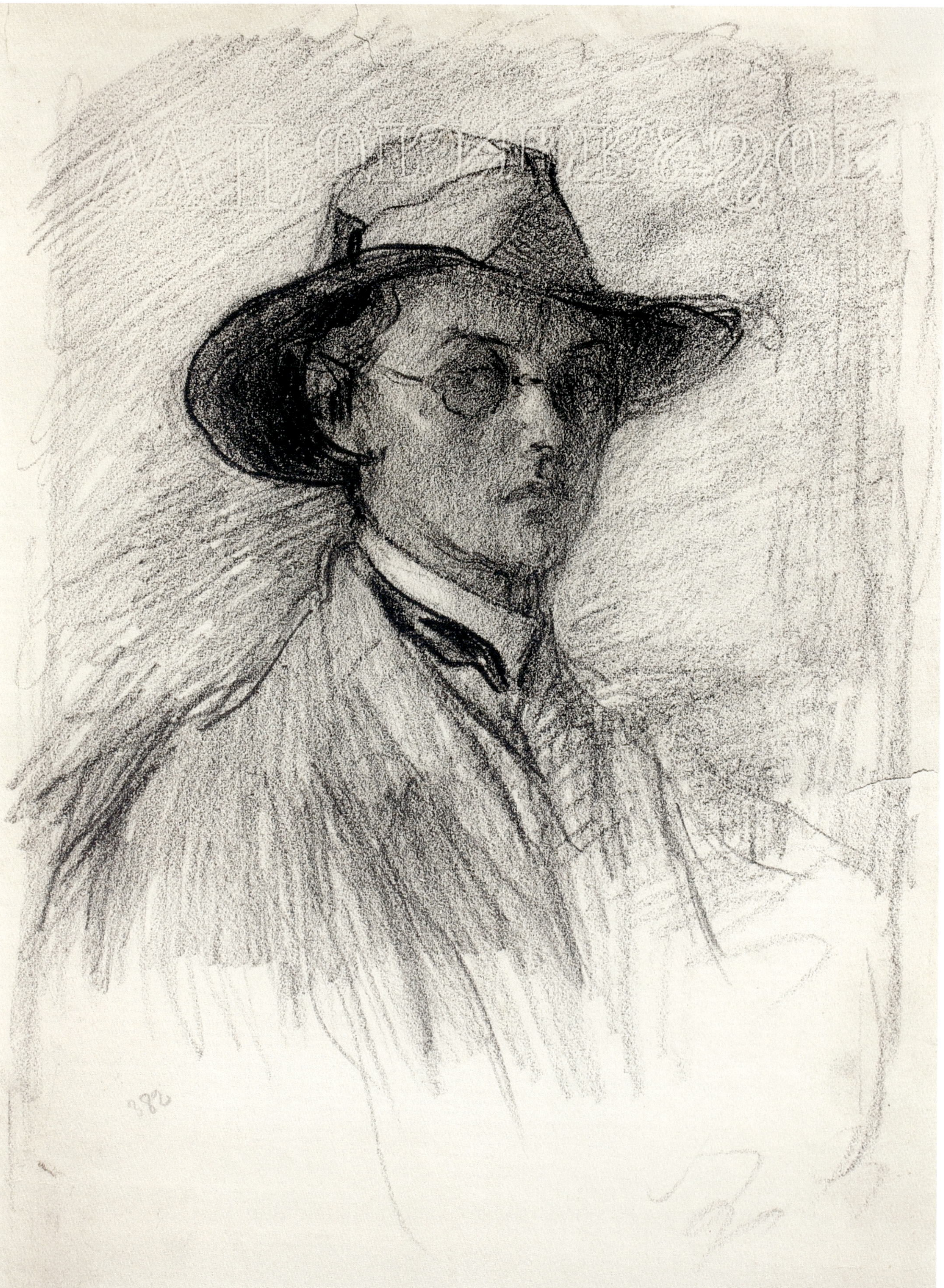

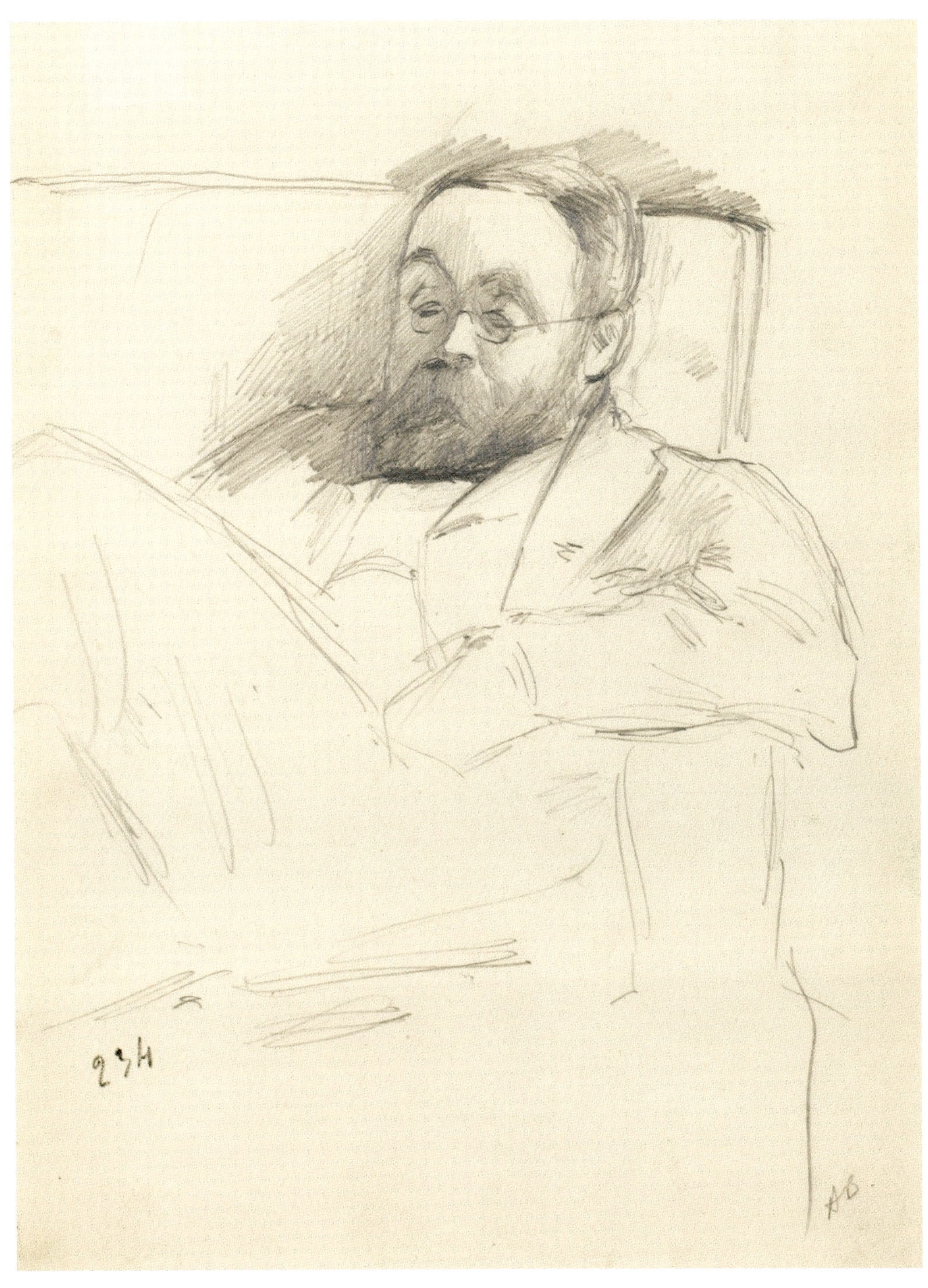

CAT. 48 – *M. Erwan Berthou, Poet*, pencil on paper, 13 ½ x 9 ½ in. (34.6 x 24 cm).

CAT. 47 – *Self-Portrait*, early 1880s, black crayon on paper, 13 1/4 x 10 3/4 in. (33.5 x 27.5 cm).

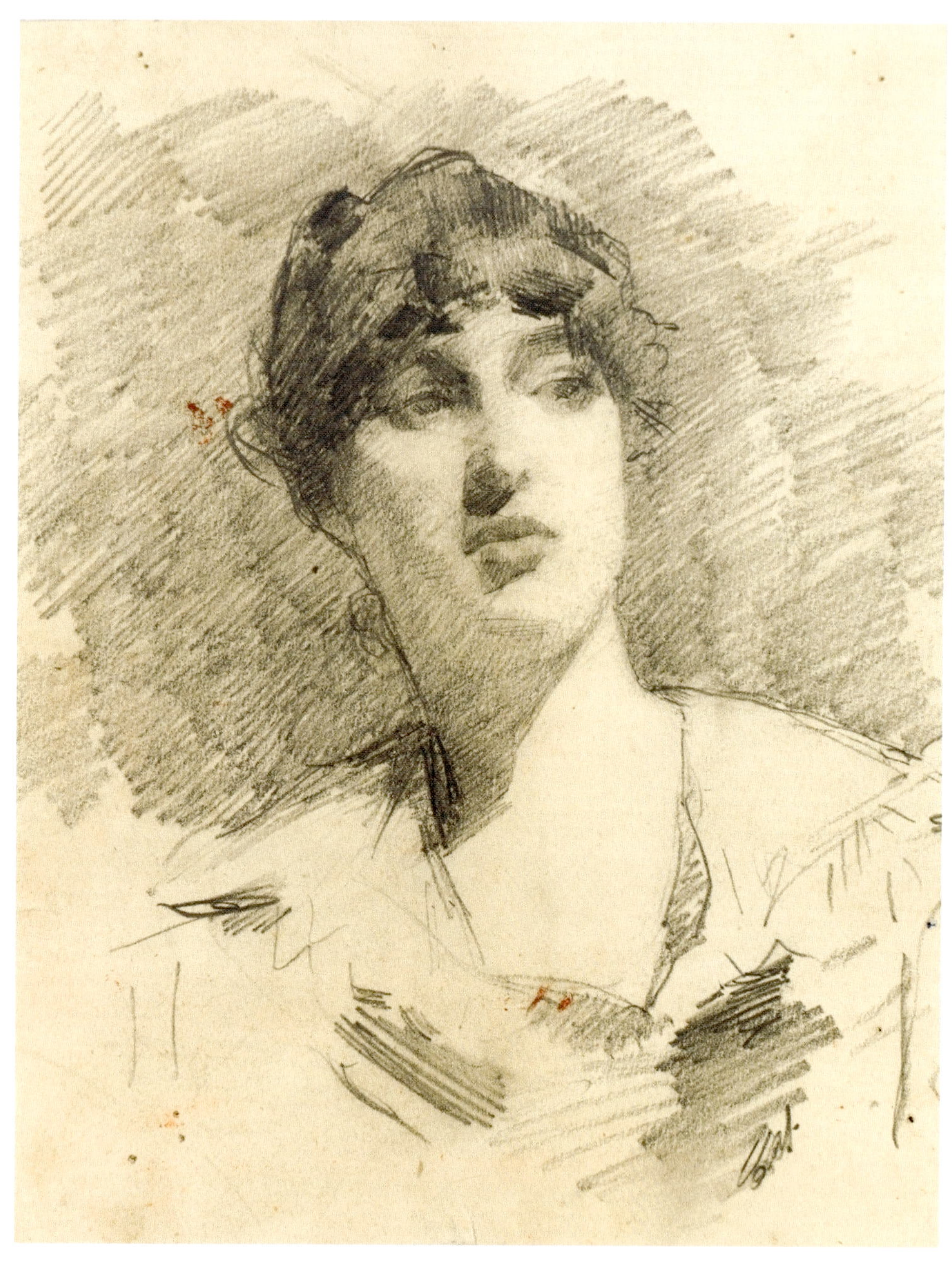

CAT. 49 – *Portrait of a Woman*, pencil on paper, 6 ½ x 5 in. (16.3 x 12.5 cm).

CAT. 50 – *Interior with Basin*, black crayon on paper, 19 ¼ x 14 ½ in. (49 x 37.2 cm).

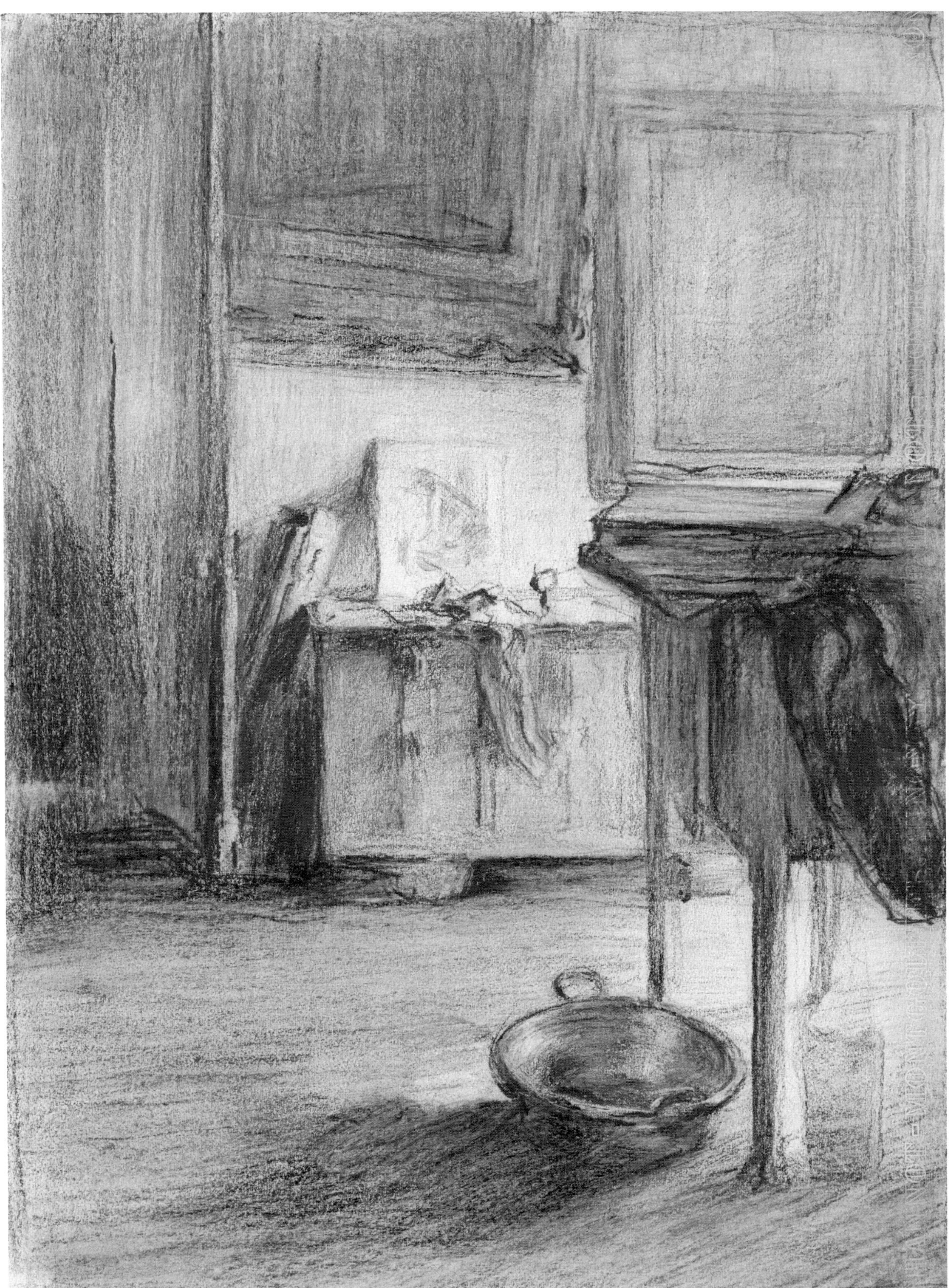

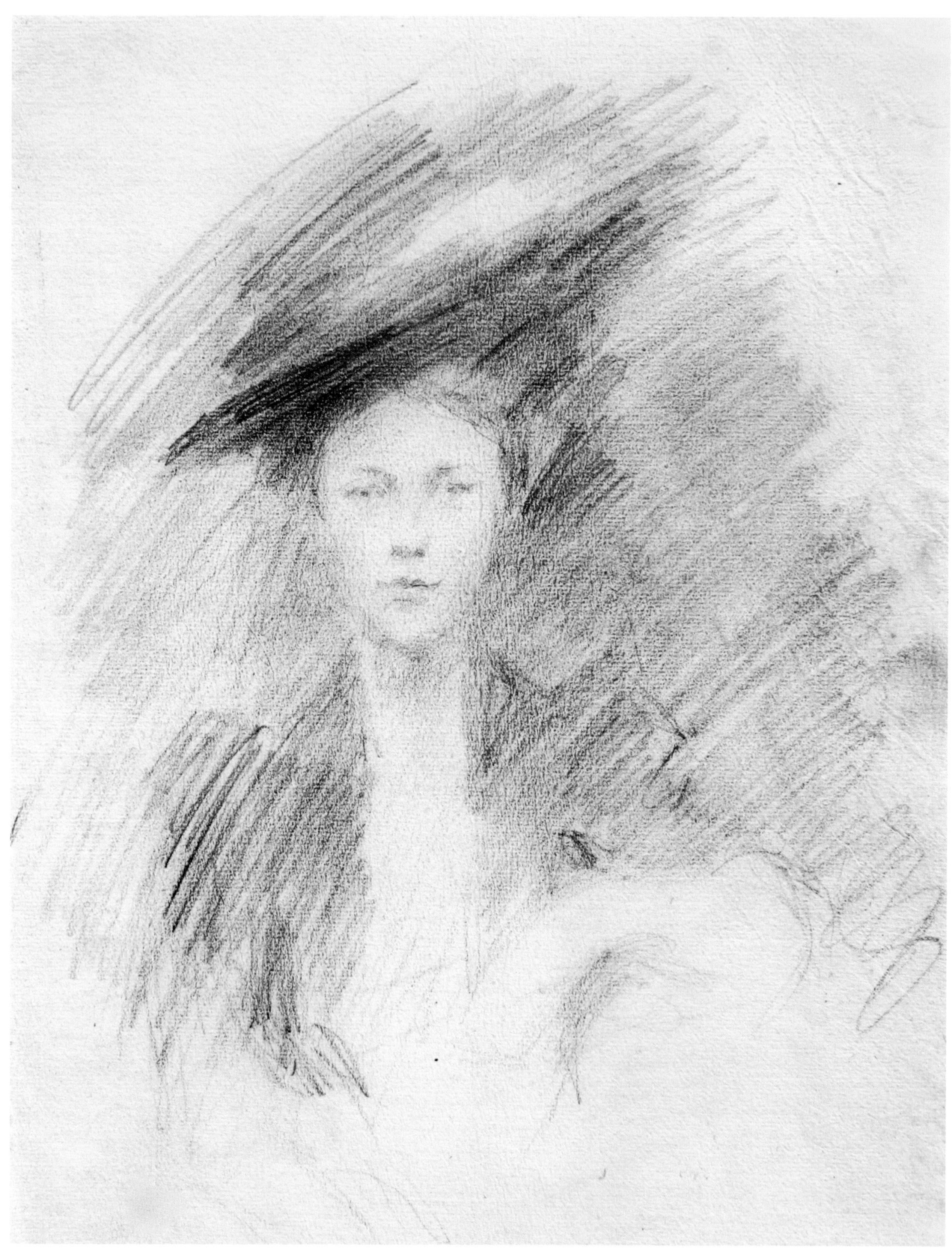

CAT. 51 – *Portrait of a Woman with Hat*, pencil on bluish paper, 17 ¼ x 11 ¼ in. (43.7 x 28.6 cm).

Other drawings in the collection

CAT. 52 – *Male nude*, black chalk on paper, 24 ½ x 18 ¾ in. (62 x 47,8 cm).

CAT. 53 – *Study of a Woman's Arm*, pencil on paper, 14 ½ x 10 ¼ in. (36.5 x 26 cm).

CAT. 54 – *Woman lying on bed*, pencil on paper, 8 ¼ x 12 ¼ in. (20.6 x 31 cm).

CAT. 55 – *Nude lying on bed*, pencil on paper, 12 x 17 ¼ in. (30.5 x 44 cm).

CAT. 56 – *Woman lying on bed*, signed, 9 ½ x 15 ½ in. (24 x 39.5 cm).

CAT. 57 – *Woman lying on bed*, pencil on paper, 12 ¼ x 18 ½ in. (31 x 47 cm).

CAT. 58 – *Standing female nude*, black chalk on paper, 9 ¾ x 6 ¼ in. (24.5 x 16 cm).

CAT. 59 – *Standing female nude*, black chalk on paper, 13 ¾ x 10 in. (35.2 x 25 cm).

CAT. 60 – *Seated female nude*, black chalk on paper, 14 ¼ x 12 ¾ in. (36 x 32 cm).

CAT. 61 – *Female nude*, black and red chalk on paper, signed, 24 ¼ x 18 ¾ in. (61.8 x 47.7 cm).

CAT. 62 – *Woman lying on bed*, pencil and black chalk on paper, 9 ¾ x 13 ¼ in. (24.5 x 33.6 cm).

CAT. 63 – *Woman lying on bed*, pencil on paper, 12 x 17 ¼ in. (30.4 x 43.5 cm).

CAT. 64 – *Standing female nude*, Black chalk on paper, 9 ¾ x 6 ¼ in. (24.5 x 16 cm).

CAT. 65 – *Seated female nude,* pencil and red pencil on paper, signed with initials, 13 ¼ x 10 in. (33.8 x 25.4 cm).

CAT. 66 – *Seated female nude*, pencil on paper, 18 ½ x 14 ½ in. (46.5 x 36.5 cm).

CAT. 67 – *Roses*, black chalk on paper, 10 ¾ x 12 ¼ in. (27.6 x 30.6 cm).

CAT. 68 – *Roses and plate*, black chalk on paper, 12 ½ x 7 ¾ in. (31.5 x 19.7 cm).

CAT. 69 – *Roses*, black chalk on paper, 18 ½ x 13 in. (47.3 x 33 cm).

CAT. 70 – *Roses*, black chalk on paper, signed and inscribed "to Andy Roses by father" 9 ¾ x 7 ¾ in. (24.8 x 19.8 cm).

CAT. 71 – *Roses*, pencil and black chalk on paper, 11 ¼ x 12 in. (28.5 x 30.5 cm).

CAT. 72 – *Tulips*, black chalk on paper, 18 ¾ x 12 ¼ in. (47.5 x 30.7 cm).

CAT. 73 – *Roses*, black chalk on paper, 13 ½ x 11 ¾ in. (3.8 x 29.8 cm).

CAT. 74 – *Roses*, pencil, black and red chalk on paper, 14 ¾ x 11 in. (37.2 x 28 cm).

CAT. 75 – *Roses*, black chalk on paper, 10 x 6 ¼ in. (25 x 16 cm).

CAT. 76 – *Roses*, black chalk on paper, 9 ½ x 8 ¼ in. (24.2 x 21 cm).

CAT. 77 – *Roses*, black chalk on paper, signed with initials, 3 ¾ x 3 ½ in. (9.5 x 9.3 cm).

CAT. 78 – *Roses*, black chalk on paper, inscribed "drawing by AB Sept 42 given to WdB", 12 ½ x 10 ½ in. (31.7 x 26.2 cm).

CAT. 79 – *Sleeping Woman*, pencil on paper, 3 ¾ x 5 ¼ in. (9.5 x 13 cm).

CAT. 80 – *Seated Woman,* black crayon on paper, 19 x 12 ½ in. (48.5 x 32 cm).

CAT. 81 – *Portrait of Regine Martial (Author)*, black chalk and scratching on paper, 17 ¼ x 11 ¼ in. (43.7 x 28.6 cm).

CAT. 82 – *Portrait of a Woman with Hat*, black chalk on paper, inscribed "Nana" on verso, 14 ¼ x 12 ½ in. (36.5 x 32 cm).

CAT. 83 – *Joyce,* black crayon, signed, 22 ½ x 16 ¾ in. (56.7 x 43 cm).

CAT. 84 – *Dorothy*, black crayon on paper, 11 x 8 in. (28 x 20.3 cm).

CAT. 85 – *Dorothy*, black crayon on paper, signed, 11 x 8 in. (28 x 20.3 cm).

CAT. 86 – *Joyce*, black crayon on paper, 11 x 8 in. (28 x 20.3 cm).

CAT. 87 – *Joyce,* black crayon on paper, 25 ¼ x 19 ¼ in. (64 x 49 cm).

CAT. 88 – *Joyce,* black crayon and colour on paper, 25 x 19 in. (63.2 x 48.2 cm).

CAT. 89 – *Joyce*, black crayon on paper, 11 x 8 in. (28 x 20.3 cm).

CAT. 90 – *Joyce*, black crayon on paper, 11 x 8 in. (28 x 20.3 cm).

CAT. 91 – *Mabel Charles*, black crayon on paper, 11 x 8 in. (28 x 20.3 cm).

CAT. 92 – *Mabel Charles,* black chalk and scratching on paper, signed with initials, 10 ¾ x 7 ¾ in. (27.7 x 20 cm).

CAT. 93 – *Joyce*, black crayon on paper, 24 ¼ x 19 ½ in. (61.2 x 49.5 cm).

CAT. 94 – *Mabel Charles*, black crayon on paper, 16 ½ x 12 ¾ in. (42.3 x 32.5 cm).

CAT. 95 – *Joyce*, black crayon on paper, signed, 23 ½ x 17 ½ in. (60 x 44.5 cm).

CAT. 96 – *Joyce*, signed, black crayon on paper, 11 x 8 in. (28 x 20.3 cm).

CAT. 97 – *Portrait of a Woman*, black crayon on paper, 11 x 8 in. (28 x 20.3 cm).

CAT. 98 – *Portrait of a Woman leaning on a Pillow*, black crayon and scratching on paper, 17 ¾ x 11 ½ in. (45 x 29.2 cm).

CAT. 99 – *Portrait of a Woman in Cowl*, black crayon on paper, 11 x 8 in. (28 x 20.3 cm).

CAT. 100 – *Alice de Belleroche*, signed, black crayon on paper, 18 x 14 ½ in. (45.5 x 37.2 cm).

CAT. 101 – *Alice de Belleroche*, inscribed: " à Willie", black crayon on paper, 25 x 19 in. (63.2 x 48.5 cm).

CAT. 102 – *Joyce*, charcoal on paper, 25 x 19 in. (63.5 x 48.3 cm).

CAT. 103 – *Seated Woman*, black crayon on paper, 12 ¾ x 9 ¾ in. (32.5 x 25 cm).

CAT. 104 – *Joyce*, black crayon and reddish tint on paper, 25 x 19 in. (63.2 x 48.5 cm).

CAT. 105 – *Harbour Front*, signed, black crayon o paper, 9 ¾ x 12 ¾ in. (24.8 x 32.5 cm).

CAT. 106 – *Seated Man Seen from Behind*, pencil on paper, 12 ¼ x 9 in. (31 x 23.3 cm).

CAT. 107 – *Standing Woman*, pencil on paper, 13 ¾ x 9 ¾ in. (35 x 25.3 cm).

CAT. 108 – *Portrait of a Womanin Profile*, signed and dated '80, black crayon on paper, 7 ¼ x 5 ¾ in. (18.8 x 15 cm).

CAT. 109 – *Couple*, pencil on paper, 13 ½ x 9 ¾ in. (34 x 25 cm).

CAT. 110 – *Woman Working in Kitchen*, pencil on paper, 9 ¼ x 5 ¾ in. (23.5 x 15 cm).

CAT. 111 – *Yvette*, pencil and colour on paper, signed, 14 ¾ x 11 ½ in. (37.6 x 29 cm).

CAT. 112 – *Yvette*, c. 1898, pencil and colour on paper, 15 × 11 ½ in. (38.1 × 28.7 cm).

CAT. 113 – *Woman in a Café*, pencil on paper, 7 ½ x 4 ½ in. (19 x 11.5 cm).

CAT. 114 – *Interior*, black crayon on paper, 25 x 19 in. (63.2 x 48.5 cm).

CAT. 115 – *Figure in Interior*, black crayon on paper, 13 x 8 in. (33 x 20.5 cm).

CAT. 116 – *Rural Scene*, black crayon, 10 x 6 ¾ in. (25.5 x 17.5 cm).

CAT. 117 – *Trees*, black crayon on paper, 8 ½ x 12 ¾ in. (22 x 33 cm).

CAT. 118 – *Trees in Garden*, black crayon on paper, 8 ¼ x 5 ¾ in. (21 x 15 cm).

CAT. 119 – *Woman in Stairwell*, black crayon on paper, signed, 19 ½ x 12 ¾ in. (50 x 32.5 cm).

CAT. 120 – *Interior*, pencil, ink and colour on paper, 5 ½ x 9 ¼ in. (14.4 x 23.3 cm).

CAT. 121 – *Buffet*, black crayon on paper, 10 x 14 ¼ in. (25.4 x 36.2 cm).

CAT. 122 – *Study of Lance,* c.1881, pen & ink on paper, signed, 4 ¼ x 7 ½ in. (11 x 18.8 cm).

CAT. 123 – *Man at a Desk*, pencil on paper, 6 ¼ x 8 ¼ in. (16 x 20.8 cm).

CAT. 124 – *In the Garden*, black crayon on paper, 8 ¼ x 5 ¾ in. (21 x 15 cm).

CAT. 125 – *Still life with Copper Pots*, black crayon on paper, 13 x 10 in. (33.2 x 25.4 cm).

CAT. 126 – *Crucible*, black crayon on paper, 14 ¼ x 10 ½ in. (36.2 x 26.6 cm).

CAT. 127 – *Still life with Seashells*, black crayon on paper, 14 ¼ x 10 in. (36.2 x 25.4 cm).

CAT. 128 – *Rustington Manor, interior*, signed, black crayon on paper, 10 ¾ x 7 ¾ in. (27.7 x 20.2 cm).

CAT. 129 – *Woman and Interior,* pencil on paper, 9 ¼ x 5 7/8 in. (23.5 x 15 cm).

CAT. 130 – *Portrait of a Woman and Various Studies of Tableware*, inscribed "to Andy", black crayon, 15 x 10 ½ in. (38 x 26.5 cm).

CAT. 131 – *Woman Behind Bar*, pencil on paper, 5 ½ x 9 ¼ in.(14.3 x 23.4 cm).

CAT. 132 – *Rustington Manor, dining room*, black crayon on paper, 7 ¾ x 10 ¾ in. (20 x 27.7 cm).

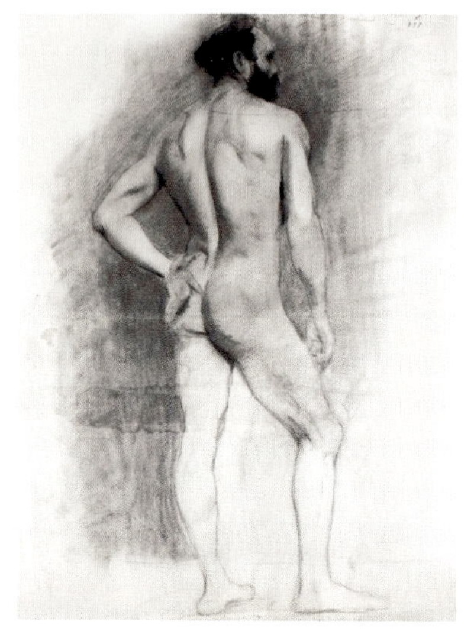

CAT. 52

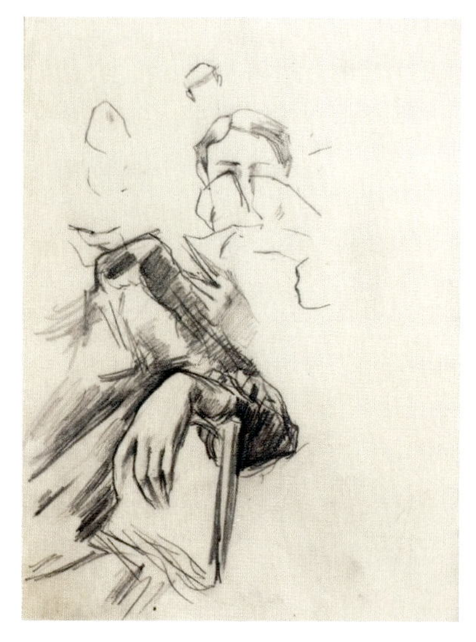

CAT. 53

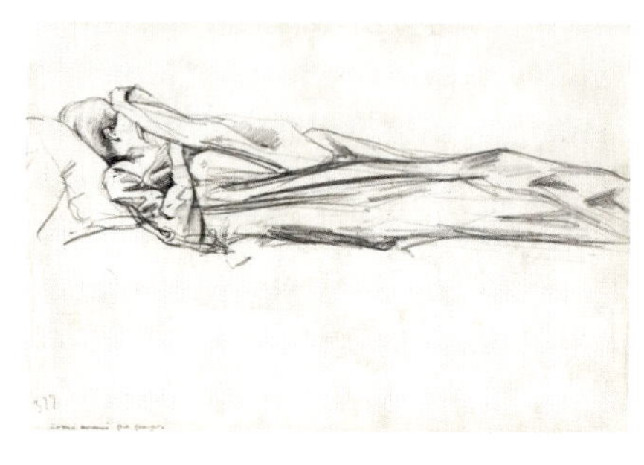

CAT. 54

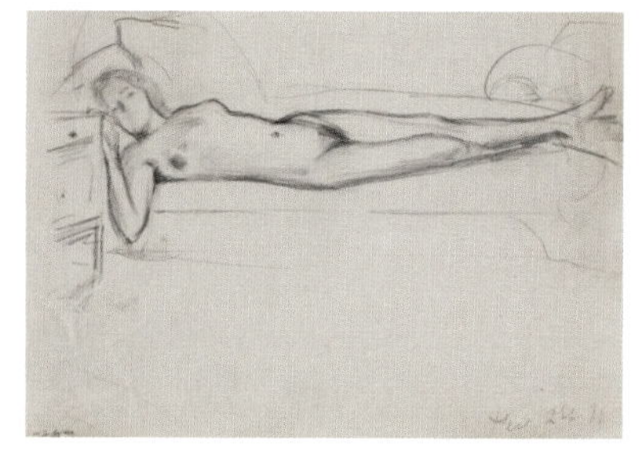

CAT. 55

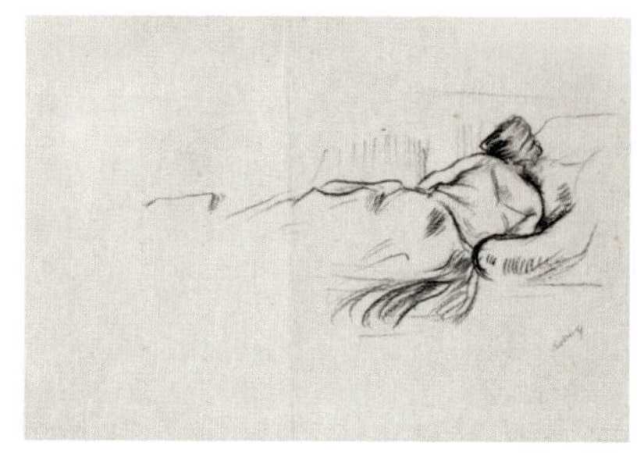

CAT. 56

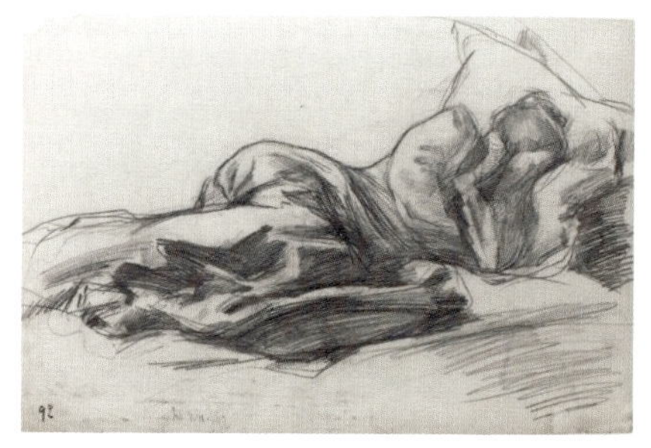

CAT. 57

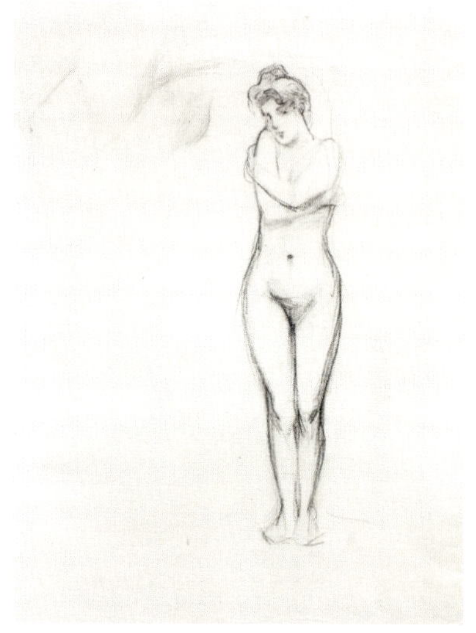

CAT. 58

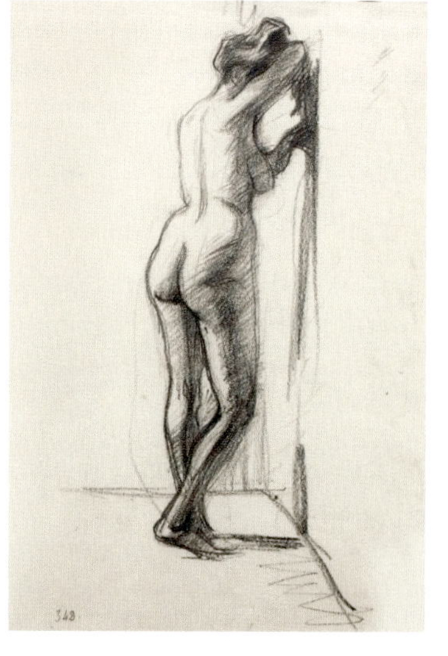

CAT. 59

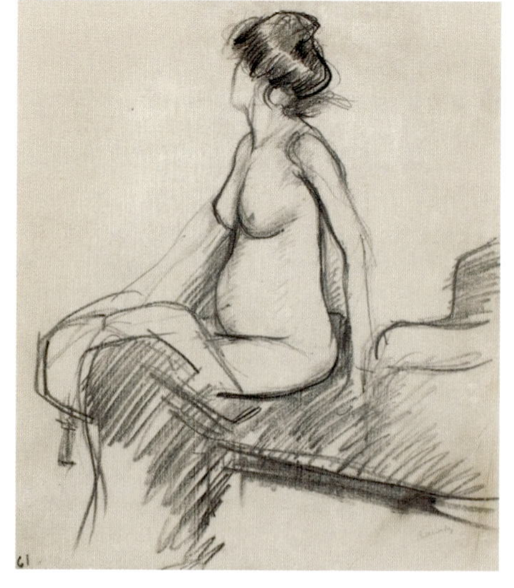

CAT. 60

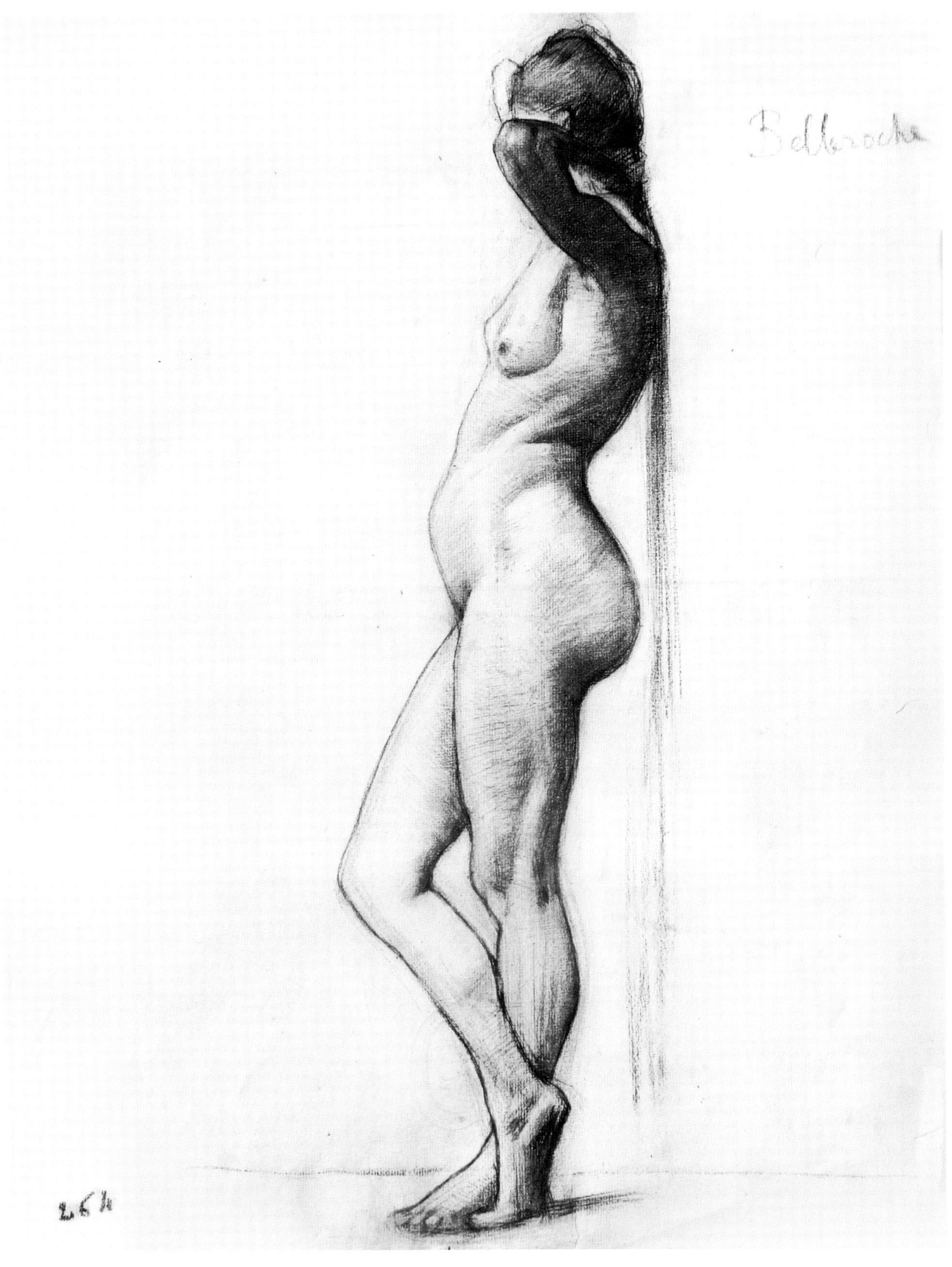

CAT. 61

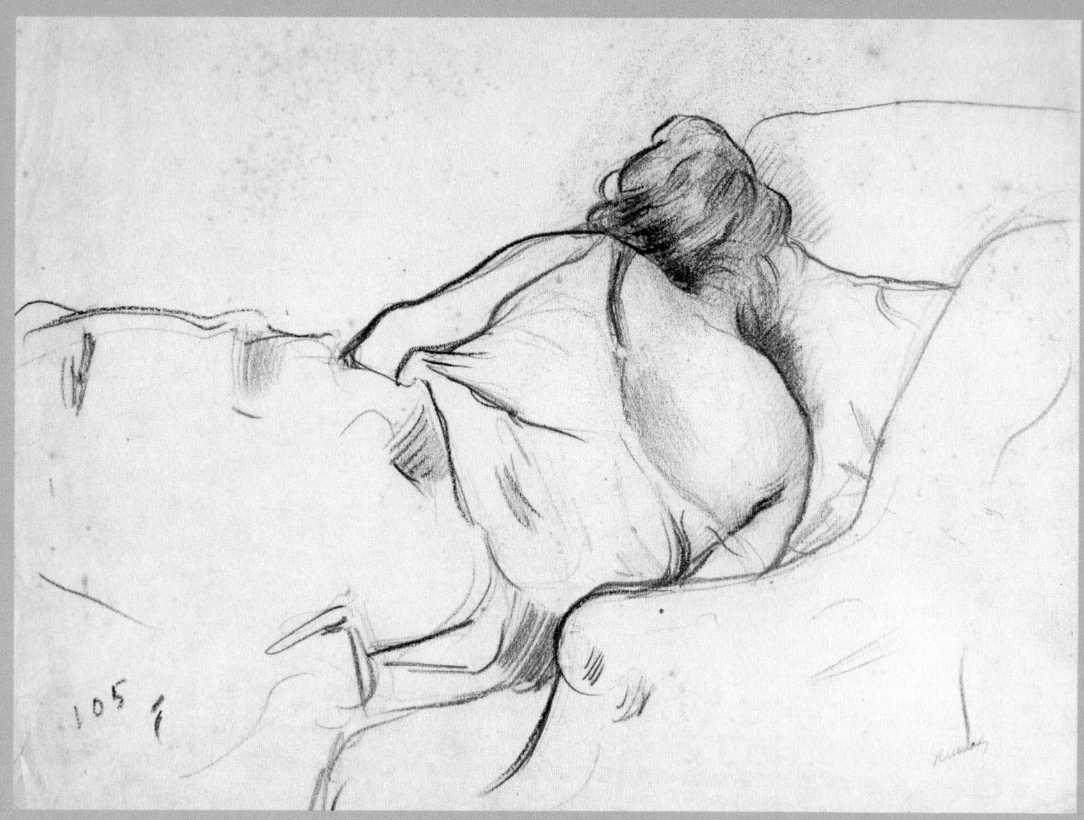

CAT. 62

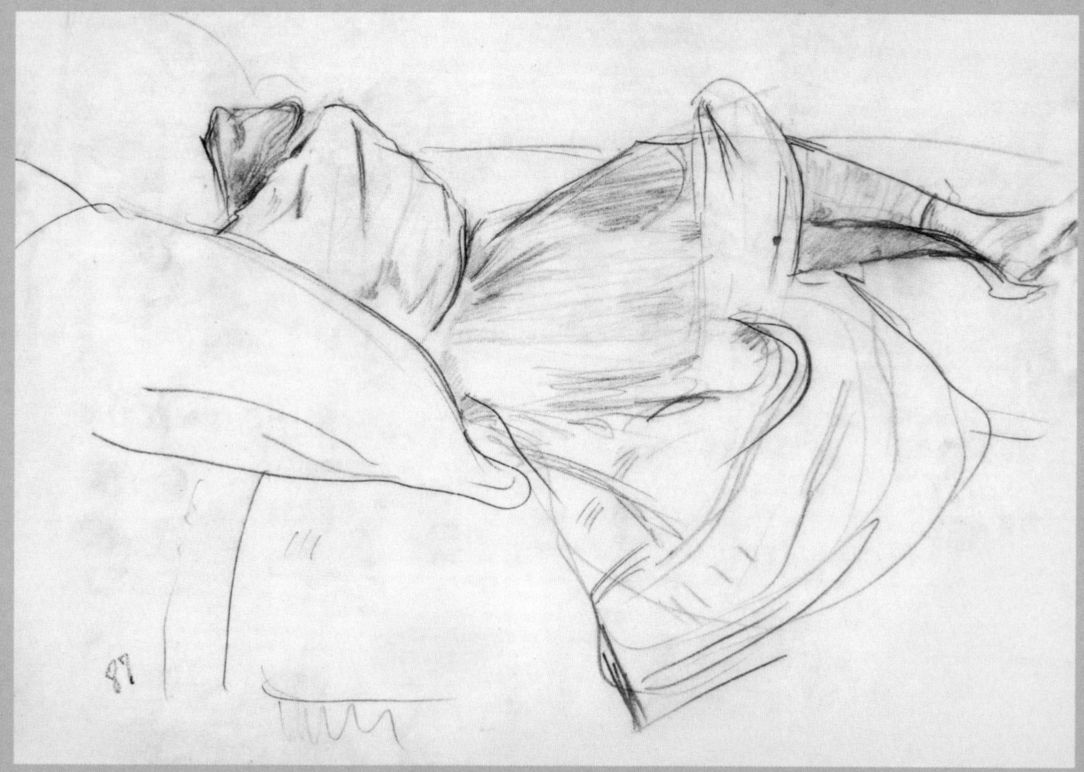

CAT. 63

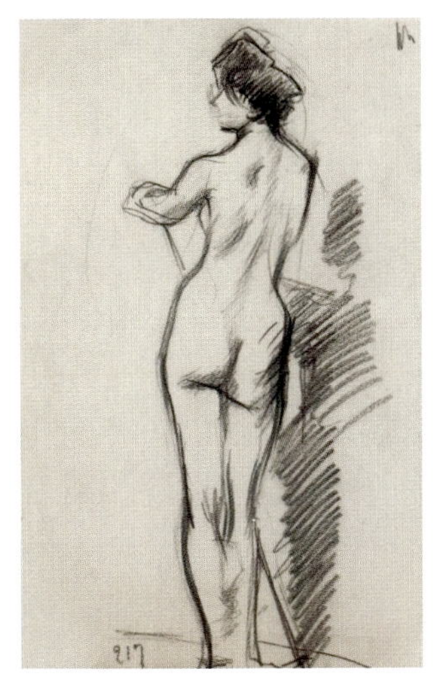

CAT. 64

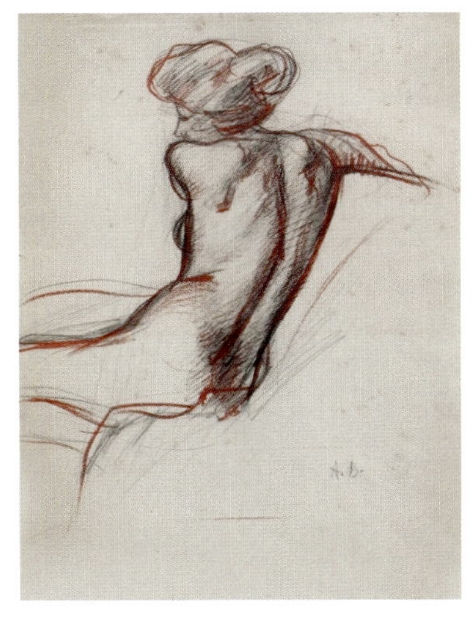

CAT.65

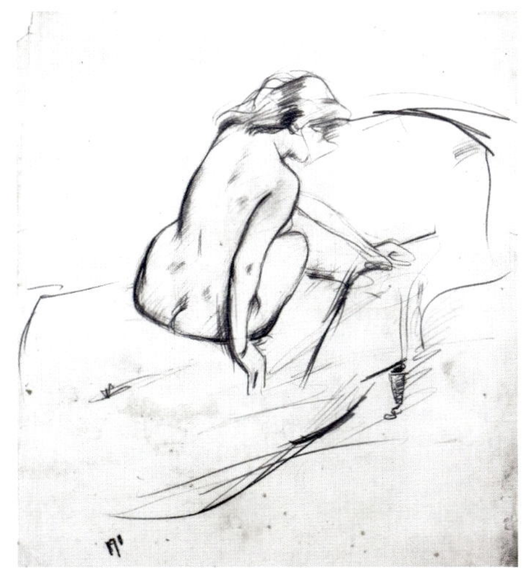

CAT. 66

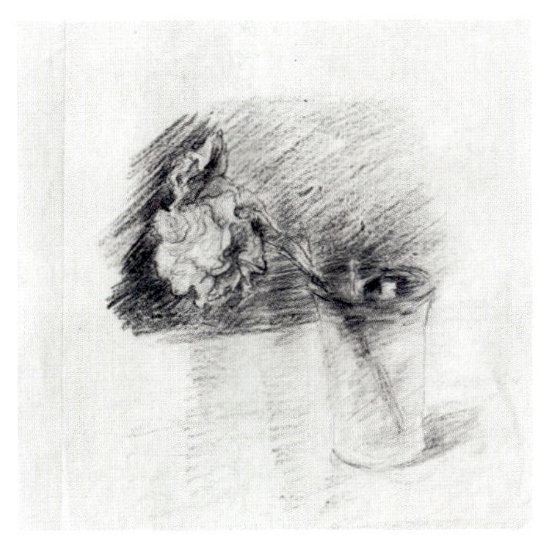

CAT. 67

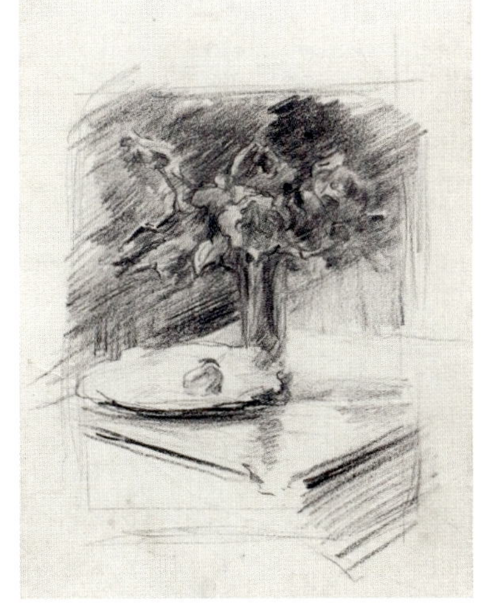

CAT. 68

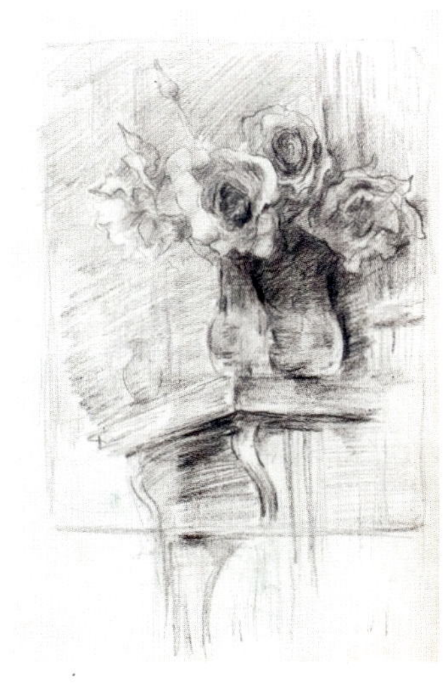

CAT. 69

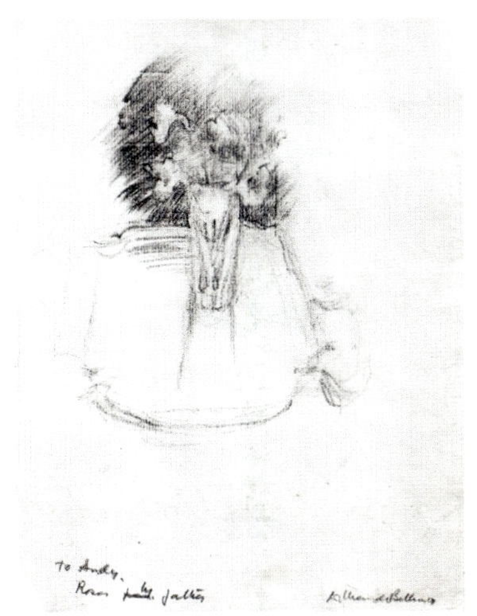

CAT. 70

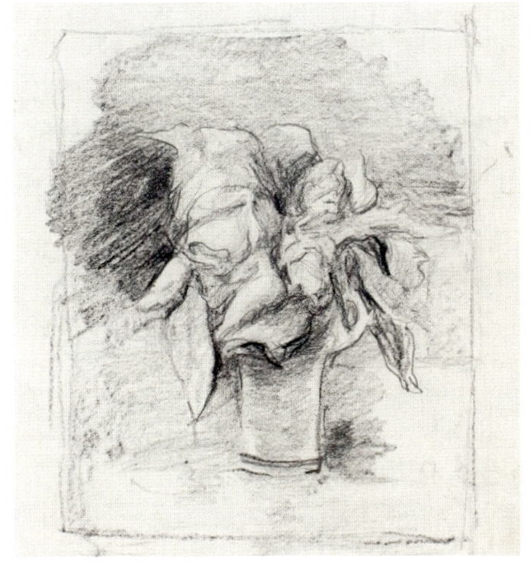

CAT. 71

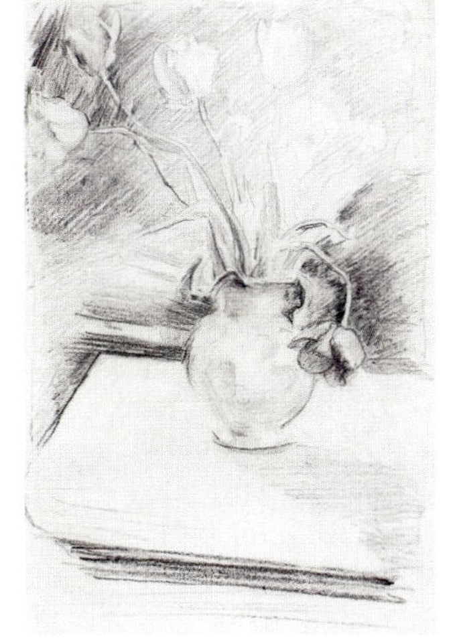

CAT. 72

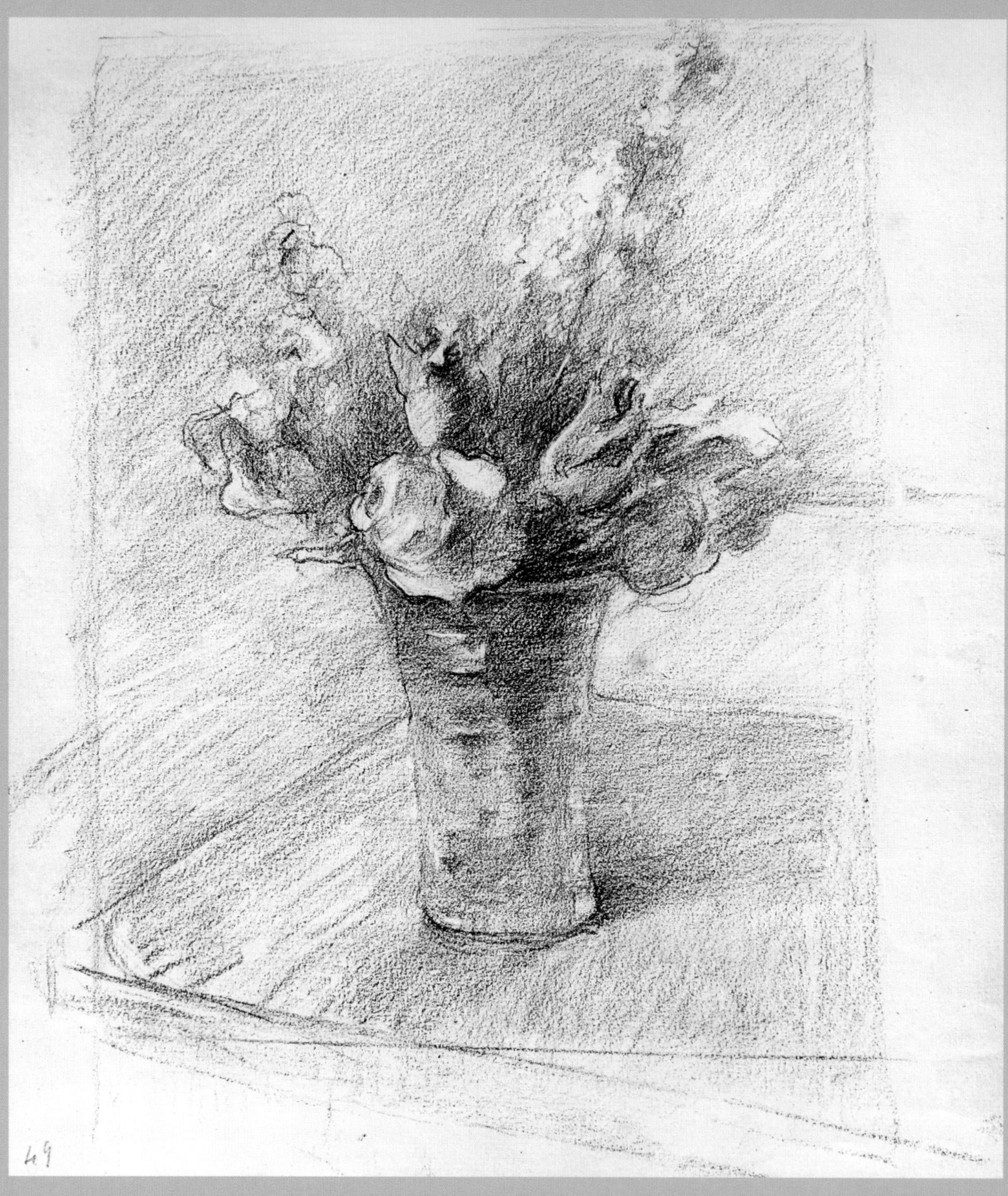

CAT. 73

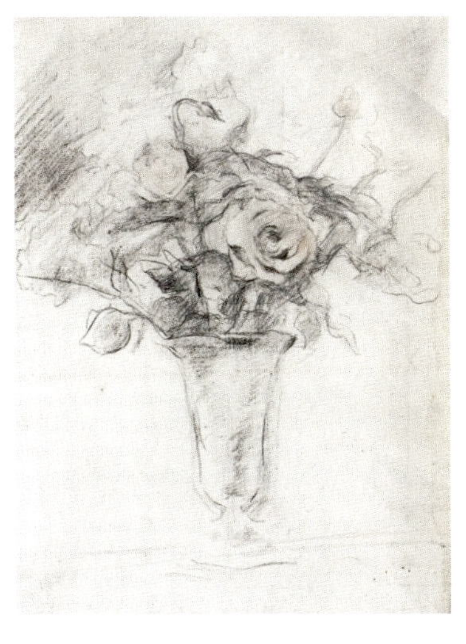

CAT. 74

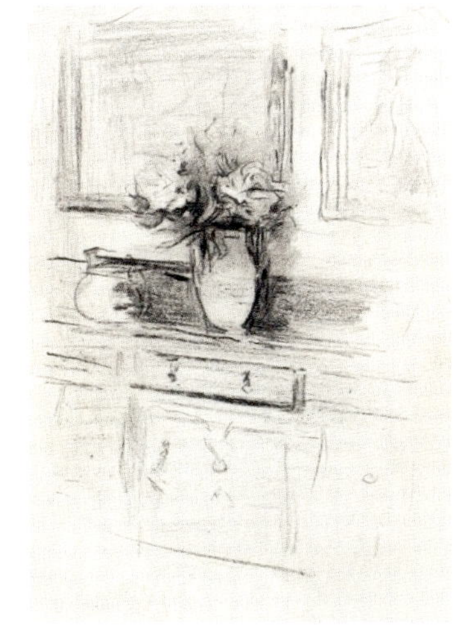

CAT. 75

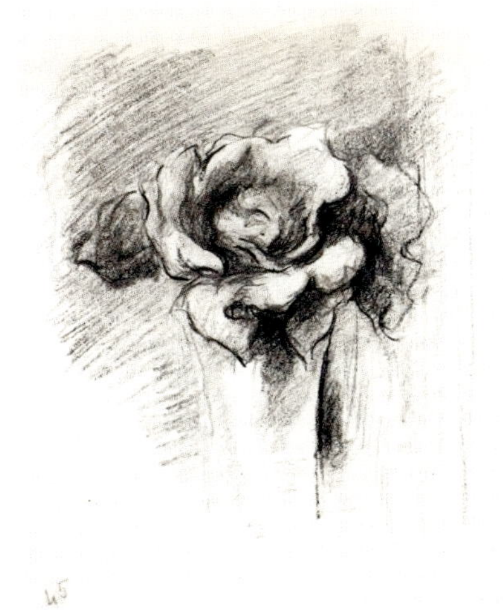

CAT. 76

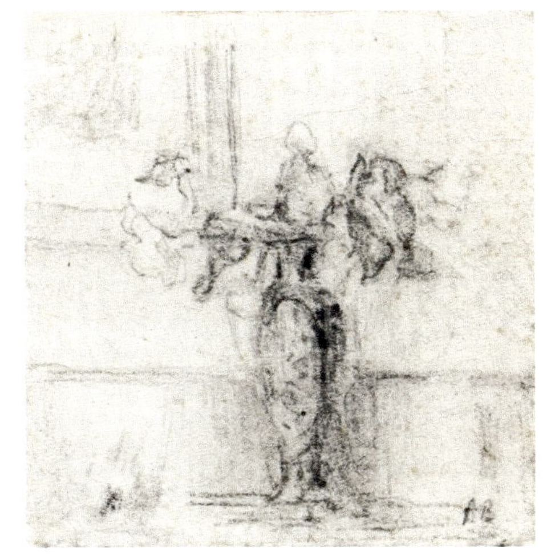

CAT. 77

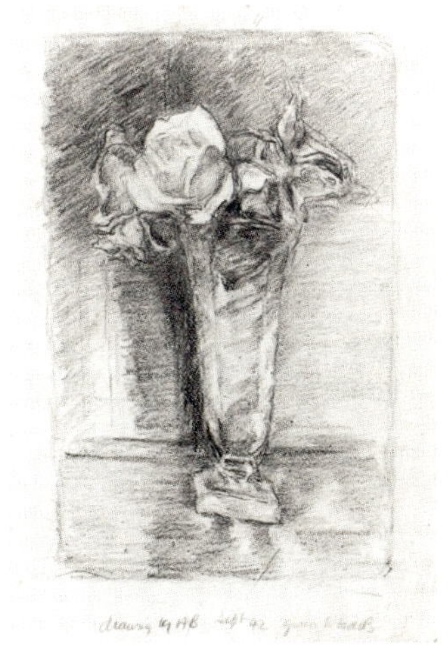

CAT. 78

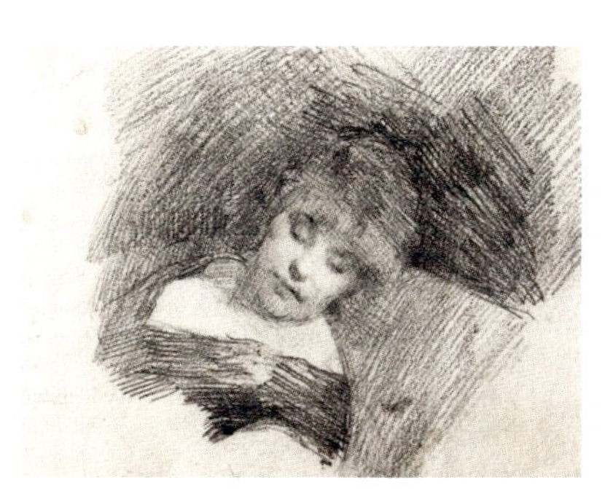

CAT. 79

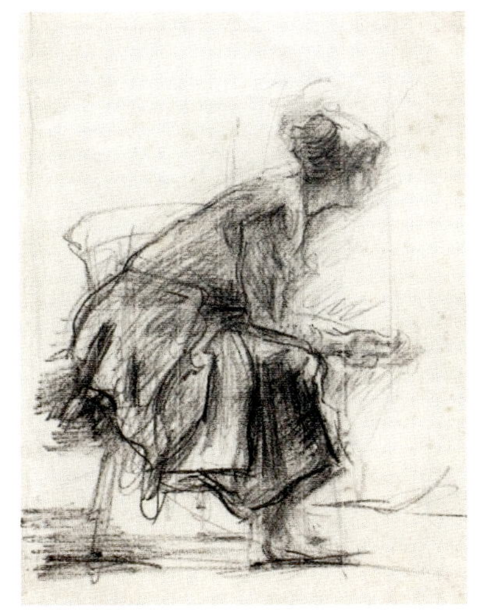

CAT. 80

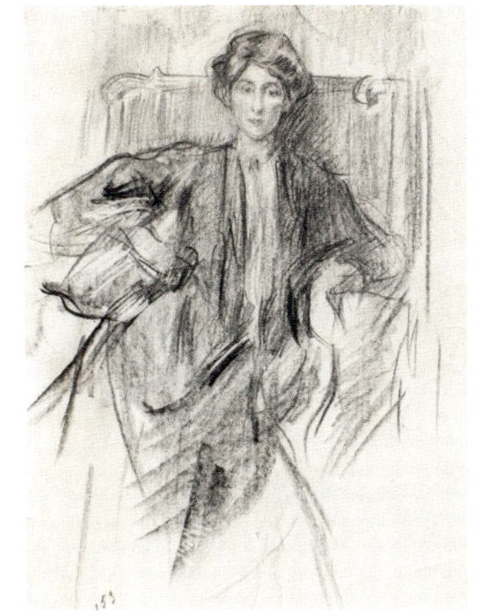

CAT. 81

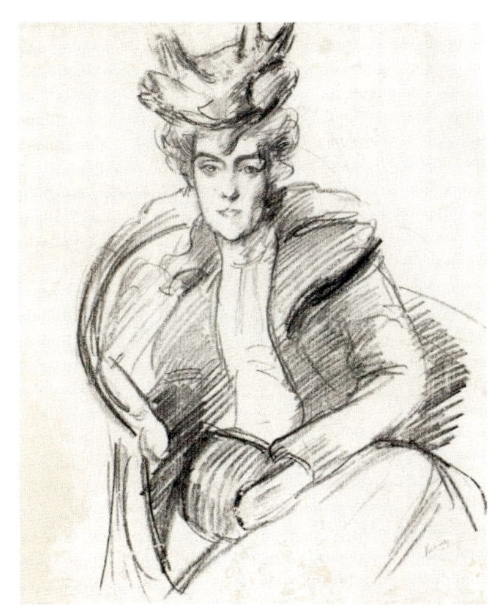

CAT. 82

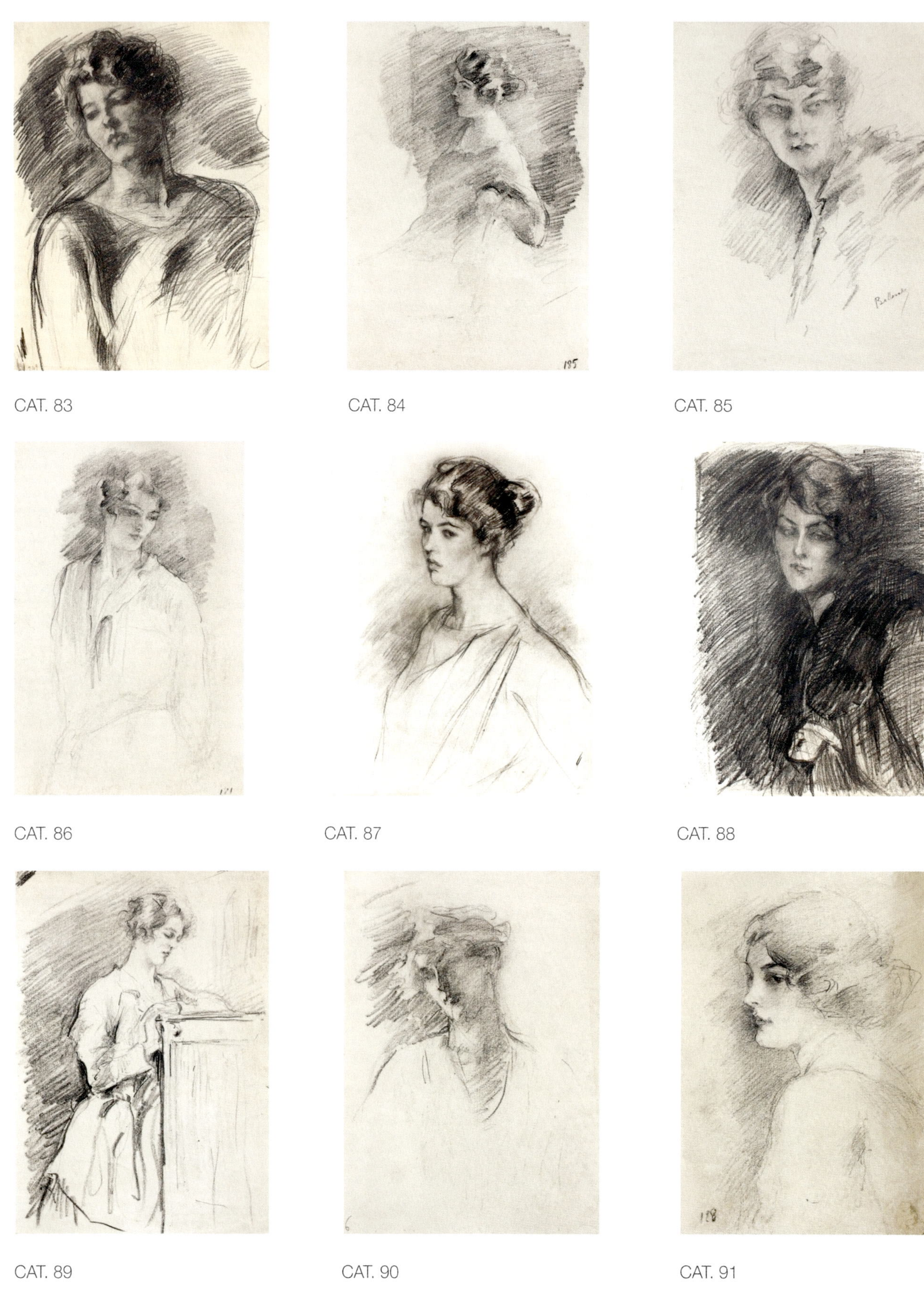

CAT. 83

CAT. 84

CAT. 85

CAT. 86

CAT. 87

CAT. 88

CAT. 89

CAT. 90

CAT. 91

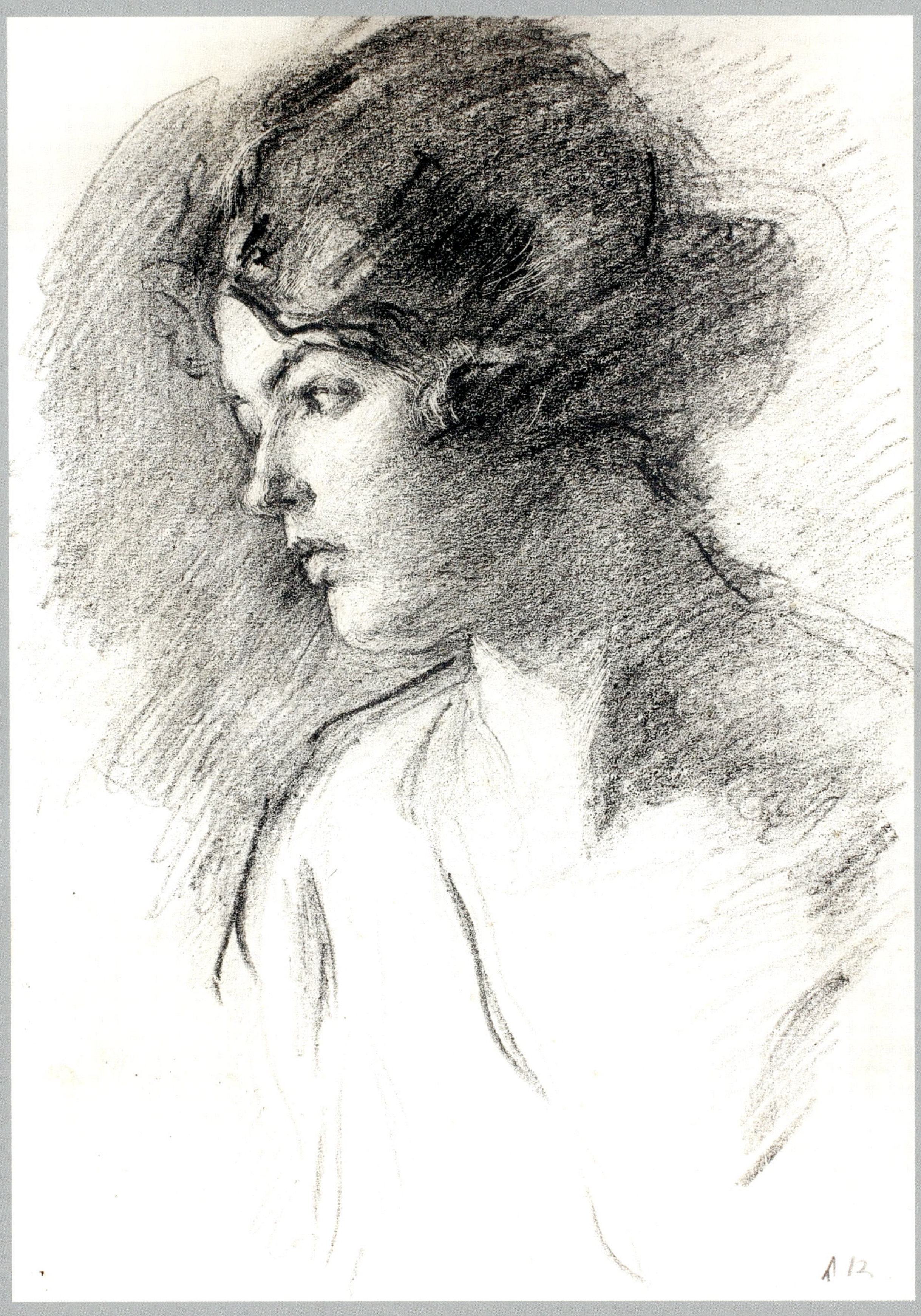

CAT. 92

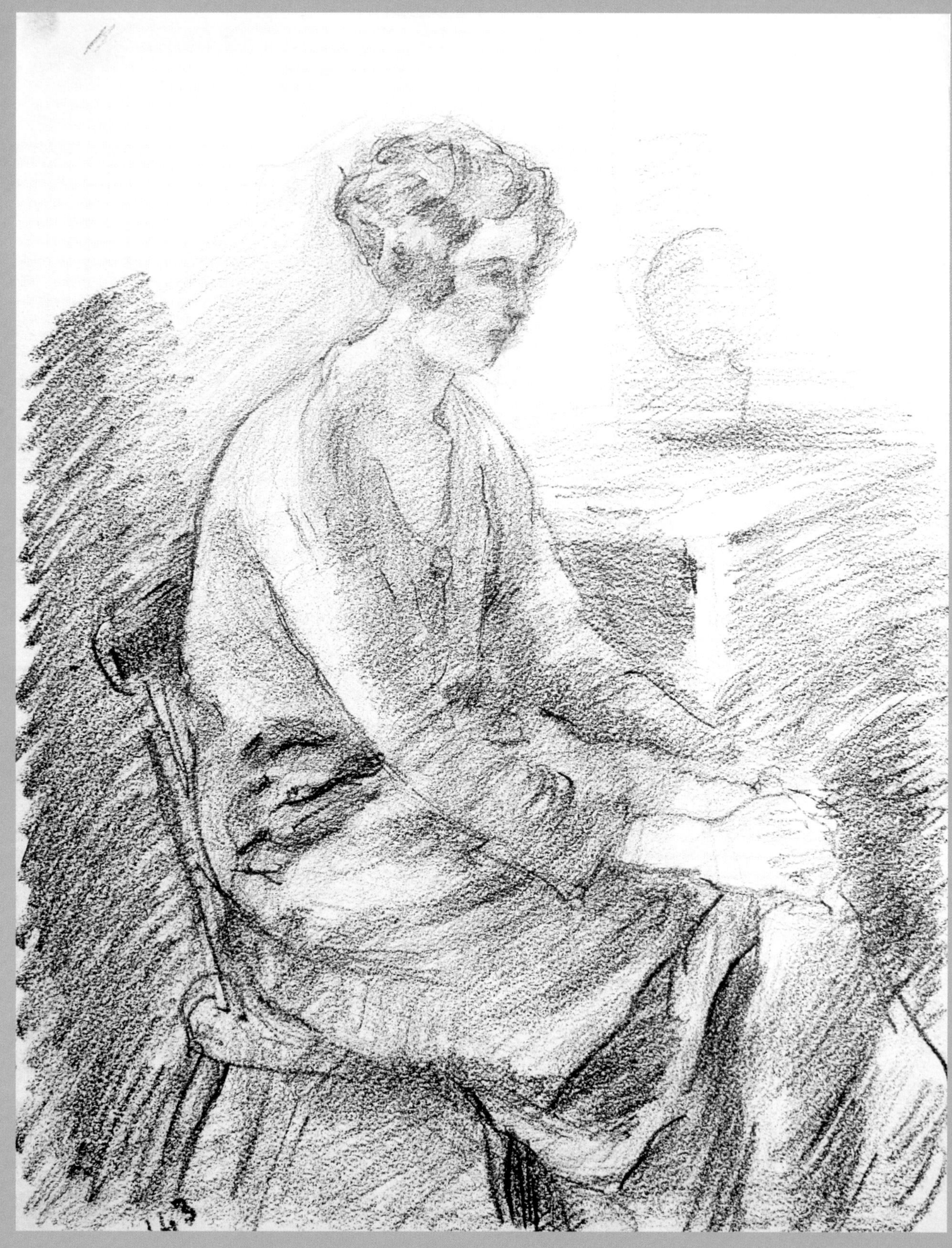

CAT. 93

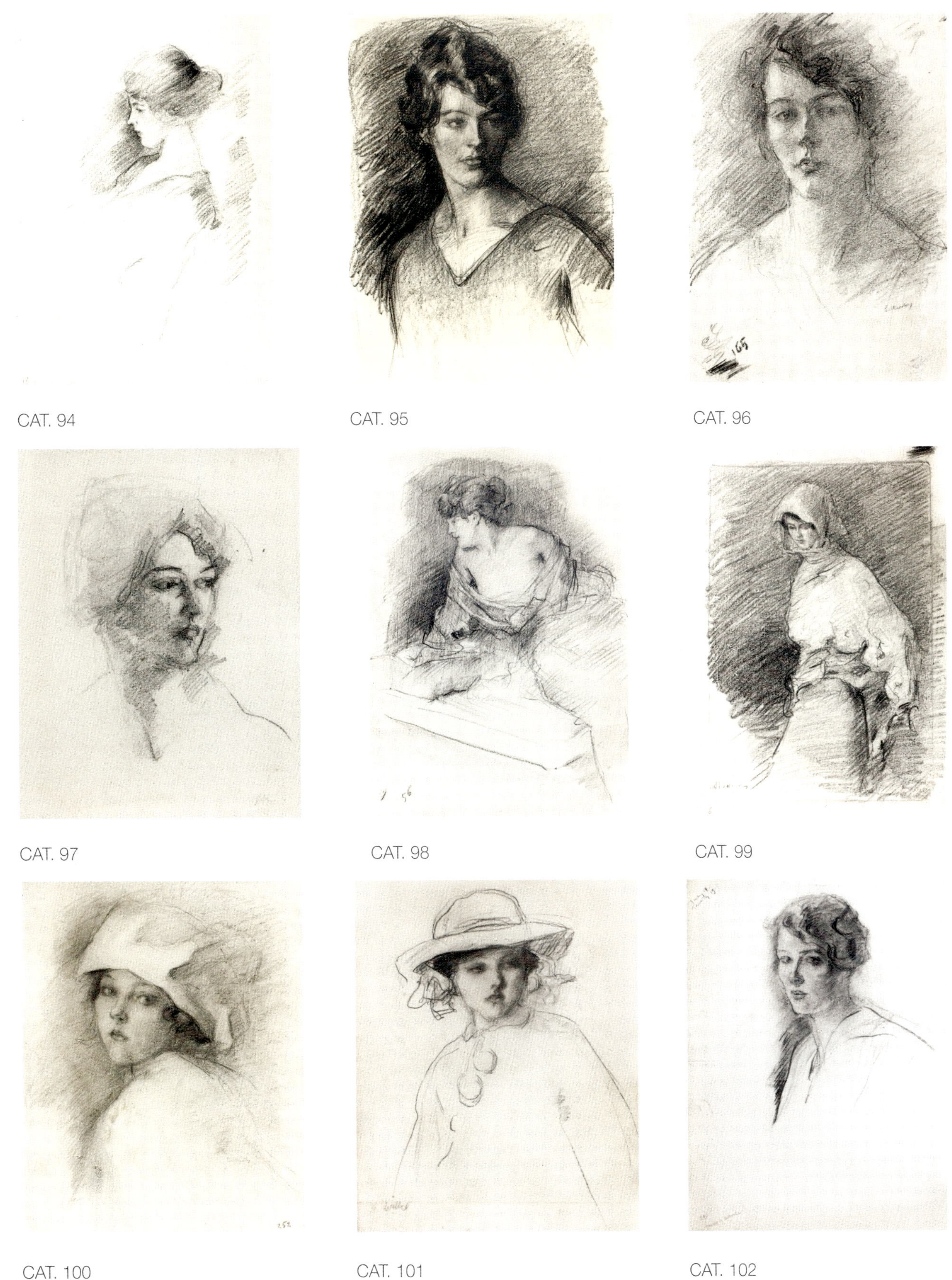

CAT. 94

CAT. 95

CAT. 96

CAT. 97

CAT. 98

CAT. 99

CAT. 100

CAT. 101

CAT. 102

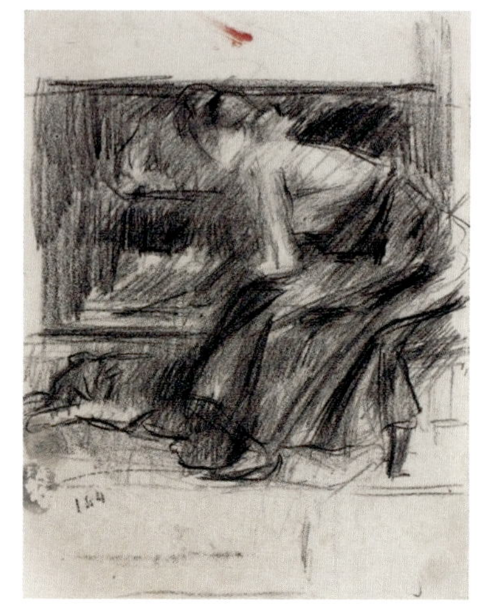

CAT. 103

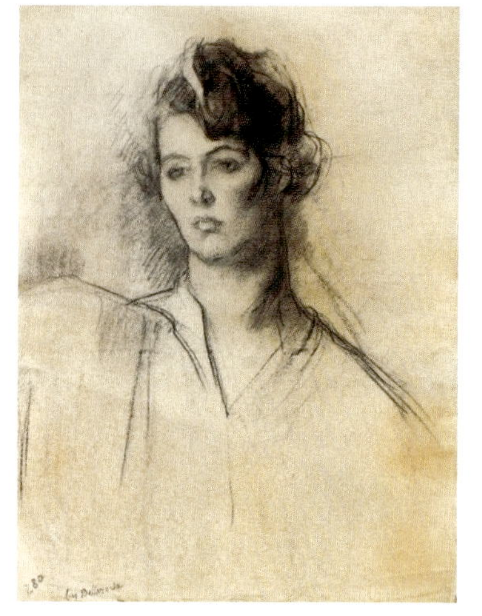

CAT. 104

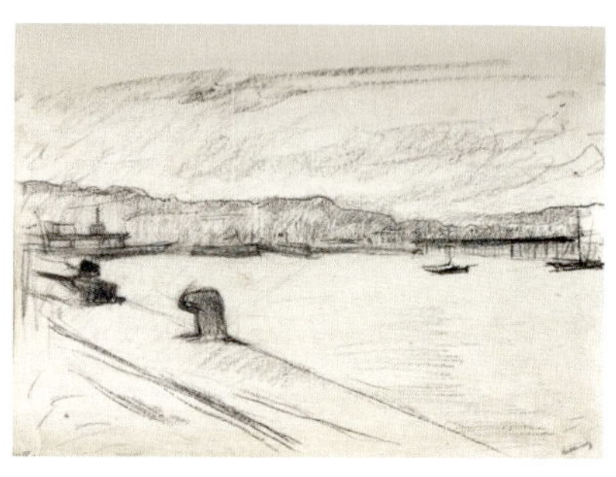

CAT. 105

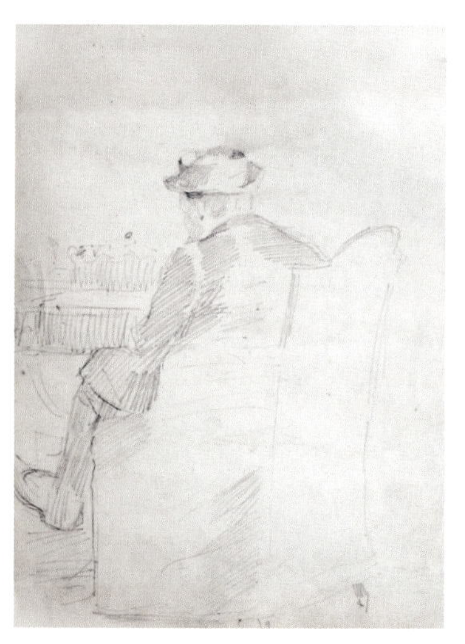

CAT. 106

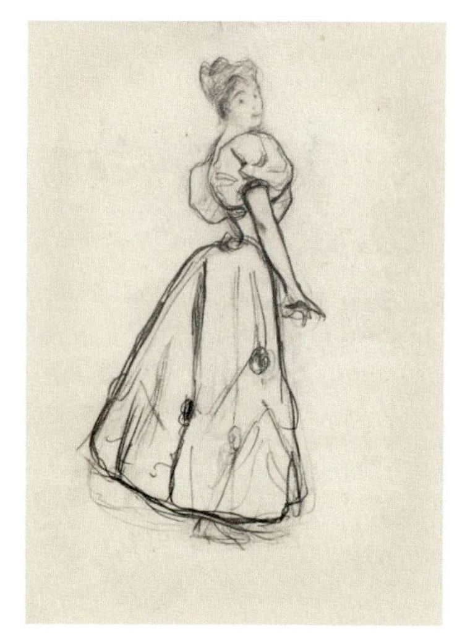

CAT. 107

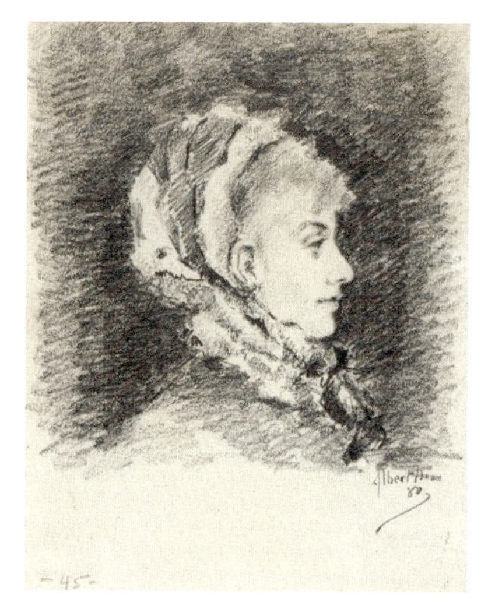

CAT. 108

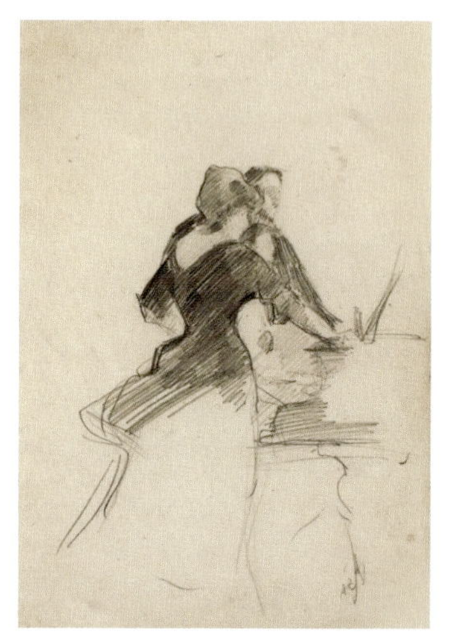

CAT. 109

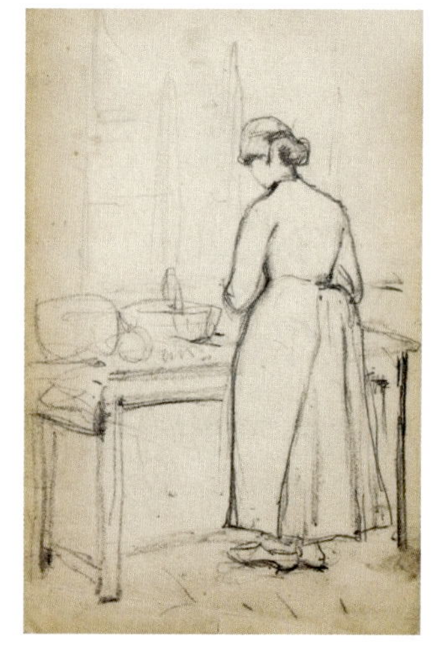

CAT. 110

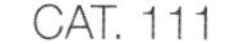

CAT. 111

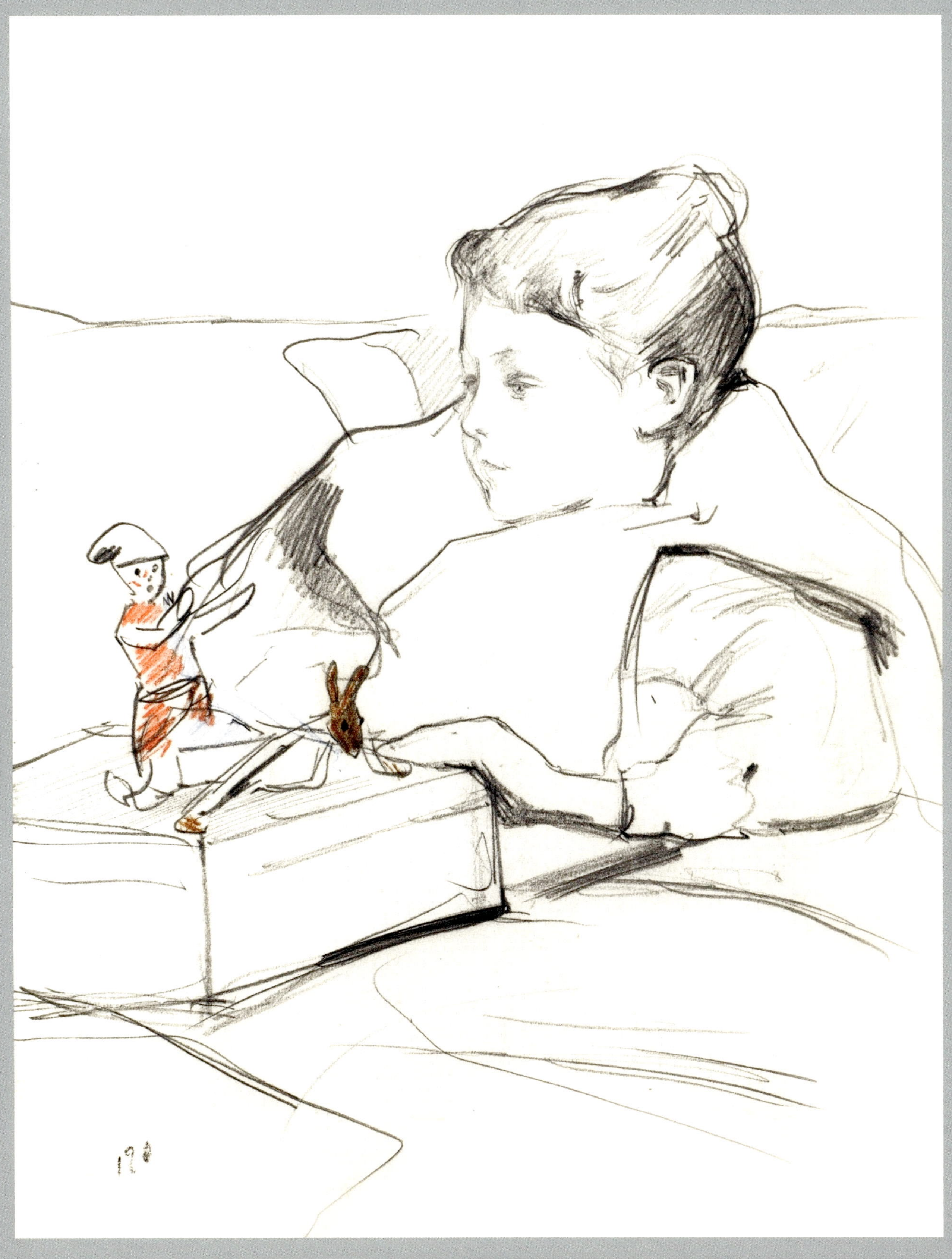

CAT. 112

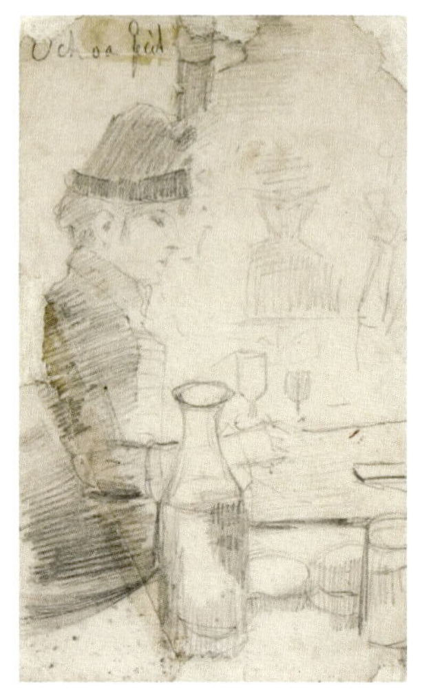

CAT. 113

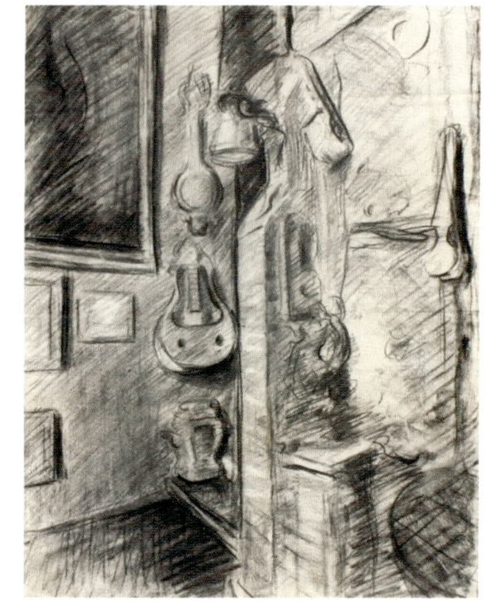

CAT. 114

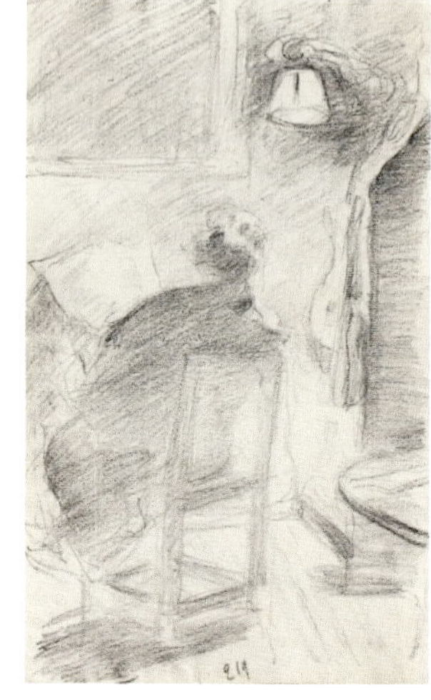

CAT. 115

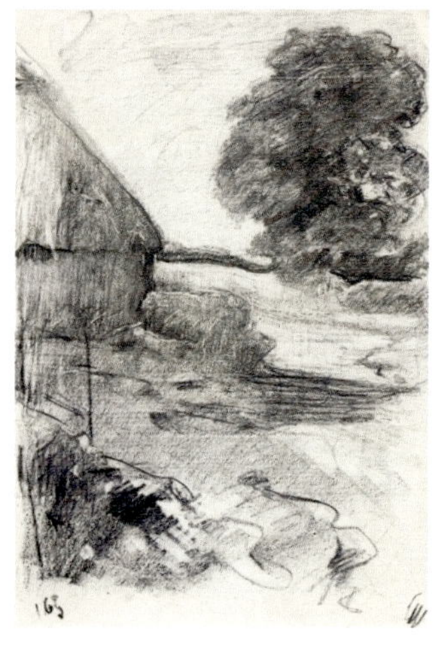

CAT. 116

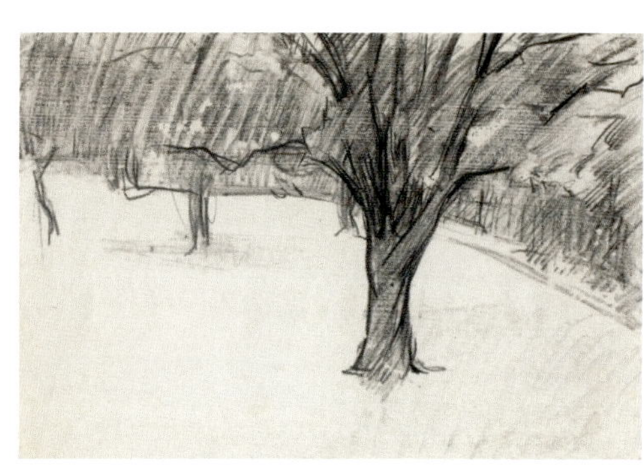

CAT. 117

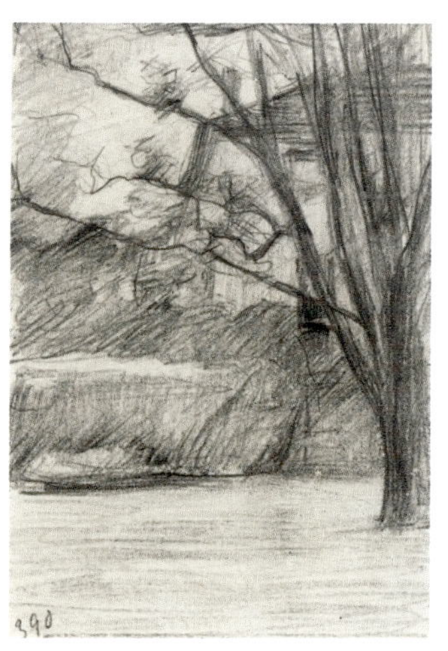

CAT. 118

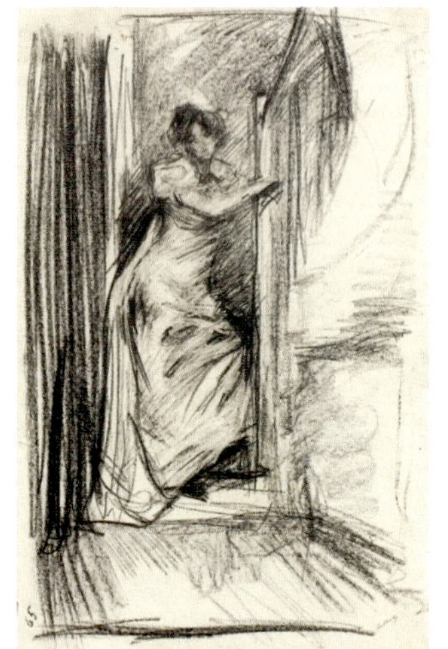

CAT. 119

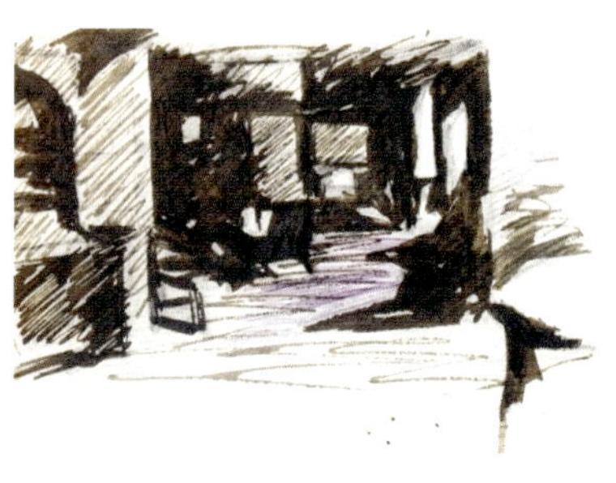

CAT. 120

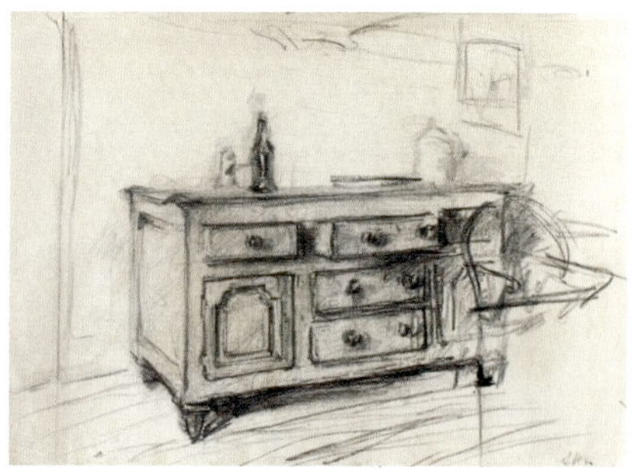

CAT. 121

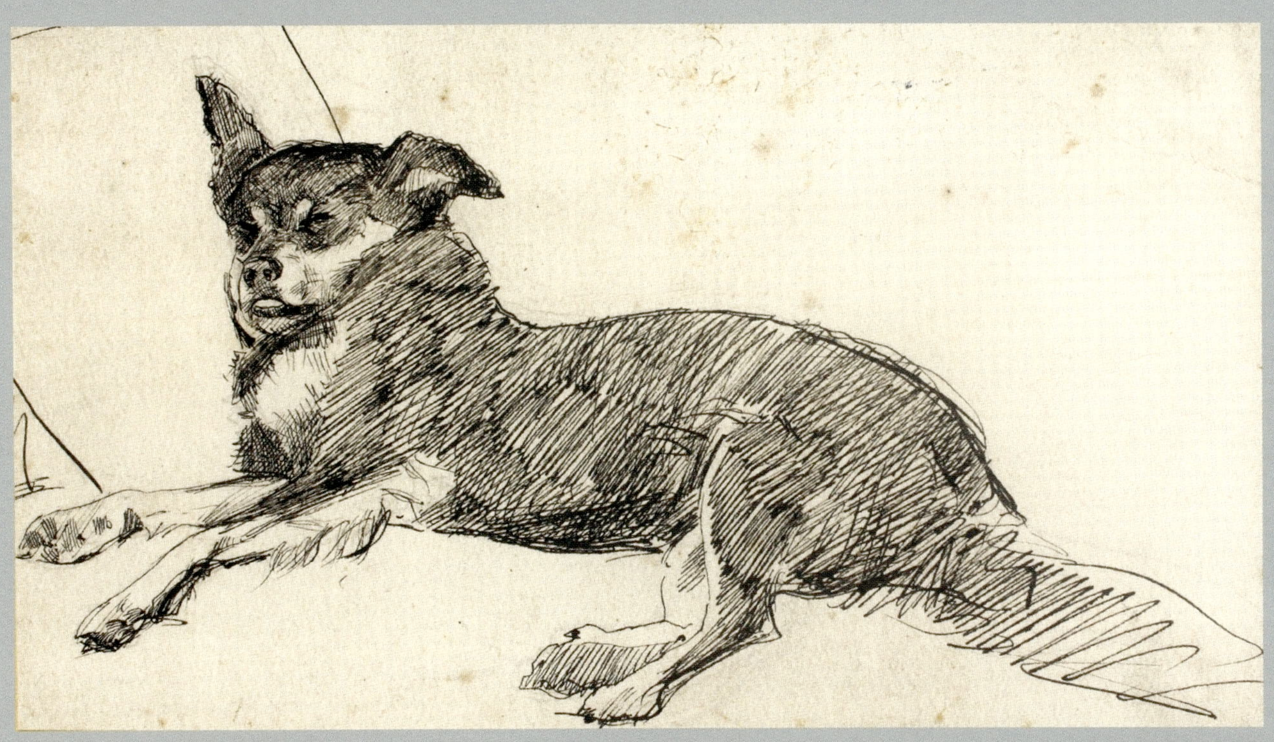

CAT. 122

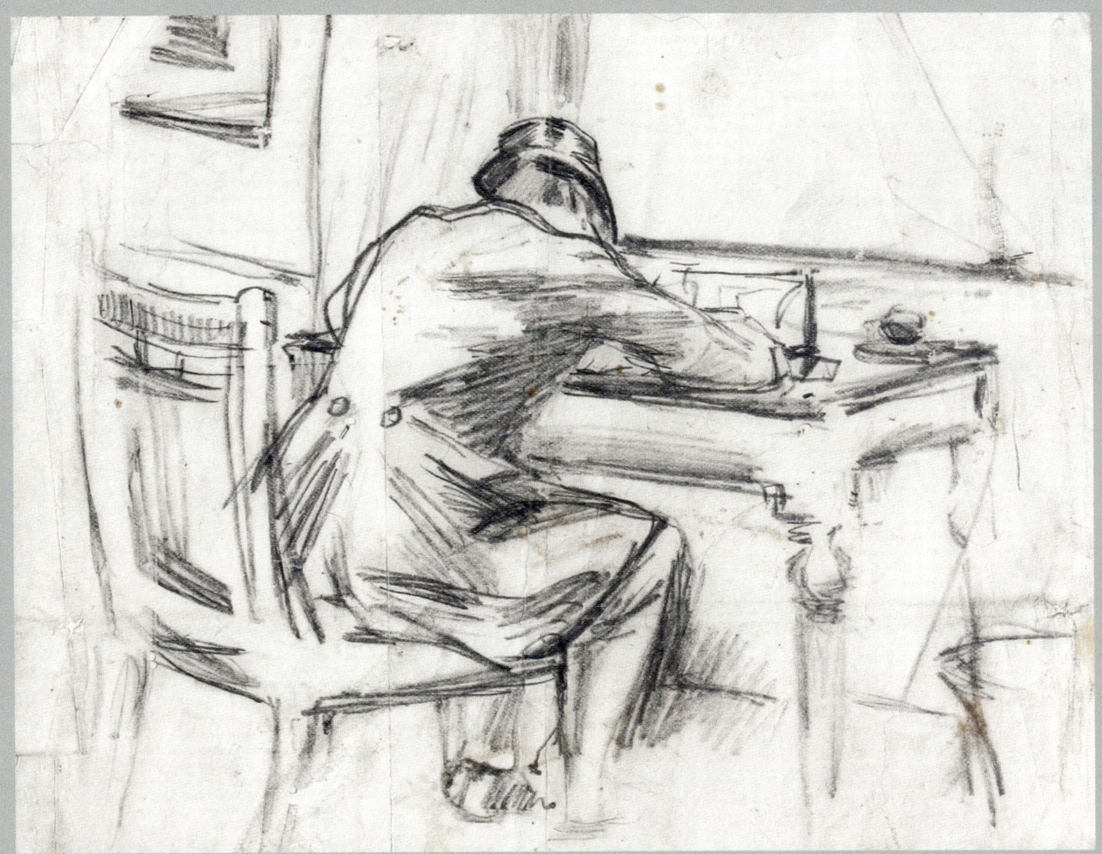

CAT. 123

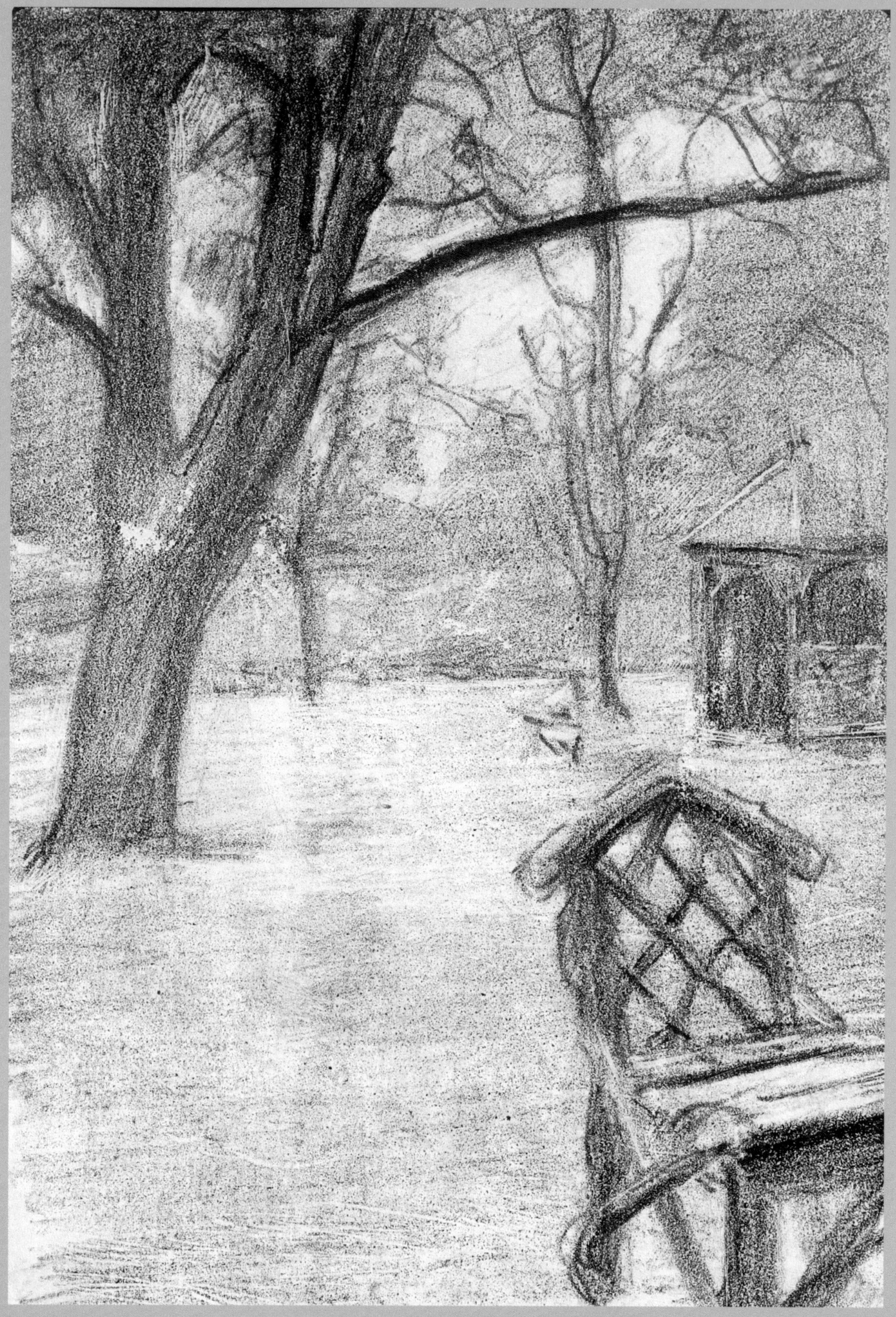

CAT. 124

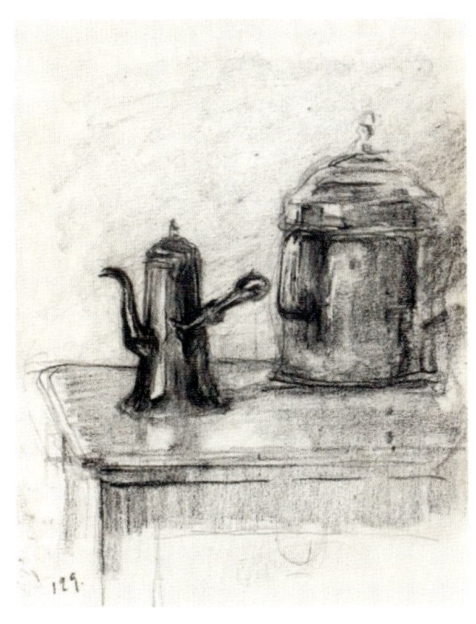

CAT. 125

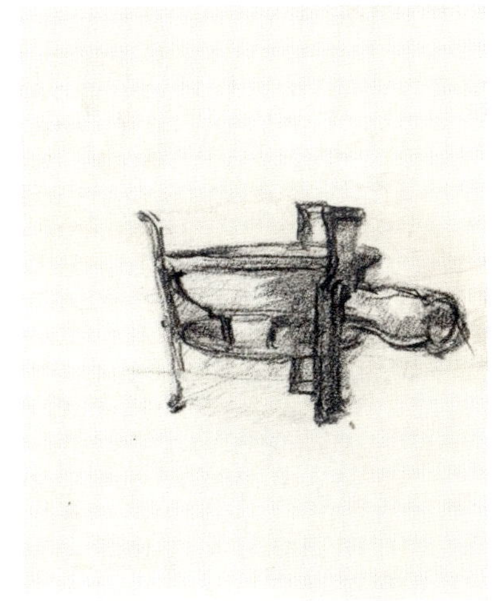

CAT. 126

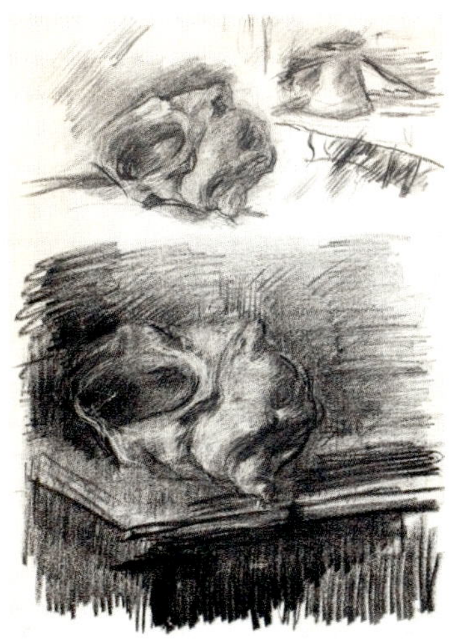

CAT. 127

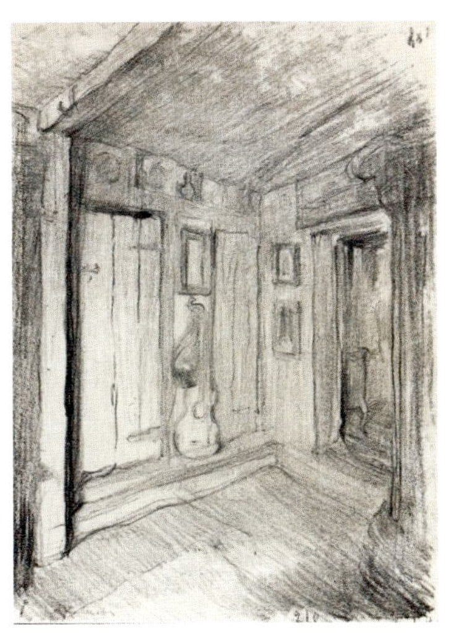

CAT. 128

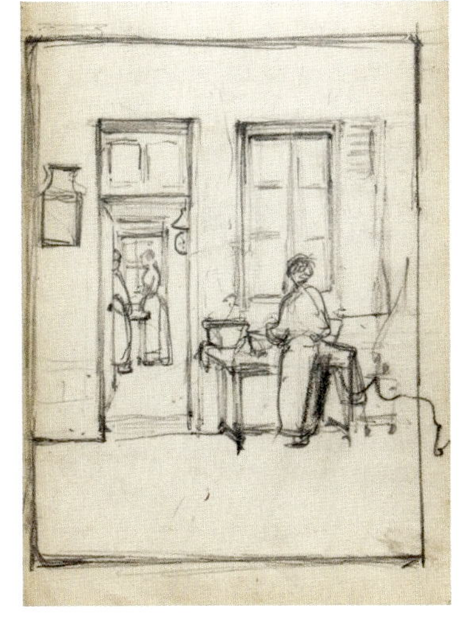

CAT. 129

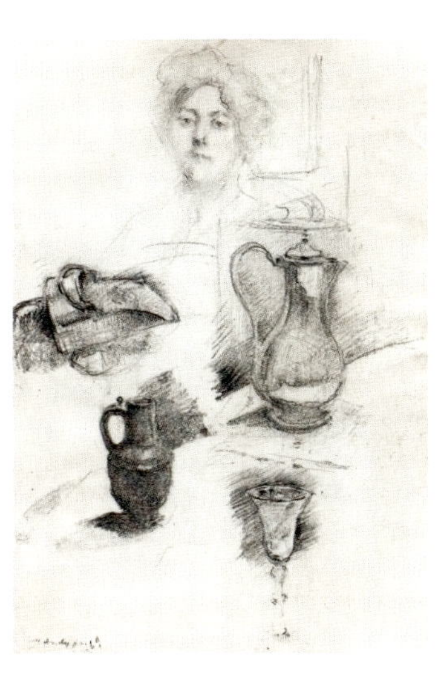

CAT. 130

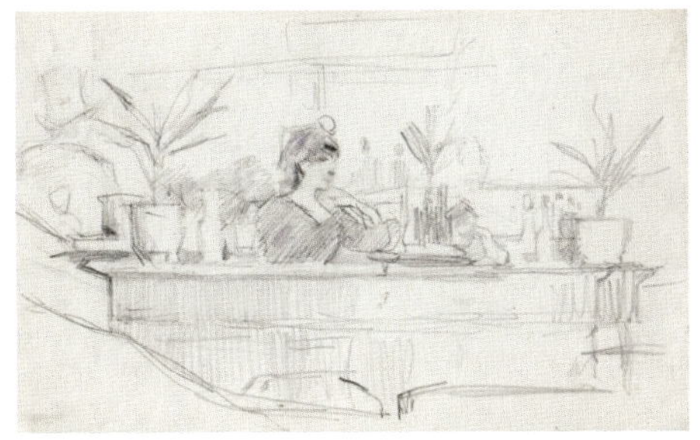

CAT. 131

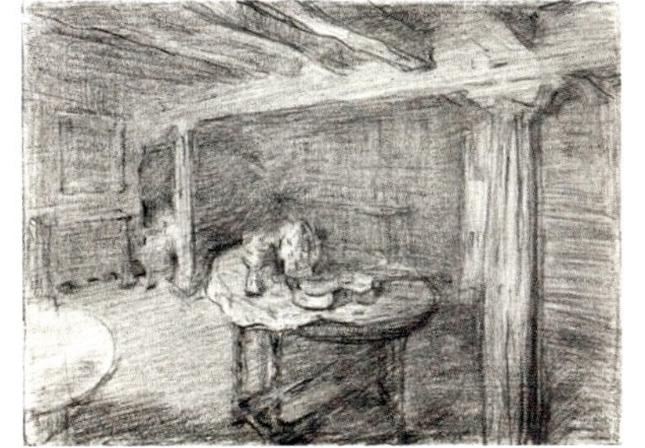

CAT. 132

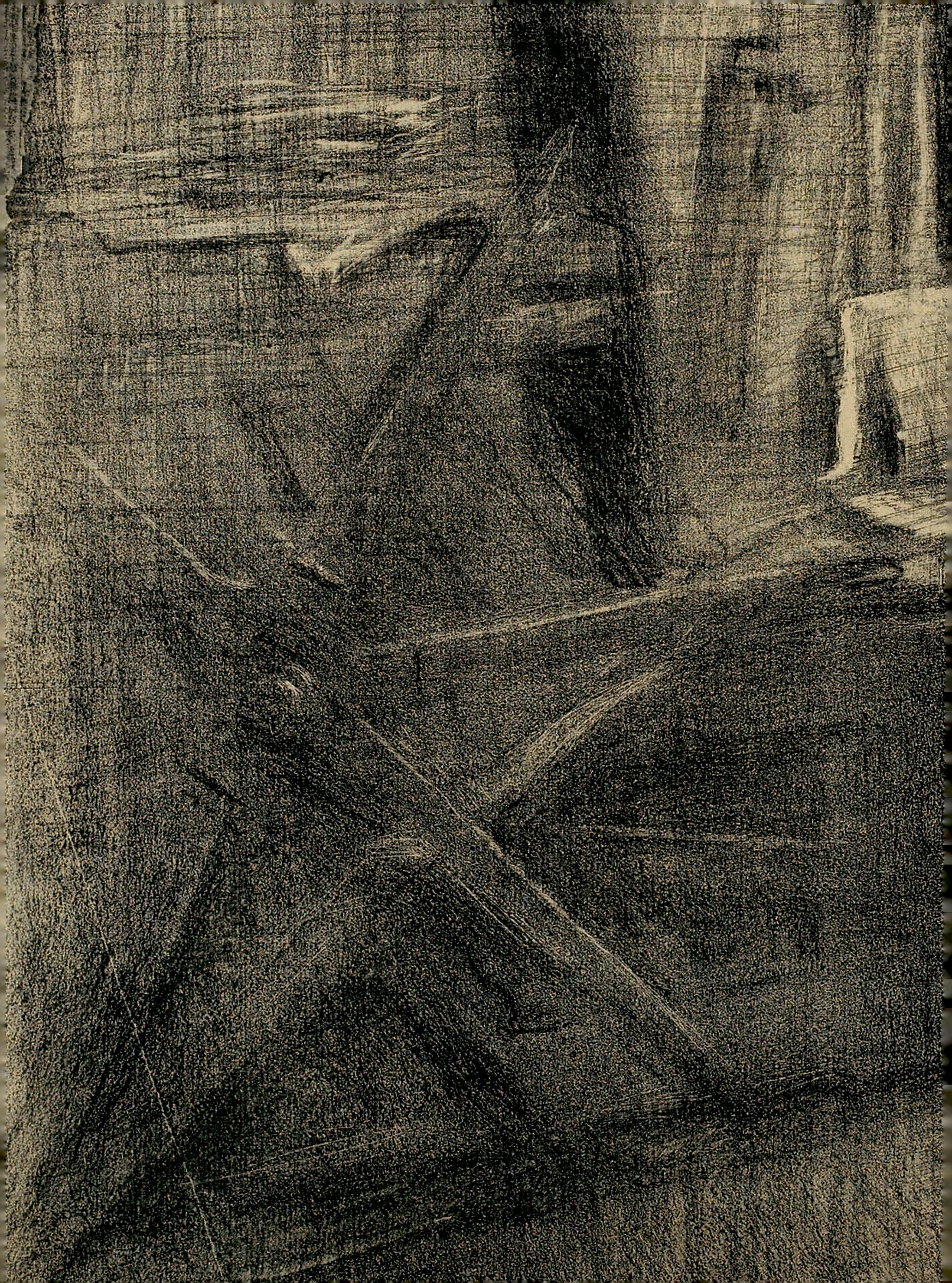

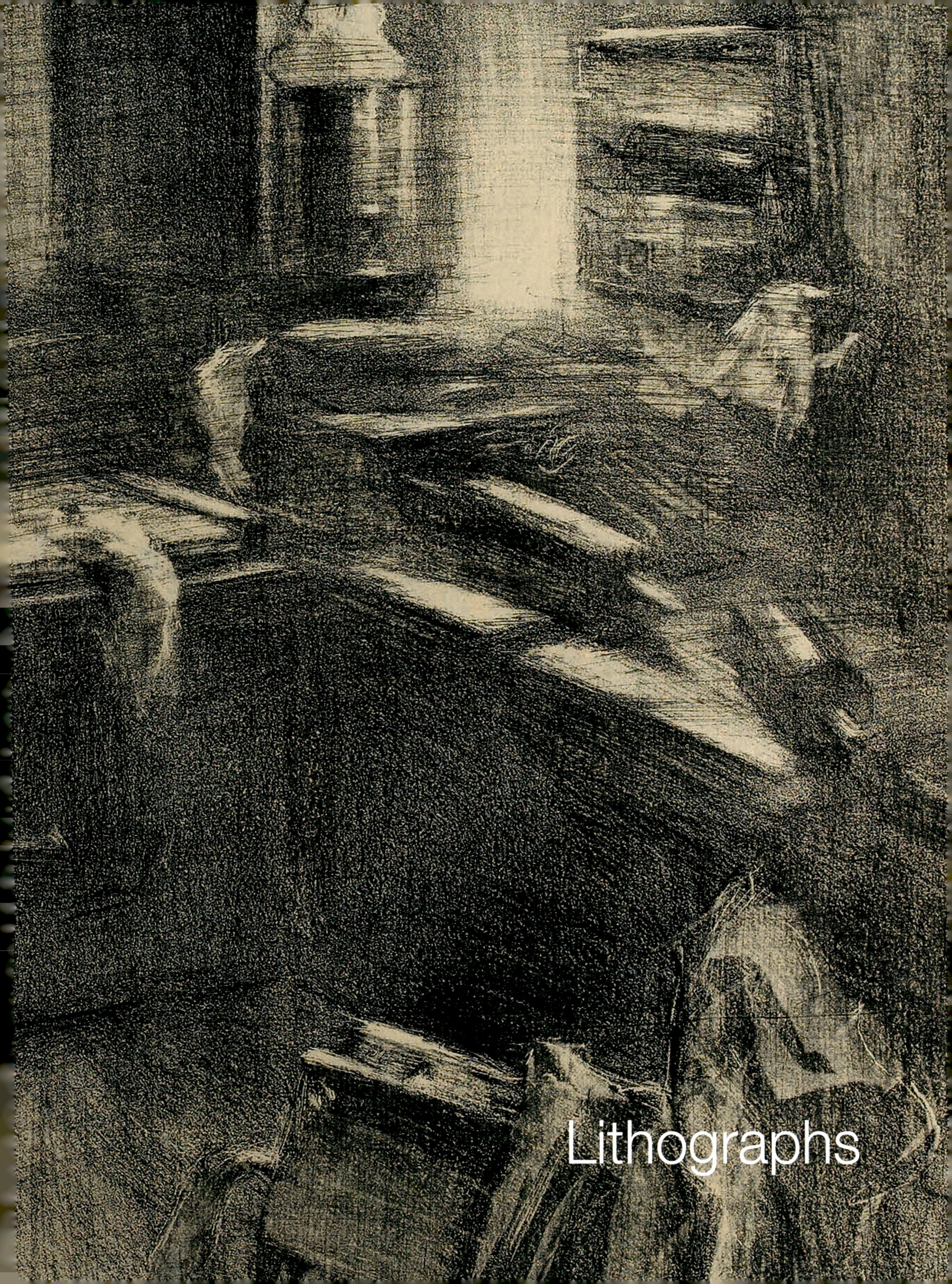
Lithographs

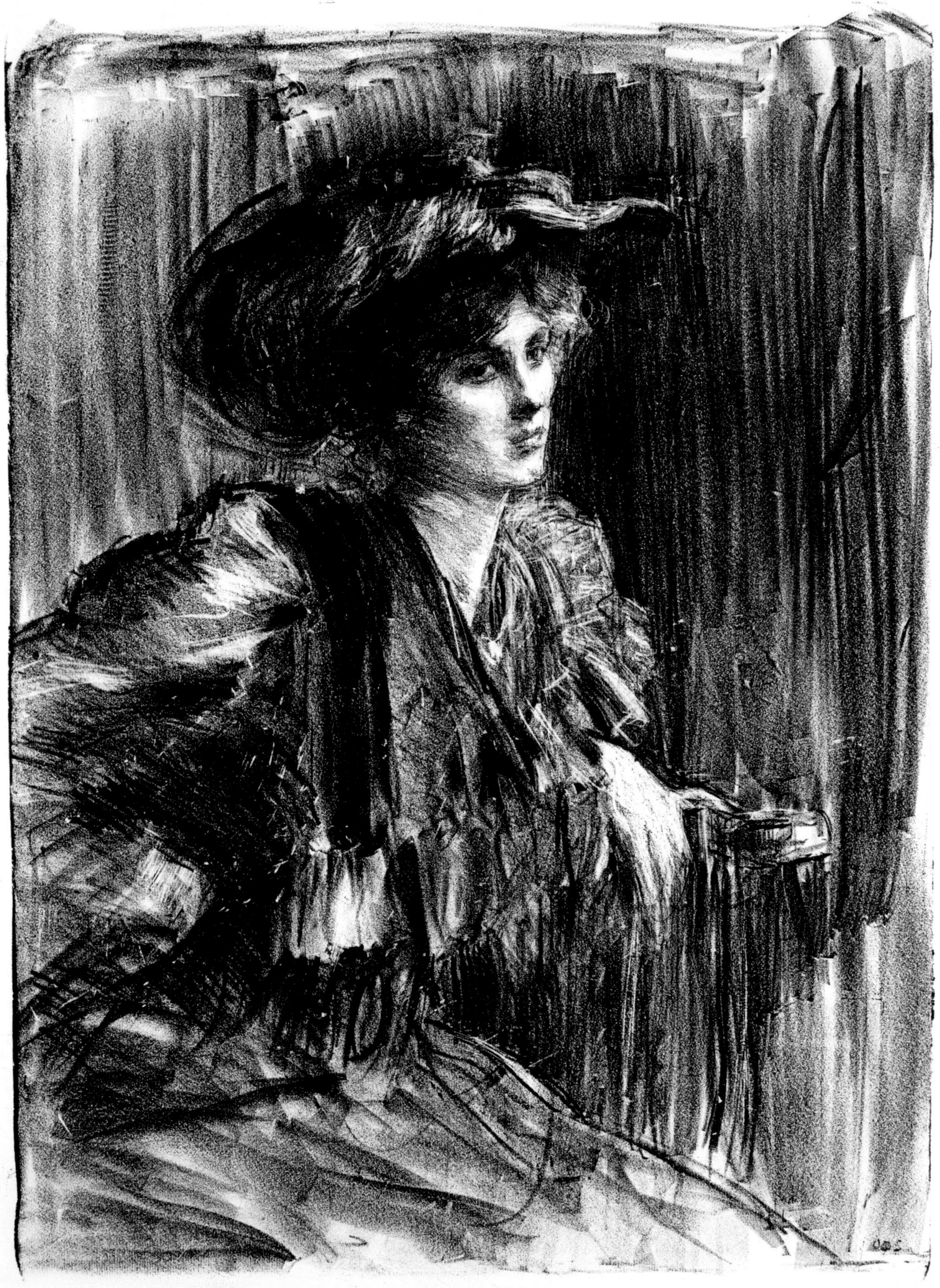

'As a lithographic artist he stands alone. No modern can touch him, either in his knowledge or the quality to be got out of the stone. No one else has succeeded in making lithography the rival of painting. His prints are full of colour and animation and subtle delicacy. He wins from the stone the utmost richness it is capable of yielding. His prints exhibit the full orchestration from light to dark.'

Frank Brangwyn, foreword to *Albert de Belleroche* by Julian A Millest, (*Apollo* 1935 XII 124 April).

In less than 25 years, starting in 1900, Belleroche produced nearly 1000 different lithographic images.The three women who most heavily influenced Belleroche's life were also his three most frequently portrayed models: Lili Grenier (1863-c.1936), his mistress of 17 years and the subject of 67 lithographs; Julia (Julie) Emile Maria Visseaux (1882-1958) his wife and the subject of 60 lithographs, produced between 1907 and 1924; and Mrs. Alice Milbank (c.1840-1916), the artist's mother, of whom Belleroche produced a dozen lithographs in the four years spanning 1900-1904 out of a total of thirty. After moving to England in 1912 Belleroche recruited new English models including Dorothy, Joyce and Mabel Charles.

According to Steven Kern, author of *The Rival of Painting: The Lithographs of Albert Belleroche*: 'The lithographs of Albert de Belleroche are complex visual discourses on light and dark, gradation and modelling. He achieved a considerable reputation during his lifetime as a printmaker, and his bravura approach to lithography remains without comparison. During a period in which artists and dealers began to seize upon the commercial application of lithography – a medium which combined low production costs with large print runs – few invested effort in further exploring its artistic idiosyncrasies. Belleroche stretched the medium beyond accepted boundaries, and the accomplishments he generated still verge on the inexplicable.'

According to George Kenney, author of the catalogue raisonné of *Albert de Belleroche, Master of Belle Epoque Lithography* (Liss Llewellyn, 2024): 'The artist's secret was his complete mastery over the entire lithographic process, starting from drawing directly on the stone to overseeing ink application and paper selection through to the final printing. He prepared his own stones, freely drawing with crayons varying from very fine to coarse. He also used, lavis, tusche, and combinations of these. He carefully selected antique and tinted paper to enhance his images and used his own press. His proficiency enabled him to craft images that exhibit a remarkable range, resembling powerful charcoals, delicate silver points, or pastel drawings. Despite predominantly creating single-colour lithographs, Belleroche's mastery of colour values truly rivals that of paintings. He brought creative legitimacy and recognition to a medium dismissed as both industrial and artisanal. For a medium tailored to produce print-runs in the thousands, Belleroche's works are uniquely singular'.

Normally, he produced about ten impressions, but sometimes he made as many as 40, and at other times he produced as few as one. According to his Log Book, Belleroche produced 49 single impressions and 46 biotypes, i.e. editions of two. The term monotype would usually refer to a unique image made by printing from a metal or glass plate, drawn or painted upon with printing ink. As the plate has not been engraved, drawn upon with a sharp point, or bitten with acid, the paper takes all of the ink on the plate; as such a second, identical copy cannot be printed.

CAT. 133 – *Gildys*, (K244, AB 200), 1906, 25 ¾ x 19 ½ in. (65.4 x 49.5 cm). Edition: 20.

Belleroche produced counterproofs by transferring a just-printed wet image on to a second dry sheet of paper; this would appear in reverse and typically softer in tone.

In addition to the lithographs Belleroche produced himself, an additional 35,000 impressions were made from "his original stones" by others during 1903-1908 for commercial use in magazines and societies. In 1907 and 1908, Belleroche exhibited at the Senefelder Club of London. The Club published *The Neolith*, a journal that produced 700 impressions of his lithograph *Mélancholie*, 1907, (K473, AB 240B).

.

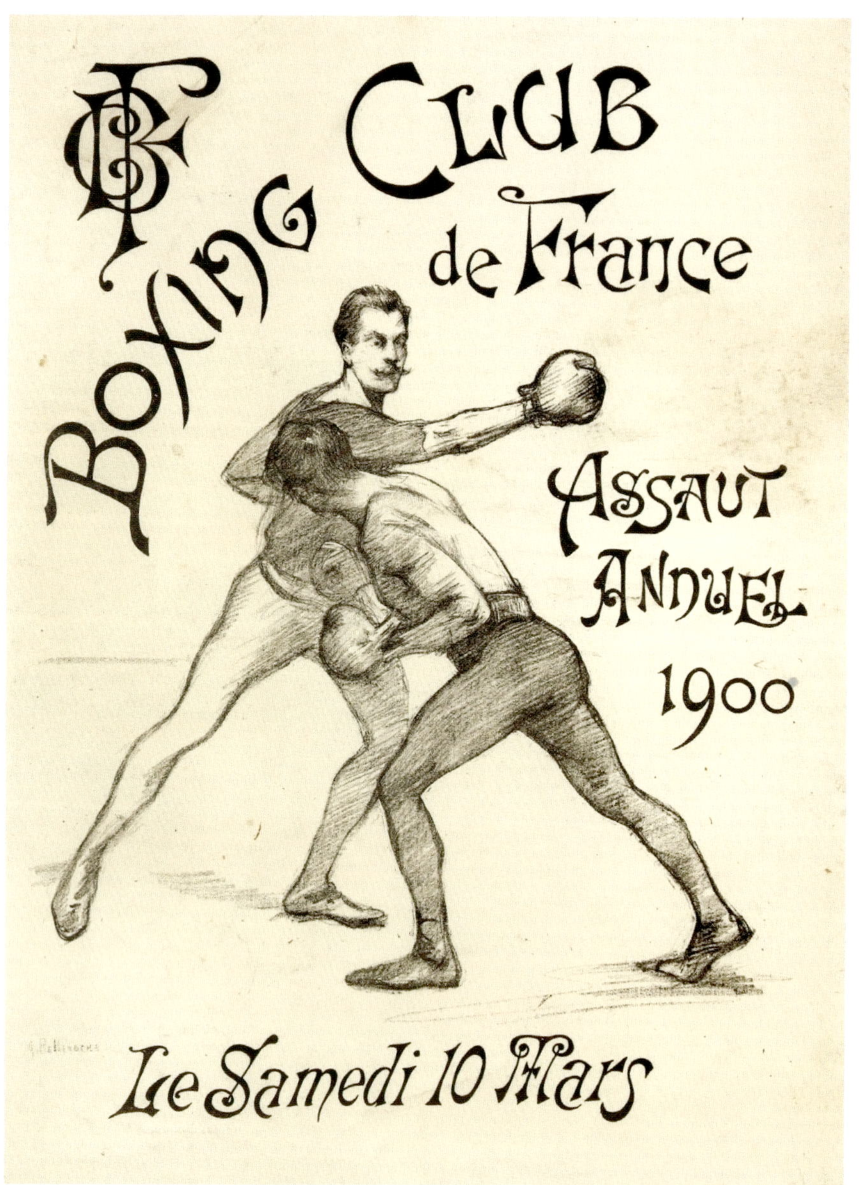

CAT. 134 – Poster for the Boxing Club de France, (K848, AB 588), 1900,
signed in the stone, 12 ¼ x 9 ½ in. (31 x 24 cm). Edition: 1.

CAT. 135 – *Henry Gazell* (?) *Pensive*, (K840, AB 581), c.1904, 24 ¼ x 20 ¼ in. (61.6 x 51.4 cm). Edition: 4.

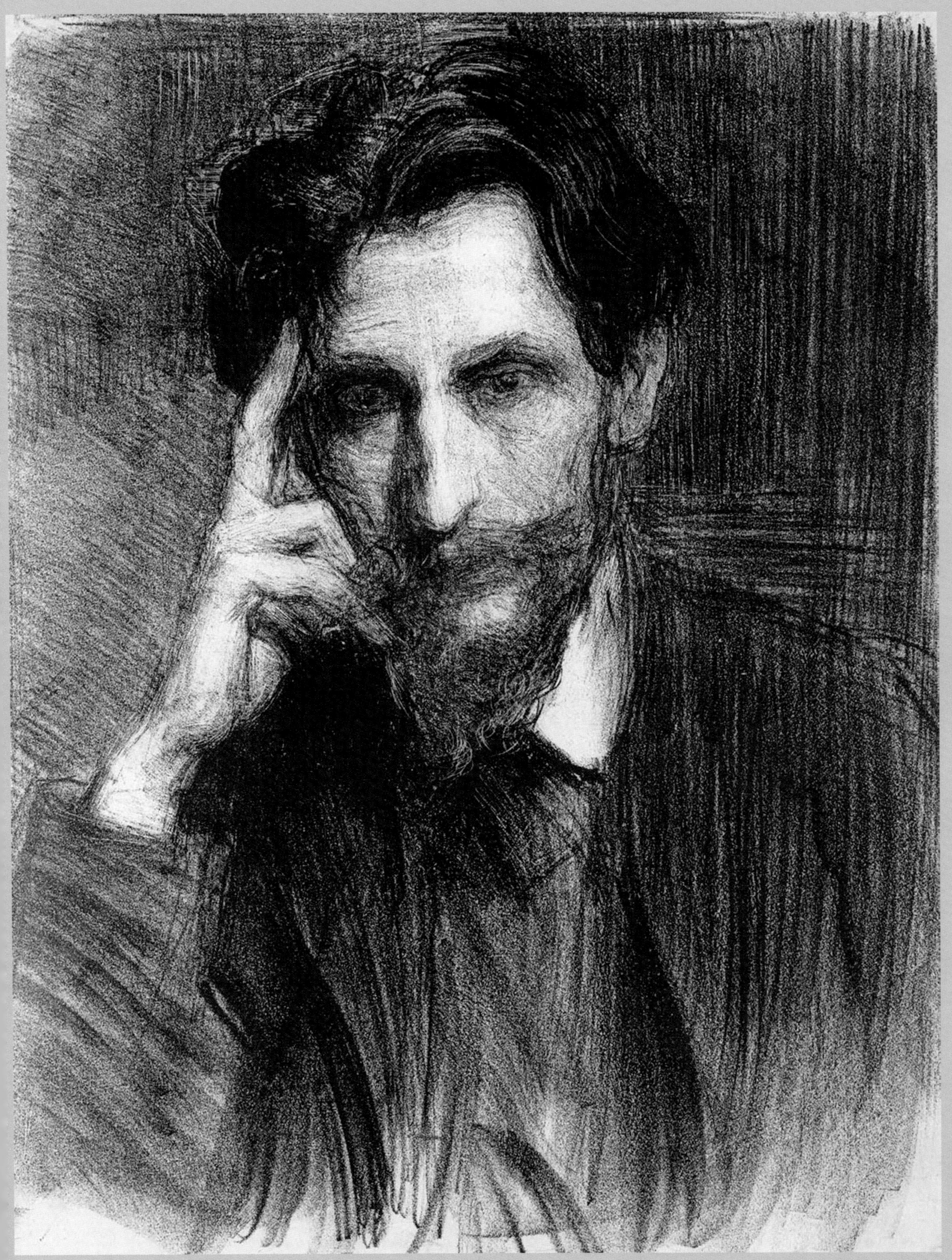

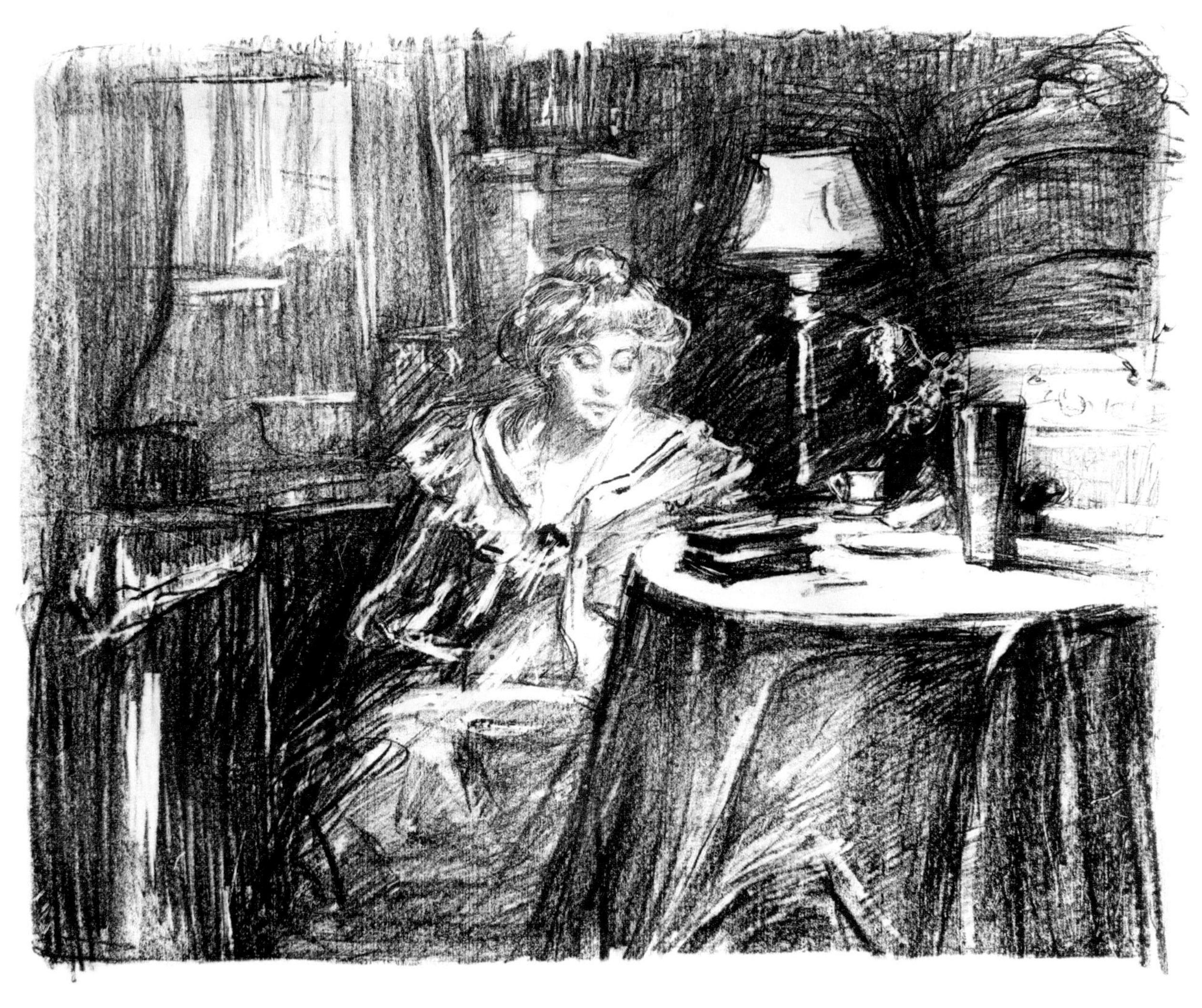

CAT. 136 – *Mrs. Millbank Reading by Lamp on Table*, (K137, AB 531), c.1904, 20 ¼ x 24 ¼ in. (51.4 x 61.6 cm).

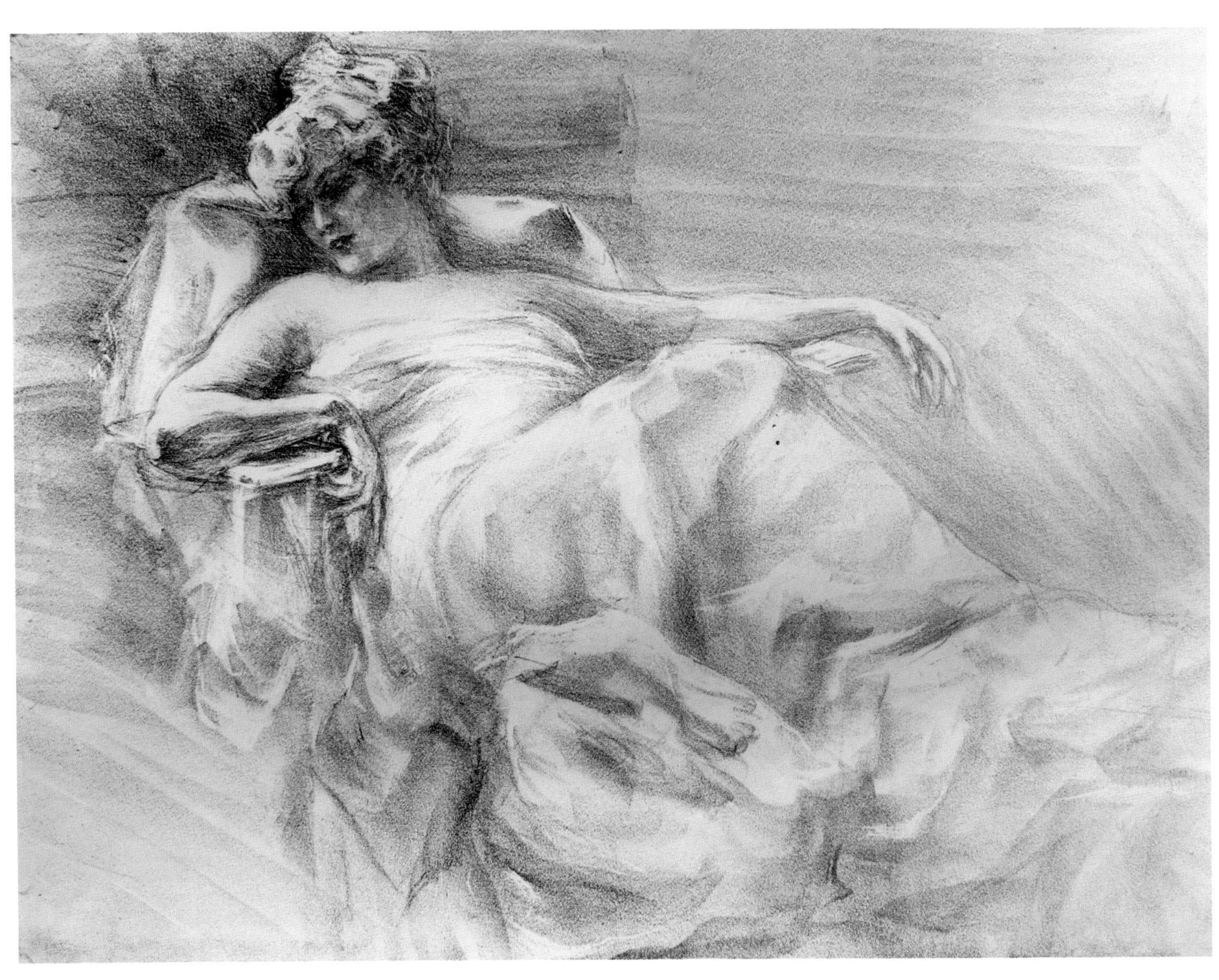

CAT. 137 – *Le Repos, la Dormeuse*, (K194, AB 306), 1909, signed, 12 ¼ x 15 ¾ in. (30.9 x 40.2 cm). Edition: 10.

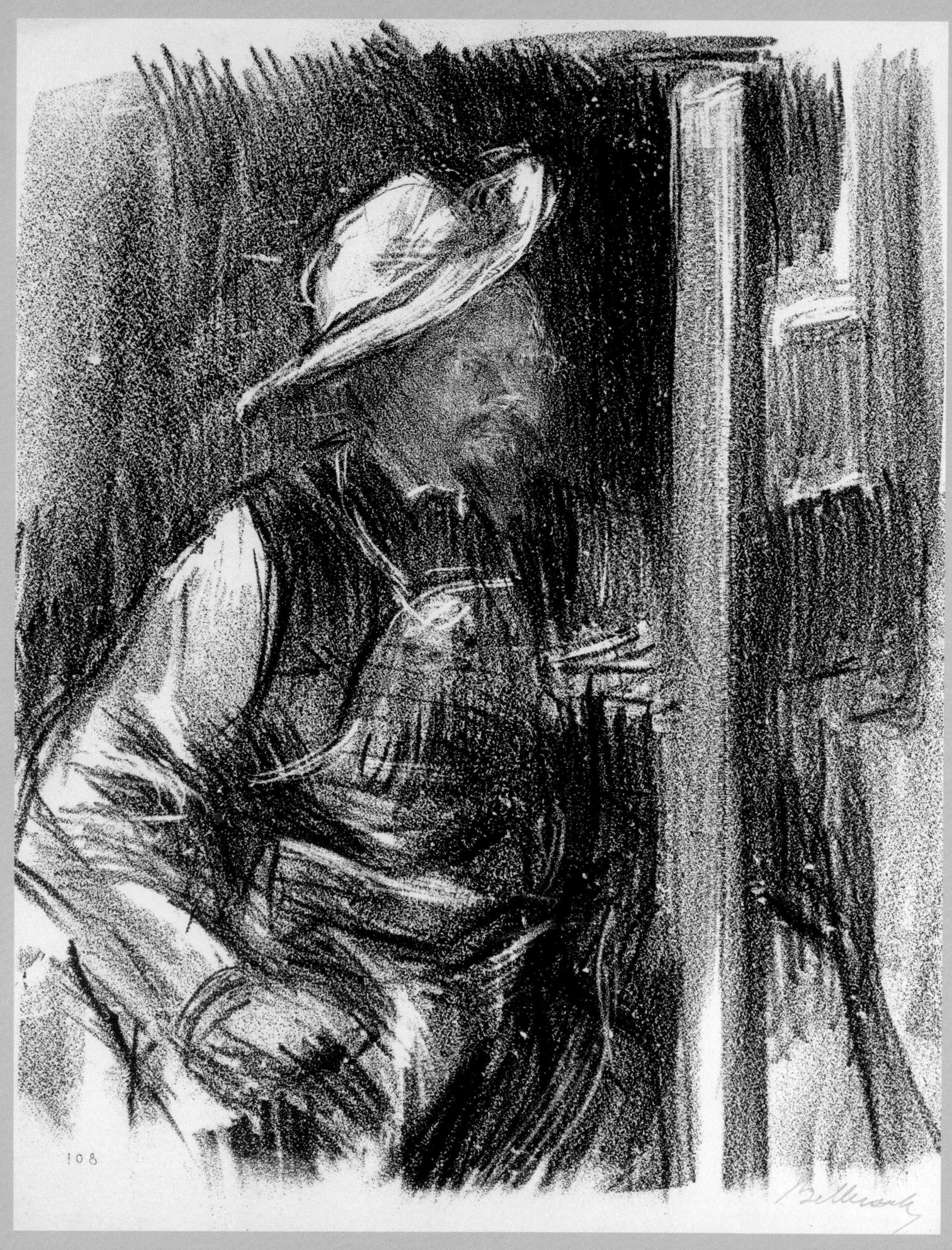

CAT. 138 – *Portait of Léandre (painter)*, (K845, AB 113), 1908, 16 ½ x 12 ¾ in. (42.2 x 32.3 cm). Edition: 5.

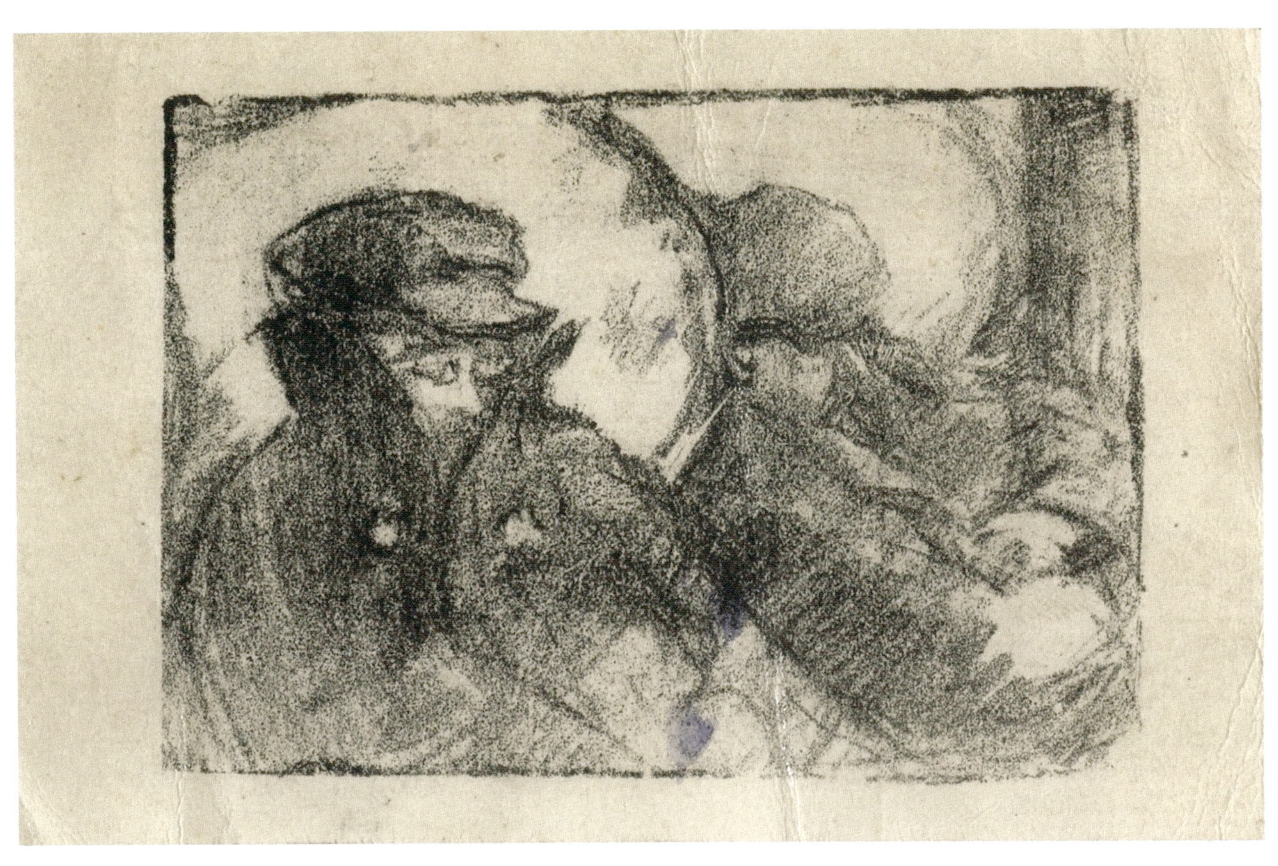

CAT. 139 – *Two Men*, 1910 (?), (K850, AB 907), 2 3/4 x 4 in. (7 x 10.2 cm). Edition: 2 (?).

OVERLEAF:

CAT. 140 – *Divine on sofa (reclining)*, (K493, AB 634.1), 1909, signed, 19 ¼ x 25 ½ in. (48.5 x 64 cm). Edition: 10.

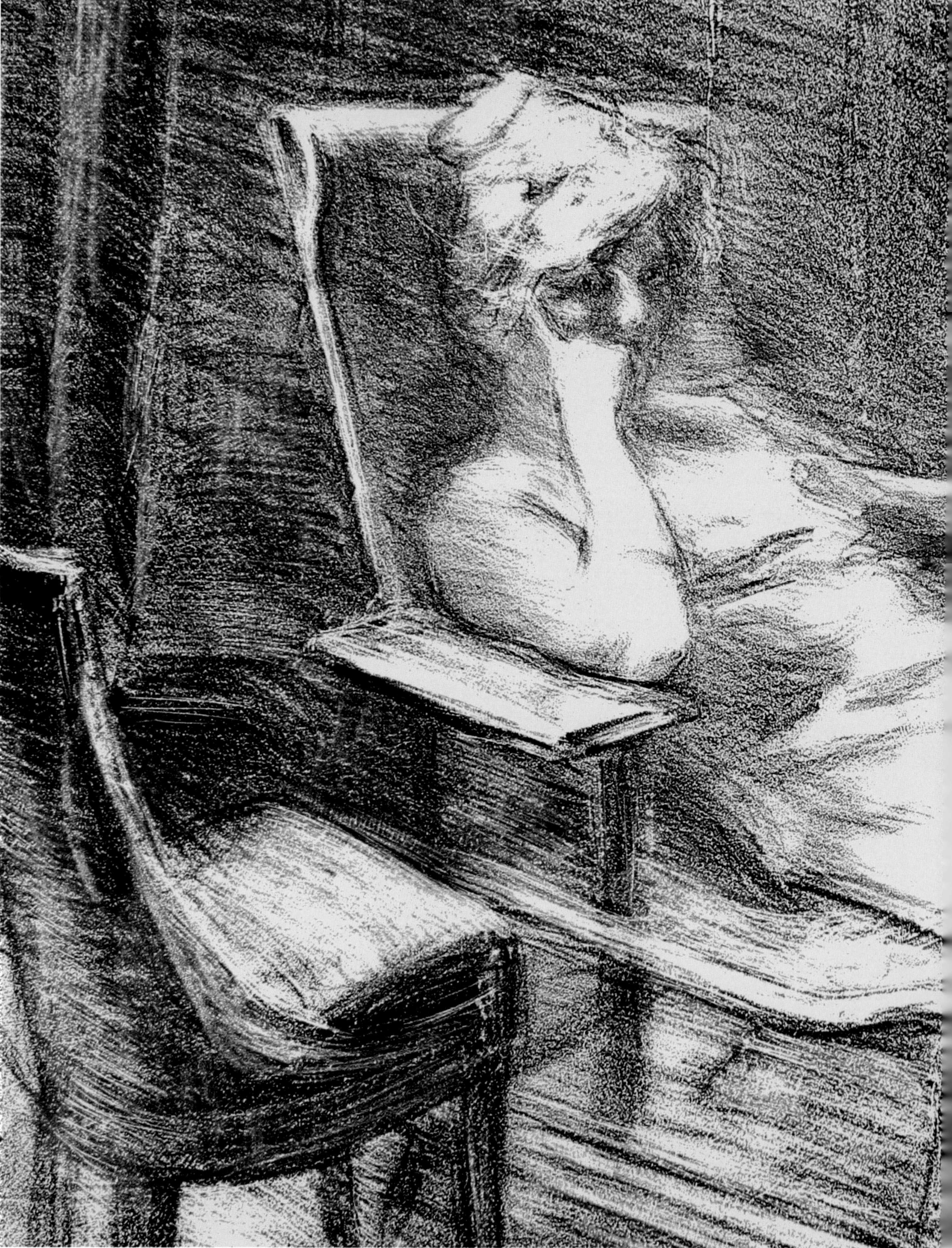

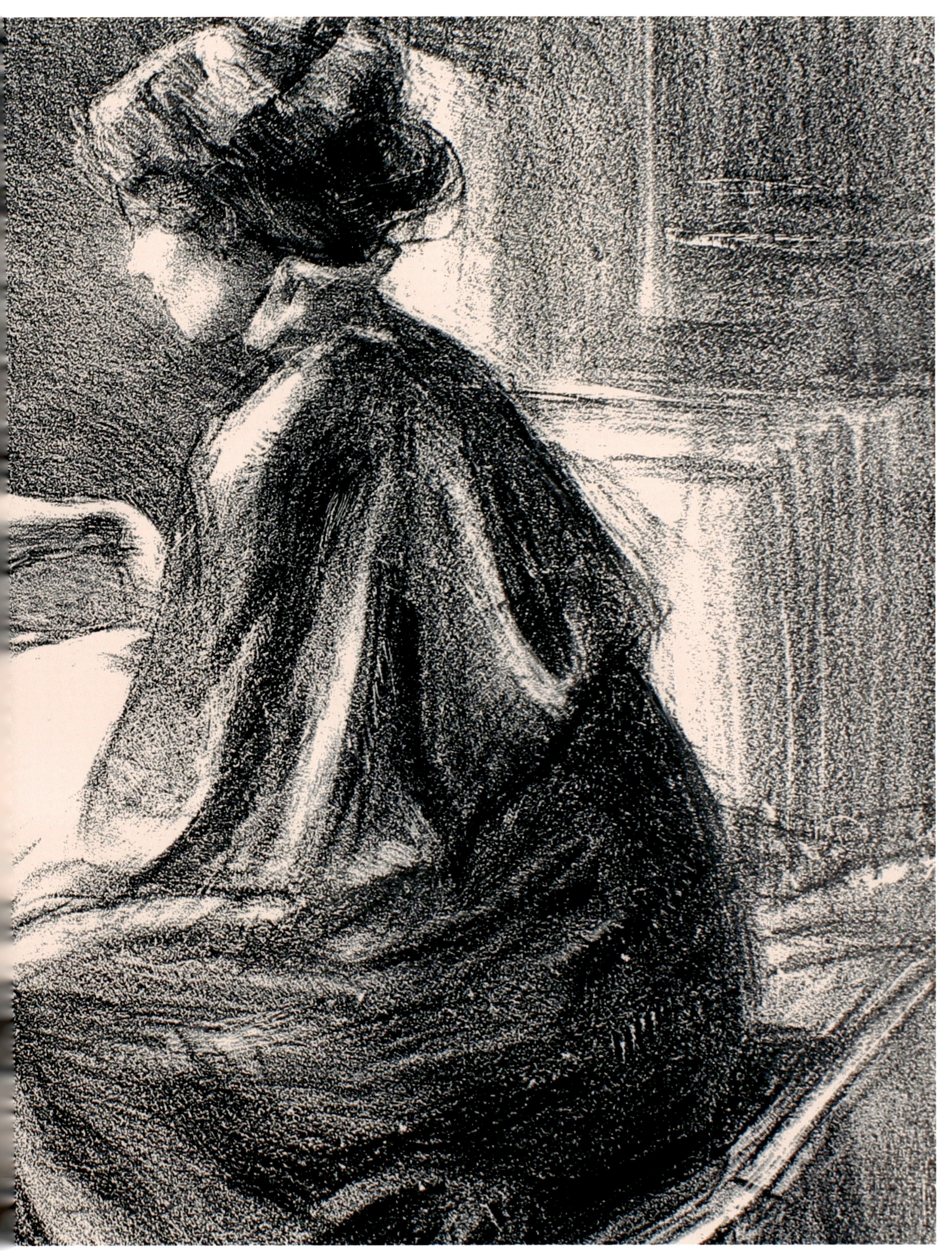

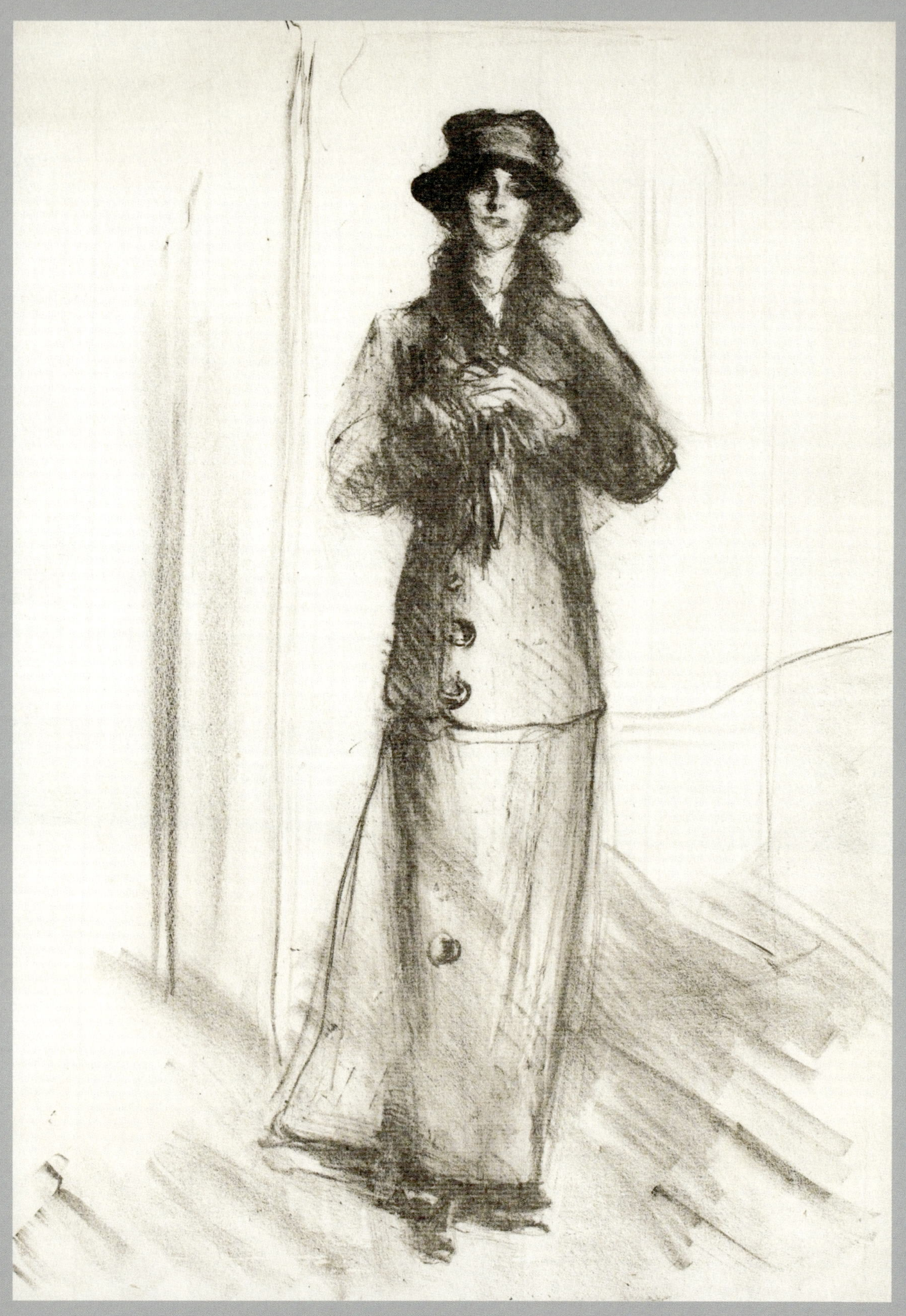

CAT. 141 – *Sortie*, (K724, AB 419), 1914, 17 ½ x 10 ½ in. (44.5 x 26.8 cm). Edition: 5.

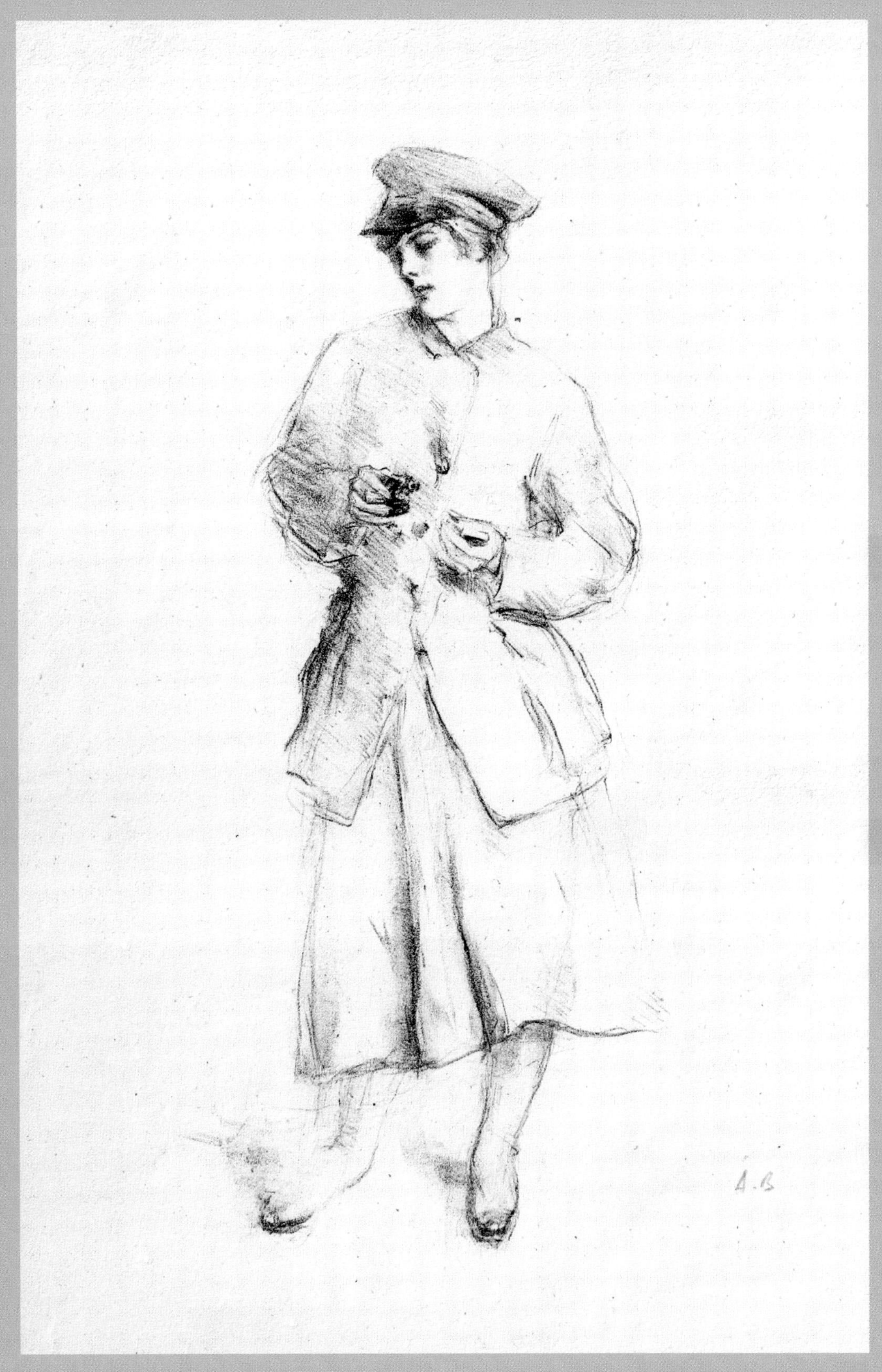

CAT. 142 – *The Ticket Collector*, (K713, AB 428B), 1915, 17 ½ x 11 ¼ in. (44.5 x 28.6 cm). Edition: 10.

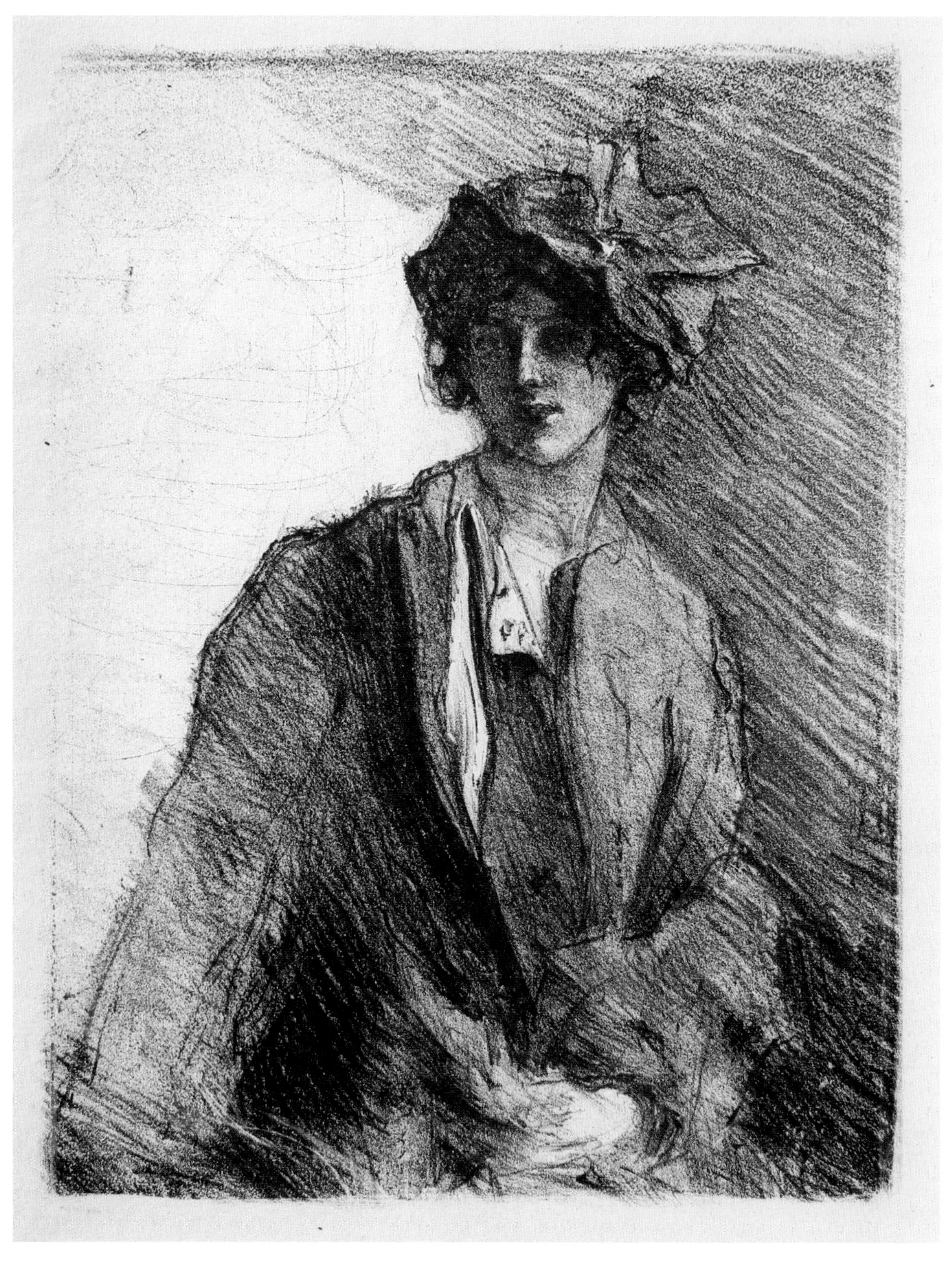

CAT. 143 – *Mabel, full length seated*, (K682, AB 421), 1916, 20 ¼ x 13 ½ in. (51.4 x 34.3 cm).

CAT. 144 – *Portrait of Mr. Anglada*, (K827, AB 156), 1907, signed, 23 ½ x 18 ½ in. (59.7 x 47 cm). Edition: 5.

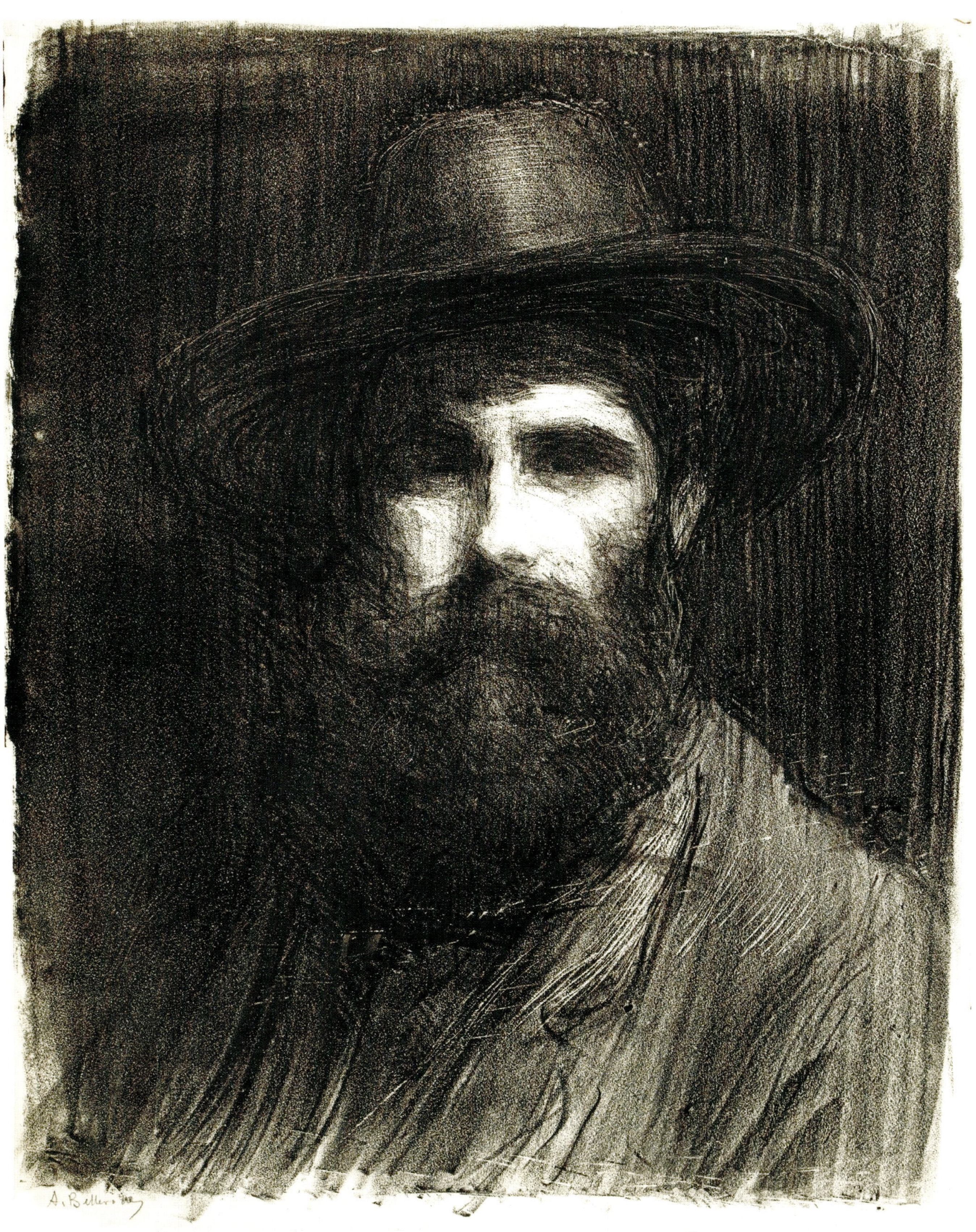

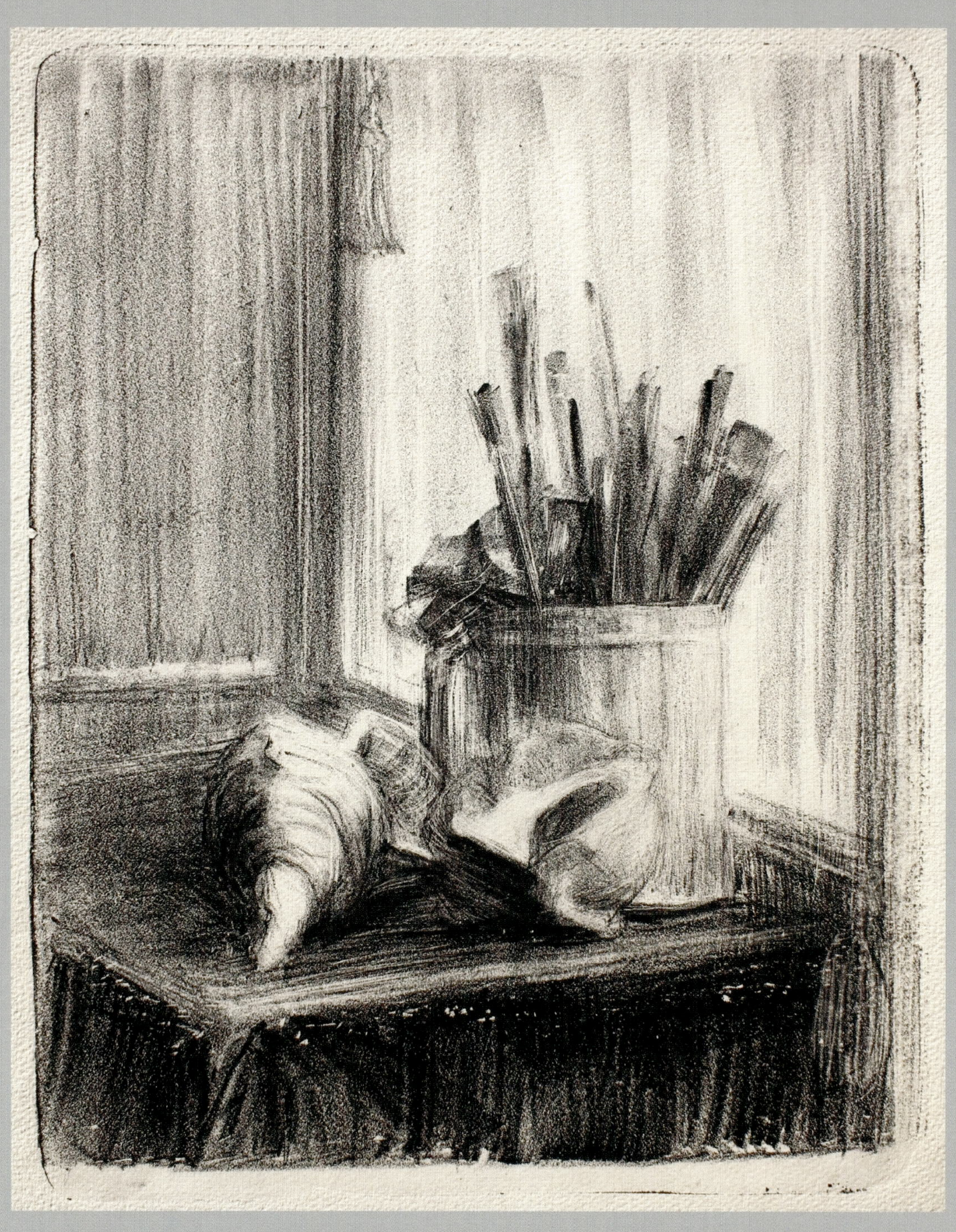

CAT. 145 – *Pinceaux et coquillages*, (K940, AB 25), 1906, 25 ½ x 19 ½ in. (65 x 50 cm). Edition: 10.

CAT. 146 – *Studio, Glencairn*, (K883, AB 665), c.1912, signed, 24 ¾ x 18 in. (62.9 x 45.7 cm). Edition: 6.

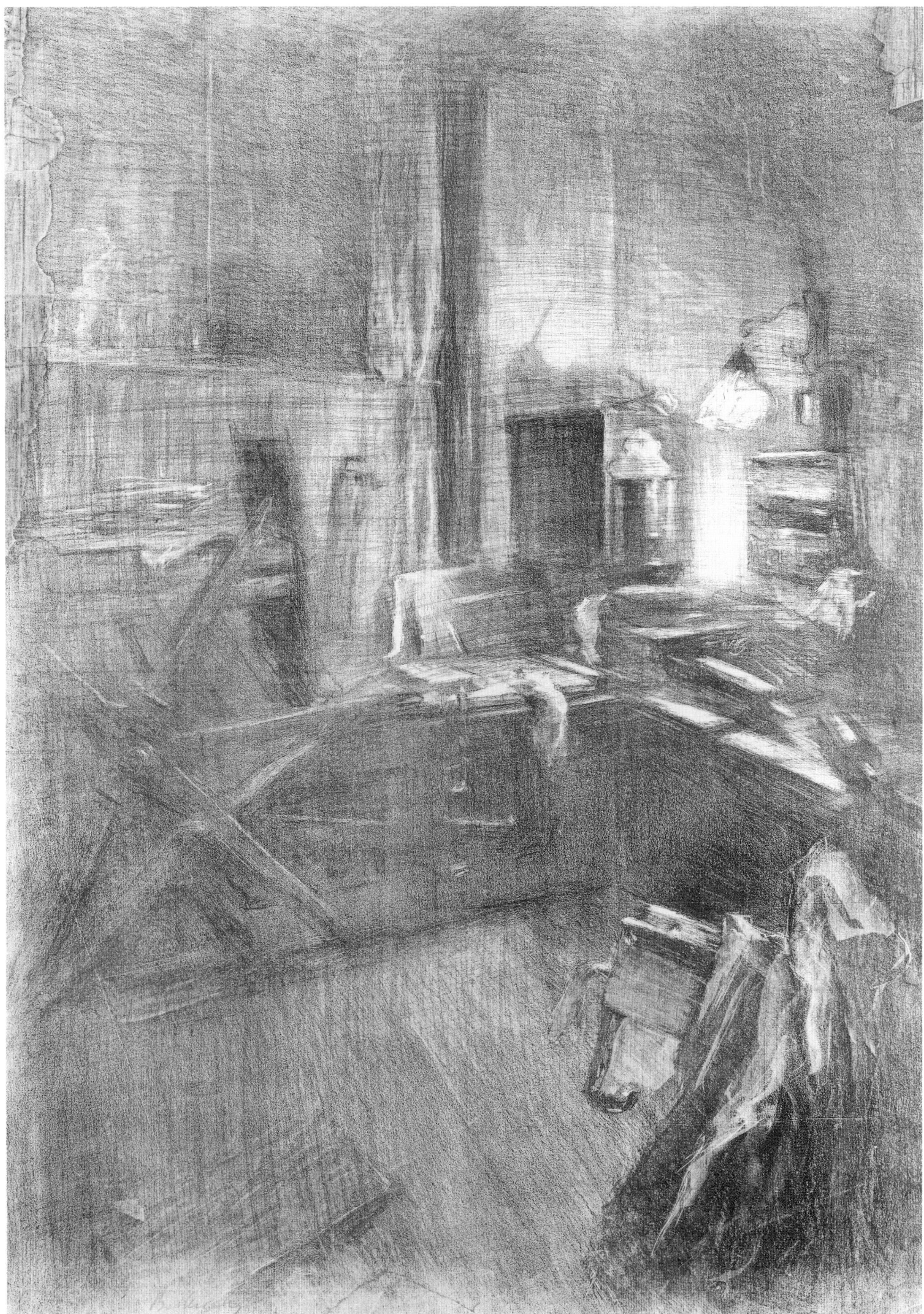

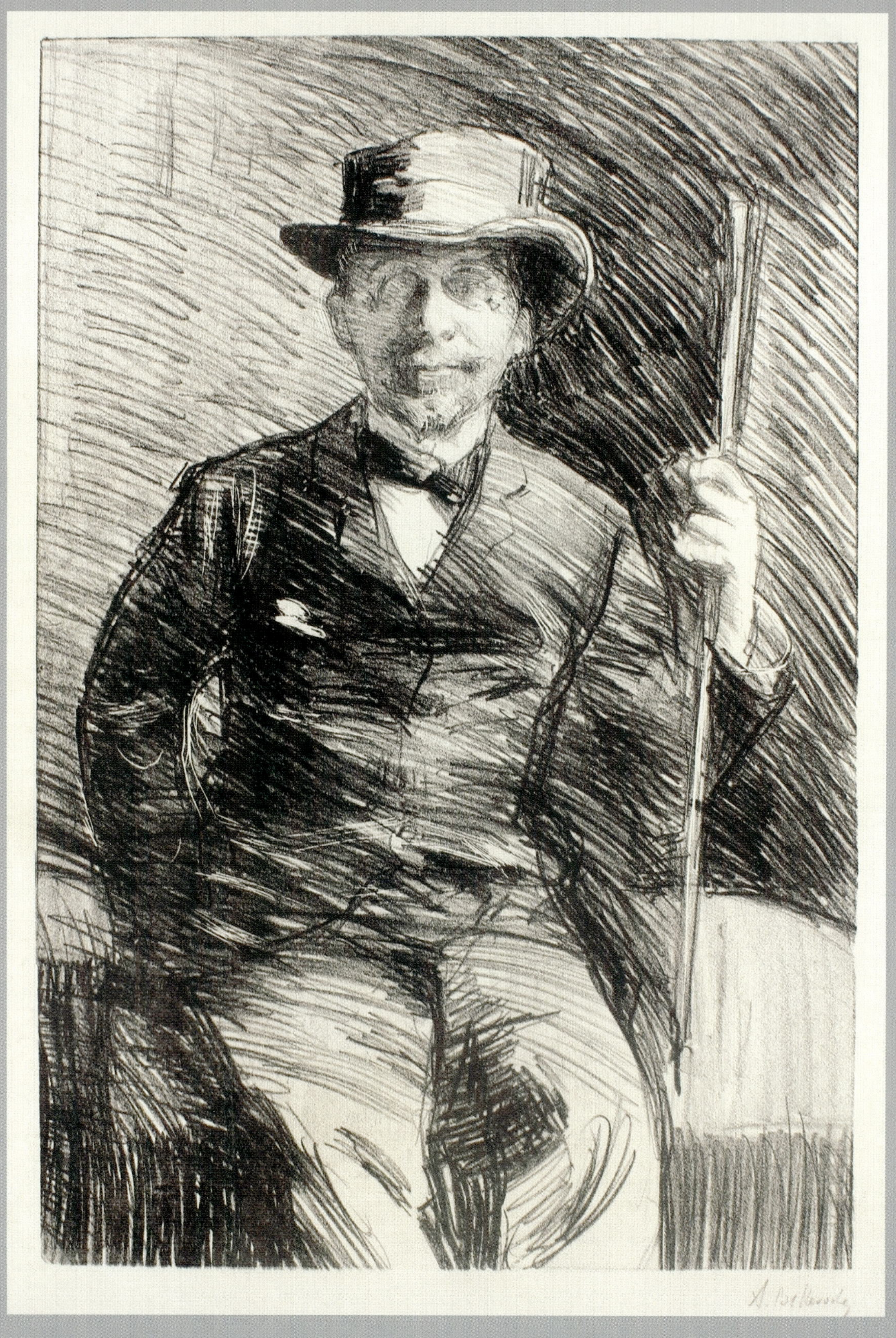

CAT. 147 – *Portrait of Jacques Rizo*, (K862, AB 37.4), 1901, (inscribed on back), signed, 17 ¼ × 13 ½ in. (44 × 34 cm). Edition: 10.

Other lithographs in the collection

CAT. 148 – *M.H. Vauxelles*, (K865, AB 575), 1910 (?), 20 x 13 ¾ in. (50.5 x 35 cm). Edition: 1.

CAT. 149 – *Mr. Pollard*, (K858, AB 289), 1907, signed with initials, 13 x 8 ¼ in. (33 x 21 cm). Edition: 5.

CAT. 150 – *Mr. Daurrerie*, (K837, AB 585), 1901, inscribed " à Dominique - A. Belleroche 1900", 17 ½ x 11 ¼ in. (45 x 28.5 cm). Edition: 1.

CAT. 151 – *Cartoon Self Portrait*, (K175, AB 568), c.1902, 10 ¼ x 6 in. (26 x 15.3 cm). Edition: 1.

CAT. 152 – *Henry Gazell, artist*, (K841, AB 578), c.1908, signed, printed recto verso, 19 ½ x 13 ¾ in. (50 x 35cm). Edition: 1.

CAT. 153 – *Joseph Pennell*, (K857, AB 430), 1909, 13 x10 in. (33 x 25.5 cm). Edition 6.

CAT. 154 – *Monsieur Le Normand*, (K851, AB 570), c.1908,signed, Inscribed verso, 24 ½ x 17 ¼ in. 62.5 x 44 cm). Edition: 1.

CAT. 155 – *La jardinière*, (K943, AB 288), 1907, 8 ½ x 7 in. (22 x 16.5 cm). Edition: 3.

CAT. 156 – *Page de croquis d'hommes au café*, (K859, AB 564), 1905 (?), signed, 17 ½ x 22 ½ in. (57 x 44.5 cm). Edition: 1.

CAT. 157 – *Le vieux verre*, (K950, AB 394), 1915, signed, 8 ½ x 7 in. (22 x 16.5 cm). Edition: 10.

CAT. 158 – *Le petit poêle au bois* (?), (K901, AB 133), 1914, signed with initials, 21 ½ x 14 ½ in. (55 x 37 cm). Edition: 10.

CAT. 159 – *Fiammette*, (K948, AB 36.5), 1902, signed, 17 ½ x 14 ¼ in. (44.5 x 36.5 cm). Edition: 20.

CAT. 160 – *The Mirror*, (K891, AB 405), 1919, 21 ¼ x 14 ½ in. (55 x 37.2 cm). Edition: 10.

CAT. 161 – *Théière (Tea Service)*, (K953, AB 36.6), 1902, signed, inscribed "Trial proof", 10 ¼ x 14 ¼ in. (26 x 36.5 cm). Edition: 10.

CAT. 162 – *Study, Glencairn (Scotland)*, (K887, AB 655), 1913, 14 ¾ x 10 ¼ in. (37.5 x 26 cm). Edition: 10.

CAT. 163 – *Intérieur la Boissière (Sawmill Studio)*, (K875, AB 443), 1909, 24 ½ x 17 in. (62 x 43 cm). Edition: 10.

CAT. 164 – *Dimanche*, (K954, AB 713), c.1902, inscribed "Dimanche 25 juin Essai au fusain", 12 ¼ x 18 ¾ in. (31 x 47.5 cm).

CAT. 165 – *Les meules de foin*, (K922, AB 155), 1907, signed, 8 ½ x 7 ½ in. (21.6 x 20.4 cm). Edition: 10.

CAT. 166 – *Dans la vieille chapelle*, (K873, AB 182), 1909, 21 x 14 1/2 in. (53.3 x 36.8 cm). Edition: 15.

CAT. 167 – *The Maid in the Doorway*, (K892, AB 640), 1920 (?), 25 ½ x 19 ¾ in. (65.2 x 50.3 cm).

CAT. 168 – *Kings-Lynns (Norfolk)*, (K926, AB 657), c.1909, 9 ¾ x 11 ¼ in. (24.7 x 28.8 cm).

CAT. 169 – *Scene from Window, Glencairn*, (K913, AB 451), 1915, 12 x 15 ¼ in. (30.5 x 38.8 cm). Edition: 10.

CAT. 170 – *Grotte Châteaudun*, (K096, AB 340), 1911, signed, 22 x 15 ¼ in. (56 x 39.5 cm). Edition: 15.

CAT. 171 – *The Old Outside Wall, Rustington*, (K935, AB 663), 1924, signed, 18 ¾ x 12 ¾ in. (47.5 x 32.5 cm).

CAT. 172 – *La Boissiere (Sawmill)*, (K903, AB 310), signed with initials, 1909, 11 ½ x 17 in. (29.7 x 43 cm). Edition: 5.

CAT. 173 – *Julie de B at St. Gedule, Brussels*, (K924, AB 359), 1911, 17 ½ x 22 in. (44.5 x 55.5 cm). Edition: 10.

CAT. 174 – *Joan, Etude de femme*, (K626, AB 406), 1913, 19 ½ x 17 ¾ in. (49.2 x 45 cm). Edition: 15.

CAT. 175 – *Applying Leeches*, (K855, AB 567), 1920 (?), 13 x 10 in. (33 x 25.4 cm). Edition: 2.

CAT. 176 – *Mrs. Millbank sitting in a room*, (K138, AB 532), 1904, signed with initials, 17 ¼ x 26 ½ in. (43.5 x 68 cm). Edition: 4.

CAT. 177 – *La Parisienne (1/2 Length)*, (K415, AB 6B), 1903, 24 ¼ x 19 in. (62 x 48 cm). Edition: 10 (?).

CAT. 178 – *Woman with hat standing in bedroom,* (K085, AB 516), 1910 (?), signed, 17 x 11 ¾ in. (43 x 30 cm).

CAT. 179 – *Early Morning*, (K725, AB 364), 1915, 1915, signed with initials, 17 ¼ x 10 ¾ in. (44.2 x 27.5 cm). Edition 10.

CAT. 180 – *Indolence (Fleury),* (K339, AB 708), c.1904, 26 ¾ x 14 ½ in. (68 x 37 cm). Edition 10.

CAT. 181 – *Rosa*, (K361, AB 27), 1902, 6 3/4 x 5 1/2 in. (17.1 x 14 cm). Edition: 10.

CAT. 182 – *Woman window cleaner*, (K716, AB 750), 1915, 19 ¼ x 12 ½ in. (49 x 32 cm).

CAT. 183 – *Miss Charles*, (K678, AB 287.1), 1916, signed, 12 ½ x 7 ¾ in. (32 x 19.5 cm).

CAT. 184 – *Woman asleep on a chair*, (K441, AB 926), 1904, signed, 15 ¾ x 12 ¼ in. (40 x 31 cm).

CAT. 185 – *Le panier a'ouvrage*, (K100, AB 426), 1911, signed with initials, 17 x 11 ¾ in. (43.5 x 29.5 cm). Edition: 10

CAT. 186 – *La fille à la fleur, Flora*, (K660, AB 377), 1914, signed, 14 x 11 in. (35.5 x 28 cm). Edition: 10.

CAT. 187 – *Woman, right profile*, (K820, AB 719), 15 x 11 ¼ in. (38 x 28 cm). Edition: 1.

CAT. 188 – *La Toilette*, (K093, AB 334), 1911, inscribed "Julie", 16 x 11 ½ in. (40.5 x 29 cm). Edition: 12.

CAT. 189 – *Croquis*, (K329, AB 74), 1903, signed, 24 ½ x 18 ½ in. (62 x 47.5 cm). Edition: 5.

CAT. 190 – *La Correspondence*, (K102, AB 433), 1911, 21 ¾ x 15 ¾ in. (55.5 x 40 cm). Edition: 4.

CAT. 191 – *Rosa*, (K696, AB 338), 1917, 28 x 21 in. (71 x 53.5 cm). Edition: 6.

CAT. 192 – *La Parisienne*, (K414, AB 6), 1903, 23 x 17 ¾ in. (58.2 x 45 cm). Edition: 20.

CAT. 193 – *Correspondence,* (K082, AB 62B), 1910, 19 ¼ x 12 ¾ in. (49 x 32.5 cm). Edition: 10.

CAT. 194 – *Standing with Necklace*, (K637, AB 11), 1924, 14 ¼ x 9 ½ in. (36 x 24.5 cm). Edition: 10.

CAT. 195 – *Nini Seated Sucking her Thumb*, (K334, AB 704), c.1904, signed, 18 ¾ x 12 ¼ in. (47.5 x 31 cm). Edition: 2.

CAT. 196 – *Regine Martial, standing in a doorway,* (K723, AB 905), 1920 (?), 12 x 7 ½ in. (30.5 x 19 cm).

CAT. 197 – *Miss Charles*, (K656, AB 427), 1913, 16 ½ x 12 ¼ in. (42.5 x 31 cm). Edition: 10.

CAT. 198 – *Fiammette*, (K002, AB 36.1), 1902, signed, 21 ¼ x 18 ¾ in. (54 x 47.5 cm). Edition: 10.

CAT. 199 – *Miss M. in a Broad Hat*, (K653, AB 369), 1912, signed, 24 ½ x 16 ¼ in. (62 x 41 cm). Edition: 10.

CAT. 200 – *Gildys accoudée*, (K247, AB 203), 1906, signed with initials, 26 x 21 in. (66 x 53.5 cm). Edition: 20.

CAT. 201 – *Fleury in a Wicker Chair*, (K337, AB 707), 1904, signed, 12 ¼ x 15 ¾ in. (31 x 40.5 cm).

CAT. 202 – *Alice with ribbon, facing right (6 yrs)*, (K161, AB 545), c.1915, signed, 12 ¾ x 10 ¾ in. (32.5 x 27.3 cm). Edition: 1.

CAT. 203 – *Flamenco Singer*, (K709, AB 526), 1915, 28 ¼ x 21 in. (71.8 x 53.4 cm).

CAT. 204 – *Résistance, Femme penchée*, (K675, AB 410), 1915, 22 x 15 in. (56 x 38.5 cm). Edition: 10.

CAT. 205 – *The Hon. Mrs. Day*, (K642, AB 114), 1924, 15 ½ x 10 ¼ in. (39 x 26 cm). Edition: 10.

CAT. 206 – *La Modiste*, (K752, AB 382), 1914, signed, 21 x 14 ¾ in. (54 x 37.5 cm). Edition: 10.

CAT. 207 – *Miss Charles, head only*, (K670, AB 374B), 1915, signed with initials, 17 x 12 in. (43 x 30.5 cm).

CAT. 208 – *The Chin Strap*, (K778, AB 385), 1916, signed with initials, 19 ¼ x 12 ½ in. (49 x 31.8 cm). Edition: 8.

CAT. 209 – *Printemps (Miss E. Spain)*, (K702, AB 400), 1915, 32 ¼ x 23 in. (82 x 58.5 cm). Edition: 15.

CAT. 210 – *Rieuse*, (K013, AB 89), 1903, signed, 22 x 17 ¼ in. (56 x 44 cm). Edition: 30.

CAT. 211 – *Reflections (Miss Charles)*, (K666, AB 57), 1915, 25 ¼ x 19 ¼ in. (64.5 x 49 cm). Edition: 10.

CAT. 212 – *Mrs. H.V. Milbank in her bedroom*, (K151, AB 188), 1908, 26 x 18 ½ in. (66 x 46.5 cm). Edition: 5.

CAT. 213 – *Madame Fleury, profile*, (K342, AB 254), 1907, 27 ¼ x 19 ¾ in. (69.5 x 50.5 cm). Edition: 10.

CAT. 214 – *The Garter*, (K113, AB 354), 1913, 19 x 12 in. (48.4 x 30.5 cm). Edition: 10.

CAT. 215 – *Lili, bust, 3/4 profile to right*, (K021, AB 562), c.1903, 15 x 10 ¼ in. (37 x 26.2 cm). Edition: 3.

CAT. 216 – *Invitation, petite tête mantille*, (K325, AB 167), 1904, signed, 16 ¾ x 12 ¼ in. (43 x 30.7 cm). Edition: 30.

CAT. 217 – *Miss Stuart*, (K710, AB 99), signed with initials, 1917, 17 x 13 ½ in. (43 x 34.3 cm). Edition: 10.

CAT. 218 – *Petite tête penchée, profile*, (K448, AB 166), 1905, 16 ½ x 12 ¾ in. (42.2 x 32.3 cm). Edition: 10.

CAT. 219 – *Le Canapé Louis XV*, (K118, AB 348), 1914, 28 x 19 ¼ in. (70.5 x 48.5 cm). Edition: 10.

CAT. 220 – *Leone*, (K276, AB 147), 1910, inscribed "Pepita", 30 ¾ x 23 in. (78 x 58.4 cm). Edition: 10.

CAT. 221 – *Holidays, Goodbye*, (K726, AB 444), 1917, signed with initials, 15 ½ x 9 ½ in. (39.5 x 24 cm).

CAT. 222 – *Le Petit velours*, (K766, AB 389), 1915, 23 x 18 in. (58.5 x 47.8 cm). Edition: 15.

CAT. 223 – *Fleury Seated Looking Right*, (K341, AB 701), 1905 (?), 17 5/8 x 11 ½ in. (44.5 x 29 cm). Edition: 1.

CAT. 224 – *Angélique*, (K119, AB 345), 1915, 24 x 16 1/2 in. (61 x 42 cm). Edition: 10.

CAT. 225 – *Tête de profile avec chapeau*, (K001, AB 111), 1901, 23 x 18 ¼ in. (58.5 x 47 cm). Edition: 10.

CAT. 226 – *Double Portrait of Woman*, (K451, AB 171C), 1905, signed, 13 ¾ x 11 1/4 in. (35.5 x 28 cm).

CAT. 227 – *Madame Newout? (Newoul?)*, (K327, AB 445), 1909, 19 ½ x 13 ¾ in. (50 x 35.3 cm). Edition: 6.

CAT. 228 – *Mabel in a Beret*, (K657, AB 363B), 1914, signed, 22 x 17 ½ in. (56 x 44 cm). Edition: 10.

CAT. 229 – *Madame Fleury, sur la table*, (K344, AB 259), 1908, signed, 23 x 17 ½ in. (58.5 x 45.5 cm).

CAT. 230 – *The Signet Way*, (K764, AB 365), 1915, 22 x 15 in. (56.3 x 38 cm).

CAT. 231 – *Joselyne, tête blonde penchée sur épaule*, (K265, AB 521), c.1903, 28 x 19 ¾ in. (71.5 x 50 cm).

CAT. 232 – *Indécision*, (K740, AB 353), 1913, signed, 20 ¼ x 14 ¾ in. (51.5 x 37.5 cm). Edition: 5.

CAT. 233 – *Woman with Bow in back*, (K496, AB 71.1), 1910 (?), 14 ½ x 10 ½ in. (36 x 26.7 cm).

CAT. 234 – *Mariane*, (K289, AB 247), 1908, signed, 10 ¼ x 7 ¾ in. (26 x 19.5 cm) printed recto verso. Edition: 25.

CAT. 235 – *Lavinia (large hat)*, (K646, AB 341), 1915, signed, 21 ½ x 14 ¼ in. (54.5 x 35.5 cm). Edition: 10.

CAT. 236 – *Sporting Style, Portrait Bust*, (K697, AB 751B), 1914, 22 x14 ¾ in. (56 x 37.5 cm).

CAT. 237 – *Madame Newout?(Newoul?)*, (K327, AB 445), 1909, signed, 7 ¾ x 5 ¾ in. (20 x 15 cm). Edition: 6.

CAT. 238 – *Maltese Cape*, (K279, AB 308), 1909, signed with initials, 13 ¾ x 8 ½ in. (35 x 21.5 cm). Edition: 10.

CAT. 239 – *Hooded woman, profile*, (K823, AB 775), signed with initials, 20 ¼ x 13 ¼ in. (51.2 x 33.3 cm). Edition: 1.

CAT. 240 – *Miss Charles 3/4 profile*, (K658, AB 374), 1914, signed with initials, 22 ¼ x 16 ½ in. (56 x 43 cm). Edition: 10.

CAT. 241 – *Marthe portrait*, (K296, AB 250), 1907, signed, 19 x 11 ¾ in. (48.5 x 30 cm). Edition: 30.

CAT. 242 – *Madame Fleury, portrait*, (K343, AB 255), 1907, 22 ¾ x 18 ¼ in. (58 x 46.7 cm). Edition: 10.

CAT. 243 – *Alice, bust portrait, with long hair (4 yrs)*, (K165, AB 543), c. 1920, 19 x 14 ½ in. (48 x 37 cm). Edition: 4.

CAT. 244 – *Pepita*, (K487, AB 276), 1908, 22 ¾ x 18 in. (58 x 45 cm). Edition: 8.

CAT. 245 – *Femme de profil, Lili*, (K053, AB 106), 1906, signed, 25 ½ x 19 ¾ in. (65 x 50 cm). Edition: 10.

CAT. 246 – *Alice, age 3-4*, (K163, AB 901), c.1916, 22 ½ x 17 ½ in. (57.2 x 44.5 cm).

CAT. 247 – *Priscilla, portrait*, (K351, AB 763), 1909 (?), 22 x 17 ½ in. (56 x 44.5 cm).

CAT. 248 – *Miss Eva Ames,* (K183, AB 319), 1909, 24 ¾ x 19 in. (63 x 48 cm). Edition: 12.

CAT. 249 – *Contemplation*, (K418, AB 33), 1903, 28 ½ x 21 ¾ in. (72.3 x 55.3 cm). Edition: 15.

CAT. 250 – *Indécision*, (K740, AB 353), 1913, signed, 20 ¼ x 14 ¾ in. (51.5 x 37.5 cm). Edition: 5.

CAT. 251 – *Alice Milbank with terrier*, (K130, AB 781), 1902 (?), 16 ¼ x 10 ½ in. (41 x 26.8 cm). Edition: 5.

CAT. 252 – *Alice, age 4-5 (?)*, (K162, AB 931), c.1915, 8 ¾ x 7 ¾ in. (22.6 x 19.8 cm).

CAT. 253 – *Tête de femme*, (K350, AB 59B), 1909, signed, 25 ¾ x 19 ¾ in. (65.5 x 50.5 cm). Edition: 5.

CAT. 254 – *Pensive Woman*, (K253, AB 364B), 1907 (?), signed, 20 ¼ x 14 ½ in. (51.5 x 37 cm).

CAT. 255 – *Berthe au café*, (K197, AB 59), 1904, signed with initials, 16 ½ x 12 ¾ in. (42 x 32.5 cm). Edition: 15.

CAT. 256 – *Rosette*, (K524, AB 299), 1909, signed, 20 ¼ x 14 ½ in. (51.2 x 36.5 cm). Edition: 10.

CAT. 257 – *Madame Leonardi, Visite Nini*, (K340, AB 191), 1905, signed, 23 ¾ x 19 ½ in. (60.5 x 49 cm). Edition: 20.

CAT. 258 – *Joyce, large portrait*, (K644, AB 629), 1924, 25 ¼ x 18 ¾ in. (64 x 47.5 cm). Edition: 10.

CAT. 259 – *Petite Julia, bust profile*, (K121, AB 538), c.1915, 13 ¼ x 10 ½ in. (33.5 x 27 cm). Edition: 1.

CAT. 260 – *Nayade*, (K523, AB 607), 1910 (?), signed with initials, 24 ¼ x 18 in. (61.5 x 45.5 cm).

CAT. 261 – *Yvette, arms not crossed*, (K390, AB 77), 1905, signed, 22 ¼ x 16 ½ in. (36.5 x 42 cm). Edition: 10.

CAT. 262 – *The Little Maid*, (K603, AB 391), 1915, 26 ½ x 19 ¾ in. (67.5 x 50 cm). Edition: 10.

CAT. 263 – *In the Evening, Dorothy* (?), (K601, AB 758), 1914, 23 ¾ x 19 ½ in. (65.5 x 50 cm). Edition: 5.

CAT. 264 – *Dorothy holding a punt*, (K604, AB 734), c.1915, 27 ¾ x 20 ¼ in. (70.7 x 51.3 cm). Edition: 10.

CAT. 265 – *Seated woman with Riding Crop on Knees*, (K425, AB 667), c.1903, 24 ¼ x 19 ¼ in. (62 x 48.8 cm). Edition: 2.

CAT. 266 – *Fiamette (Salvat)*, (K367, AB 235), 1907, 28 ¾ x 20 in. (73 x 50.5 cm). Edition: 20.

CAT. 267 – *The Boa*, (K145, AB 148), 1906, signed, 28 x 19 ½ in. (71 x 49.5 cm). Edition: 20.

CAT. 268 – *Croquis (Lili)*, (K016, AB 558), c.1903, signed with initials, 19 ¾ x 14 ½ in. (50.5 x 36.5 cm). Edition: 1.

CAT. 269 – *Femme nue de dos*, (K544, AB 5), 1905, 27 ½ x 18 in. (70 x 45.5 cm). Edition: 10.

CAT. 270 – *Petite femme accoudée "Mantille"*, (K745, AB 472), 1913, 19 x 13 in. (48.2 x 32.8 cm). Edition: 6.

CAT. 271 – *Alice Leclanche*, (K271, AB 208), 1906, signed with initials, 23 ¾ x 15 ½ in. (60.5 x 39.5 cm). edition: 15.

CAT. 272 – *Chiffon Pregnant with Alice*, (K097, AB 351), 1911, 16 ¼ x 11 ¾ in. (41.5 x 29.8 cm). Edition: 10.

CAT. 273 – *Deux femmes assises, by Fin Lodge*, (K150, AB 102), 1908, signed, 22 x 15 in. (56.2 x 38 cm). Edition: 10.

CAT. 274 – *Mrs. Shaw*, (K378, AB 70), c. 1909, signed with initials, 19 ¾ x 14 ¼ in. (50.5 x 36.5 cm). Edition: 10.

CAT. 275 – *Miss Charles Clifton, profile*, (K319, AB 104), 1906, signed, 22 ¾ x 18 ½ in. (58 x 47 cm). Edition: 15.

CAT. 276 – *Double portrait of woman w. hand on head*, (K727, AB 687), signed with initials, 21 x 16 ¼ in. (53.5 x 41 cm). Edition: 1.

CAT. 277 – *Miss Joan*, (K627, AB 680), 1917, 13 ¼ x 10 ½ in. (33.5 x 26.7 cm).

CAT. 278 – *Tête de femme penchée*, (K099, AB 417), 1911 (?), 12 ¾ x 10 ¼ in. (32.5 x 25.7 cm). Edition: 10.

CAT. 279 – *Portrait of Julie*, c.1913, (K115, AB 601), 17 ¼ x 11 in. (44 x 28 cm). Edition: 4.

CAT. 280 – *Profile Portrait of a Woman*, (K181, AB 198), 1906, signed 13 ¼ x 10 ½ in. (33.5 x 26.5 cm). Edition: 15.

CAT. 281 – *Mlle Sabon, musical actress*, (K363, AB 698), c.1907, 24 ½ x 19 ¾ in. (62.5 x 50 cm). Edition: 10 (?).

CAT. 282 – *Convalescence*, (K089, AB 105), 1911,13 ¼ x 18 ½ in. (33.3 x 47.3 cm). Edition: 10.

CAT. 283 – *Femme accoudée, Lucienne (Petite Lili ?)*, (K520, AB 284), 1908, signed, 25 x 19 ¾ in. (63.7 x 50.5 cm). Edition: 5.

CAT. 284 – *Pensive, 1914*, (K663, AB 384), 1914, 23 x 17 ¾ in. (56.5 x 48.5 cm). Edition: 15.

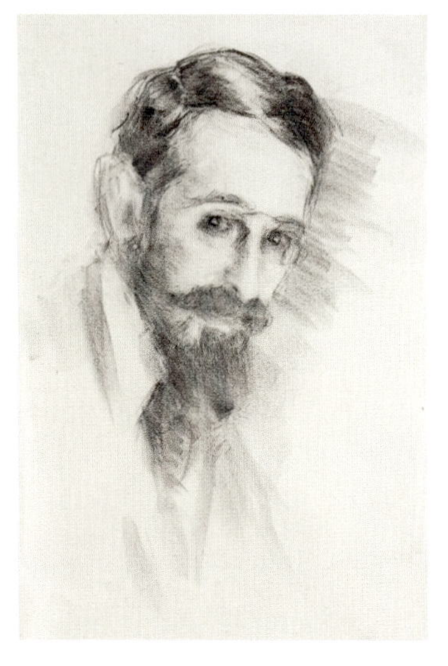

CAT. 148

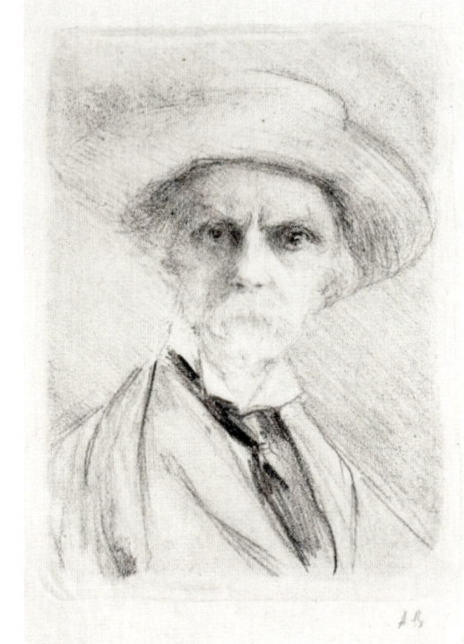

CAT. 149

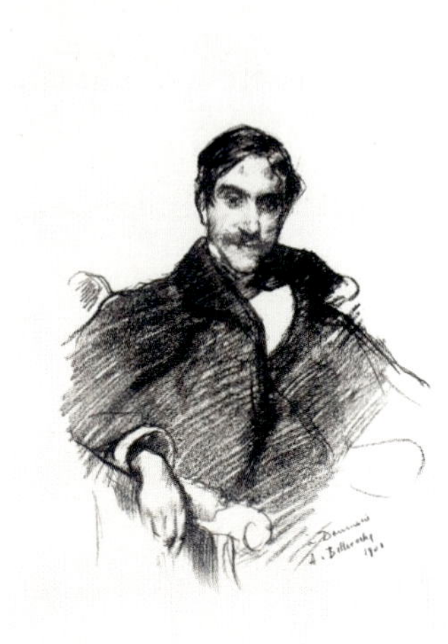

CAT. 150

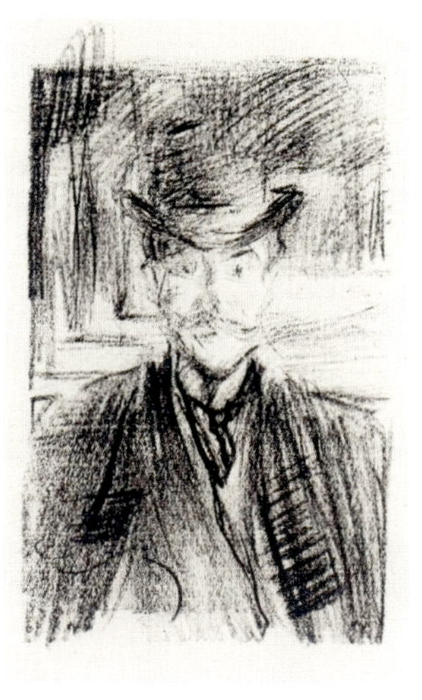

CAT. 151

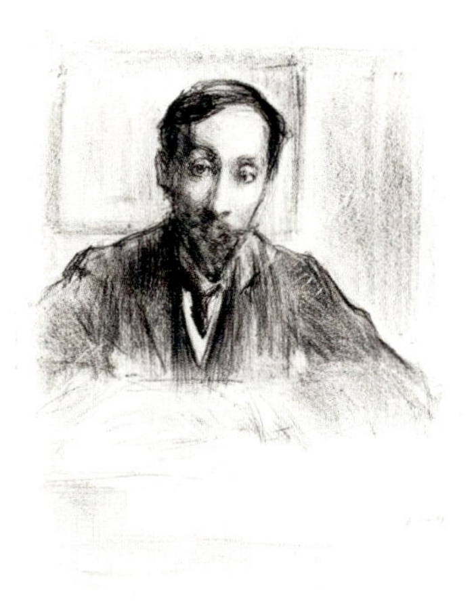

CAT. 152

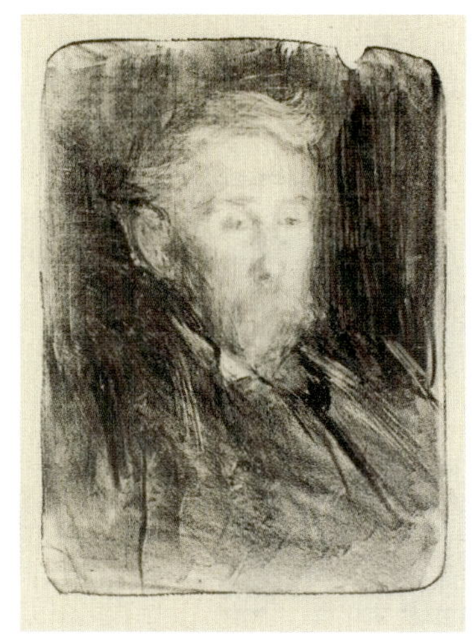

CAT. 153

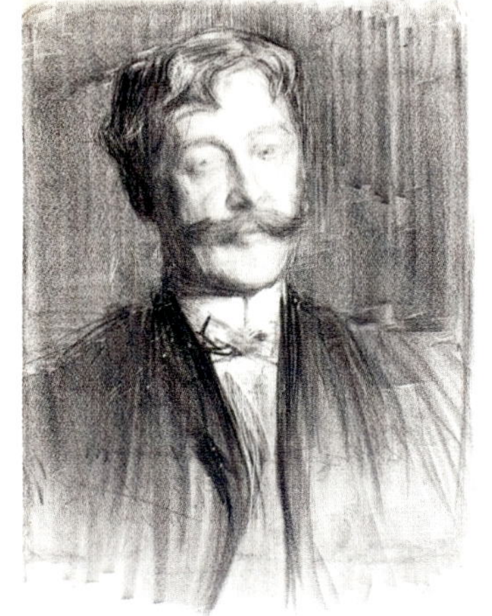

CAT. 154

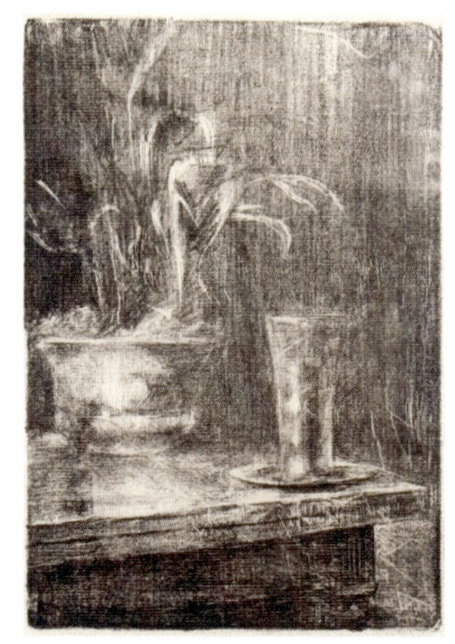

CAT. 155

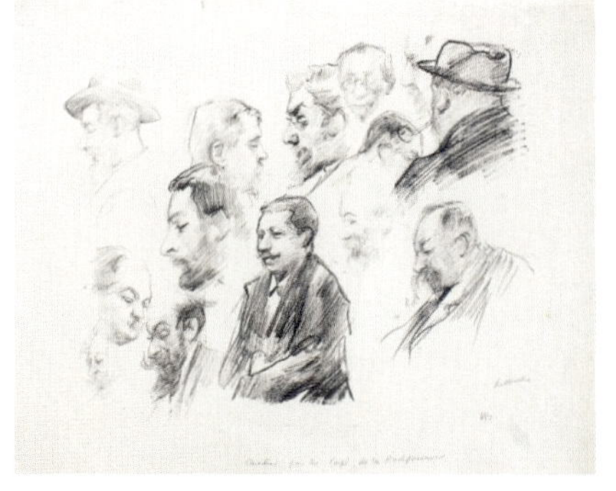

CAT. 156

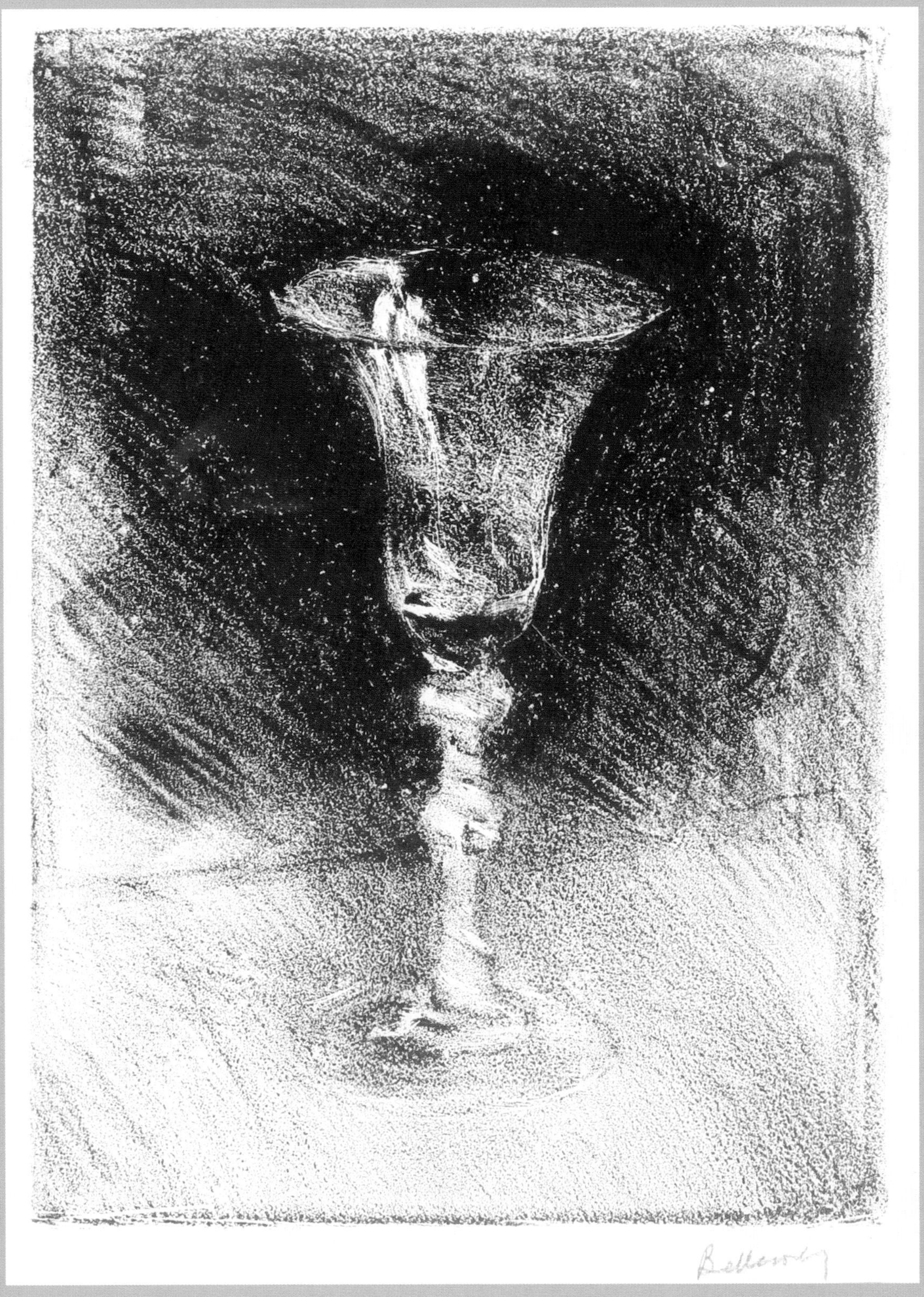

CAT. 157

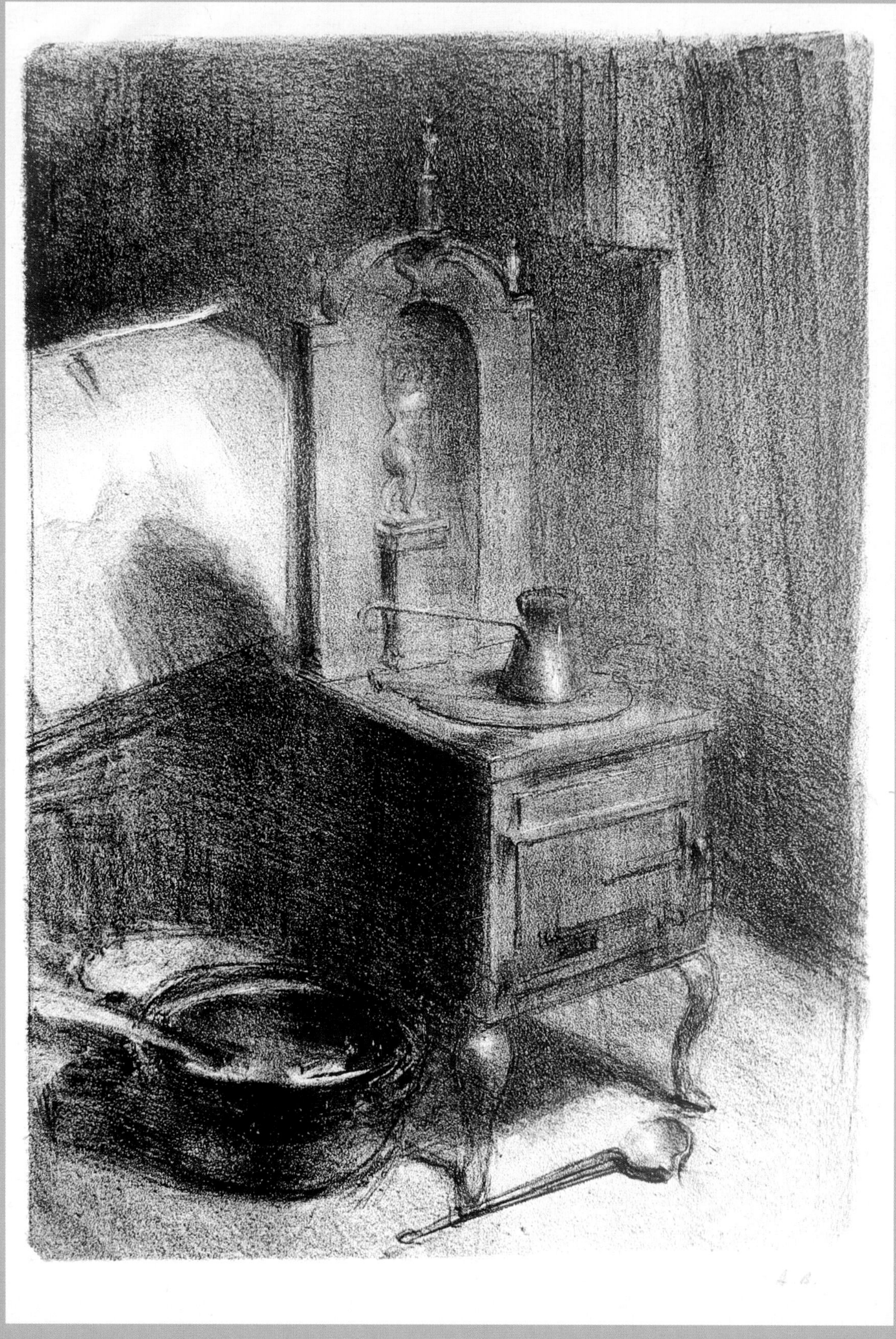

CAT. 158

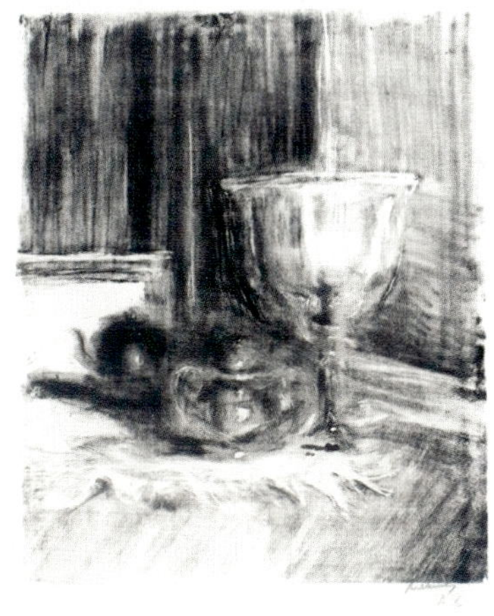

CAT. 159

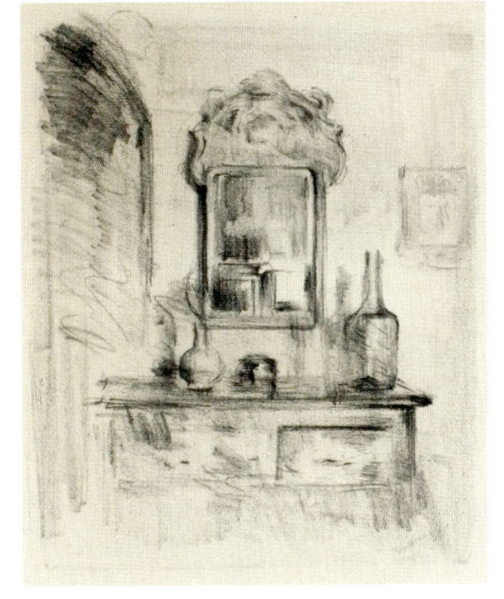

CAT. 160

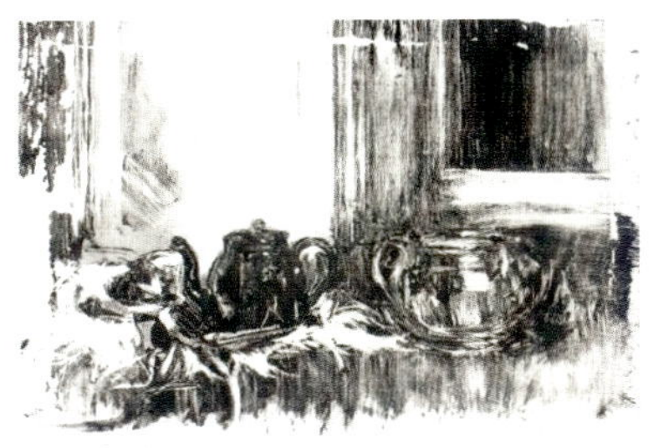

CAT. 161

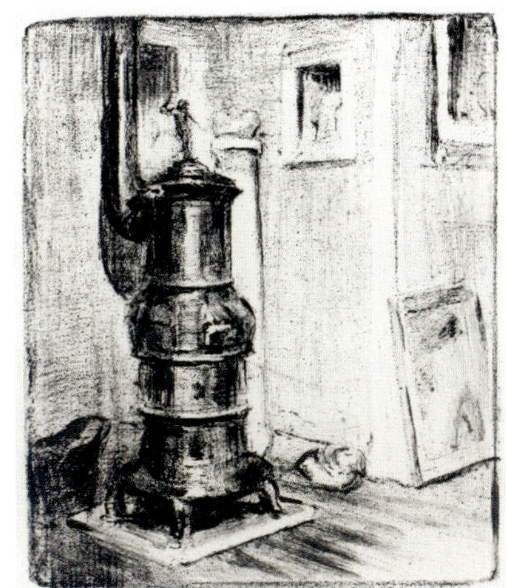

CAT. 162

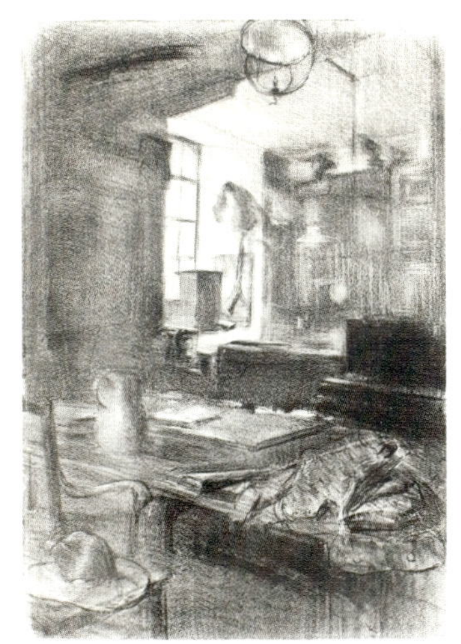

CAT. 163

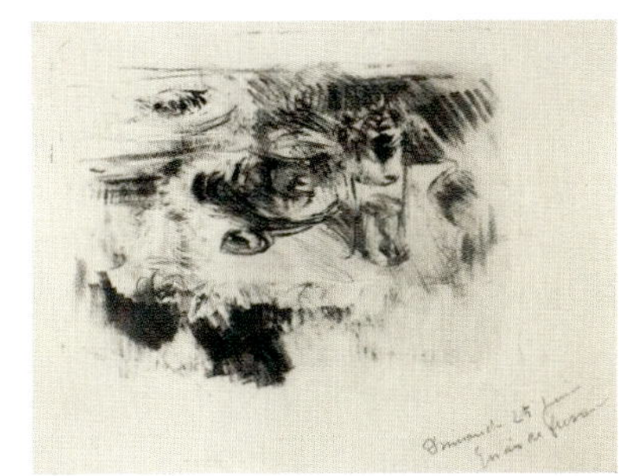

CAT. 164

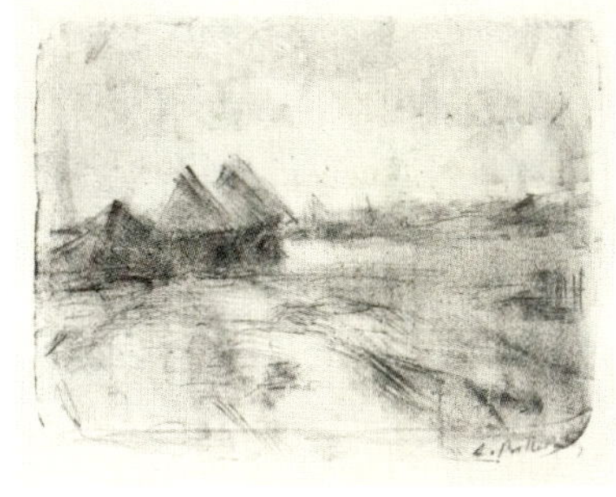

CAT. 165

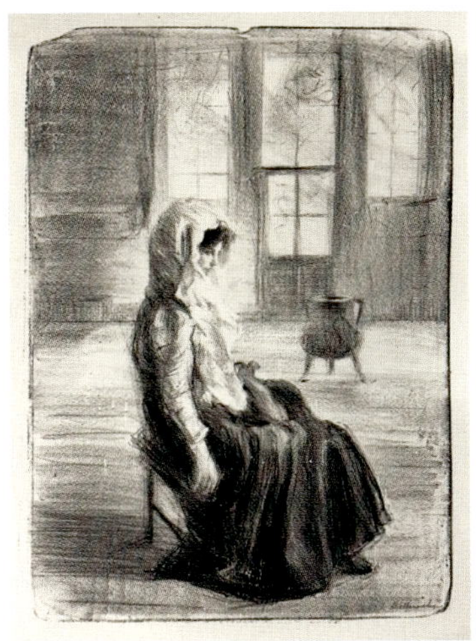

CAT. 166

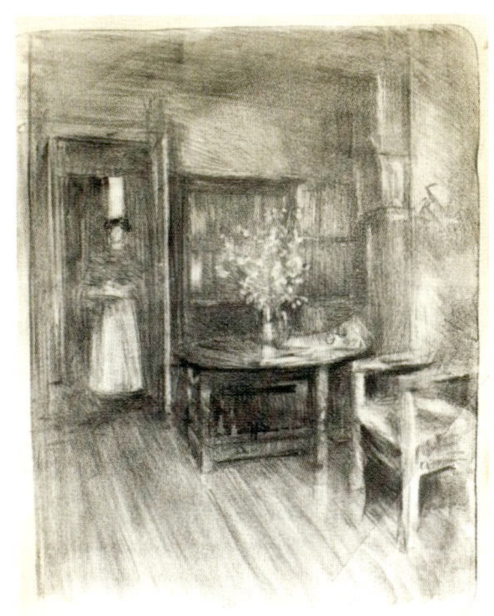

CAT. 167

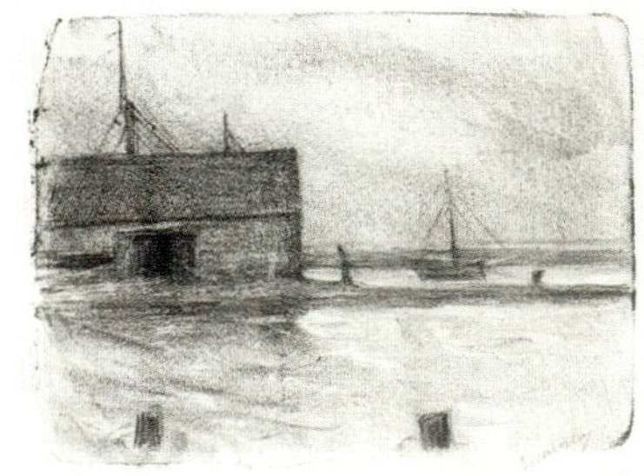

CAT. 168

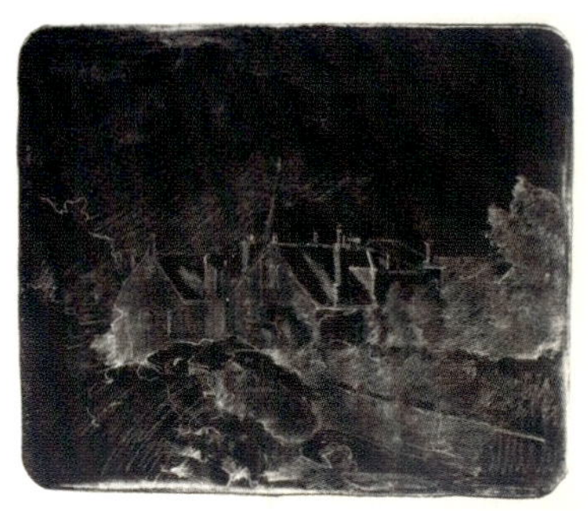

CAT. 169

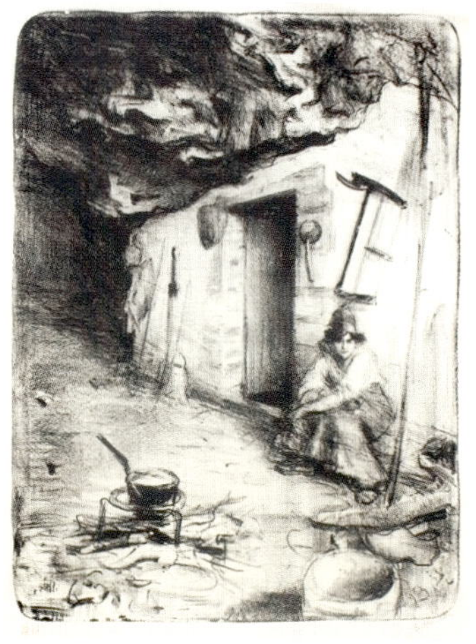

CAT. 170

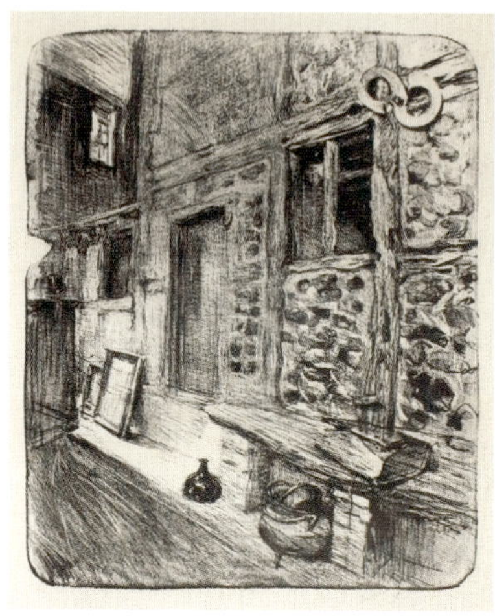

CAT. 171

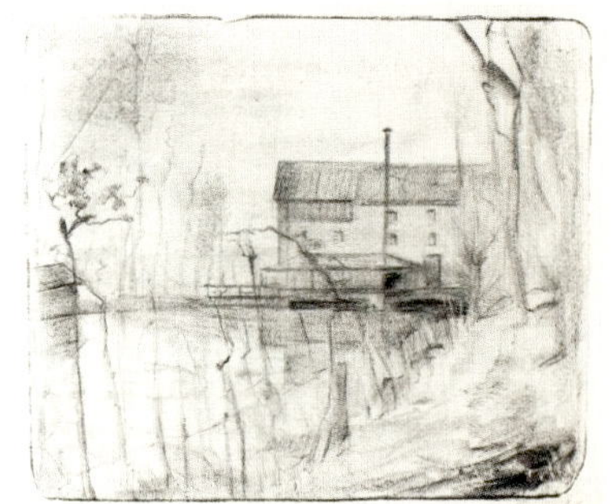

CAT. 172

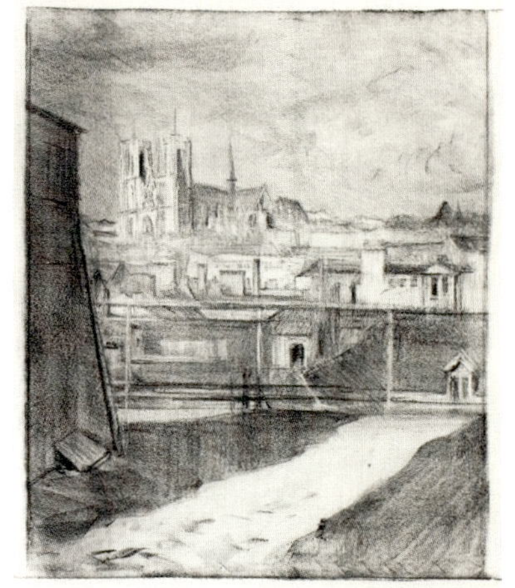

CAT. 174

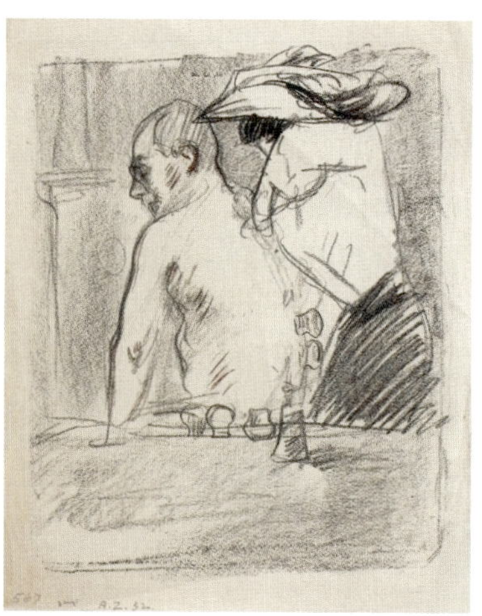

CAT. 175

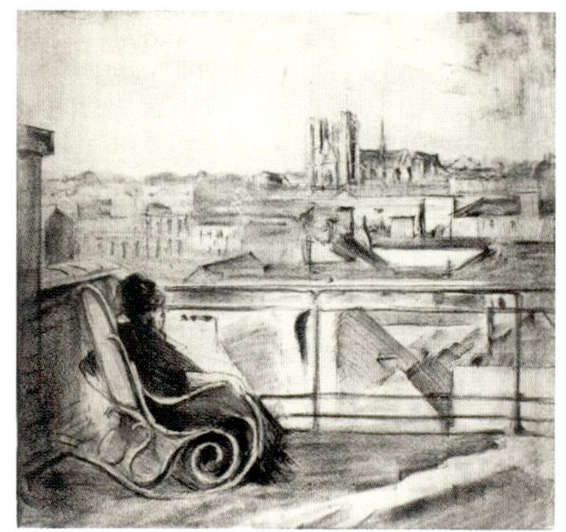

CAT. 173

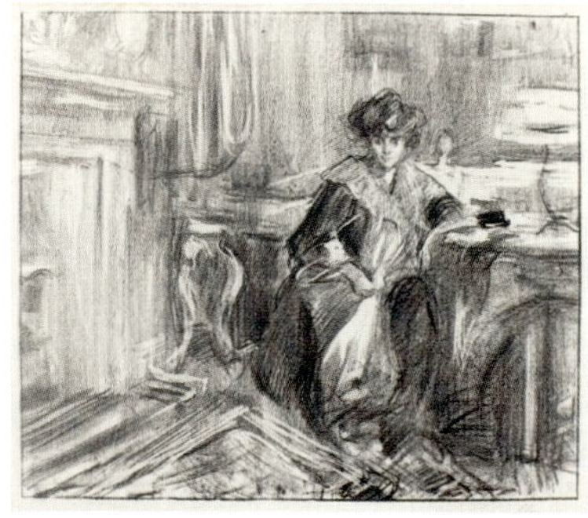

CAT. 176

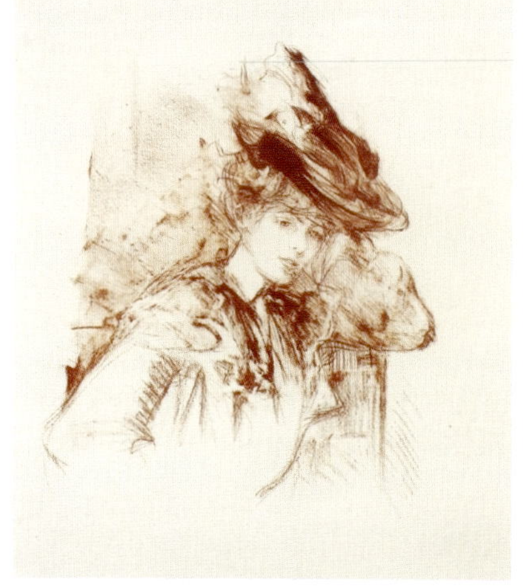

CAT. 177

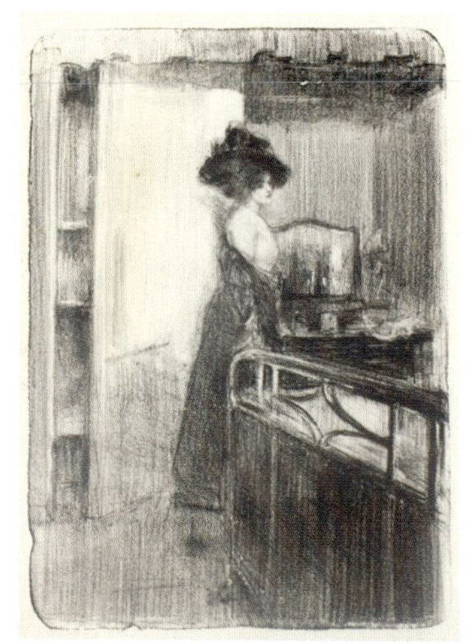

CAT. 178

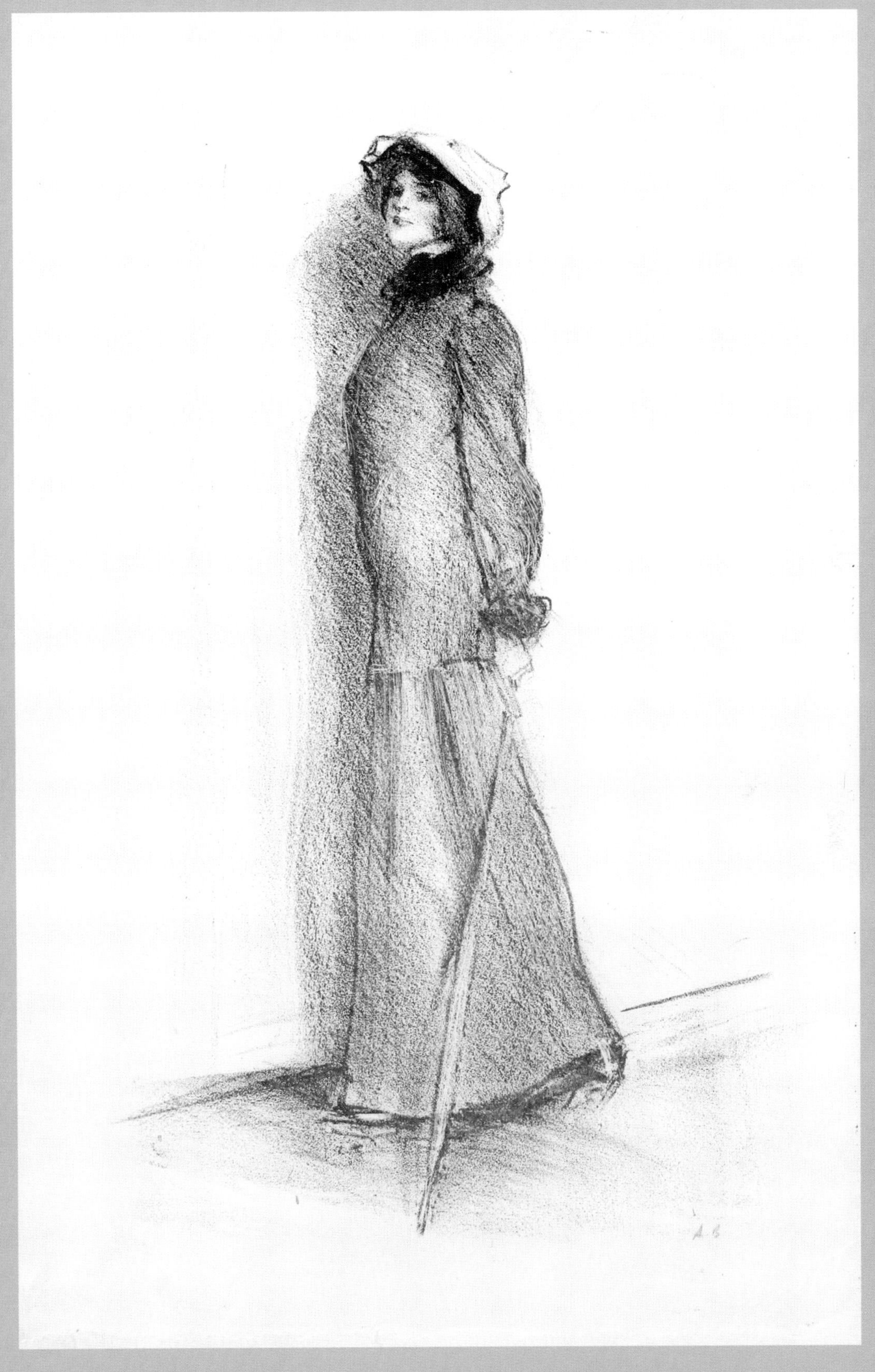

CAT. 179

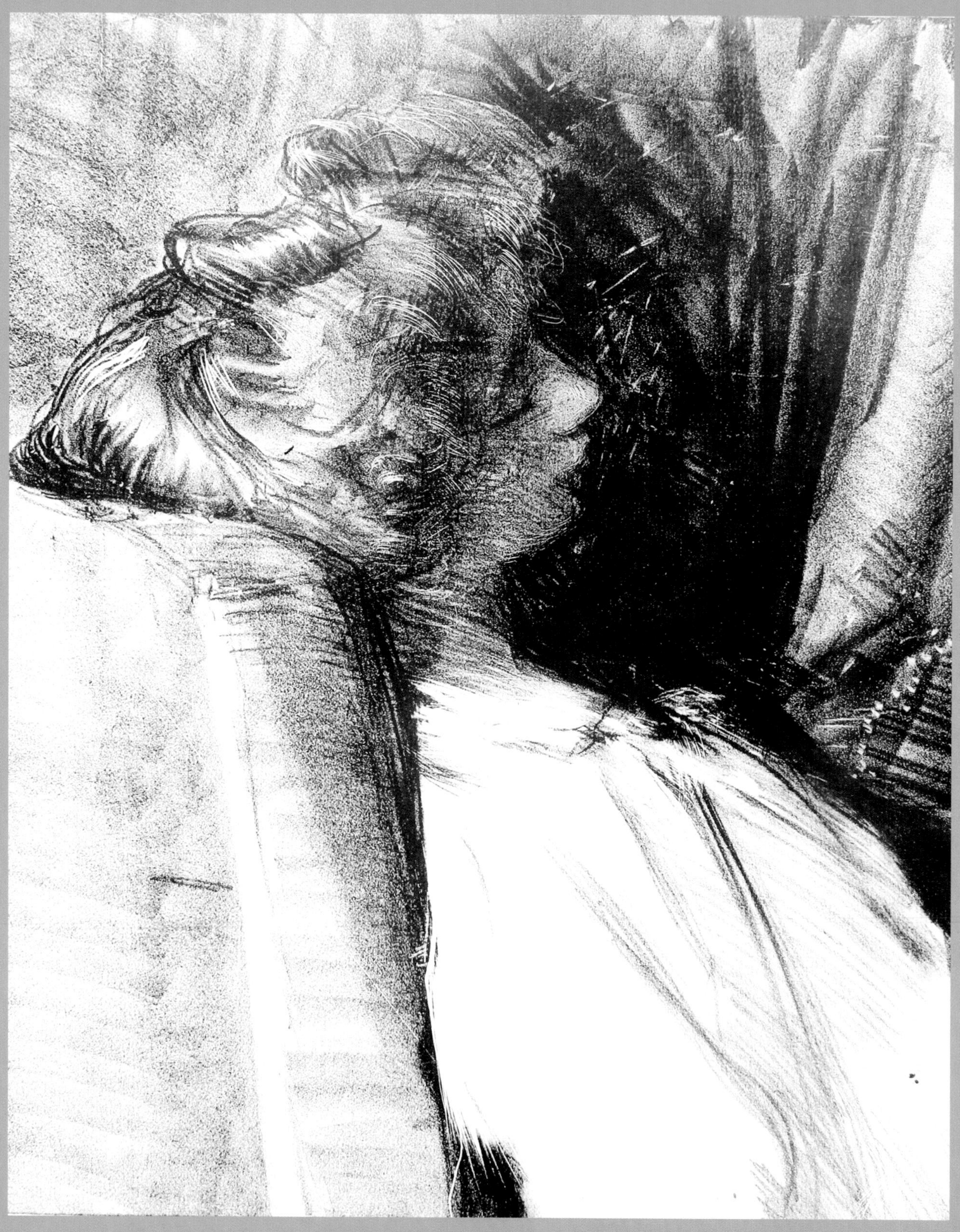

CAT. 180

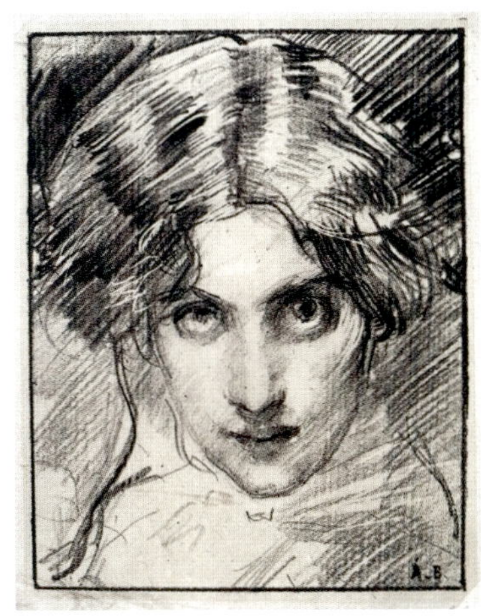

CAT. 181

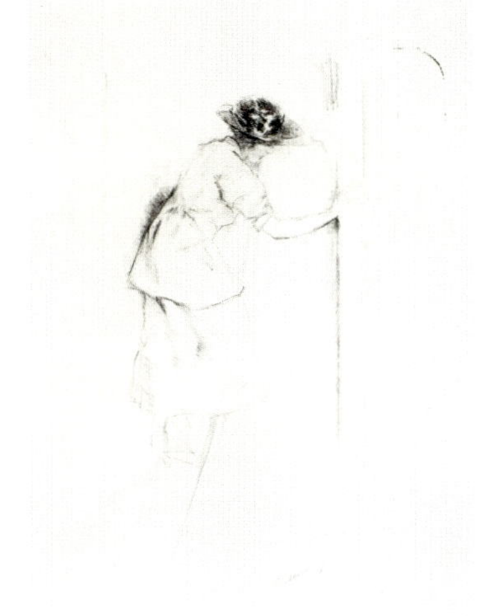

CAT. 182

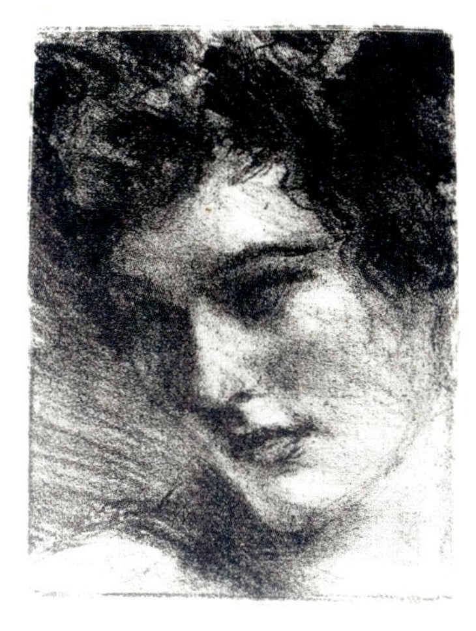

CAT. 183

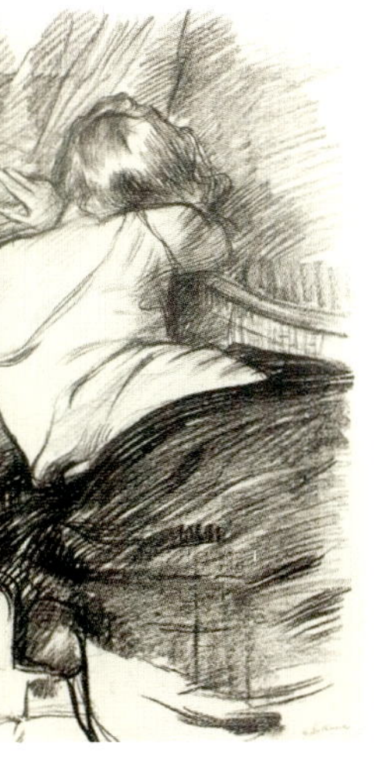

CAT. 184

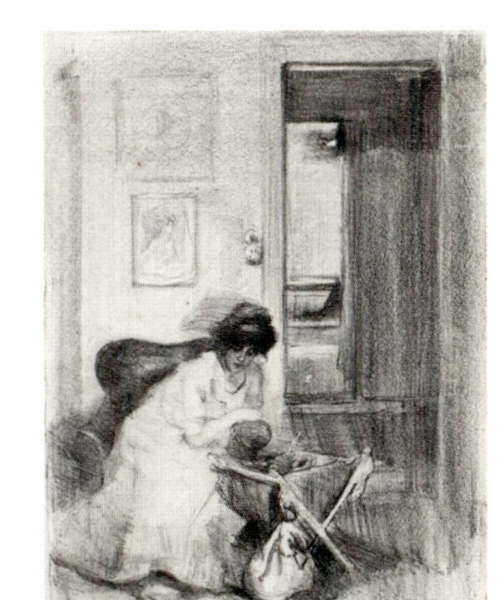

CAT. 185

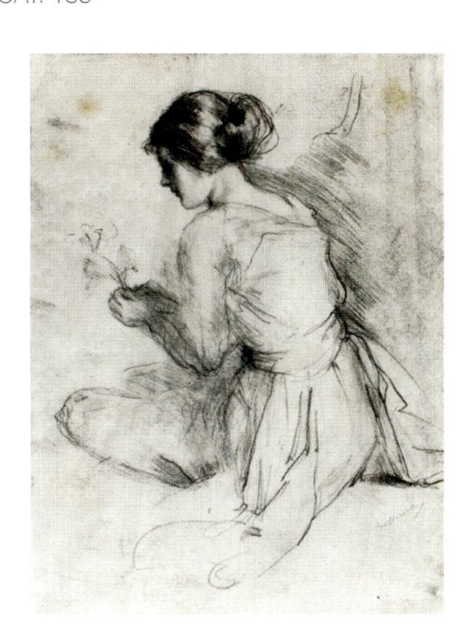

CAT. 186

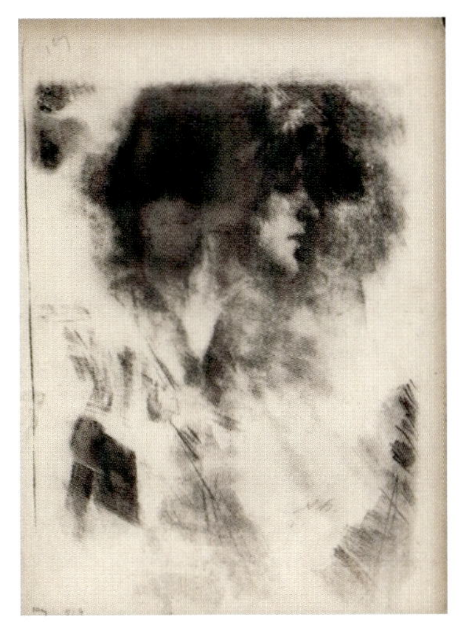

CAT. 187

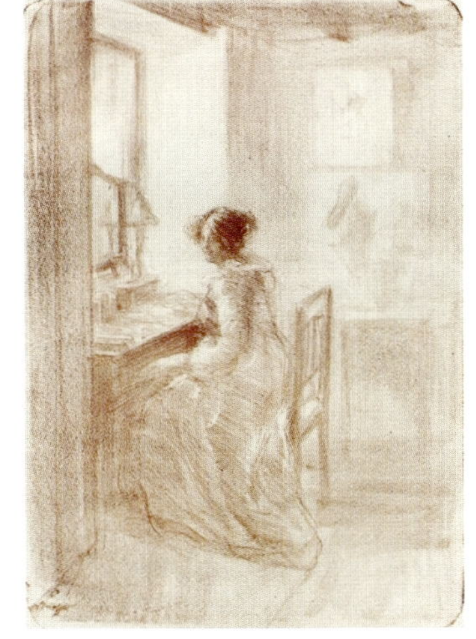

CAT. 188

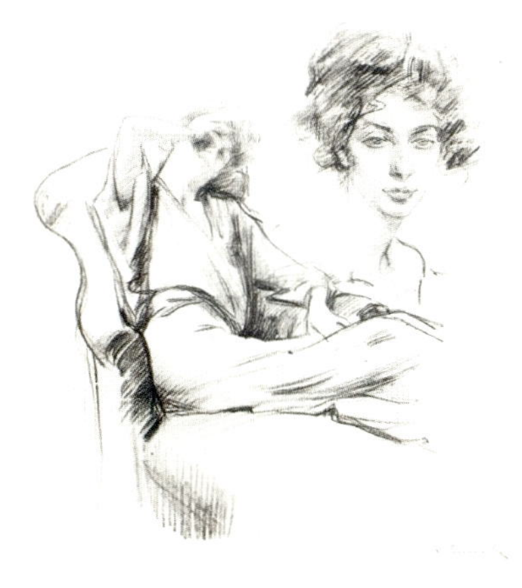

CAT. 189

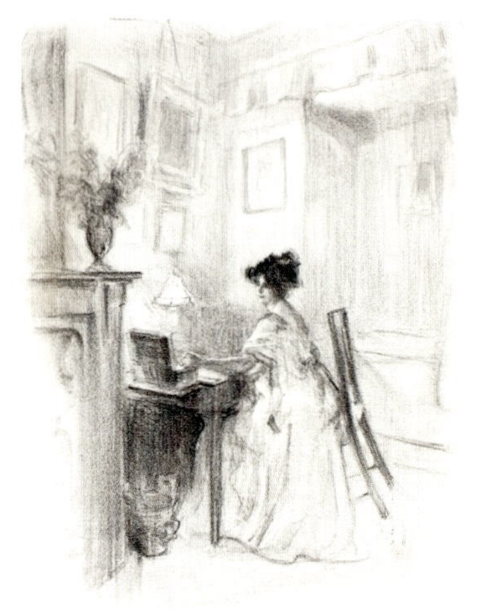

CAT. 190

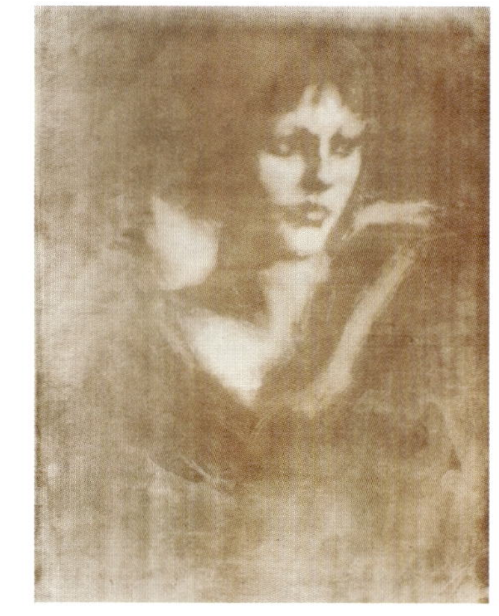

CAT. 191

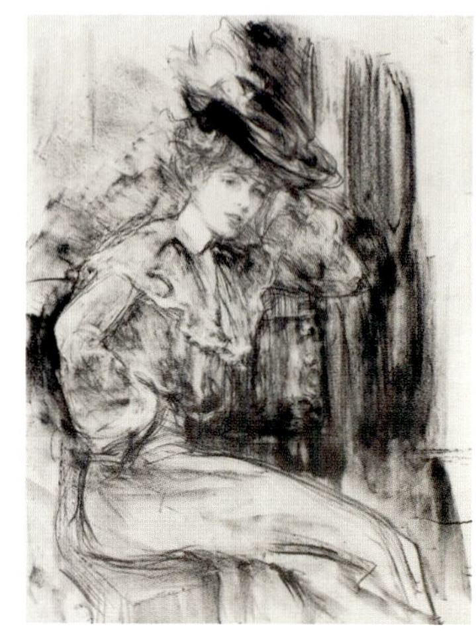

CAT. 192

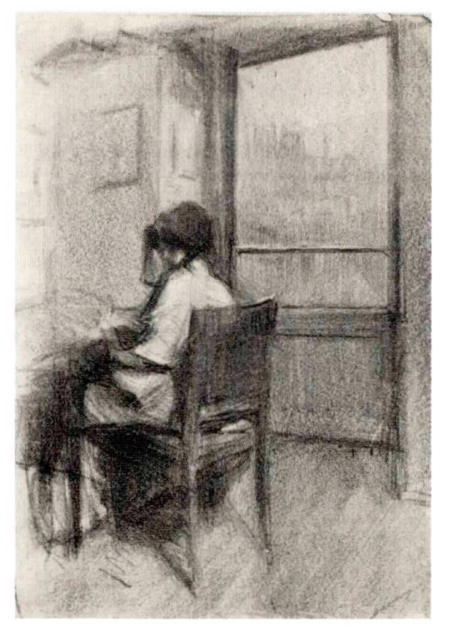

CAT. 193

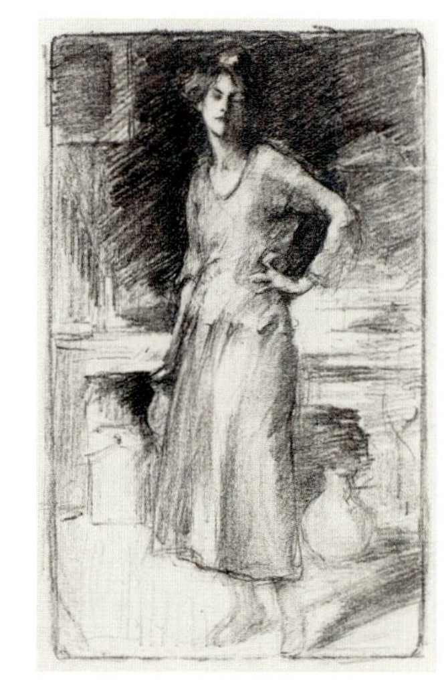

CAT. 194

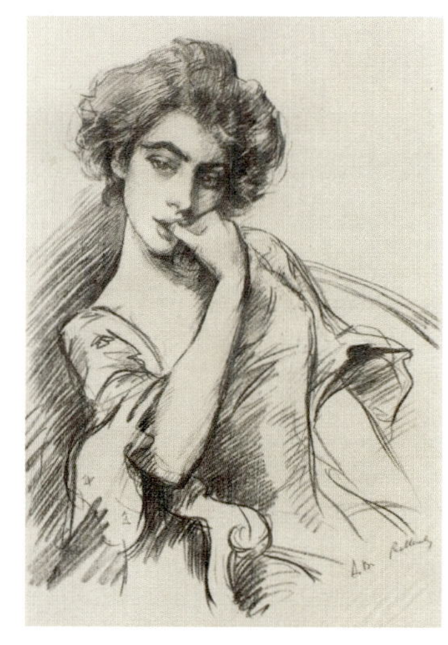

CAT. 195

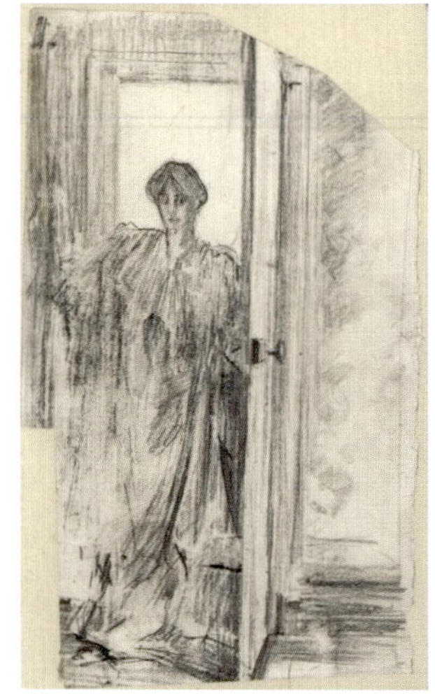

CAT. 196

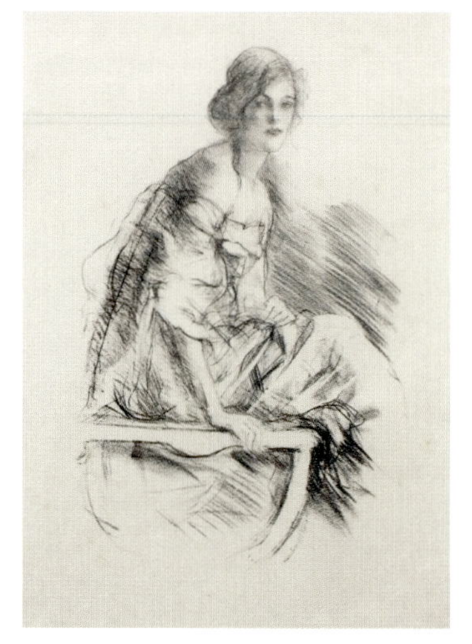

CAT. 197

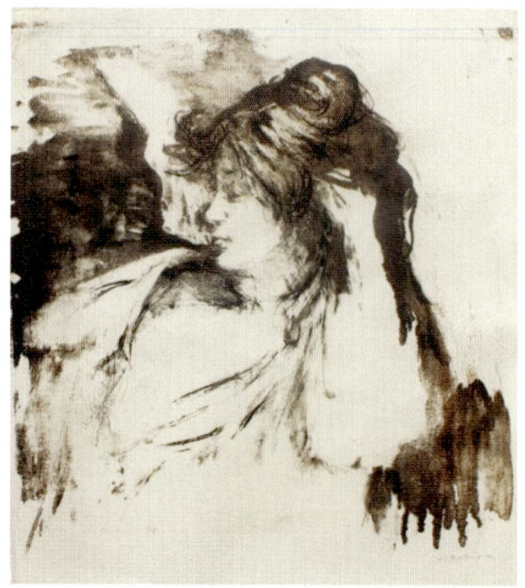

CAT. 198

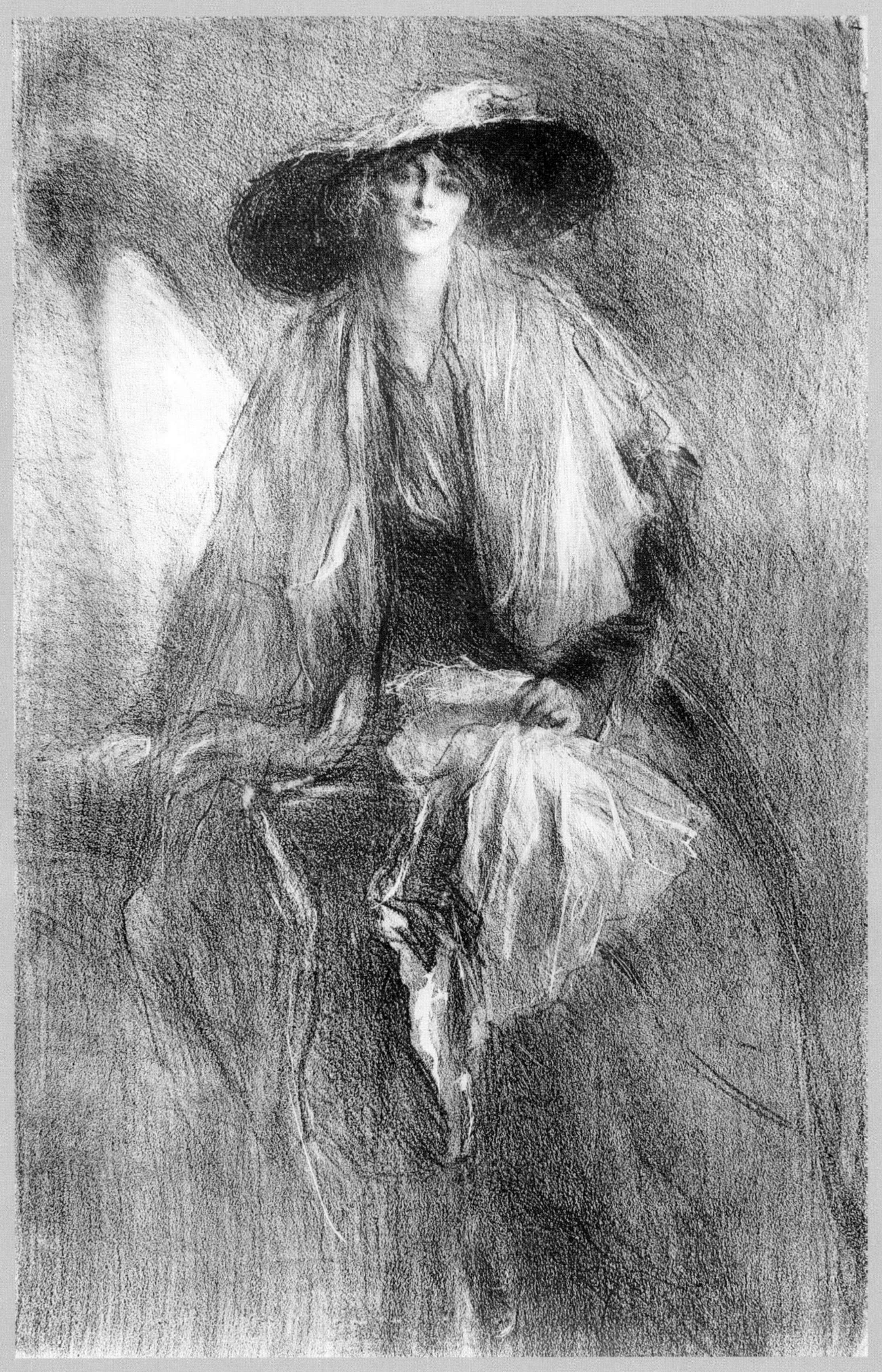

CAT. 199

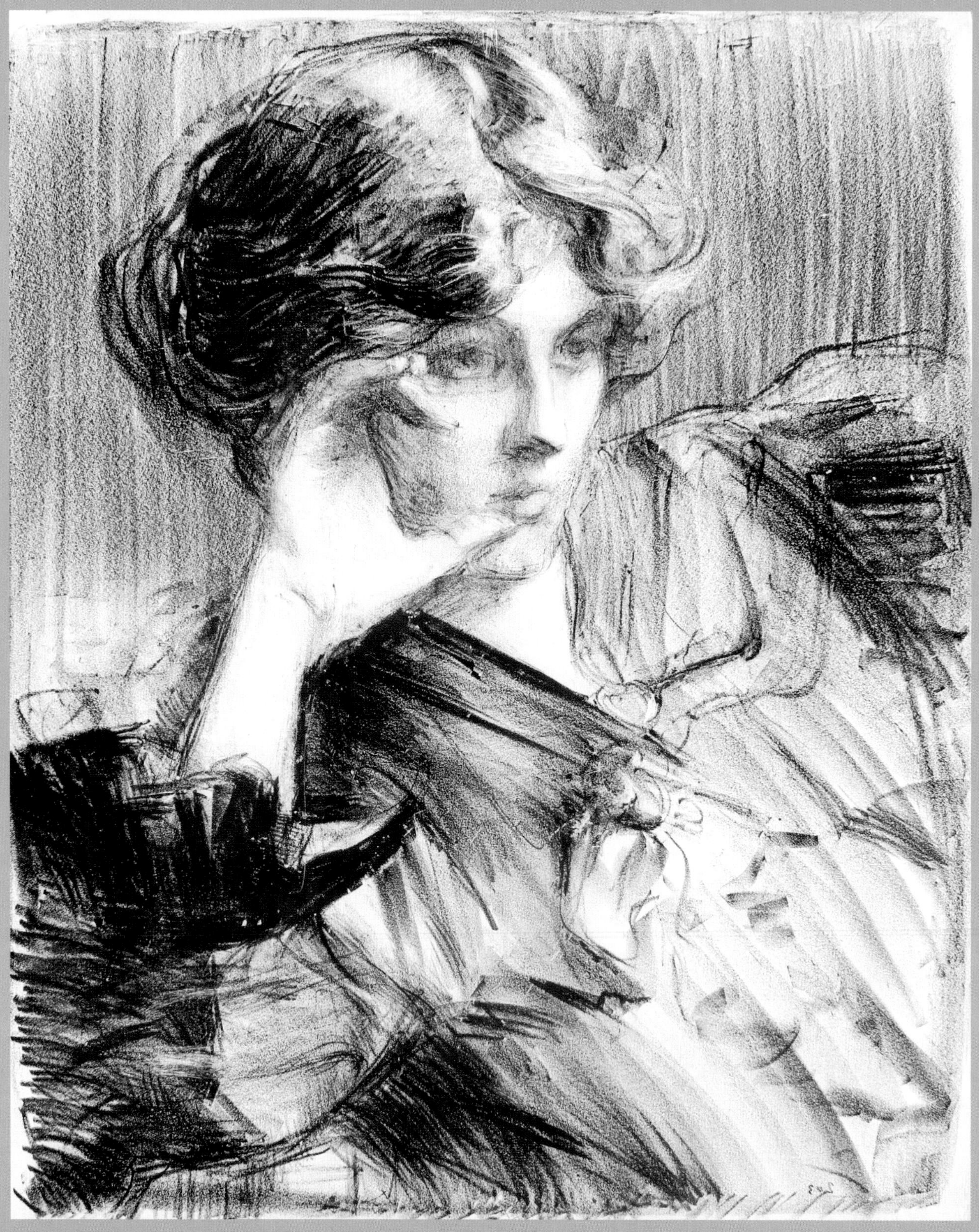

CAT. 200

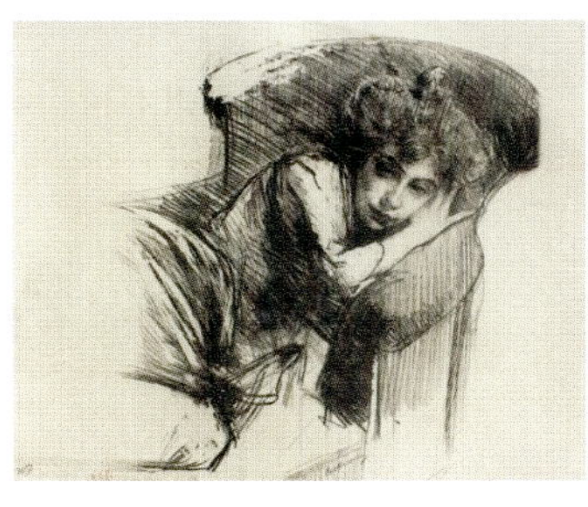

CAT. 201

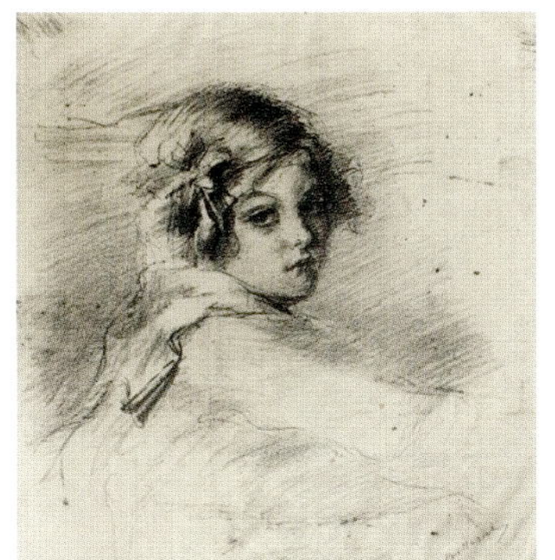

CAT. 202

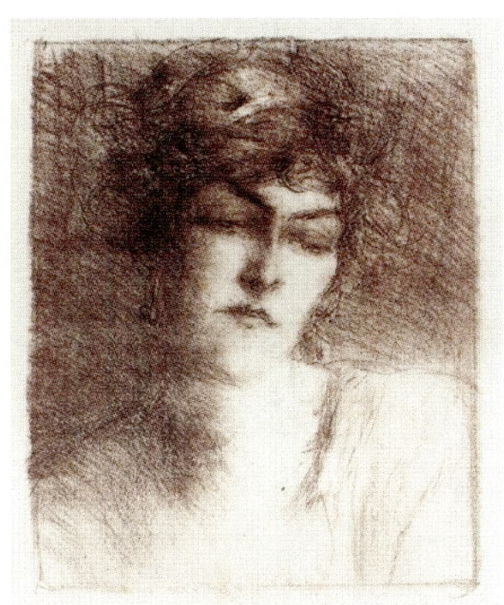

CAT. 205

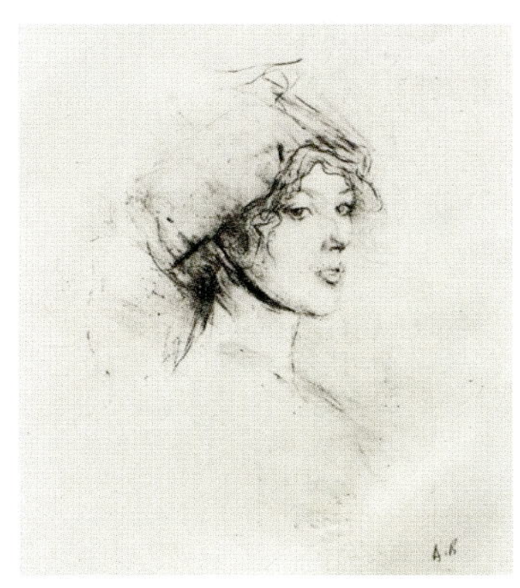

CAT. 208

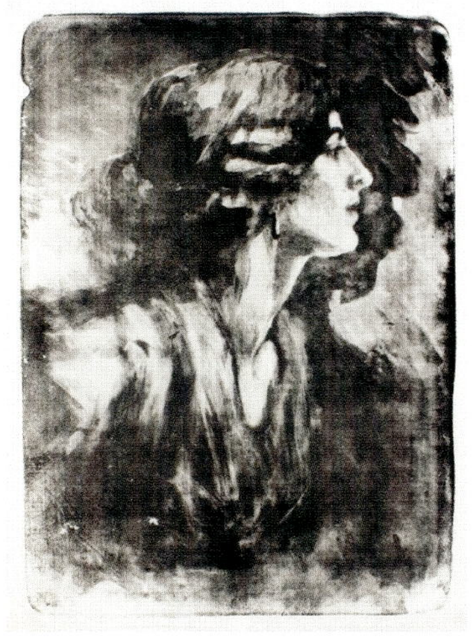

CAT. 203

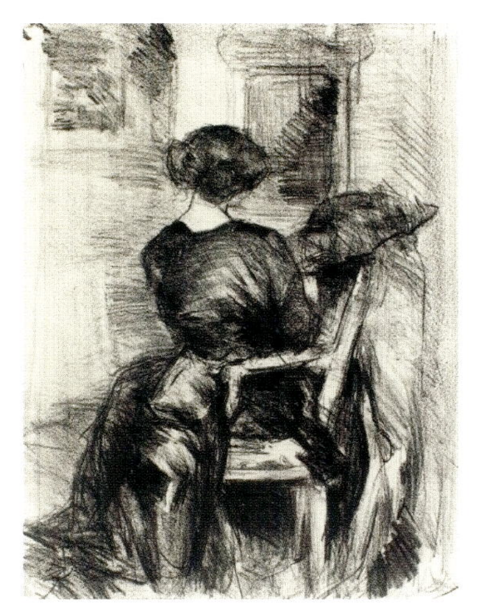

CAT. 206

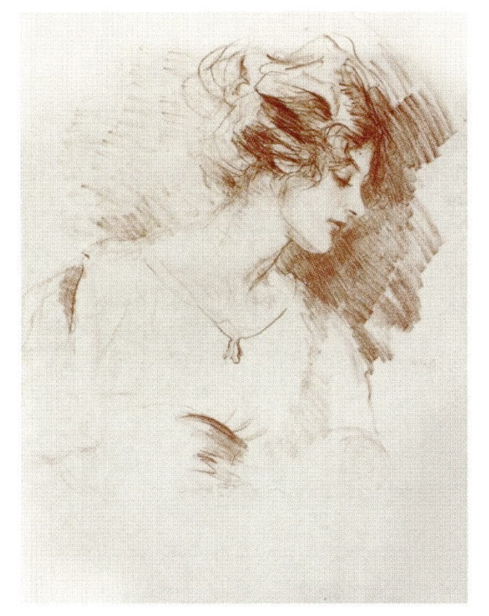

CAT. 209

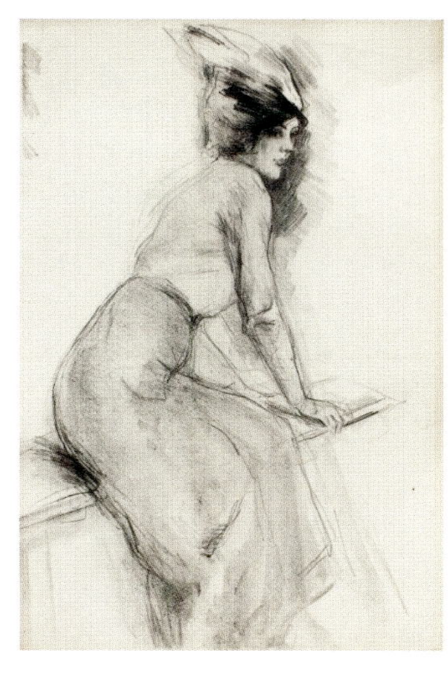

CAT. 204

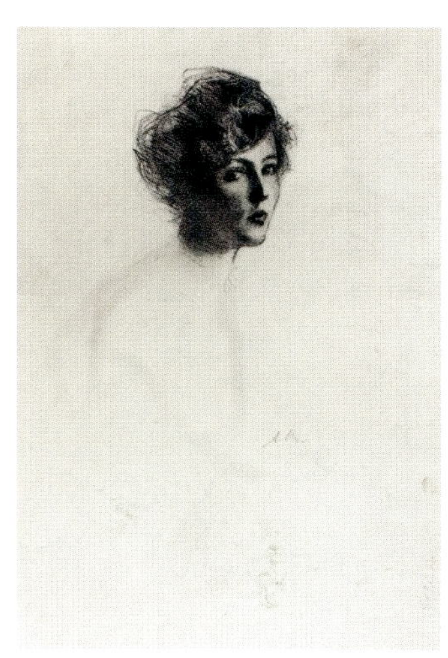

CAT. 207

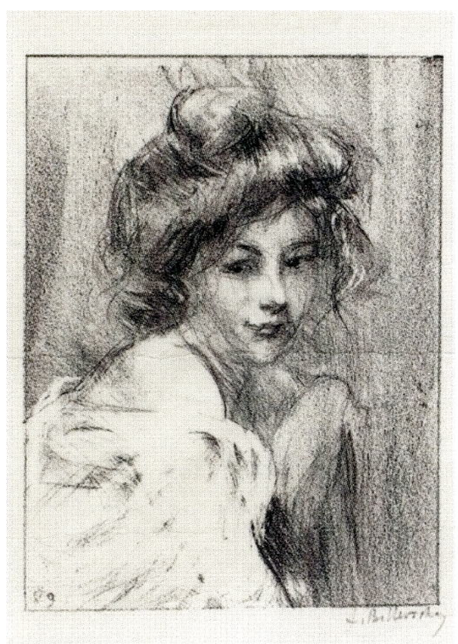

CAT. 210

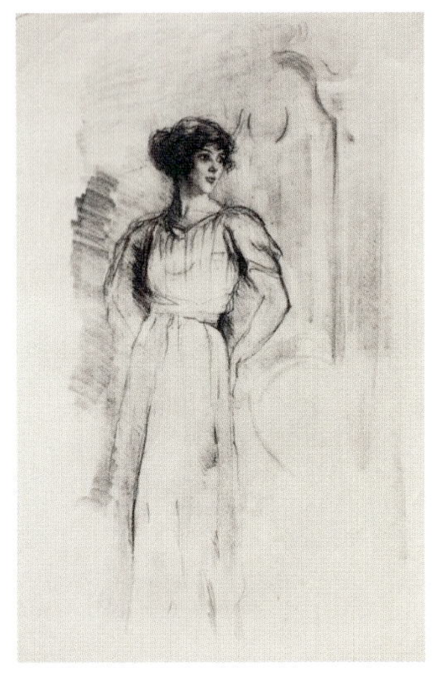

CAT. 211

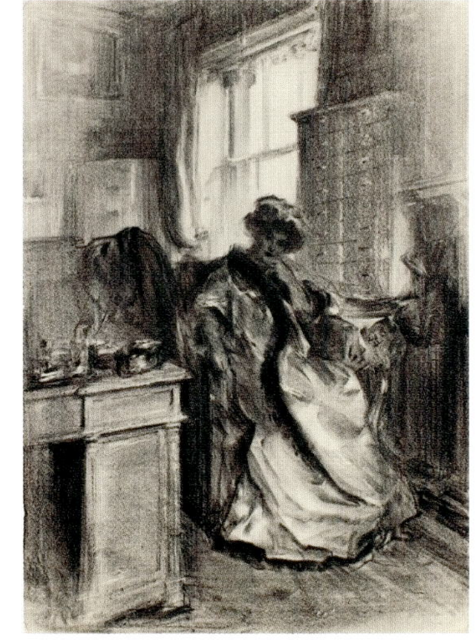

CAT. 212

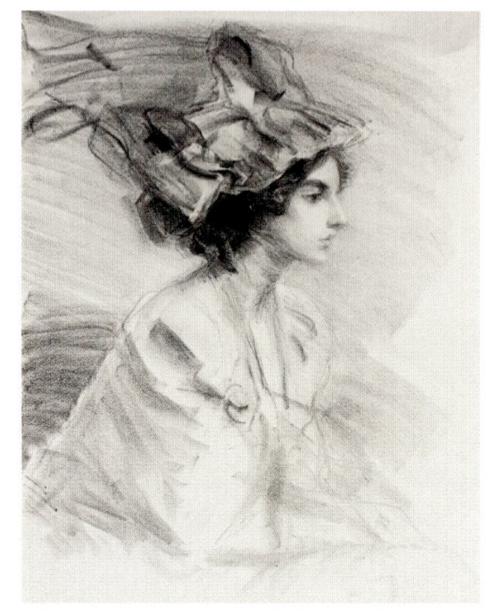

CAT. 213

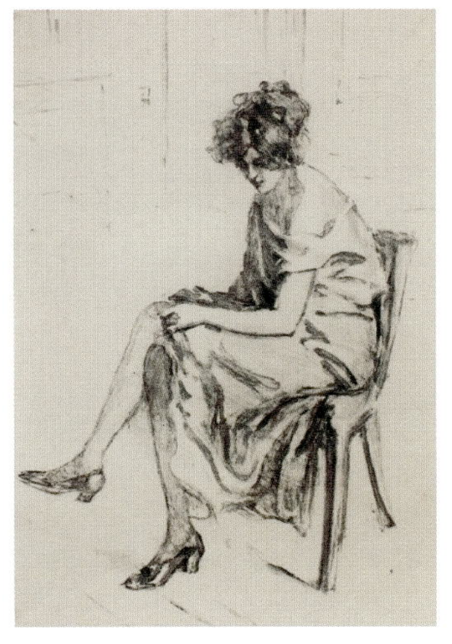

CAT. 214

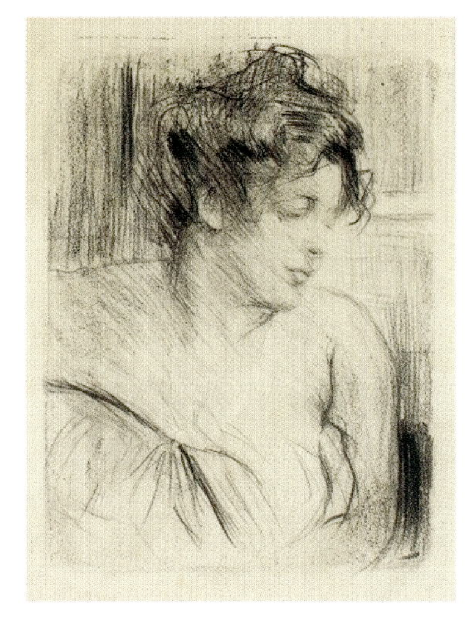

CAT. 215

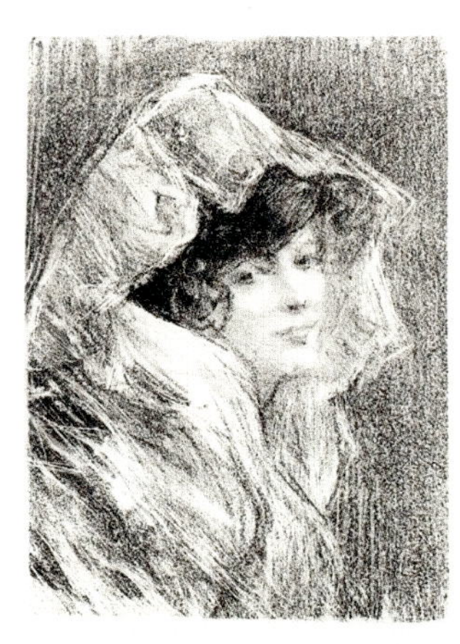

CAT. 216

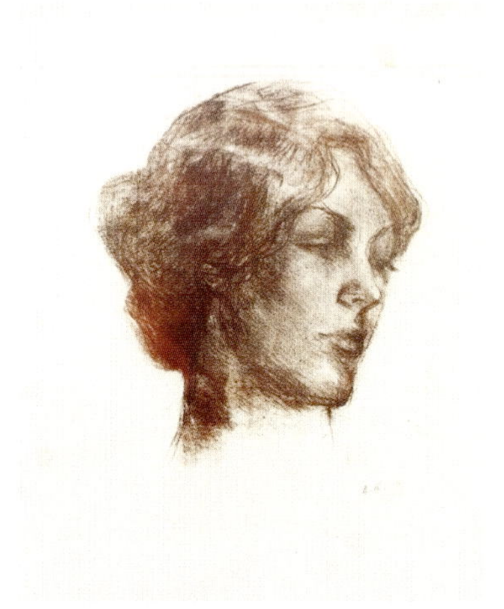

CAT. 217

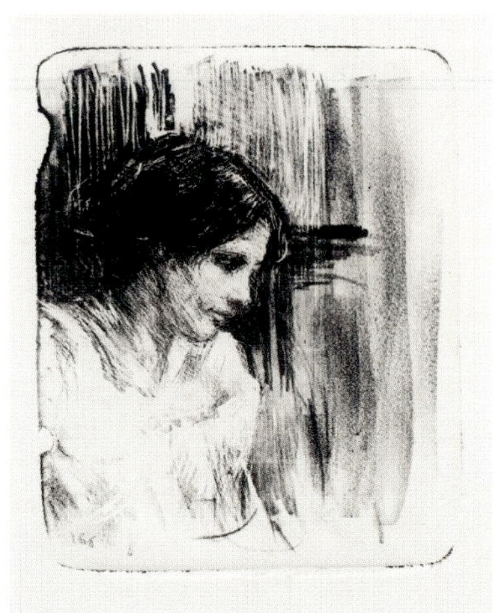

CAT. 218

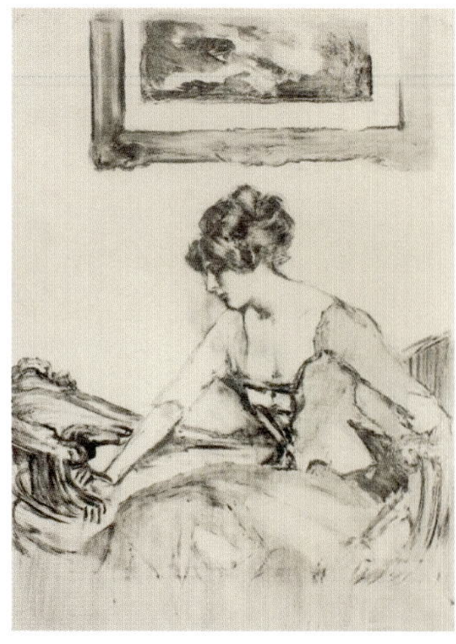

CAT. 219

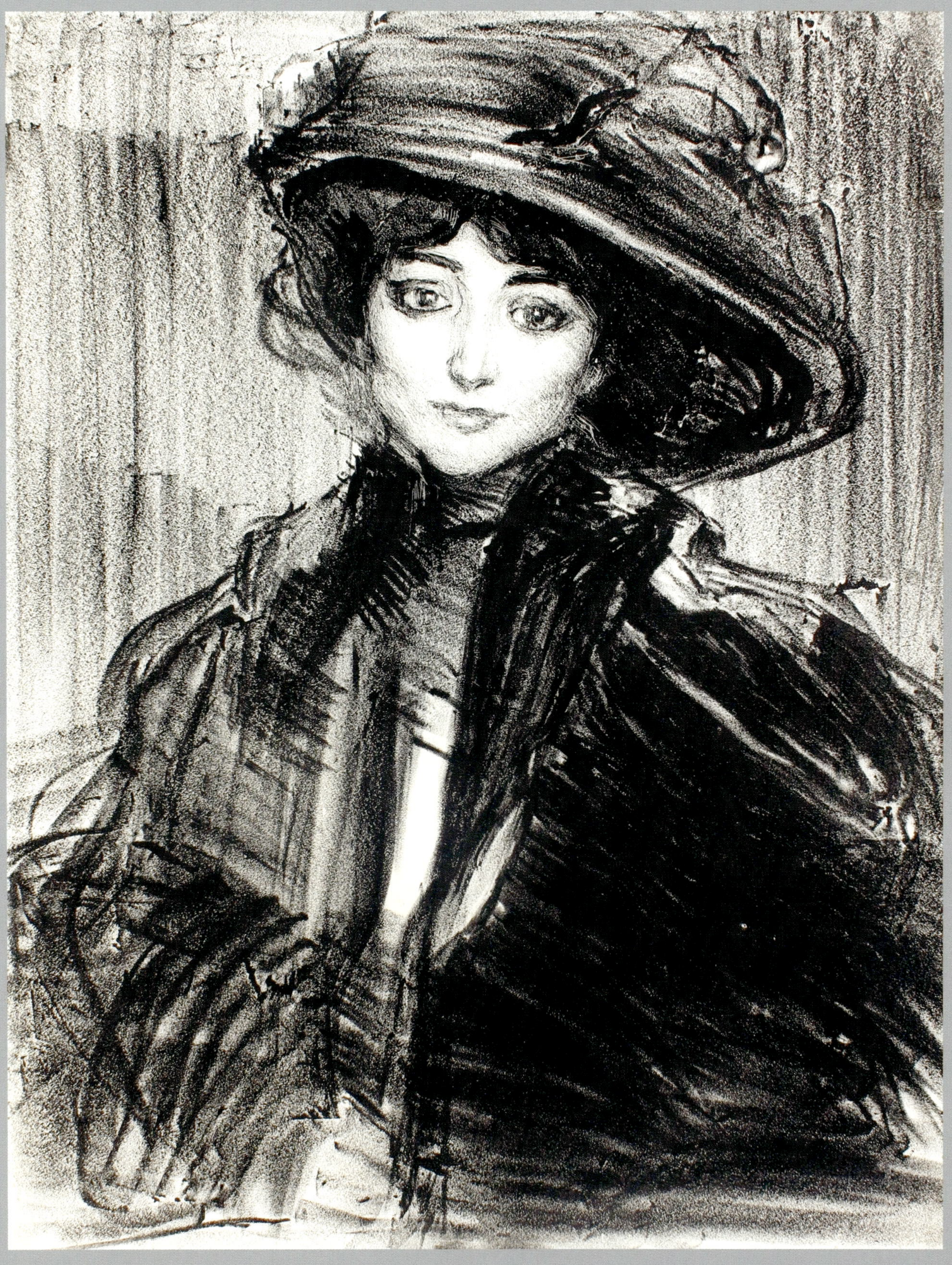

CAT. 220

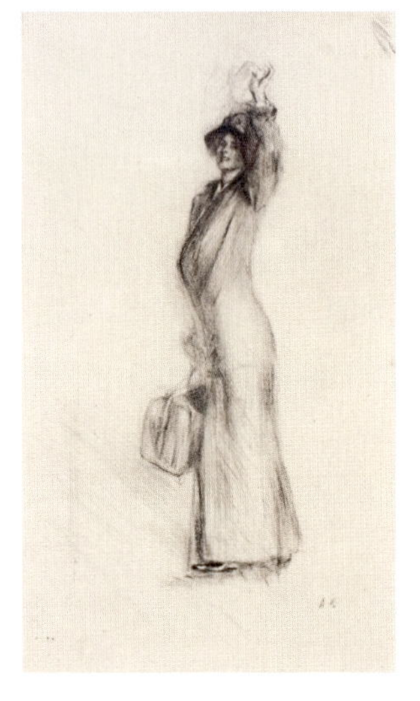

CAT. 221

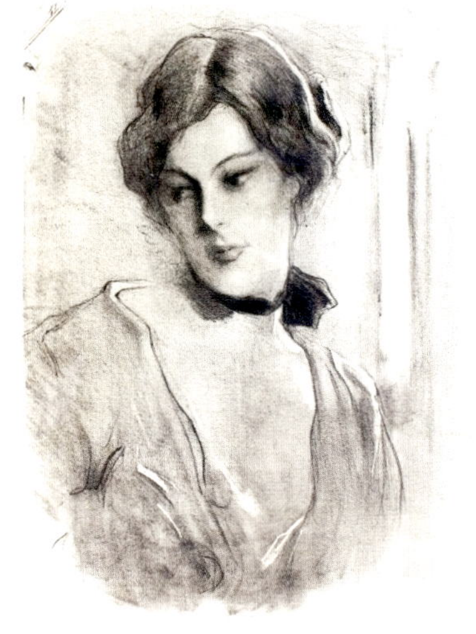

CAT. 222

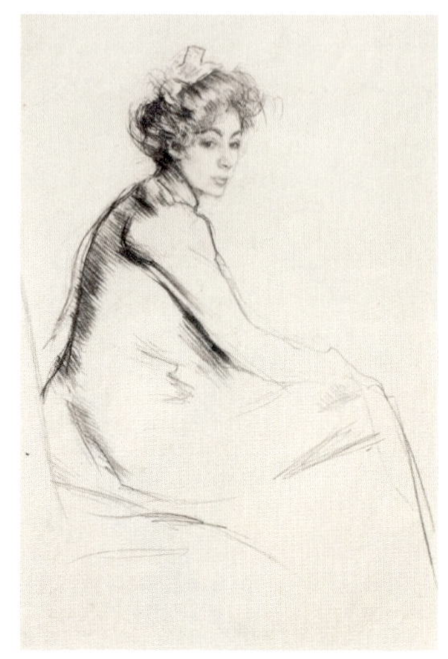

CAT. 223

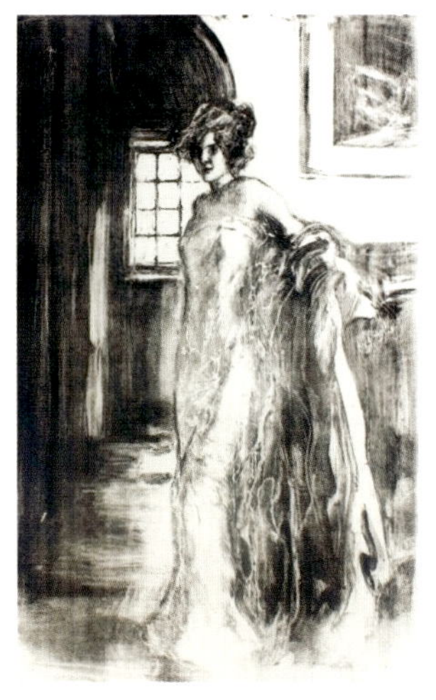

CAT. 224

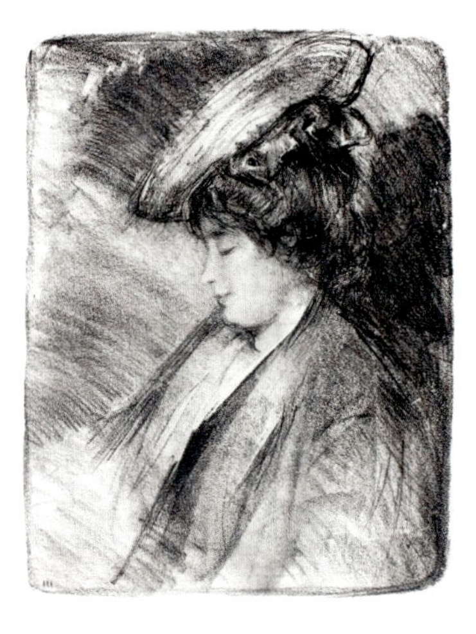

CAT. 225

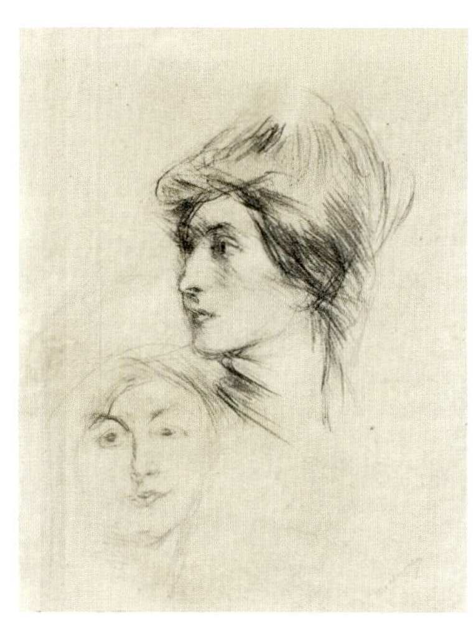

CAT. 226

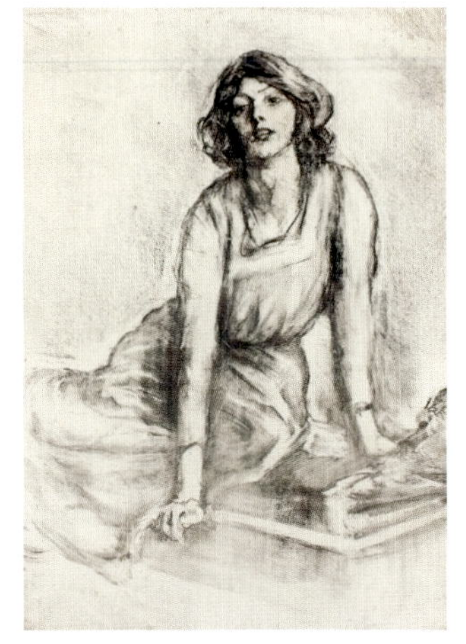

CAT. 227

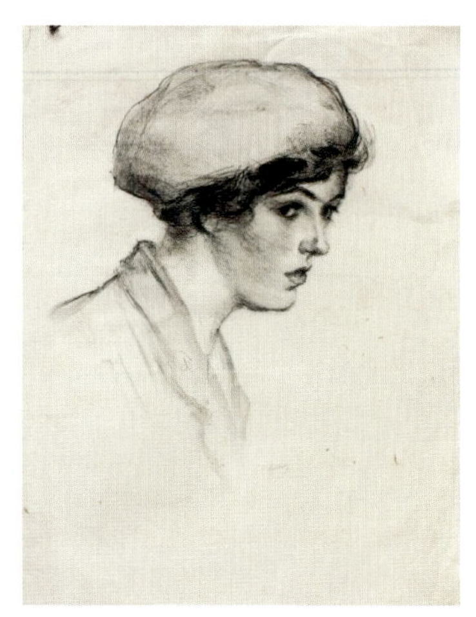

CAT. 228

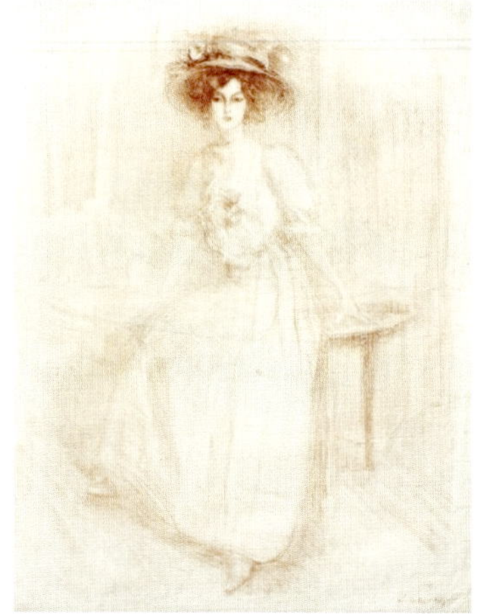

CAT. 229

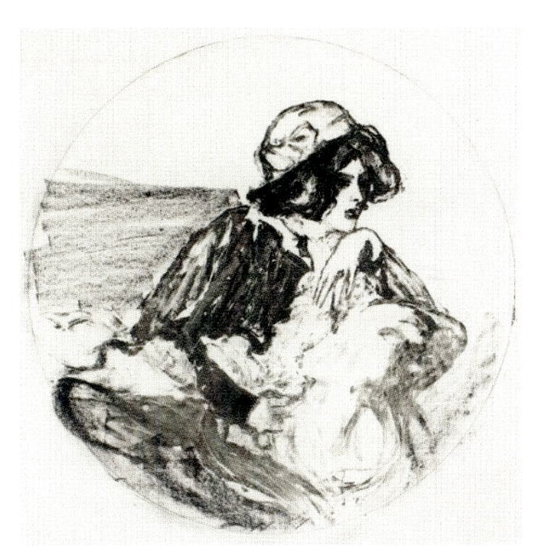

CAT. 230

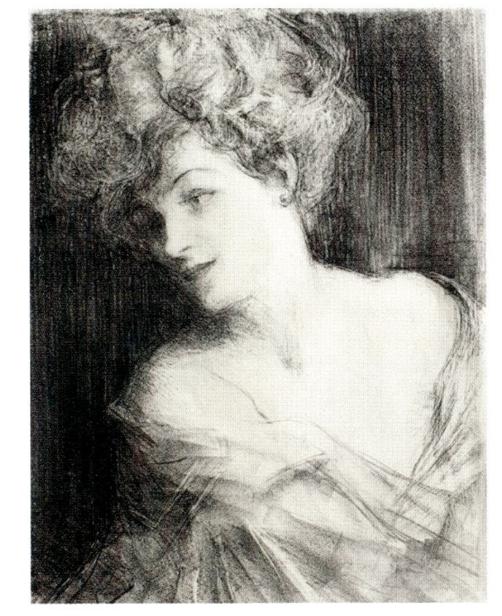

CAT. 231

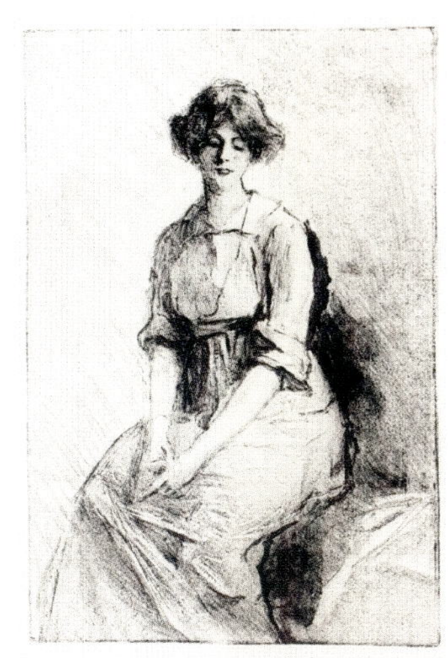

CAT. 232

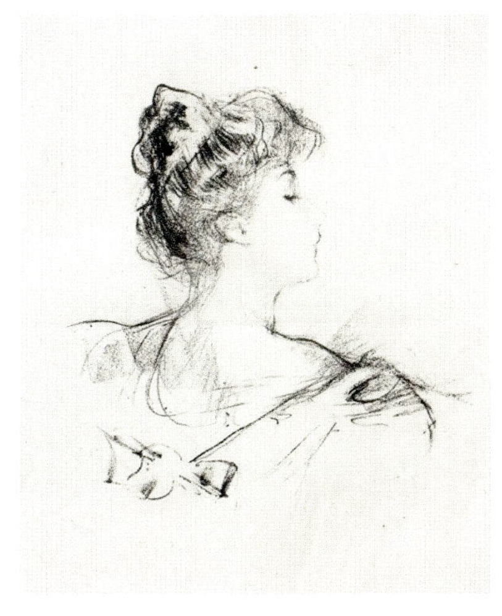

CAT. 233

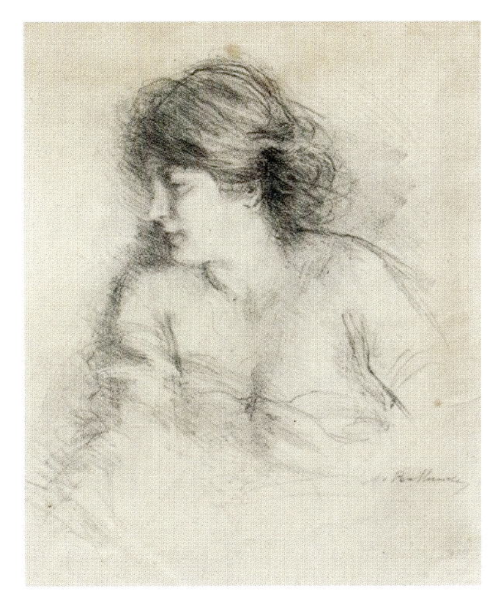

CAT. 234

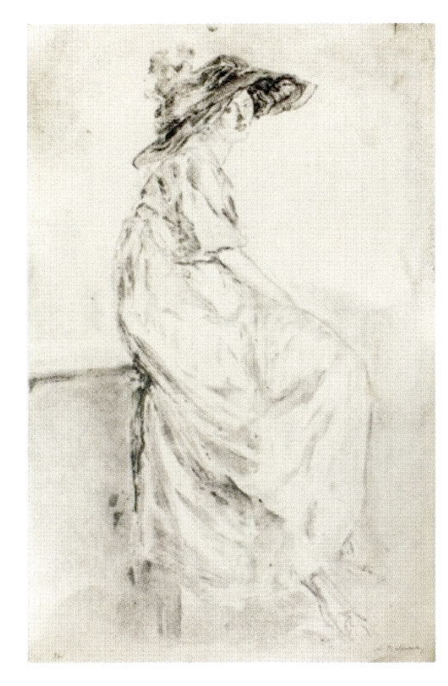

CAT. 235

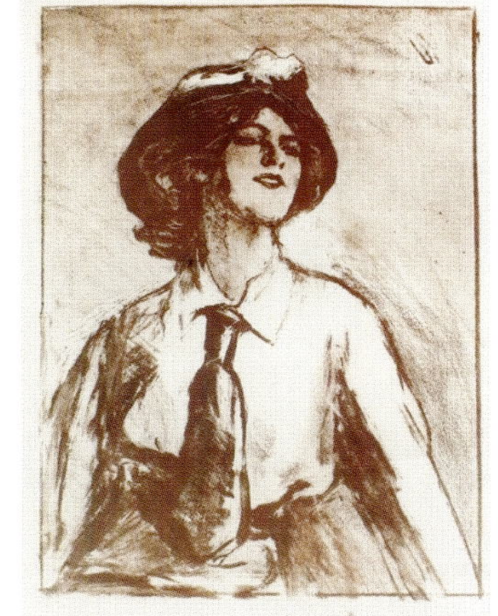

CAT. 236

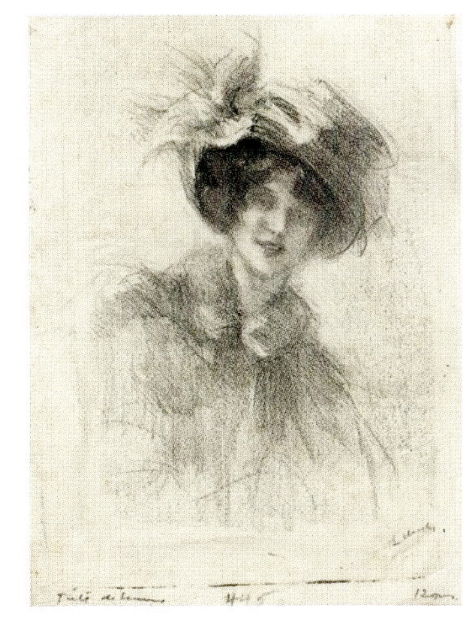

CAT. 237

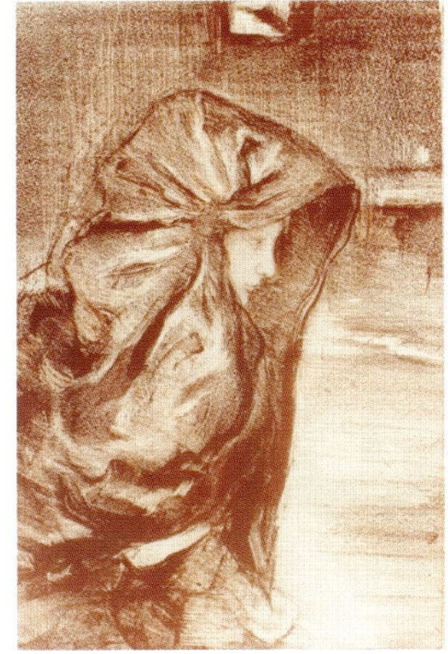

CAT. 238

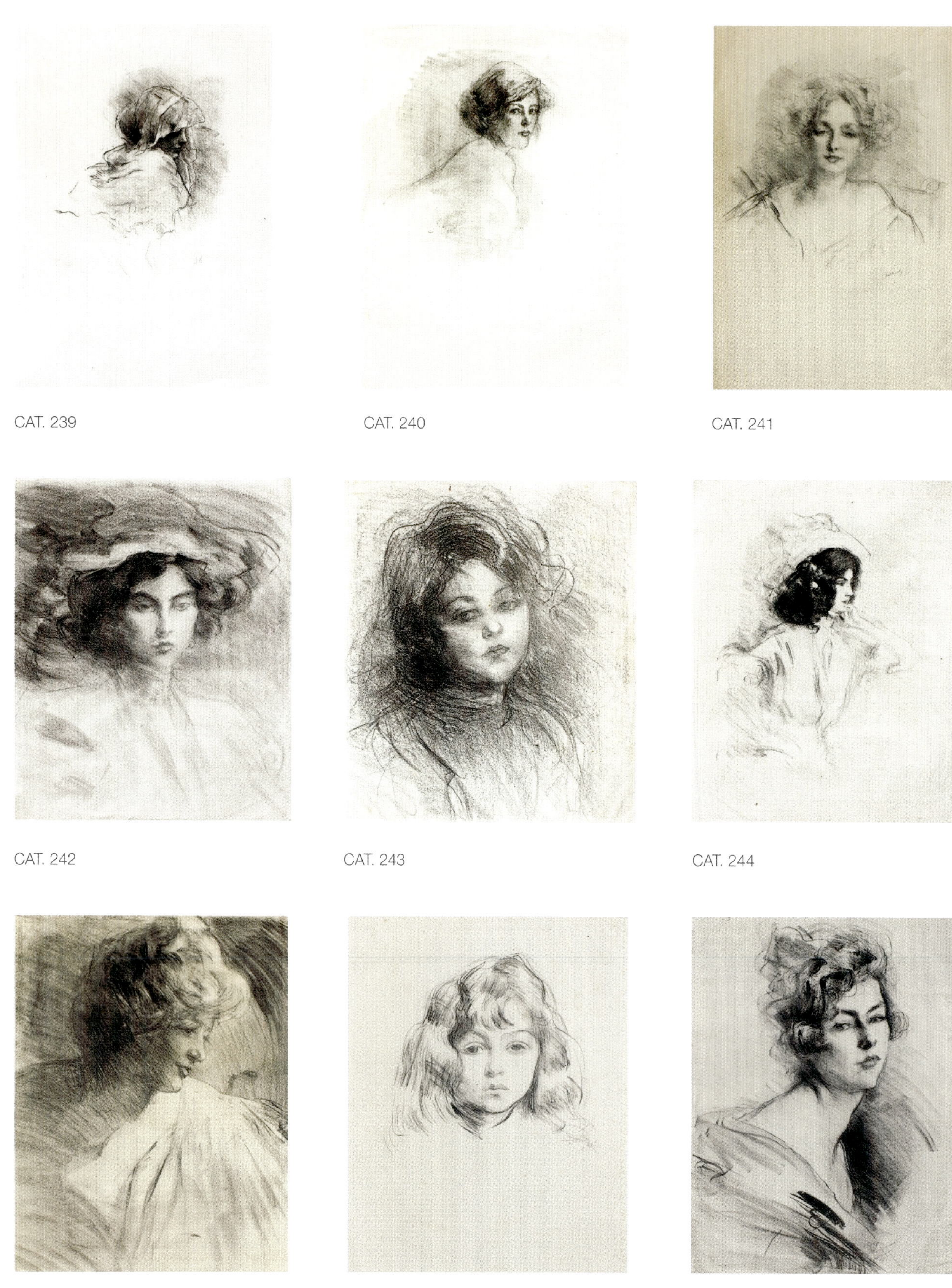

CAT. 239

CAT. 240

CAT. 241

CAT. 242

CAT. 243

CAT. 244

CAT. 245

CAT. 246

CAT. 247

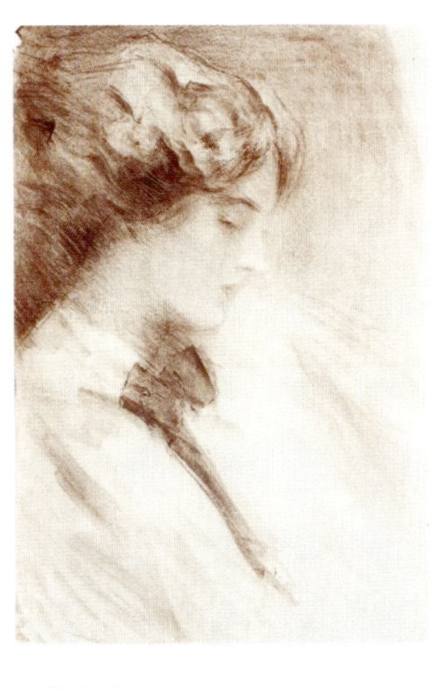
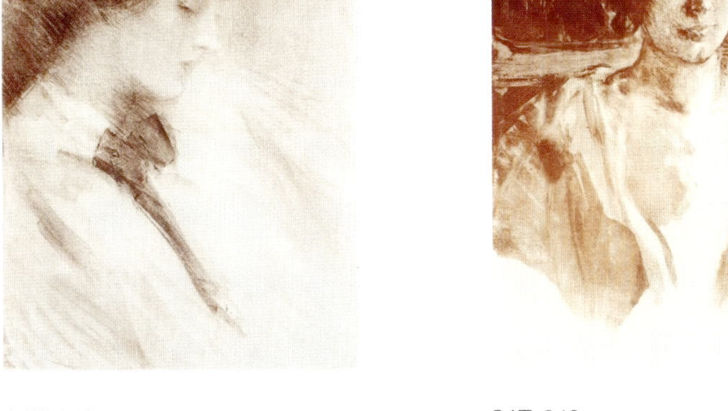

CAT. 248

CAT. 249

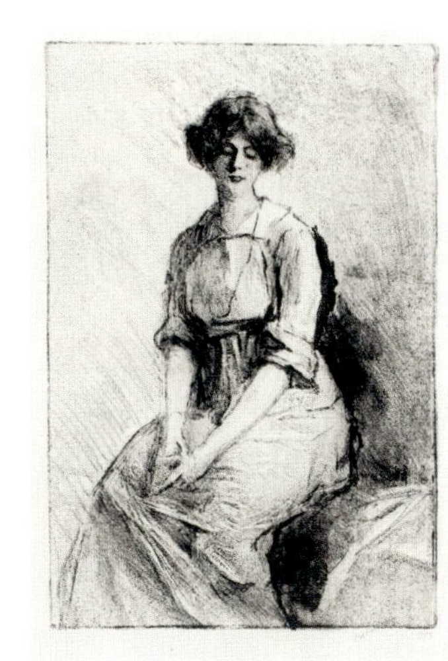

CAT. 250

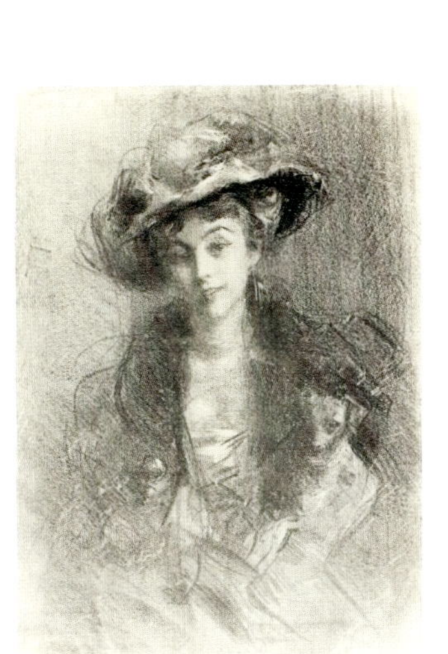

CAT. 251

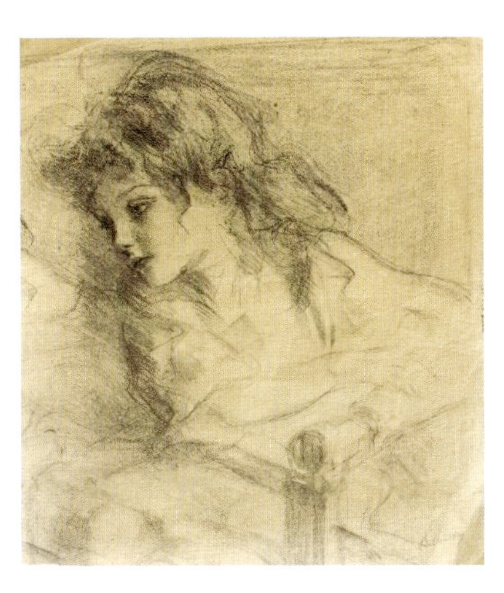

CAT. 252

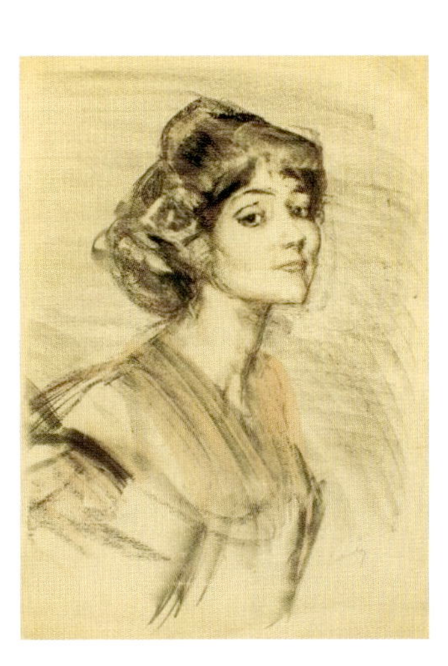

CAT. 253

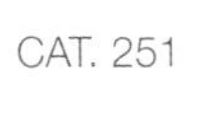

CAT. 254

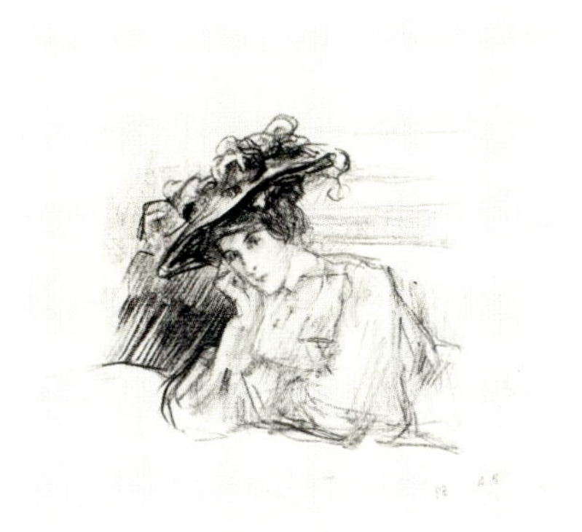

CAT. 255

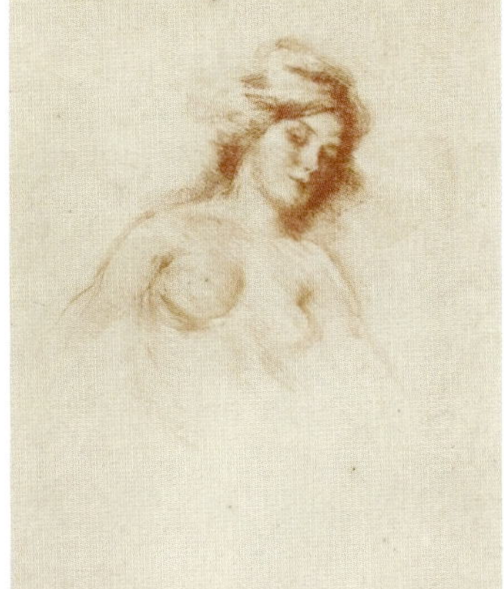

CAT. 256

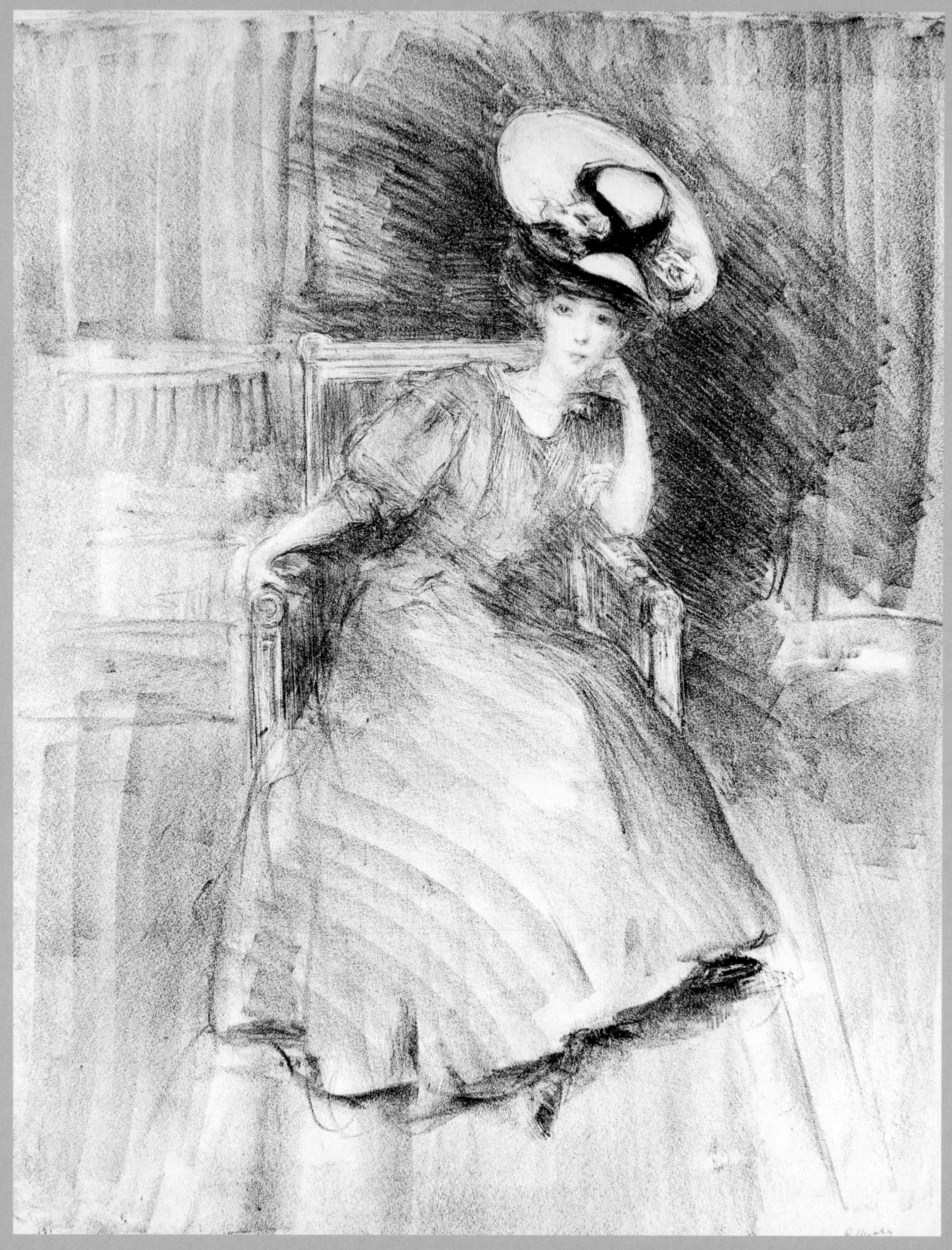

CAT. 257

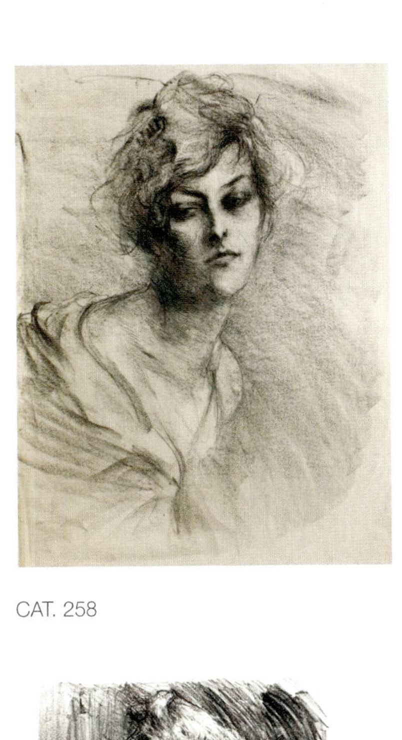

CAT. 258

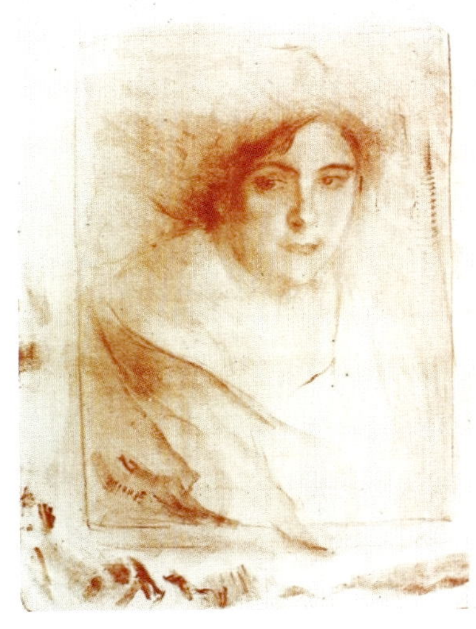

CAT. 259

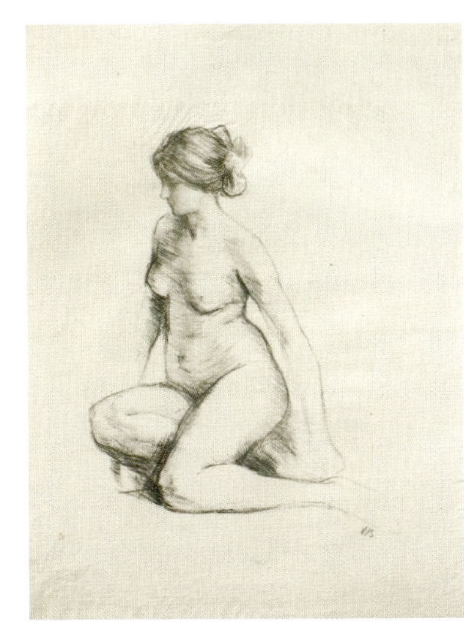

CAT. 260

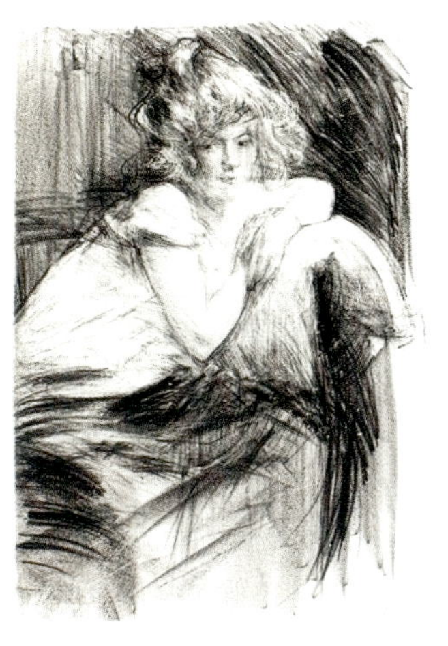

CAT. 261

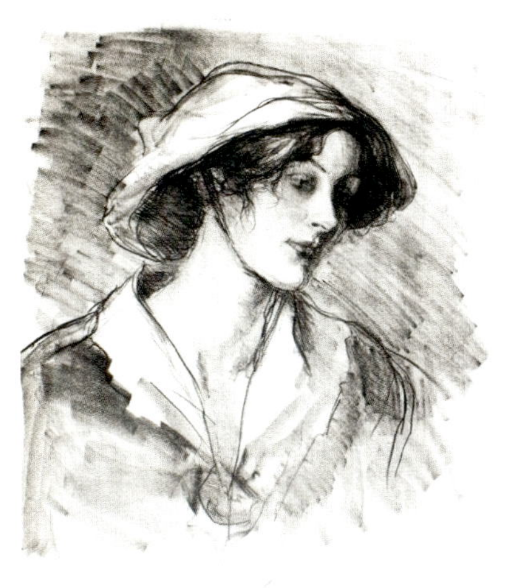

CAT. 262

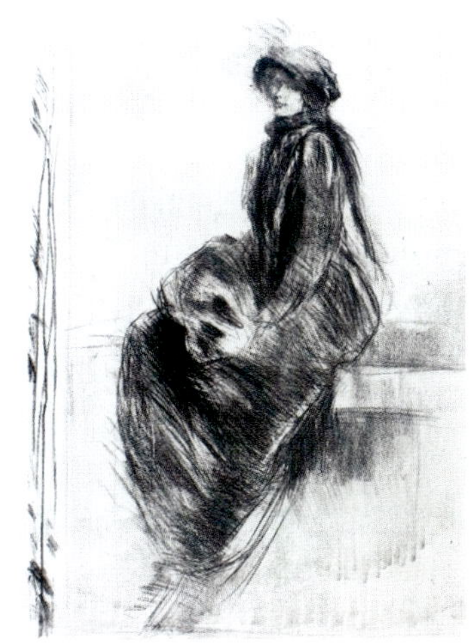

CAT. 263

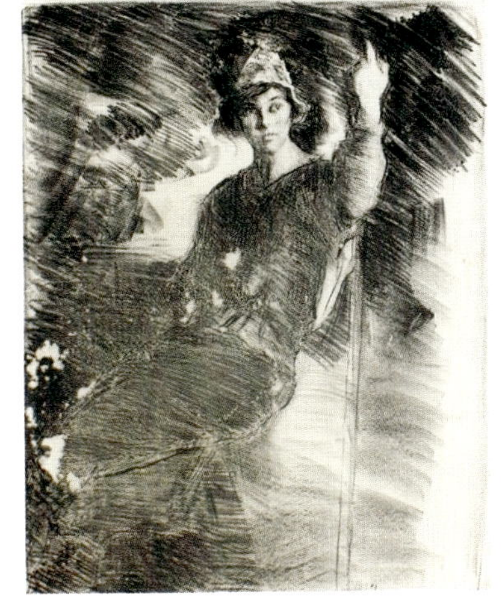

CAT. 264

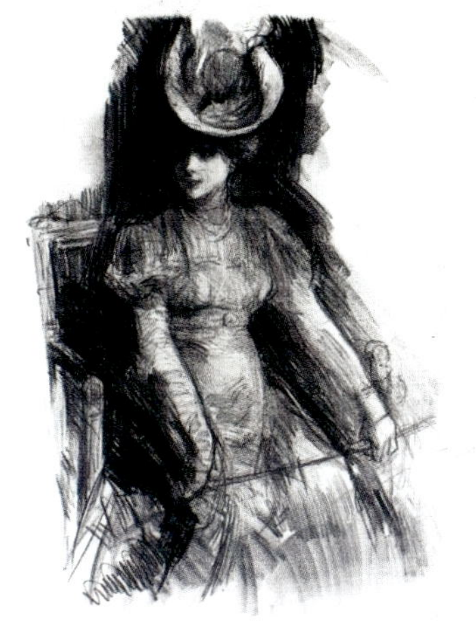

CAT. 265

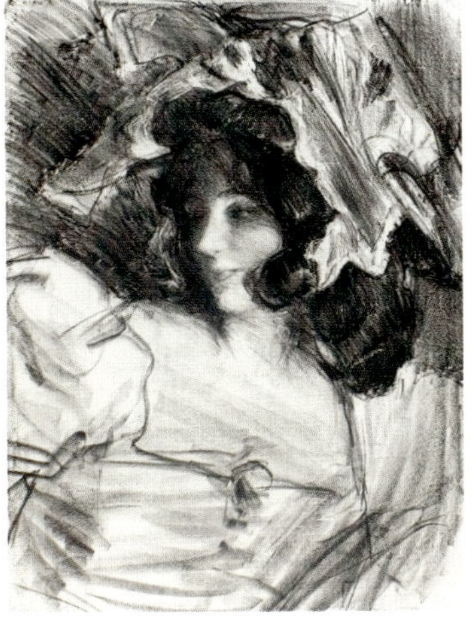

CAT. 266

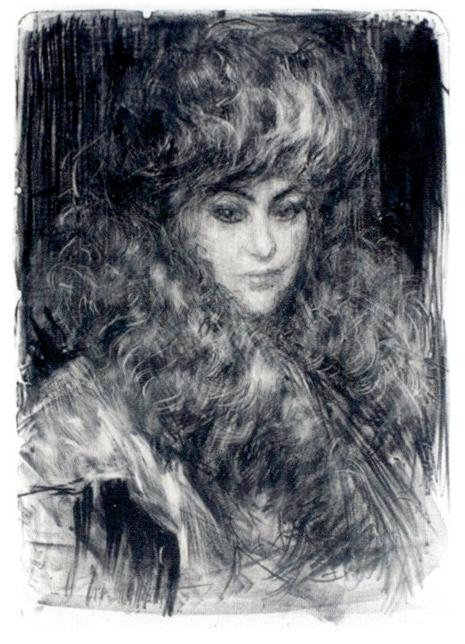
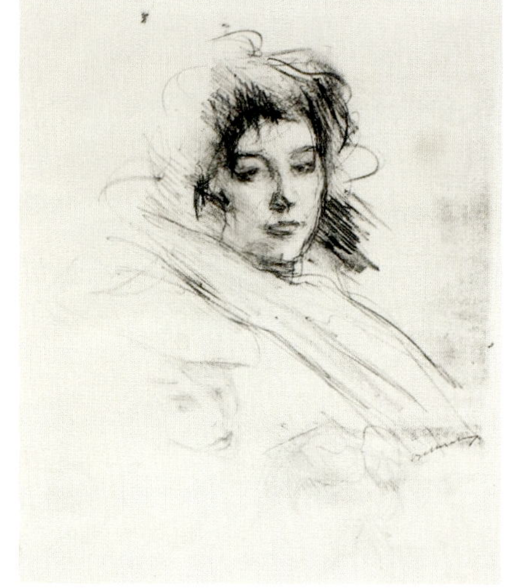
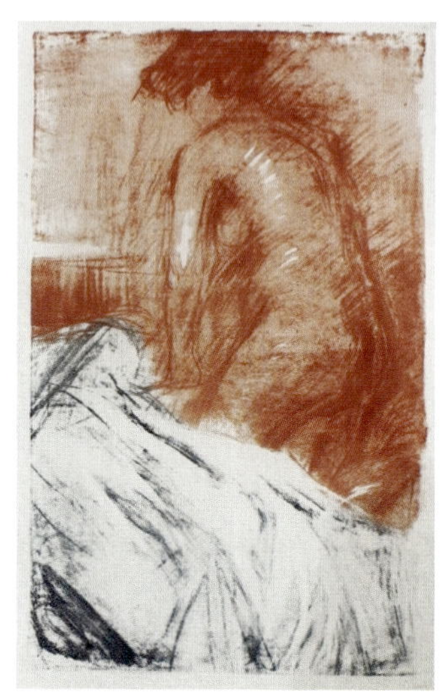

CAT. 267   CAT. 268   CAT. 269

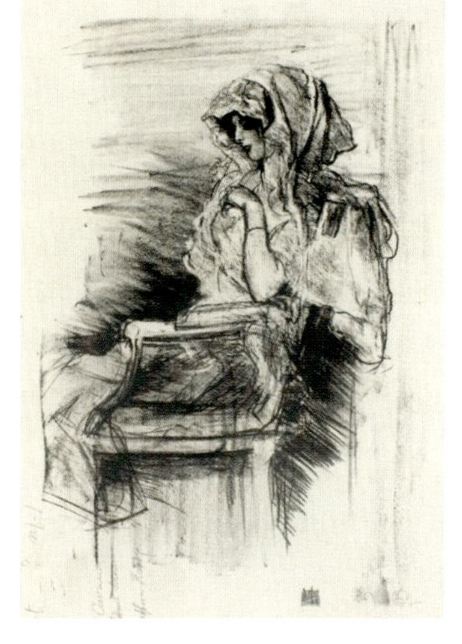
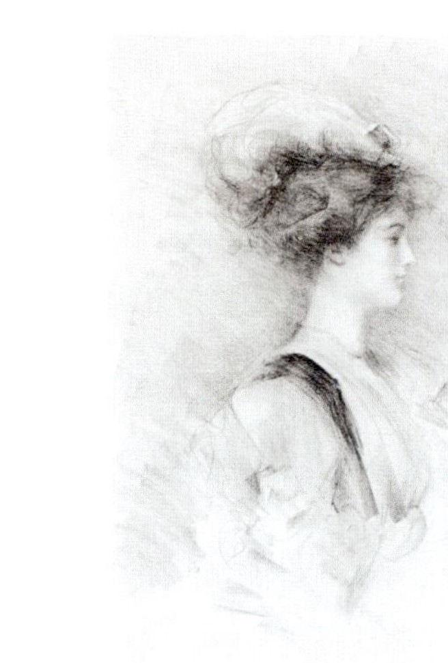
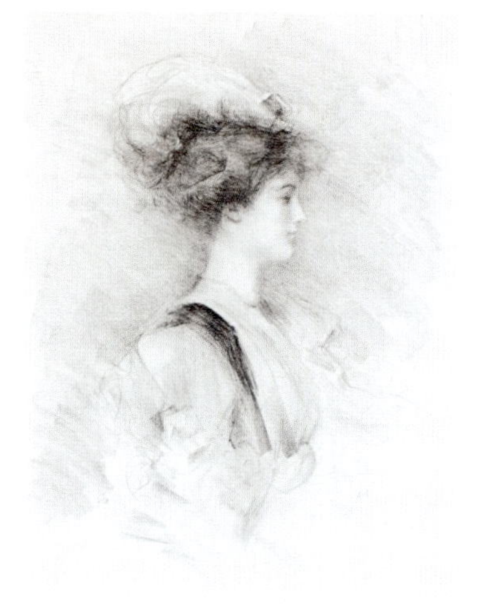
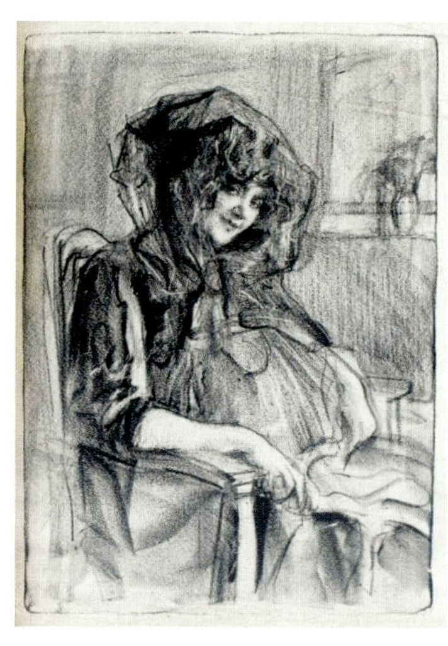

CAT. 270   CAT. 271   CAT. 272

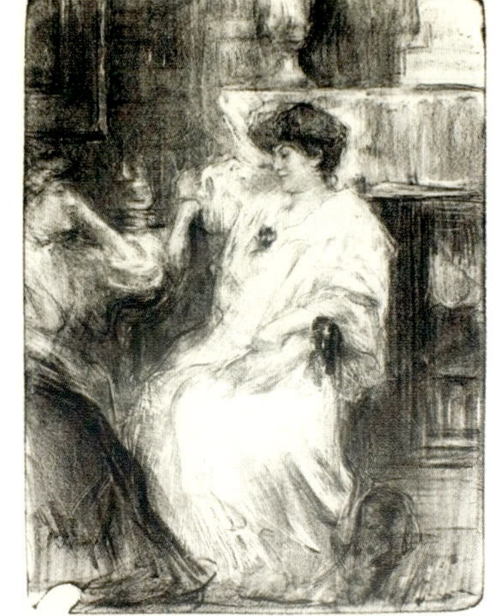
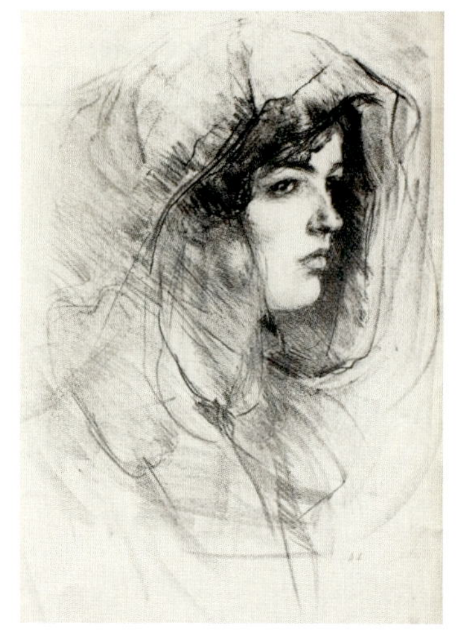
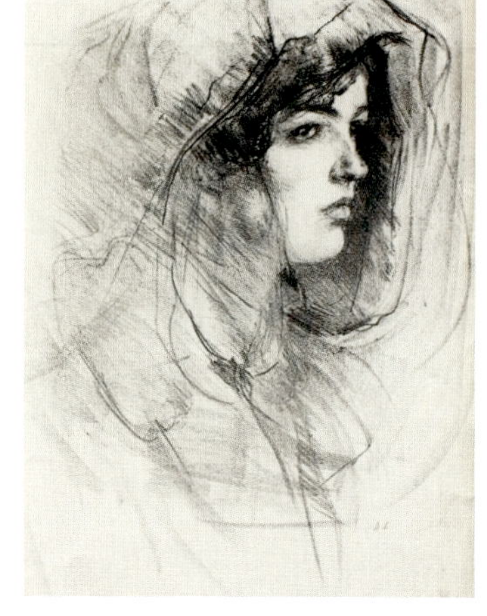
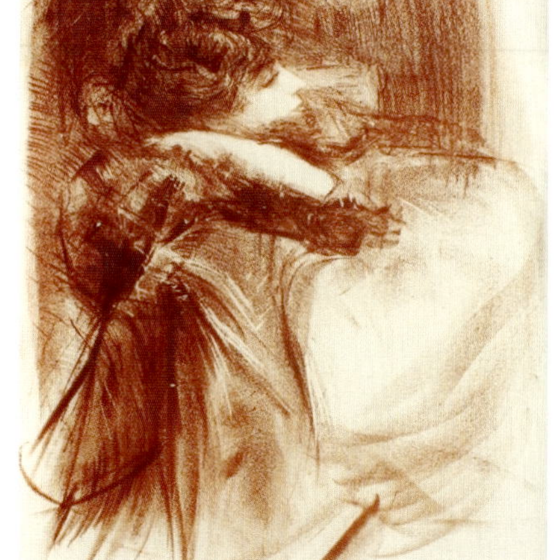

CAT. 273   CAT. 274   CAT. 275

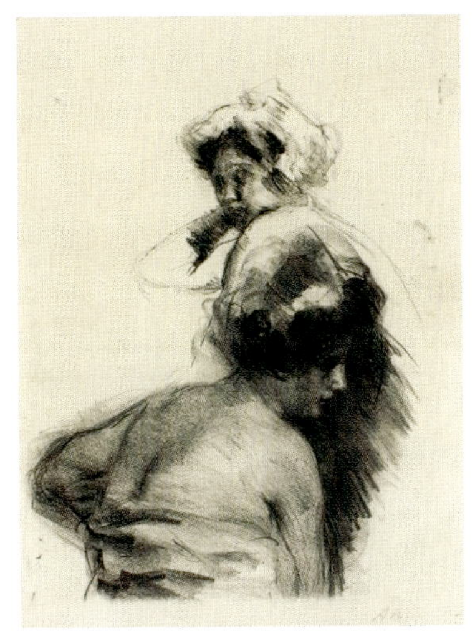

CAT. 276

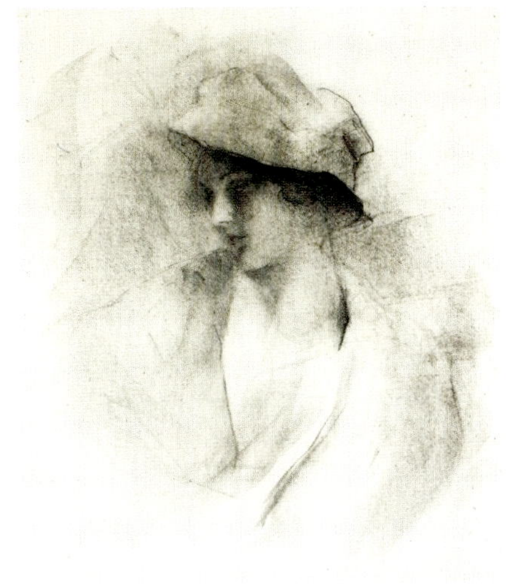

CAT. 277

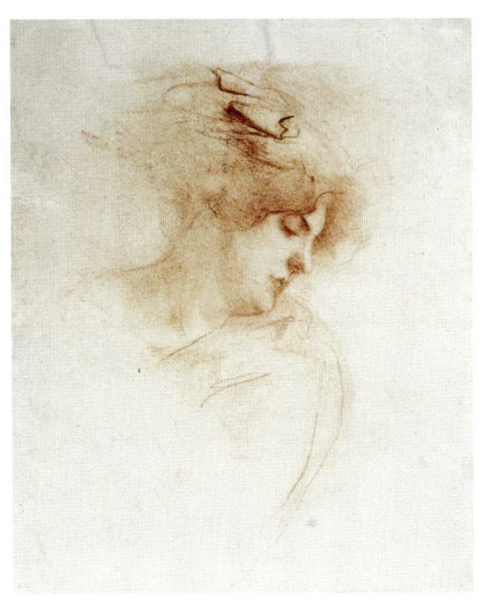

CAT. 278

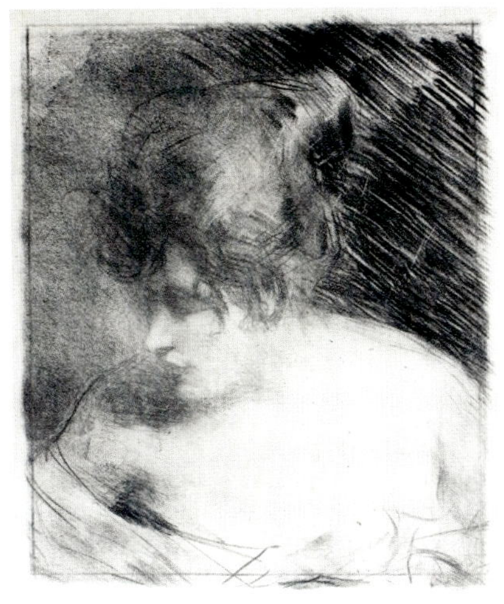

CAT. 279

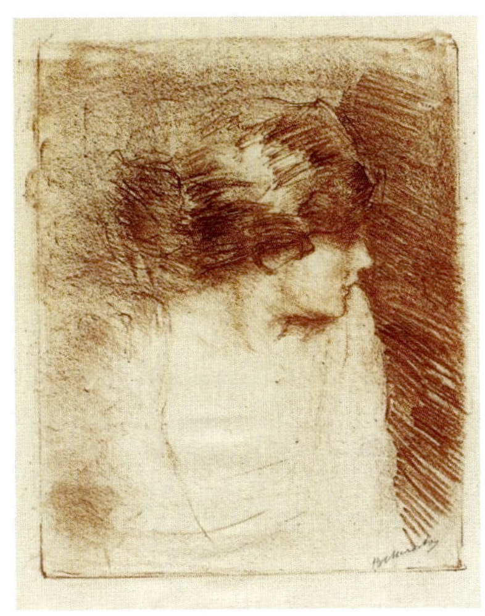

CAT. 280

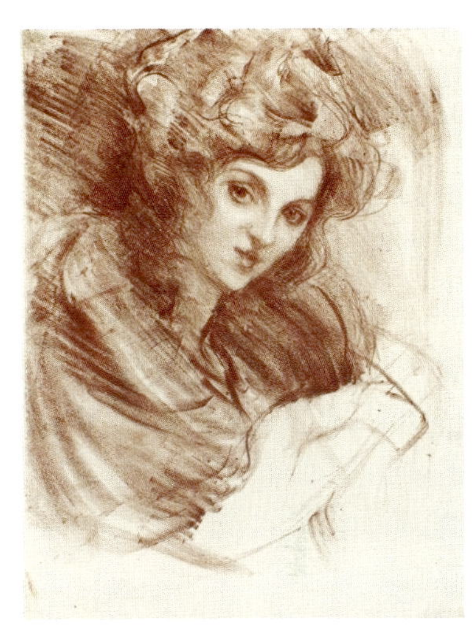

CAT. 281

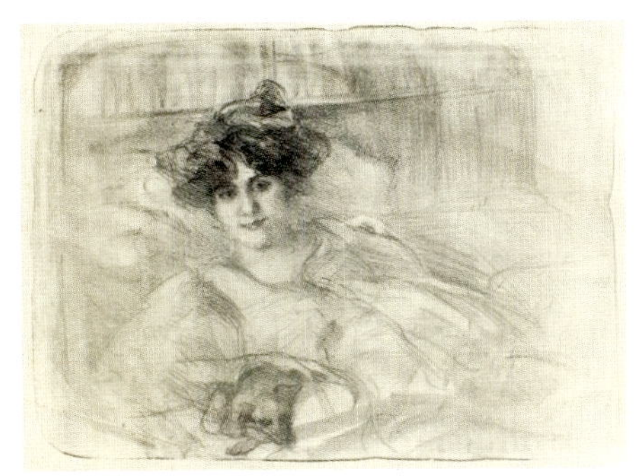

CAT. 282

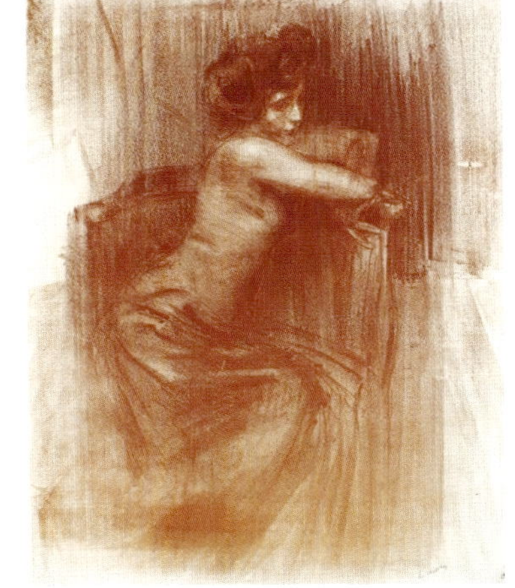

CAT. 283

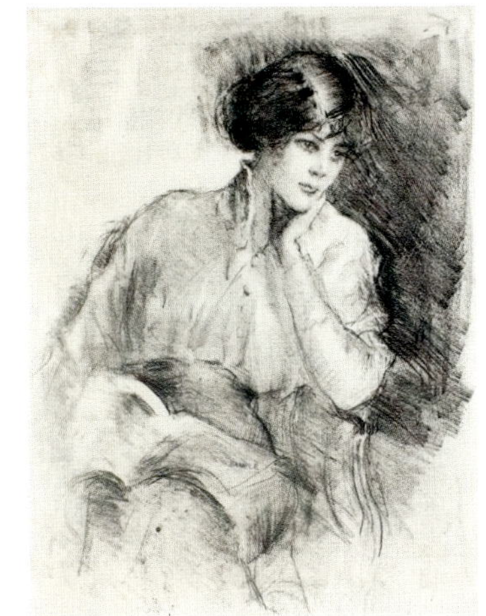

CAT. 284

Like many printmakers, Belleroche experimented with lithography and printed his stones on different types of paper using lithographic inks of different colours.

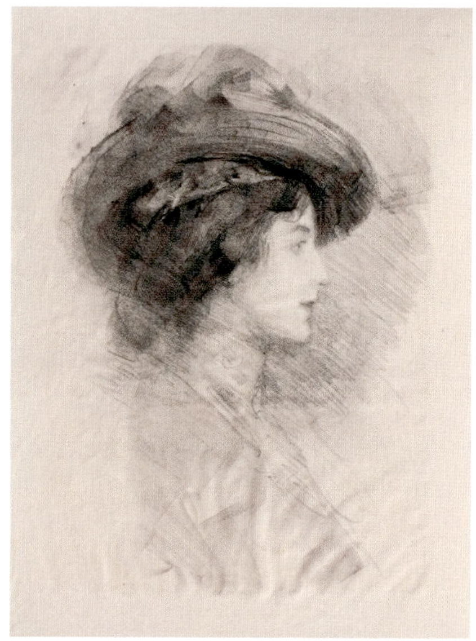
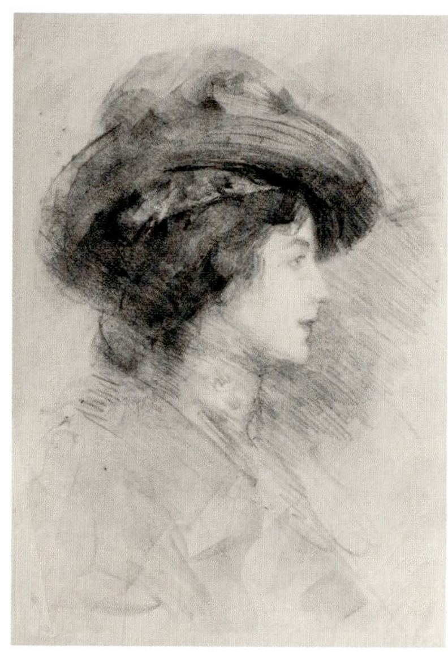

CAT. 285 - 286 – Two variations of *Woman in Hat, Profile*, (K491, AB 291), 1909. Edition 8.

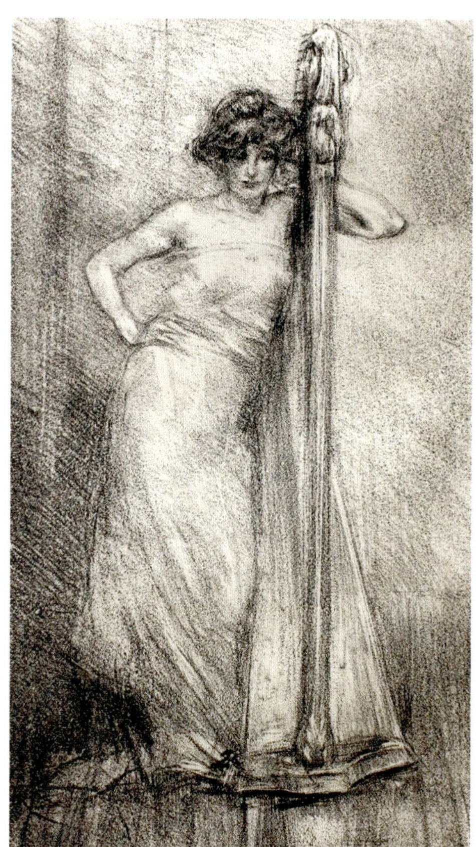
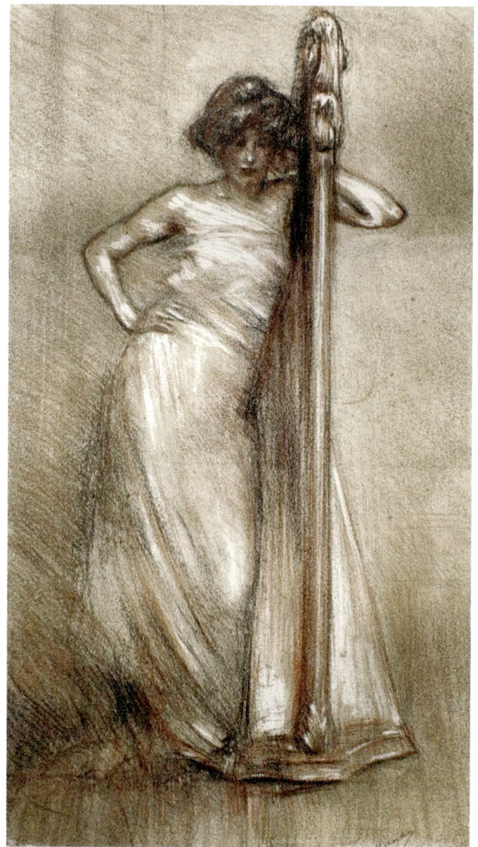

CAT. 287 - 288 – Two versions of *Femme à la harpe*, (K052, AB 66), 1906, 25 ½ x 20 in. (65 x 50.8 cm). Edition: 30.

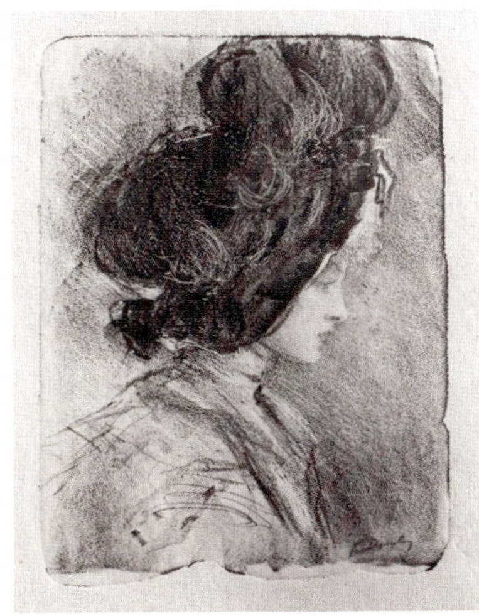 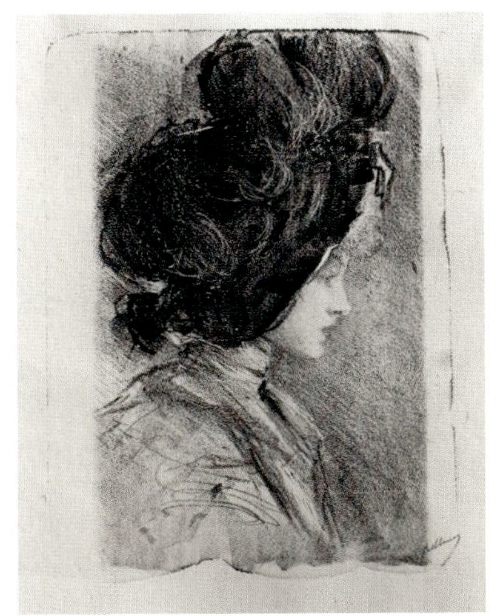 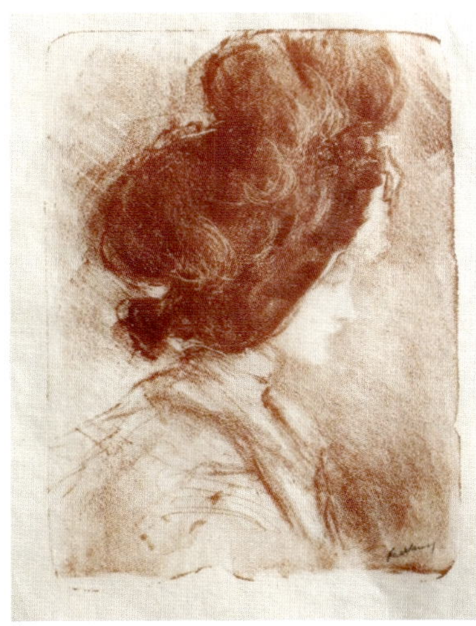

CAT. 289 - 291 – Three variations of *Petite Manon*, (K288, AB 260), 1908, 13 ½ x 10 ½ in. (34.3 x 26.7 cm). Edition: 30.

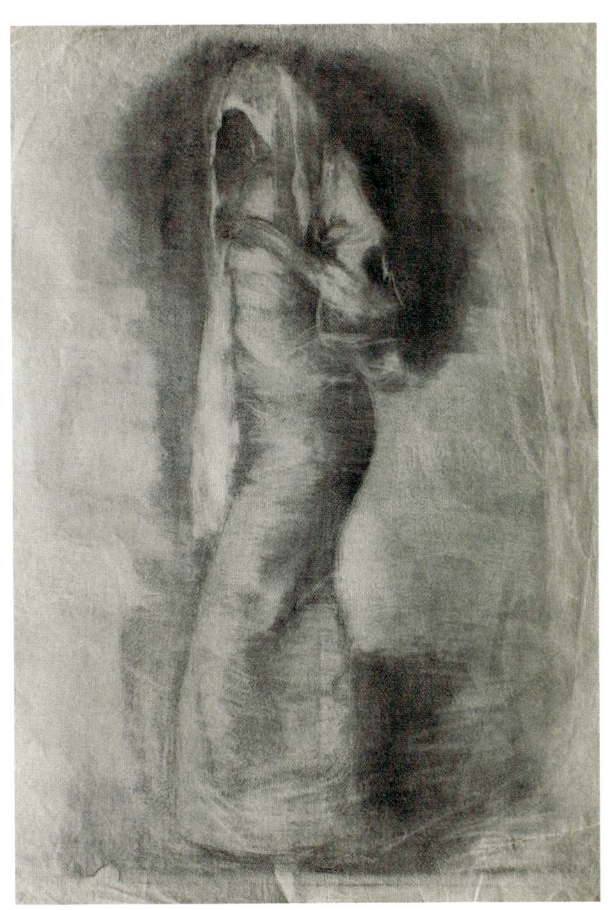 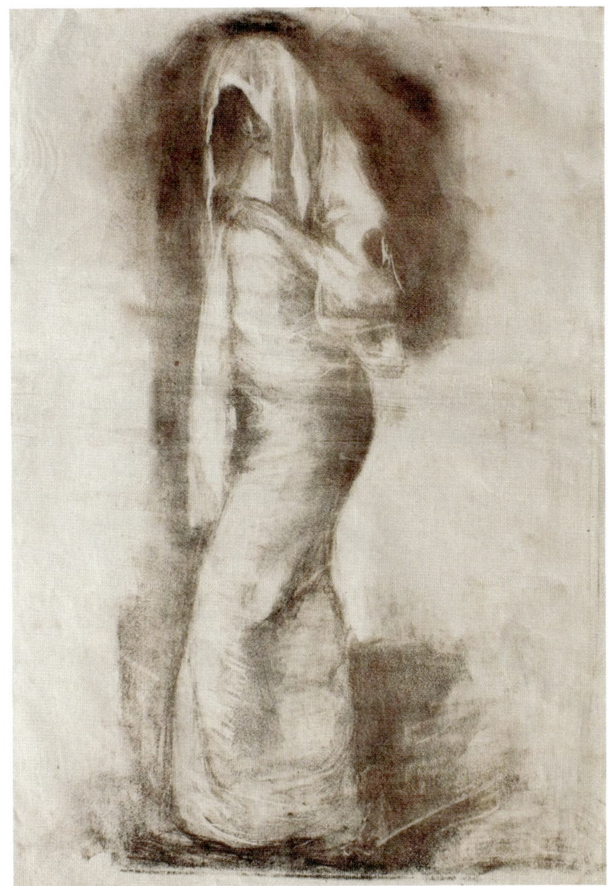

CAT. 292 - 293 – Two variations of *Danseuse mystérieuse*, (K305, AB 358), 1908, 24 ½ x 18 ½ in. (63.2 x 47 cm). Edition: 4.

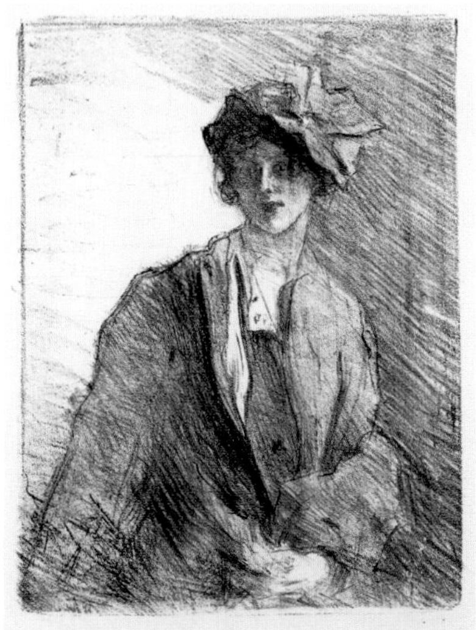 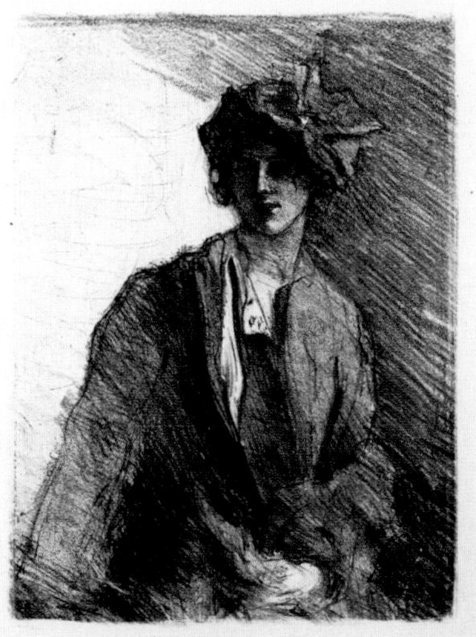 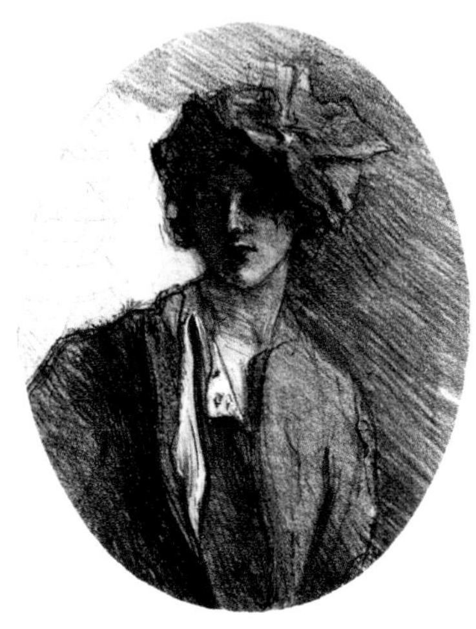

CAT. 294 - 296 – Two versions of *Mabel, full length*, (K681, 682, 683, AB 421B-421), 1916. Edition: 10 and *Mabel, half length* (oval), (K683, AB 421C), 20 x 13 ½ in. (51 x 34.5 cm)

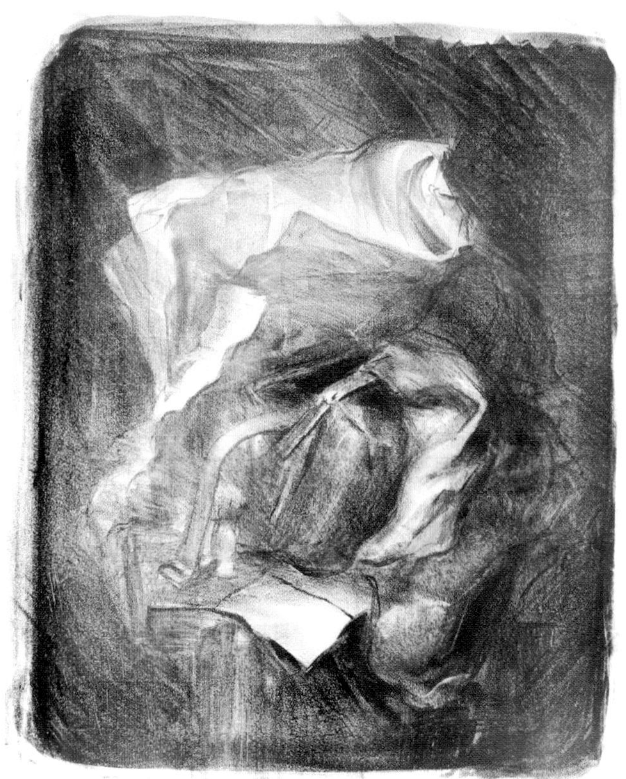 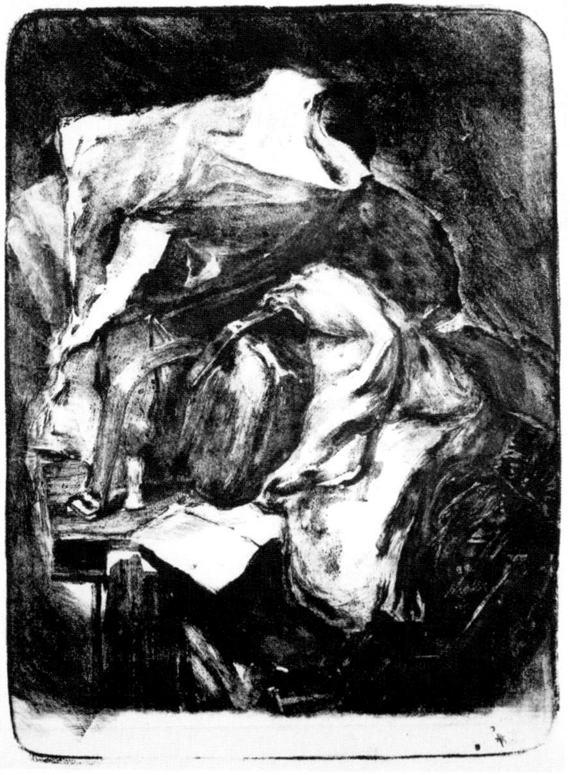

CAT. 297 - 298 – Two versions of *Open Bag on a Table*, (K942, AB 496), c.1900, 25 ¼ x 19 ¼ in. (64 x 48.8 cm).

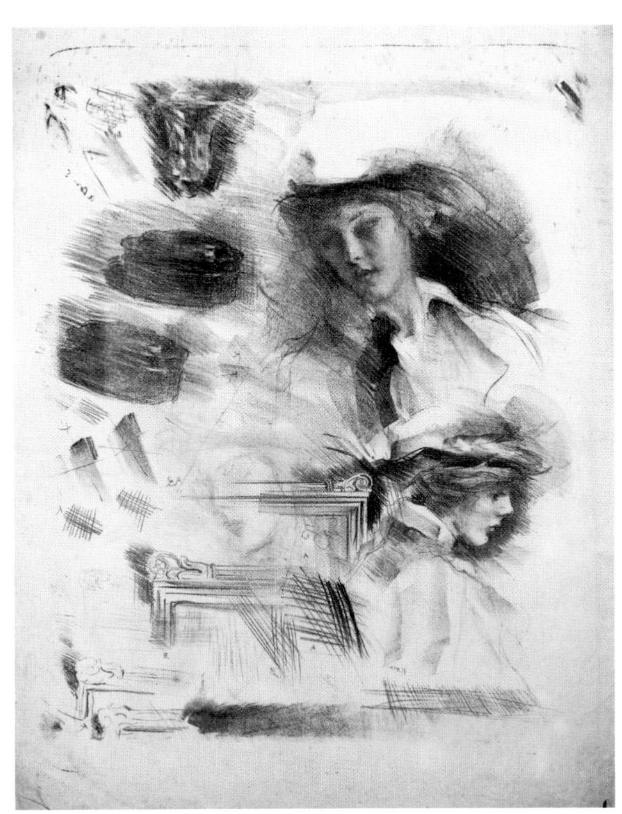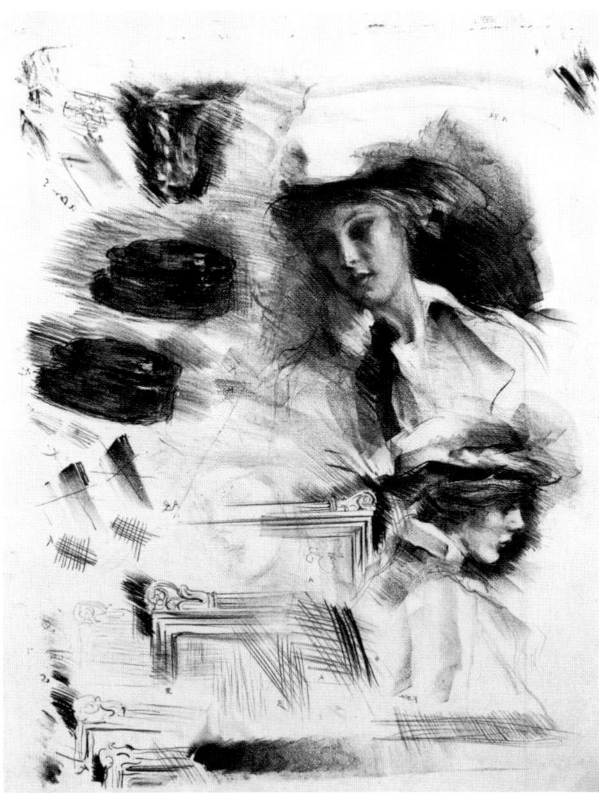

CAT. 299 - 300 – Two versions of *Collage with woman's portrait/profile*, (K773, AB 681), c.1915, 22 ¾ x 20 in. and 25 ¼ x 19 in. (58 x 51 cm and 64 x 48 cm)

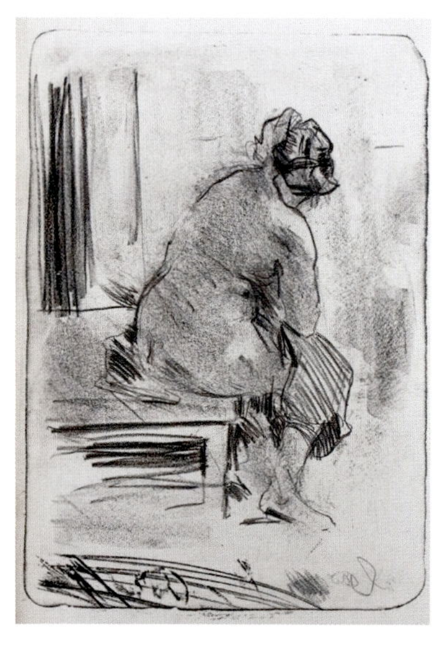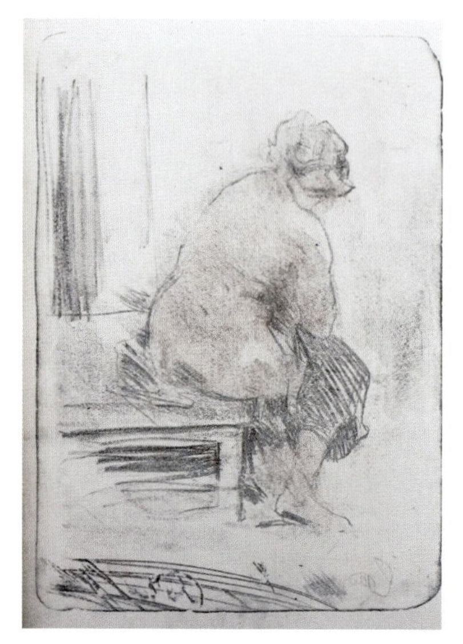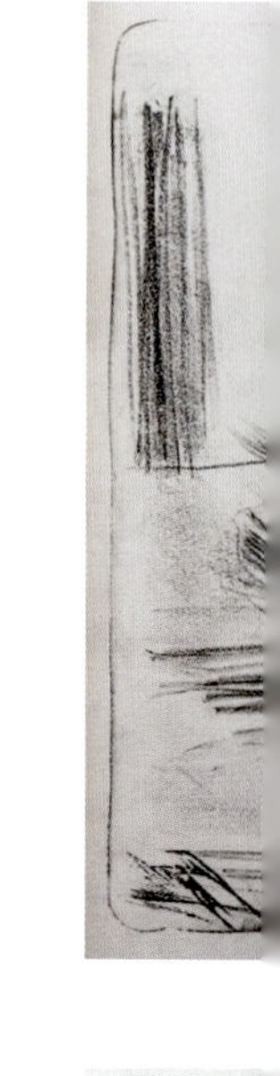

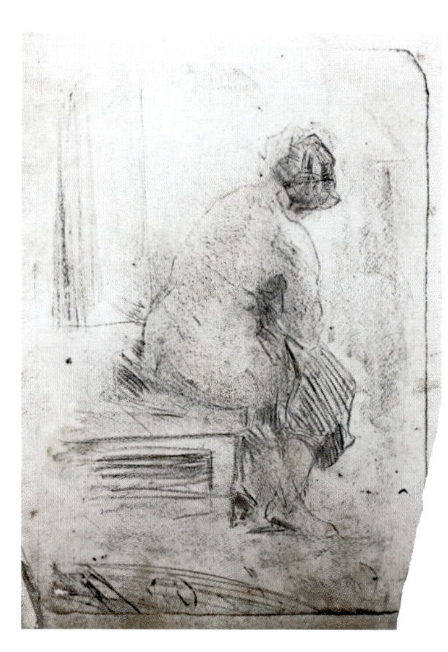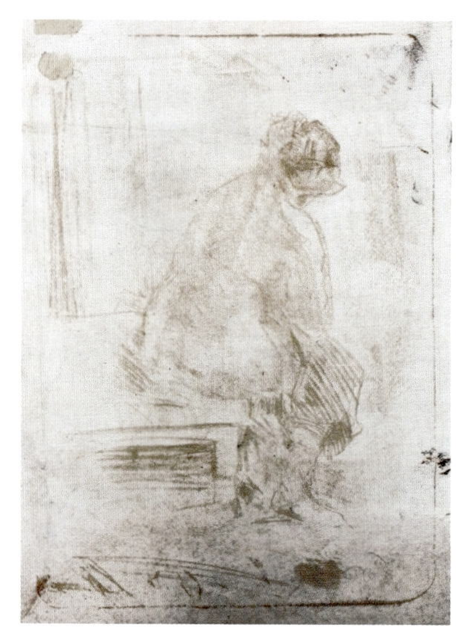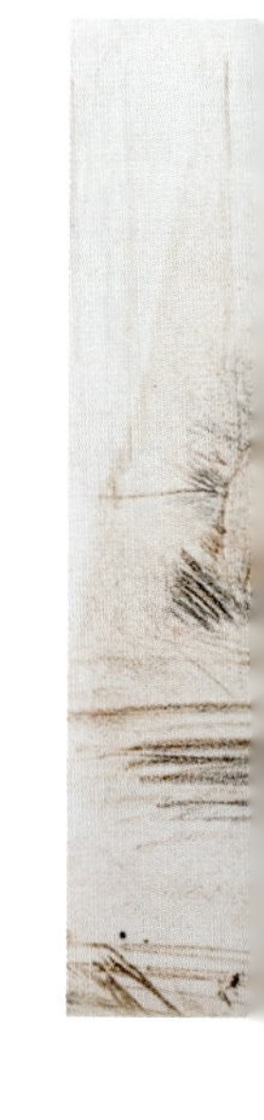

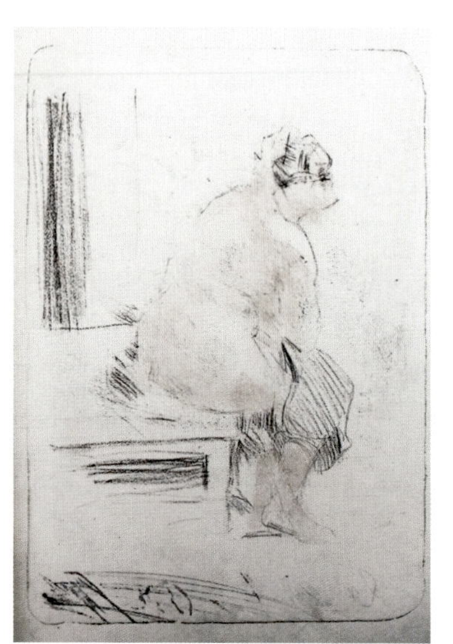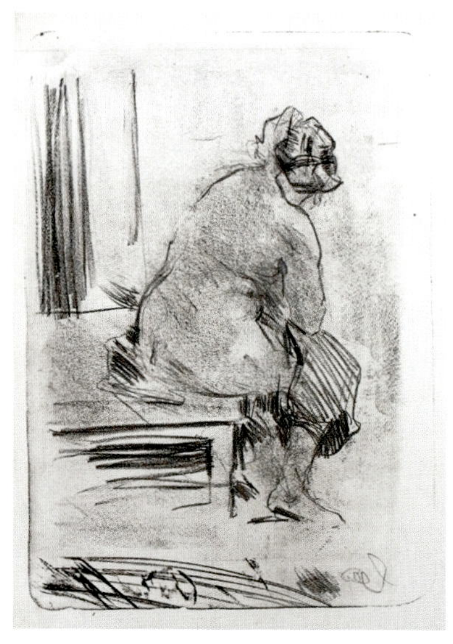

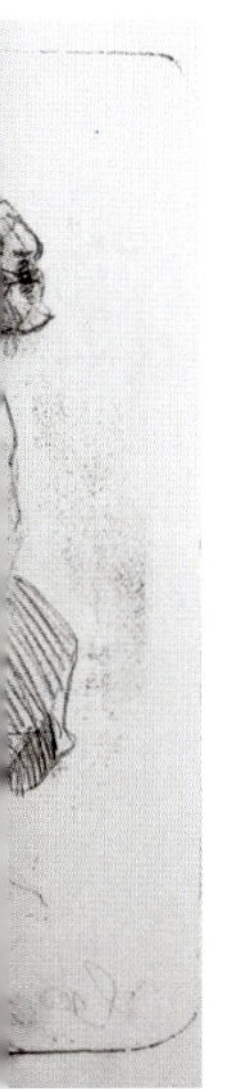
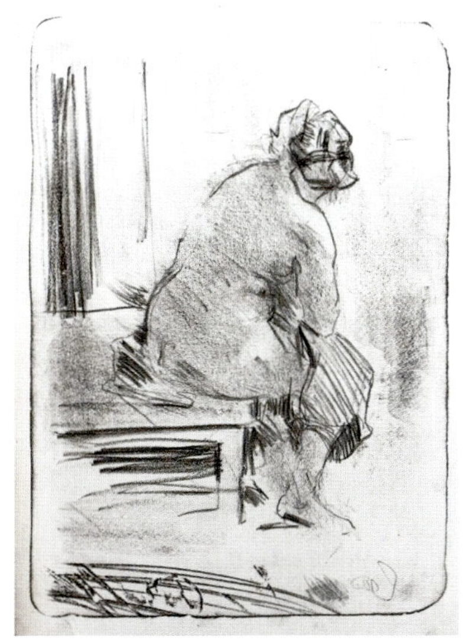
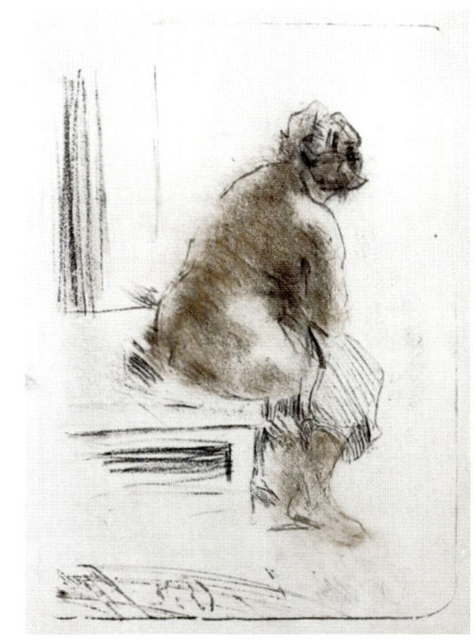
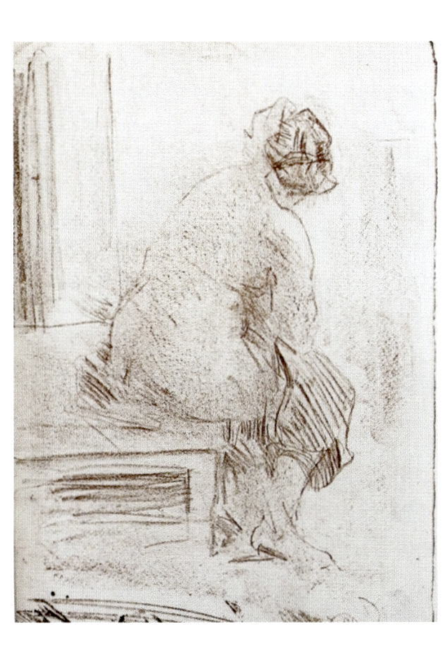
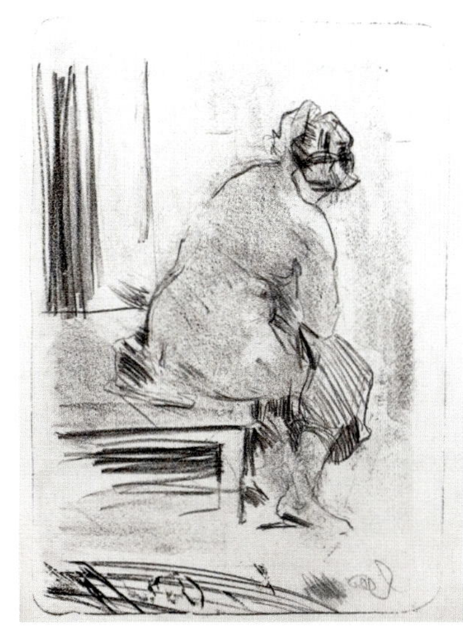
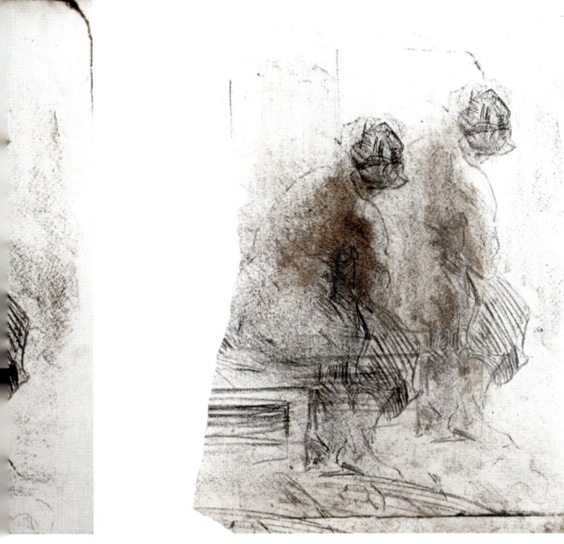

CAT. 301 - 314 – Fourteen versions of *Side of Nude Sitting on a Bed*,
(K578, AB 600A), (fiinished,1913),
each approximately 19 ½ x 12 ¾ in. (50 x 32.5 cm)

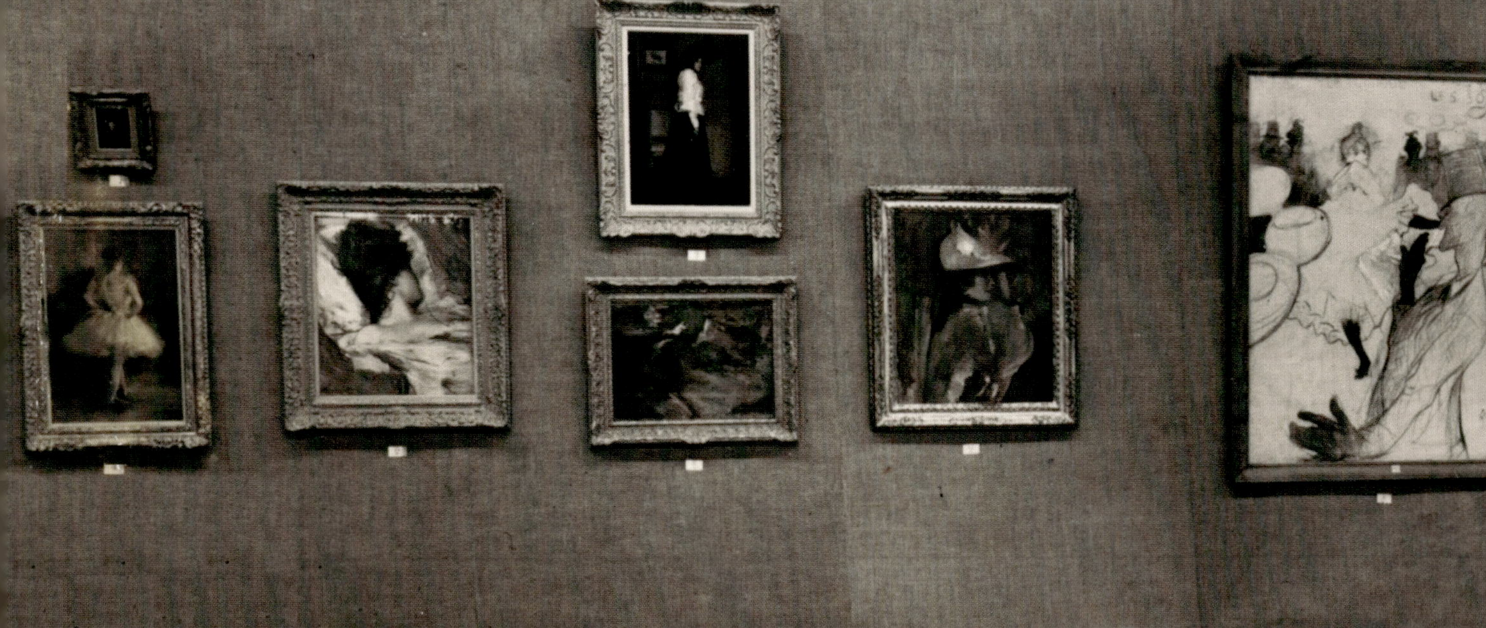

FIG. 19 – Joint retrospective exhibition of Toulouse-Lautrec and Belleroche at the Salon d'Automne, 1956

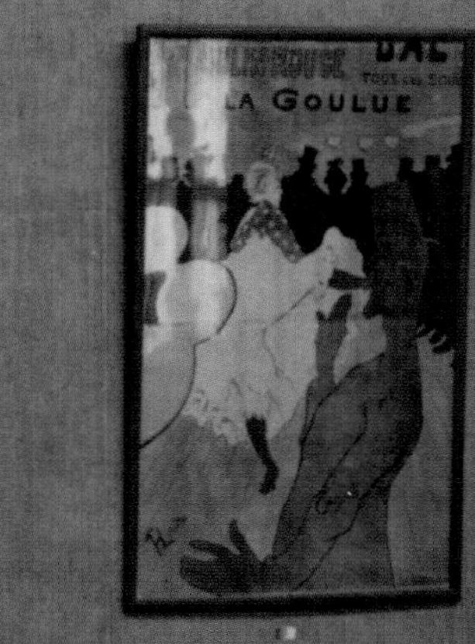

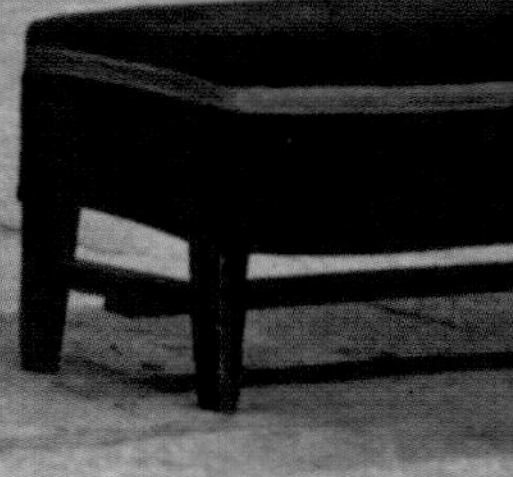

Chronology

Albert de Belleroche

1864 — Born October 22 in Swansea, Wales.

1871 — Begins to reside mostly in Paris.

1882 — Begins art studies at Carolus Duran's atelier and meets Sargent.

1890-1910 — Exhibits with the Société des Artistes Françaises, the New English Art Club, the Salons d'Automne (in 1903 he was the only English founding member) and art gallleries such as Goupil and Graves in Paris and London. Critical reviews are all complimentary.

1910 — Marries Julie Visseaux and leaves Paris for Brussels

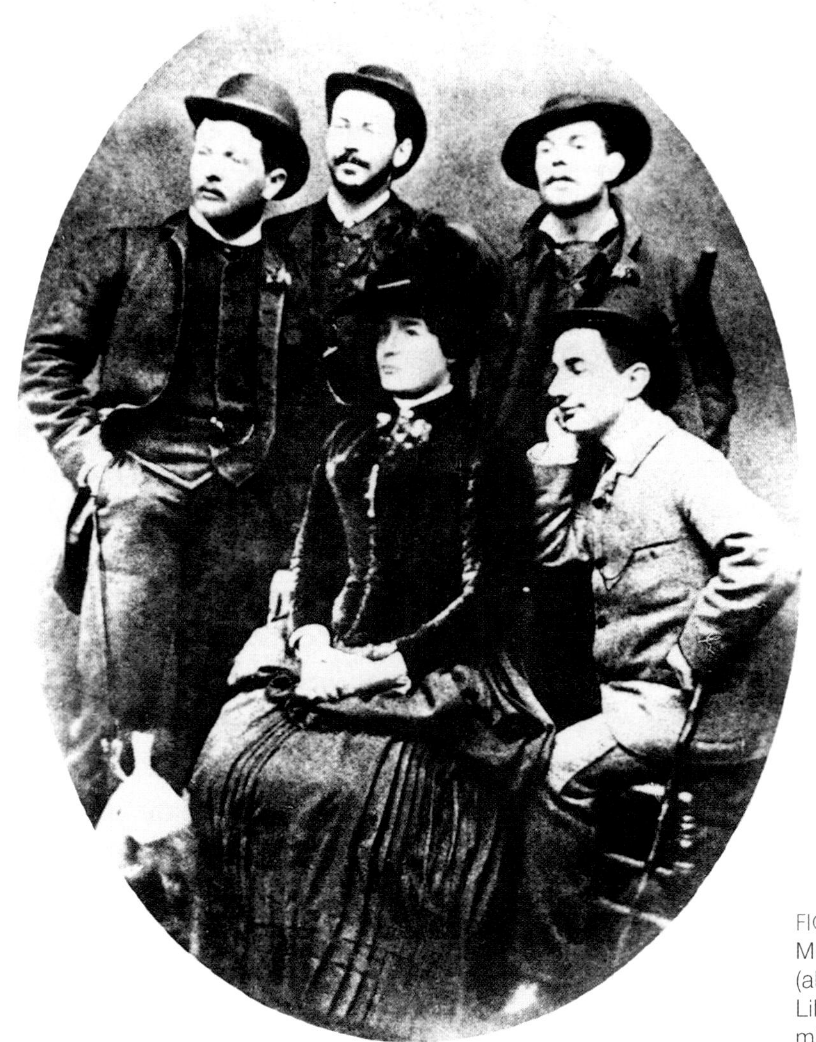

FIG. 20 – Grenier, Rabache, Metivet and Toulouse-Lautrec (all students of Cormon) with Lili, Belleroche's model and mistress.

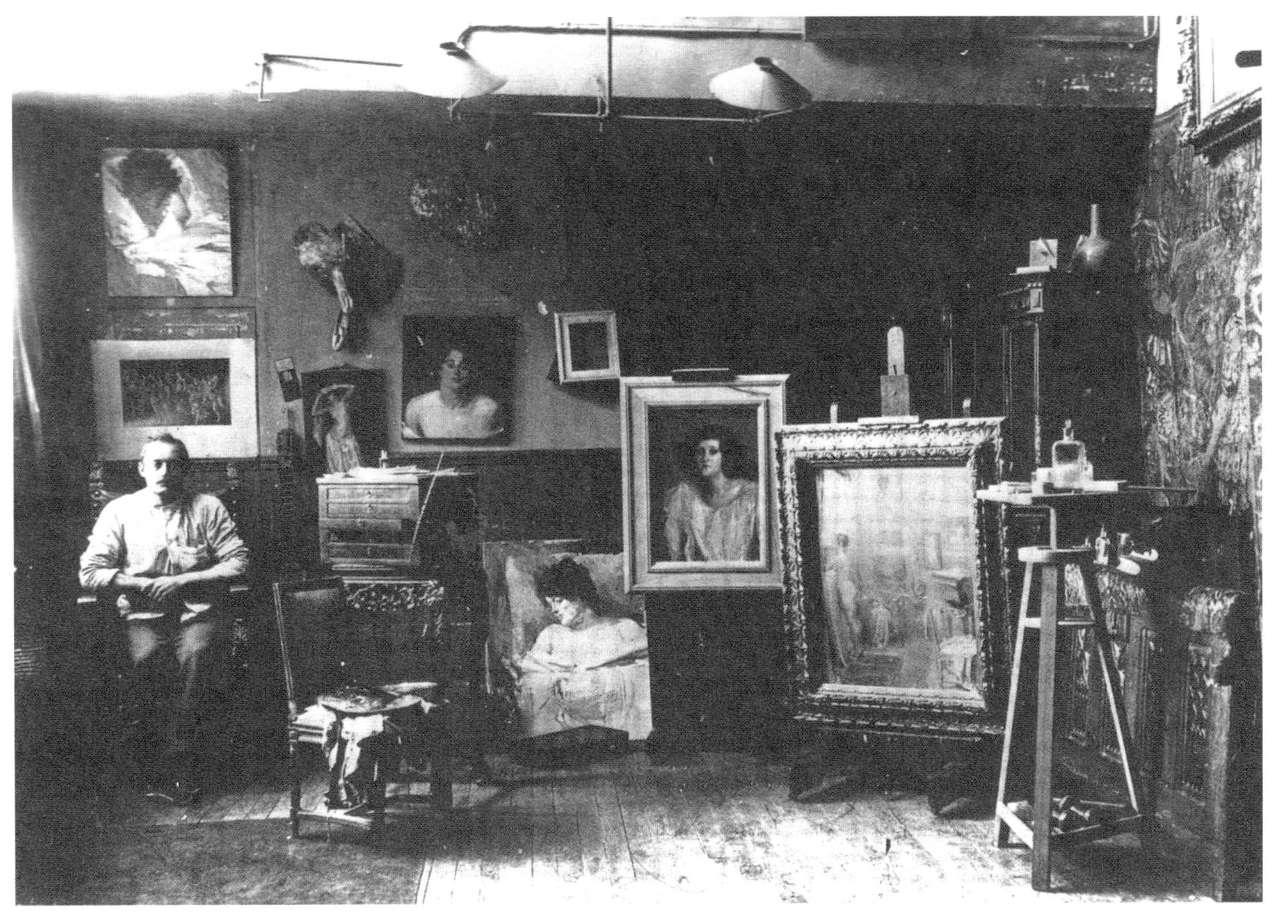

FIG. 21 – Albert Belleroche in his Paris studio, c 1900

1912	Moves to Hampstead, London.
1913-14	Exhibits at Dowdeswell Galleries, London.
1914	Exhibits at Kennedy Gallery, New York.
1918	Moves to Rustington, Sussex
1933	Retrospective exhibition of lithographs at the Bibliothèque Royale de Belgique, Brussels.
1934	Exhibition of lithographs at Worthing Art Gallery in Sussex.
1939	Gift of art to establish the Brangwyn-de Belleroche Museum in Orange, France.
1941	Exhibits at Colnaghi's Gallery, London.
1942	Retrospective exhibition of art at the National Museum of Wales, Cardiff.
1943	Exhibits at the Leicester Galleries, London.
1944	Albert Belleroche dies, 14 July, at the Crown Hotel, Southwell.

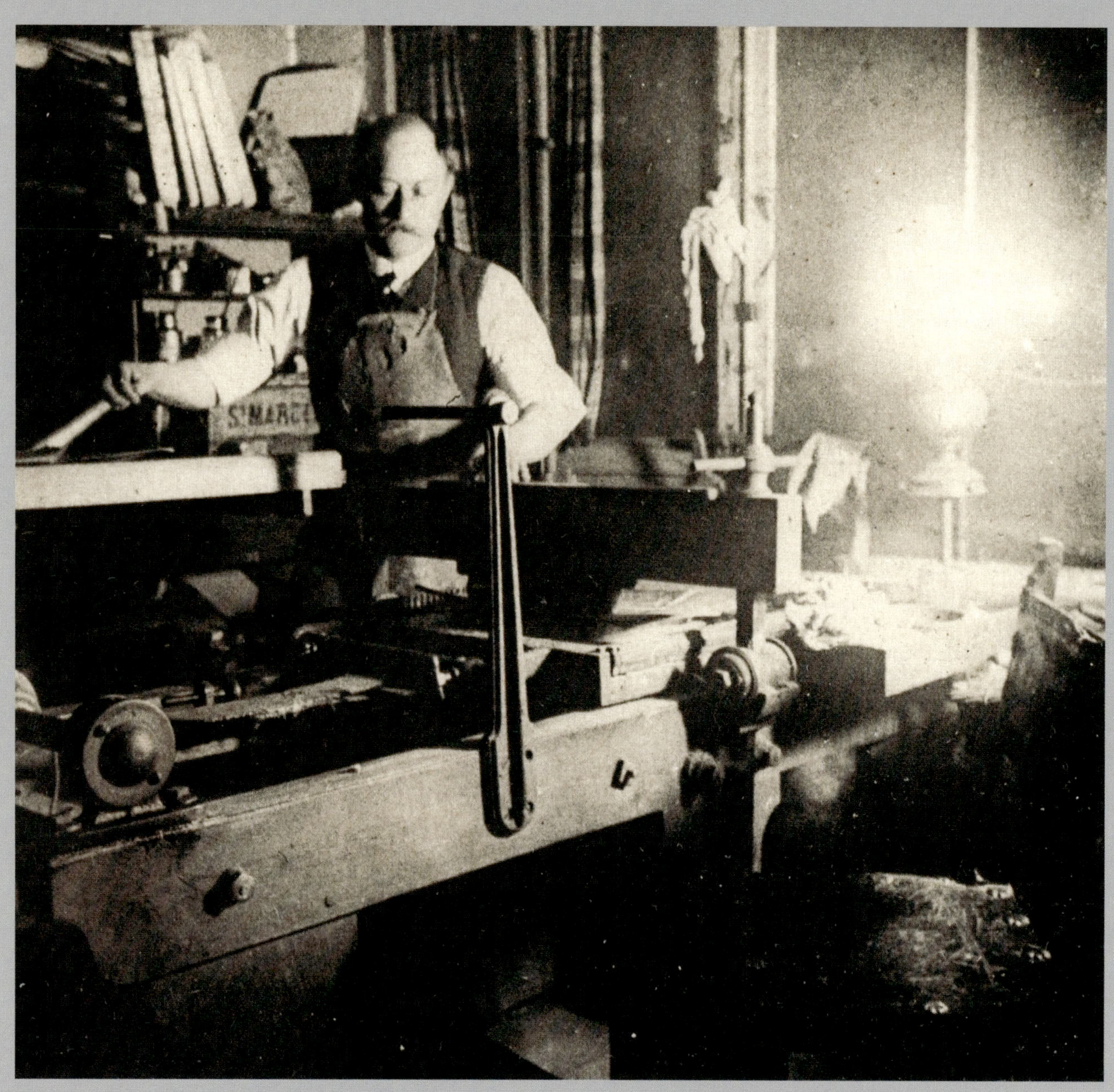

FIG. 22 – Albert de Belleroche working in his studio.

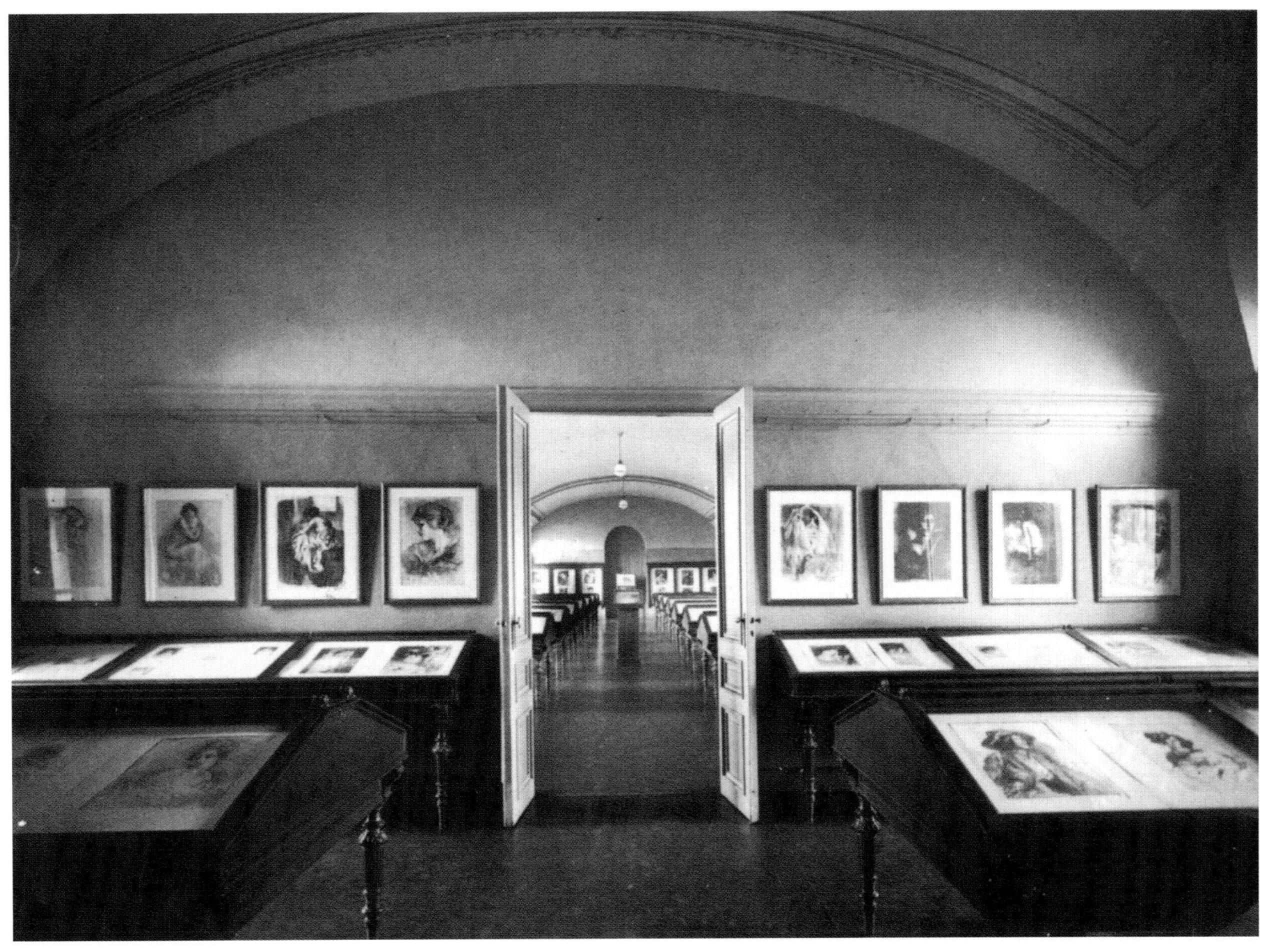

FIG. 23 – Retrospective exhibition of lithographs at the Bibliothèque Royale de Belgique, Brussels, 1933.

1947	Retrospective exhibition at the Salon d'Automne.
1954 - 68	Exhibitions in various London art galleries promoted by son William.
1956	Joint retrospective exhibition of Toulouse-Lautrec and Belleroche at the Salon d'Automne.
1996	*Women of the Belle Epoque*, Theodore B. Donson Ltd., New York.
2001	*Rival of Painting: the Lithographs of Albert Belleroche*, The San Diego Museum of Art.
2024	*Albert de Belleroche: A painter in Paris*, Rusell-Cotes Museum & Art Gallery

Albert Belleroche's Studio Log Book

Belleroche's handwritten notes from his work Log Book include titles, subject names, dates, edition numbers printed, dimensions, inks and papers used, sales to galleries, museum gifts, and general comments.

In the Log Book Belleroche included data on 618 of his lithographs. After he died Julie, his wife, added a supplement of 285 further lithographs. 26 more were added by Alice, his daughter, and 33 by George Kenney. This brings the total number of known lithographs to 962. His print oeuvre can be divided into two periods: 1900 to 1910 in Paris and 1912 to 1944 in England. The pivot event occurred in June, 1910, when the 28-year-old Julie Visseaux married Albert Belleroche and the couple left Paris to live in Brussels and then in England.

During this period, he only produced about 380 lithographs, as opposed to the 580 he produced in Paris between 1900 and 1910. In the Log Book titles of works executed in France are in French and titles of works executed in England are in English.

From January 1912-1916 Julie and Albert de Belleroche lived in Hampstead, London, in a house called Glencairn. From 1917-1940 in the Old Manor, in Rustington, Sussex, and from 1940-1944 in the Crown Hotel, Southwell, Nottingham. After the move to Rustington, until his death in 1944, Belleroche produced fewer than 80 lithographs, mostly of his family, a few models and local landscapes.

In 1940, during World War II, Belleroche evacuated his family from Rustington on the coast to Southwell in Nottingham. He took rooms at the Crown Hotel where his friends continued to visit. He also rented a room in town where he painted a few oils. Belleroche became ill at the Crown Hotel and died in 1944. He was buried at Southwell Minster.

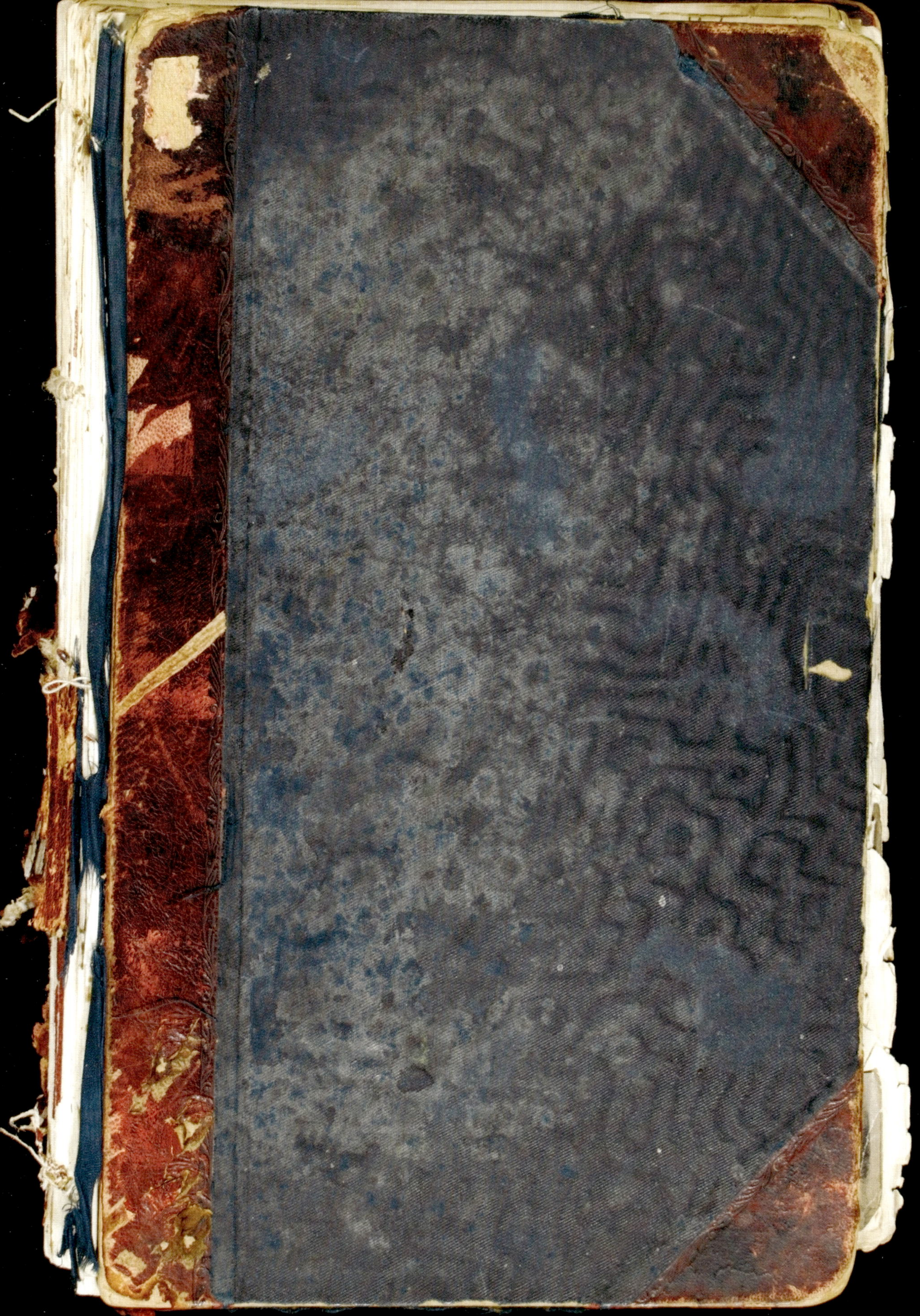

144　　(5)　　24×19"

Coll: Biblioteque Royal, Brussels

Coll. Biblioteque Royal, Brussels
145　X.52.
　　　　　　　　　　　　　　　　　　　　　Coll:
　　　　　　　　　　　　　　　　　　　British Museum
mai 7th 1906　about 10 on old paper
　　　　seven Japon 5 or 6 China
　　　　about 20 before　　"La Mantille"
Giraudy　　　(20)　30.　　Madame Anglada
　　　　　　　　　　　　18×22½"

146　Coll: Biblioteque Royal, Brussels
　　　18×13　"British Museum　(5)
1905　only two on Japon
147 "Léone"　(10)　British Museum
　　　　　　　　　　　2 China
X.76.
148　　　(20)
×3
24×17¾" Portrait　14½×24"
　　　　　　"The Boa"
　　　　　(Mrs. Milbank)
149　　　(4)

Tete de femme

mai 1906　8 on Japon

Coll: Biblioteque Royal, Brussels
　　　Br. Museum

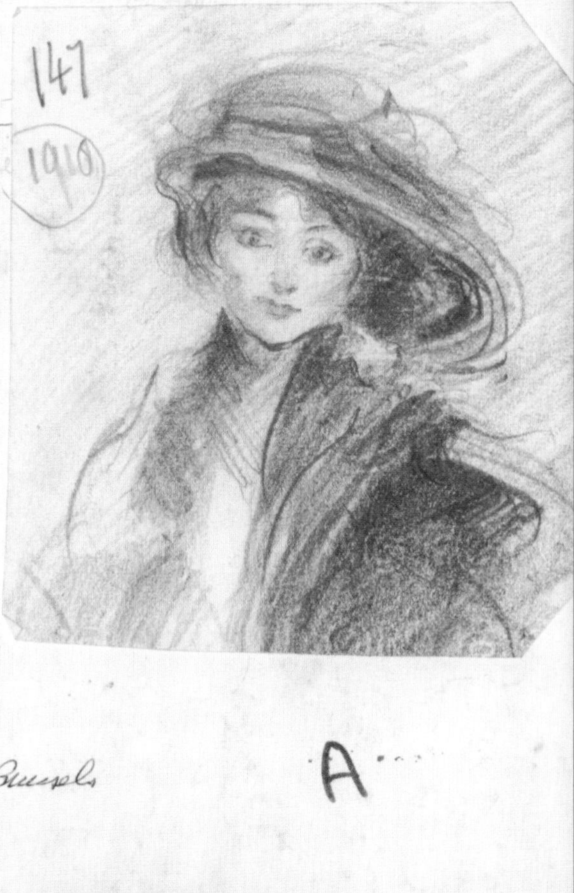

147
(1910)

A

144 .   feuille de croquis taid femme.
                              Leone .   1902

145 £2.12.6   £.3.3.   1905
P. Litho - Salon d'Aut 1906. - Graves P.L.   30
Achete mai Melbourne -
International -
Estampe
Kensington
                        Madame
                        Mantille

146 £5.5   146 —   1907
        La Toque noir Lili
                      1920   5
147 dup.
    X 155
   14½ X 19" with Frago   Julie Frago
   14½ X 9 ¾"

148 £5.5   ≠ 666 British Museum   1906
P. Litho. International — Graves P.L.
Salon 1906
Estampe 1909
Kensington   1910   Portrait

149

441. Etude Nu - Lavis

442. Petite tête de femme
Coll: Bibliotèque Royal, Brussels

444

443. Interieur La Boissiere. Chateaudun
British Museum 21 x 14½"

Coll: Bibliotèque Royal, Brussels

444. 7 x 13"

445. 8 x 5
Coll: Bibliotèque Royal, Brussels

446. Petite Etude de femme
9 x 11"

447. Coll: Bibliotèque Royal, Brussels
11 x 7" British Museum "Dorothy"

448. Coll: British Museum

449. Petite tête de femme
Coll: Bibliotèque Royal, Brussels

448

441.

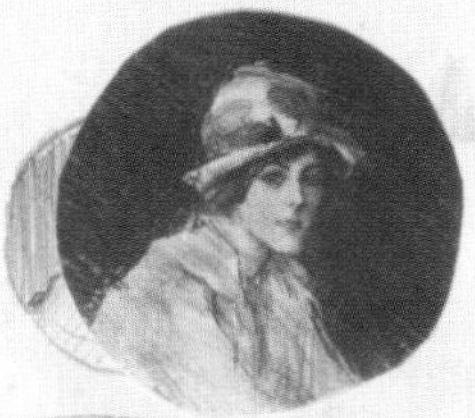

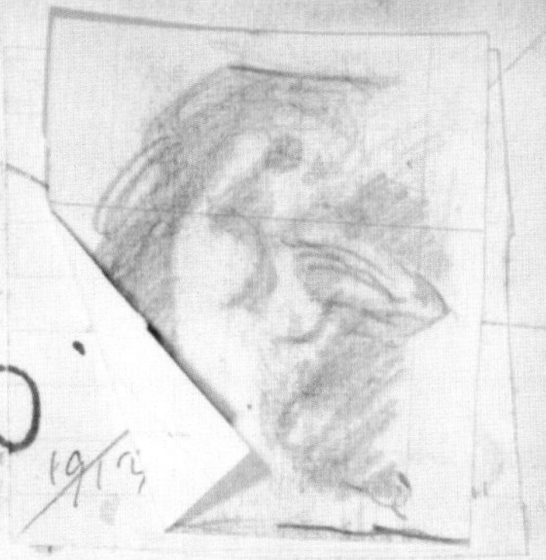

442 (10) →   1913

443. (8) →
intérieur la Boissière
Chateaudun
old 509

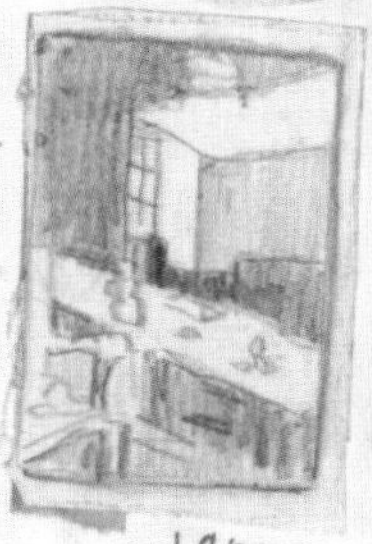

444 Hollamp
good →

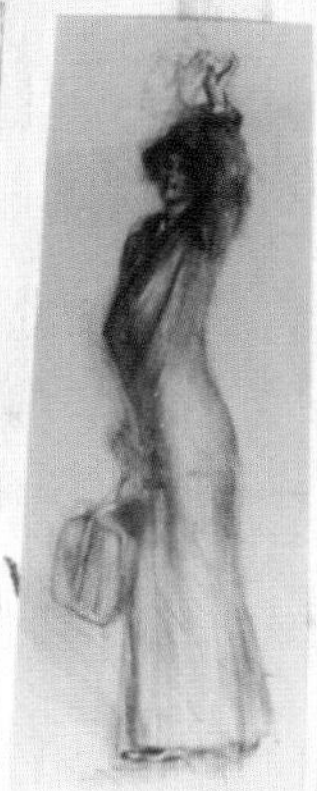

445 madame Newmont →   1917

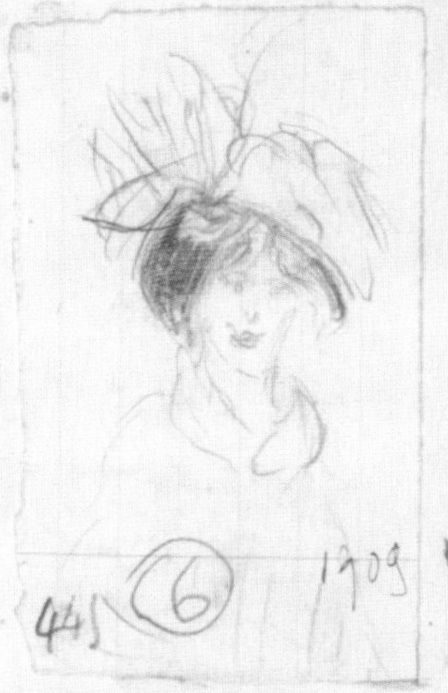

445 (6)   1709 M.

446 → (10)
1914 —

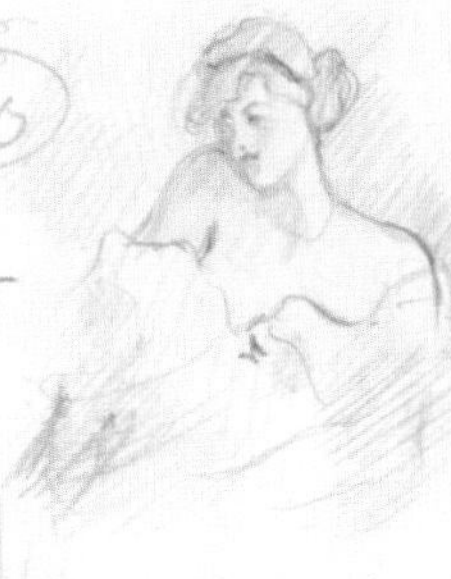

447 — (4) 1914 —

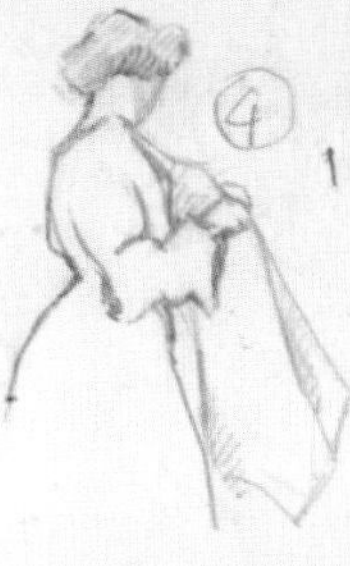

448 → (4)

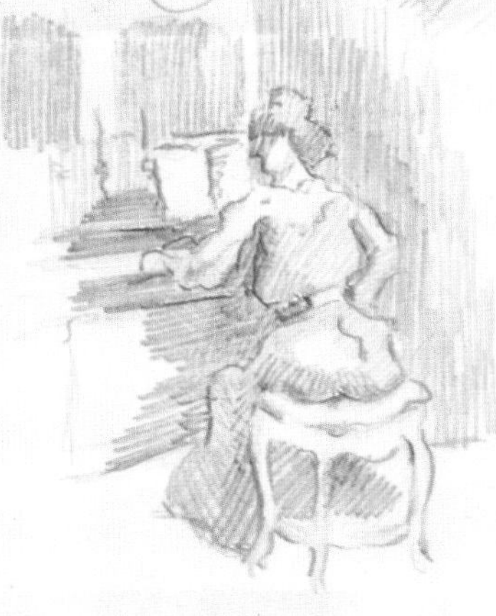

449   1924

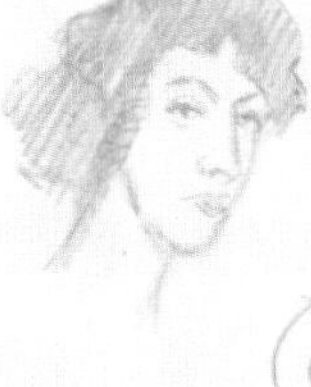

109a

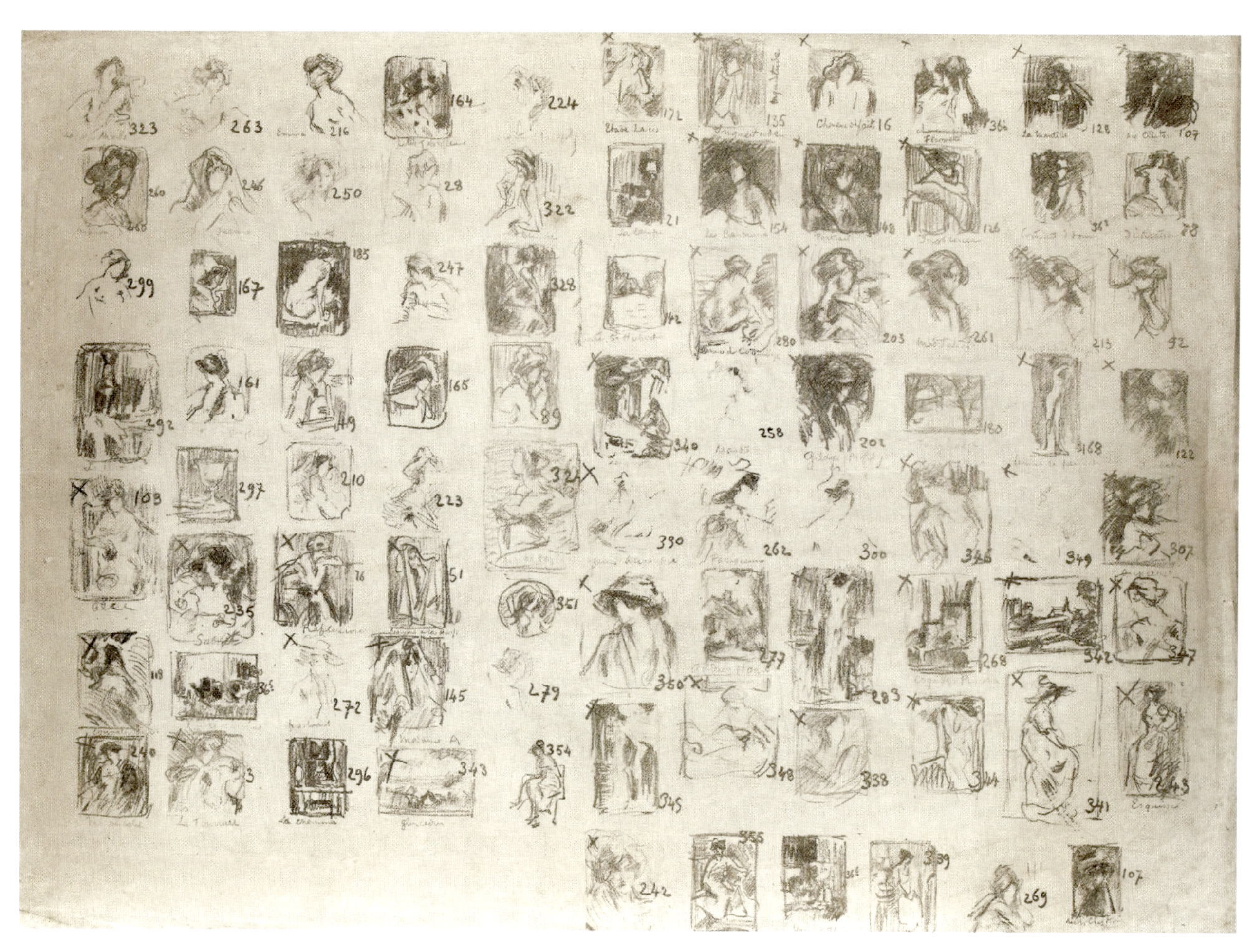

CAT. 315 – Lithograph of lithographs, (K961, AB 549), 22 1/8 x 30 1/8 in. (56.4 x 76.7 **cm**). Edition: 1.

Public collections possessing works by Albert de Belleroche:

The French National Collections

The Royal Museum, Brussels

The State Picture Galley, Dresden

Bibliothèque Nationale, Paris

Bibliothèque Royale, Brussels

Print Room, Berlin

Graphische Sammlung, Munich

The Albertina, Vienna

The Metropolitain Museum, New York

The British Museum, London

The Victoria and Albert Museum, London

The National Museum of Wales, Cardiff

The San Diego Museum
Ashmolean Museum, Oxford

Cornell, Ithaca

Cooper Hewitt Museum, New York

Art Institute, Chicago

Museum of Fine Arts, Boston

Brangwyn - de Belleroche Musée (Musée Municipal), Orange

National Gallery of Victoria, Melbourne

Santa Barbara Museum of Art, Santa Barbara

Tate Gallery, London

National Gallery, Washington DC

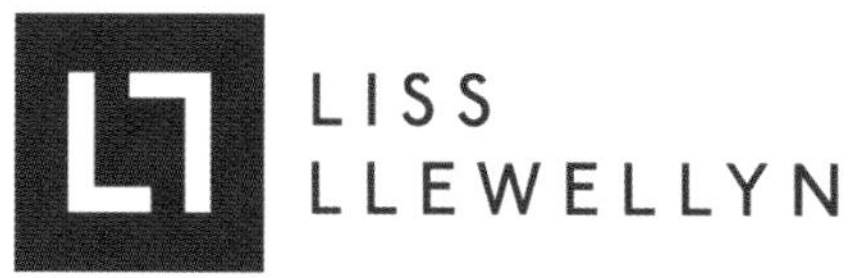